THE GERMAN POLITY FOURTH EDITION

THE GERMAN POLITY FOURTH EDITION

David P. Conradt
University of Florida

Longman
New York & London

AHV 3340-5/4

ourth Edition M-448

Longman Inc., 95 Church Street, White Plains, N. Y. 10601

Associated companies:
Longman Group Ltd., London
Longman Cheshire Pty., Melbourne
Longman Paul Pty., Auckland
Copp. Clark Pitman, Toronto
Pitman Publishing Inc., New York

Senior editor: David J. Estrin
Production editor: Carol Harwood
Text design: Jill Francis Wood
Cover design: Kevin C. Kall
Production supervisor: Judith Stern

Library of Congress Cataloging-in-Publication Data

Conradt, David P.
    The German polity / David P. Conradt.—4th ed.
        p. cm.

    Bibliography: p.
    Includes index.
    ISBN 0-8013-0125-4 (pbk.)
    1. Germany (West)—Politics and government. I. Title.
JN3971.A2C63 1989   88-22749
320.943—dc19   CIP

ISBN 0-8013-0125-4

94 93 92 91 90 89 9 8 7 6 5 4 3 2

To Ingeborg, Phillip, Tommy, and Elisabeth

Contents

Tables and Figures   *xi*

Preface   *xiii*

Introduction   *xv*

1 THE HISTORICAL SETTING   1

The First Reich   1
The Rise of Prussia   2
The Empire (1871–1918)   3
World War I and the Collapse of the Second Reich   4
The Weimar Republic (1919–1933)   5
The Nazi Third Reich and World War II   9
Foreign Occupation and National Division   12
The Formation of the Federal Republic   14
Notes   17

2 THE SOCIAL AND ECONOMIC SETTING   18

Area and Population   18
Urbanization and Industrialization   19
The Rural Sector   20
Regionalism   21
Occupational and Class Structure   22
The Economy   24

Religious Composition   29
Age and Family Structure   31
The Educational System   35
Mass Media   38
Summary and Conclusion   40
Notes   41

3 POLITICAL CULTURE, PARTICIPATION, AND
   CIVIL LIBERTIES   44

Political Values   45
Political Interest and Involvement   55
Civil Liberties and Human Rights   59
The "Radicals" in Public Service Controversy   61
Civil Liberties and the Census   63
The Status and Role of Minority Groups   65
Summary and Conclusion   77
Notes   77

4 THE PARTY SYSTEM AND THE REPRESENTATION
   OF INTERESTS   82

The Party State   82
The Party System   85
The Christian Democrats   85
The Social Democrats   90
The Free Democrats   96
The Greens   99
The Representation of Interests   101
Extent of Interest Groups   101
Importance and Style of Interest Representation   101
Major Interest Alignments   103
Summary and Conclusion   112
Notes   112

5 ELECTIONS AND VOTING BEHAVIOR   115

Electoral Mechanics   116
The Electoral System   117
Nomination and Candidate Selection   119
Electoral Politics and Campaign Styles   122
Campaign and Party Finance   123
The Pattern of Federal Elections 1949–1987   124
The Basic Orientations of the Electorate   127
The Determinants of Voting Behavior   129
Summary and Conclusions   136
Notes   136

6 POLICYMAKING INSTITUTIONS I: PARLIAMENT AND EXECUTIVE 138

Legislative Institutions 139
The Bundestag 139
The Bundesrat 148
Executive Institutions: Chancellor and Cabinet 151
Chancellor Democracy 151
Summary: The Formal Lawmaking Process 167
Preparliamentary Stage 167
Parliamentary Stage 168
Notes 169

7 POLICYMAKING INSTITUTIONS II: ADMINISTRATION, SEMIPUBLIC INSTITUTIONS, AND COURTS 172

The Development of the West German Administrative and
  Judicial System 173
State Administration 175
Semipublic Institutions 182
The Judiciary and the Court System 187
Summary and Conclusion 196
Notes 197

8 SUBNATIONAL UNITS: FEDERALISM AND LOCAL GOVERNMENT 200

The Development of German Federalism 200
State-Level Politics 202
The Future of Federalism 211
Local Government 212
The Urban Crisis, West German Style 214
Summary and Conclusion 216
Notes 217

9 CONCLUSION: THE GERMAN POLITY FACES THE FUTURE 219

Change in Foreign Policy 219
Change in Inter-German Relations 224
Constitutional Change 225
Policy Issues and Processes 228
Notes 234

Select Bibliography 235

Appendix: The Basic Law of the Federal Republic 247

Index 267

Tables and Figures

Tables

2.1 Occupational Composition of the Work Force, 1882–1986   23
2.2 German Economic Trends, 1950–1987   24
2.3 Income by Occupation, 1984   26
2.4 Capital Resources by Occupation   27
2.5 Equality in Marriage, 1954–1979   34
3.1 Feelings of National Pride in Major European Countries, 1985   50
3.2 Changes in Attitudes toward Previous Regimes (Monarchy and Dictatorship) and Key Values of the Bonn Republic (Political Competition and Representation), 1950–1978   52
3.3 Public Opinion and the Limits of Free Expression   64
3.4 "Politics Should Be Left to Men." Major European Countries, 1983   68
3.5 Discrimination Experienced by Working Women: Major West European Countries, 1980   70
5.1 Seat Distribution in the 1987 Federal Election   118
5.2 Group Affiliation of the Top Fifty Candidates on the Christian Democrat List for North Rhine–Westphalia   121
5.3 Party Vote in Federal Elections, 1949–1987, Second Ballot   124
5.4 Continuity and Change in Voting Behavior, 1965–1987   129
5.5 Party Vote by Social Class, 1980–1987   131
5.6 Support for CDU/CSU by Religion, 1976–1987   132
5.7 Rank Order of Major Campaign Issues by Salience to the Electorate, 1983 and 1987   135

6.1 Importance of Parliament: Major West European Countries, 1983   147
6.2 West German Chancellors, 1949–1989   158
7.1 Hierarchical Structure of the Ministry of Economics   176
7.2 Distribution of Public Employees by Governmental Level and Rank   179
7.3 The German Court Structure and Judiciary   191
8.1 The Länder of the Federal Republic   204
8.2 Expenditures of State and National Governments by Policy Area   209
8.3 Sources of Tax Revenues by Governmental Level   210

Figures

1.1 Political Map of Germany   13
2.1 Age Structure of the Population   31
3.1 Levels of Interest in Politics, 1952–1983   57
5.1 Ideological Self-Estimate of the Electorate, 1987   128
9.1 Change in Popular Attitudes toward Acceptance of the German-Polish Border (Oder-Neisse Line)   222

Preface

Developments since the publication of the third edition of this book, the gratifying response of colleagues and students, and the appearance of new research on German politics by social scientists on both sides of the Atlantic are the major factors that necessitate this new edition. The work has been updated, and the findings of recent research have been incorporated into the text. A discussion of the role of the Bundesbank, the health and pension systems, and the federal employment agency in the policy process have been added to Chapter 7. Sections on the 1987 federal election, changes in the party system, and expanded treatments of major policy problems have also been added to this edition.

The book's general thesis and approach, however, remain. The Federal Republic, now entering its fifth decade, has become an established liberal democracy with all the problems and potential of many other "late capitalist" societies: reduced economic growth, increased unemployment, the financial crisis in social welfare programs, the decay of the inner cities, housing shortages, the maintenance of civil liberties and human rights, an alienated youth subculture, terrorism, and environmental protection. In addition, West Germany must deal with its special problems of national identity, German reunification, and its future relationship to the Soviet Union and Eastern Europe. These issues should be at the center of any analysis of modern German politics, rather than concentration on neo-Nazism or speculations about defects in the German "character."

This study has benefited greatly from the stimulation and research support provided by colleagues in Germany and the United States. In the Federal Republic, I am especially indebted to Jürgen W. Falter, Hellmut Hoffmann, Max Kaase, Jürgen Kalkbrenner, Werner Kaltefleiter, Hans-Dieter Klingemann, Franz-Urban Pappi, Walter Picard, Lutz Reuter, Erwin K. Scheuch, and Rudolf

Wildenmann. Special mention must go to the founder and director of the Institut fur Demoskopie, Elisabeth Noelle-Neumann, who has, over the years, generously shared her invaluable archive of public opinion surveys. Frau Marianne Strenger of the Inter-Nationes organization in Bonn promptly fulfilled my innumerable requests for information and publications. In the United States, all or parts of the manuscript were carefully read by Henry Albinski, Charles R. Foster, M. Donald Hancock, Dwight Lambert, Peter Merkl, Ferdinand Mueller-Rommel, Peter Speser, and James H. Wolfe. Their comments saved me from many embarrassing mistakes. I am, of course, solely responsible for any remaining errors of fact or judgment.

David P. Conradt

Introduction

This book seeks to provide an introduction to the modern West German polity that will enable the student of comparative politics to acquire a detailed knowledge of this particular system and to compare it meaningfully with others.

This study departs from earlier treatments of the Federal Republic in its emphasis on the institutionalized character of the postwar system and the multiplicity of policy changes and conflicts that are now taking place within the Republic. In short, the key question is no longer whether Germany will remain a liberal democratic society but, rather, what kind of democracy the Federal Republic has been and will be in the future. Thus this book will not deal extensively with the possibilities of neo-Nazi revivals, or portray right-wing extremism as a problem that still troubles the system and occupies the attention of its political leadership, simply because neo-Nazism is no longer a significant issue.

This does not deny the influence of the past on present institutions and processes; throughout the work, and especially in the treatment of national identity in Chapter 3, I have attempted to relate historical factors—particularly the Third Reich and World War II—to the present politics of the Republic. But it does suggest that a portrayal of the Republic as one that is "in suspense" or as one in which the leadership is insecure or anxious about its capabilities to maintain the liberal democratic order is misleading. To American and British students whose image of Germany derives largely from movies and television programs dealing with the Third Reich, this approach may be surprising, but it provides a more realistic portrait of how the West German political system functions.

Some commentators still regard any increase in political conflict or polarization in the Federal Republic as an indicator of a "system crisis"—as a sign that the values, institutions, and processes of liberal democracy are being called into question.[1] An everyday observation about politics in countries such as the United States or Great Britain, that there can be conflict within a consensus on the "rules of the game," is still difficult for some observers to make about the Federal Republic. This has been especially true in recent years as German politics becomes more "interesting," or less "dull" for foreign analysts—with the rise of the Greens, the political machinations surrounding the 1983 election, the peace movement, the massive and sometimes violent protests surrounding the stationing of new missiles on German soil, and the general increase in opposition to American foreign and defense policies. None of these developments is inconsistent with the stability of the Republic's liberal democratic structure. Indeed, one could consider these developments as an expression of the vitality of the West German democracy. The fundamental changes in political values and attitudes since 1945, discussed and documented in Chapter 3 and elsewhere by the author and others, have made these new "interesting" developments possible. The growth of grass-roots citizen-initiative groups in the 1970s, from which the Greens of the 1980s emerged, is fully consistent with the remade political culture thesis.

This study of the German polity will not include the internal politics of the German Democratic Republic (GDR), or East Germany, as it is also termed. East Germany, like the Federal Republic (West Germany), was founded in 1949. Unlike the Federal Republic, it is a one-party state whose political institutions and processes are modeled after those of the Soviet Union. The characteristics of what political scientists term political democracy and that we will use in the book—freedom of expression, freedom to form and join organizations, the right to vote in free and fair elections, the right of political leaders to compete for support, the availability of alternative sources of information, and the presence of institutions that make government policies dependent on votes and other expressions of preference—are not present in the German Democratic Republic.[2] Thus an examination of East German politics belongs more properly to the study of communist political systems, one-party totalitarian societies, or the "Eastern European pattern" of politics. Where relevant, however, references to East Germany, as it relates to the domestic and foreign policies of the Federal Republic, will be made.

THE STUDY OF GERMAN POLITICS

To the student of comparative politics, a knowledge and understanding of the West German polity is important for several reasons:

First, Germany offers an excellent example of the complexities, difficulties, and tragedies of political development. Unlike the United States or Great Britain, political stability, much less democratic political stability, has been a rarity in the German political experience. Frequently throughout its history, Germany has faced the basic problem, now confronting many less-developed countries, of establishing a political order that achieves a balance between conflict and consensus, liberty and order, individualism and community, unity and diversity.

Second, German politics offers the student a "laboratory" in which to study political change. Within the last century not only specific governments but also the entire regime or form of government has been subject to frequent and sudden change. The empire proclaimed in 1871 collapsed with Germany's defeat in World War I and was followed by a democratic republic in 1919. This first attempt at political democracy lasted only fifteen years and was replaced in 1933 by the Nazi dictatorship. The Nazis' "thousand-year" Reich lasted only twelve years with catastrophic consequences for Germany and the world. In 1945, the destruction of the Nazi system brought a system of military occupation to Germany, which was followed in 1949 by the creation of two German states: a Federal Republic of Germany, composed of the American, British, and French zones of occupation; and a communist state, the German Democratic Republic, in the Russian zone. Thus in less than a century, Germany has had two republics, one empire, one fascist dictatorship, one communist dictatorship, and one period of foreign military occupation. Few countries present the student with a better opportunity to examine the causes and consequences of such political change.

Third, German politics illustrates the effects of the international political system upon domestic politics. As we discuss in Chapter 1, the present political organization of the German people is the by-product of the postwar struggle between East and West. The basic decisions that established the two German states and ceded large portions of the prewar *Reich* (literally "kingdom") to the Soviet Union, Poland, and Czechoslovakia were not made by German political leaders. And throughout the postwar period the politics of West Germany, more than that of any other Western European country, has been affected by decisions made in Washington, Moscow, and elsewhere outside Germany.

Fourth, the study of West German politics gives the student an opportunity to examine one of the most important capitalist or market economies in the world today and particularly the relationship between the policies of government and this economic system. Although not immune to the problems of inflation, unemployment, and economic growth common to all advanced industrial societies, West Germany has confronted these issues more successfully than any of its major Western European neighbors. Economic performance has also been cited as a prime factor in the postwar growth of popular support for the values and institutions of liberal democracy.

Finally, West Germany is an increasingly important country in the international political system. At present it is the strongest member of the European Economic Community (Common Market), as well as the most powerful ally of the United States. A knowledge and understanding of West

German politics offer the student insights into a key "actor" in the future of Western Europe and the international political system.

THE PLAN OF THE BOOK

A knowledge of the major historical developments that preceded the establishment of the Federal Republic is essential background information for the later chapters. This is provided in Chapter 1. The social and economic structure of the Federal Republic is then examined in Chapter 2. Emphasis in this chapter is placed on postwar changes and their impact on political attitudes and behavior. German political culture and participation as well as the role and status of minority groups are discussed in Chapter 3. The postwar party system, the key role of the three "established" parties (Social Democrats, Christian Democrats, and Free Democrats), the recent emergence of the Greens, and the activity of the major postwar interest groups are the topics of Chapter 4. Postwar elections and electoral politics are discussed in Chapter 5. The major national policymaking institutions—the parliament, executive, bureaucracy, courts, and semipublic institutions—are the subjects of Chapters 6 and 7. West Germany's subnational governmental units—the states and local communities—are treated in Chapter 8. The work concludes with an examination of several present and future policy problems confronting the Federal Republic, including a brief examination of recent foreign policy developments.

This study attempts to develop two major themes: (1) Since 1949 the Federal Republic has achieved a degree of legitimacy and consensus unmatched by any other German regime in this century; Germany and the Germans have changed. (2) Within this context, the political system is now dealing with a variety of policy problems that, because of the importance of first achieving a consensus on political democracy, could not be addressed earlier. The manner in which these issues are resolved will determine the quality and the extent of political democracy in West Germany.

This latter issue is, however, by no means a uniquely German question. Today, having achieved democratic political stability, Germany must confront the complex challenges facing modern democracies in Europe and elsewhere. A recent study of the "crisis of democracy" lists some of these[3]. One is "overloaded government": the expansion of popular participation and involvement has greatly increased citizen demands on government; the resultant expansion of governmental activities has in turn strained the economic resources of the society. Another crisis is "consensus without purpose": although there is consensus on the basic rules of the democratic political game, there is less "sense of purpose as to what one should achieve by playing the game."[4] The emergence of grass-roots political protest movements and new political parties in the Federal Republic and elsewhere in Western Europe is an expression of this dissatisfaction with traditional party and state structures.[5] The postwar development of the Federal Republic, examined in this book, is indeed a success story, but whether the past is of value in helping to meet the problems of the future is in Germany, as elsewhere, an open question.

NOTES

1. John Vinocur, "Signs of Instability Cloud Germany's Future," *New York Times,* August 2, 1982, p. 1. Also H.P. Secher, "Trend Changes in a 'Remade' Political Culture: Whither the Federal Republic?," unpublished paper presented at the State Department, *Germany in the 1980s* Conference, Washington DC, May 12,1983; and Peter J. Katzenstein, "Problem or Model? West Germany in the 1980s," *World Politics* 32, no. 4 (July 1980): 597.
2. Robert A. Dahl, *Polyarchy, Participation and Opposition* (New Haven: Yale University Press, 1971), p. 3.
3. Michael Crozier, Samuel P. Huntington, and Joji Watanuki, *The Crisis of Democracy* (New York: New York University Press, 1975), p. 161.
4. Ibid., p. 159.
5. Suzanne Berger, "Politics and Antipolitics in Western Europe in the Seventies," *Daedalus,* no. 4 (Winter 1979), pp. 27–50.

THE GERMAN POLITY FOURTH EDITION

CHAPTER 1

The Historical Setting

The Federal Republic of Germany was established in 1949 and is certainly one of Europe's and the world's newer states. But the people within its borders belong to one of Europe's oldest linguistic, ethnic, and cultural units—the German nation. This nation dates back at least to A.D. 843, when Charlemagne's empire was partitioned following his death into West Frankish (much of modern France), Central Frankish (the modern Netherlands, Belgium, Alsace, and Lorraine), and East Frankish (modern Germany) empires. The East Frankish empire under Otto the Great (936–973) was later termed the Holy Roman Empire and lasted until about 1250. But neither this first empire, or *Reich,* nor any of its successors has ever united all of Europe's German-speaking peoples into a single state with a strong central government.

THE FIRST REICH

The medieval Reich was in fact a very loose-knit collection of many different tribes, each with distinct dialects and varying degrees of economic and military strength. While this empire, even after 1250, formally held together and was not finally abolished until the time of Napoleon, it had in fact ceased to exist as a viable political entity by the end of the thirteenth century. The first German Reich then became little more than a fragmented collection of literally hundreds of principalities and free cities.[1] While the process of building a unified nation-state continued in Britain and France, the German peoples of Central Europe were deeply divided. This decentralization of political authority, characteristic of feudalism, meant that many separate and distinct political institutions and processes took root within the German nation.

1

The Lutheran Reformation of the sixteenth century brought, through Luther's translation of the Bible into High German, a uniform style of written German, but it did little else to facilitate unity and integration. Indeed, it divided Central Europe still further into Protestant and Catholic territories. The Thirty Years War (1618–1648), which followed the Reformation, was fought largely on German soil, with the different German states, allied with various foreign powers, fighting each other. The war thus severely weakened the states individually and collectively. On the eve of Europe's transformation from an agrarian-feudal to a capitalist-urban society, Germany, unlike Britain or France, remained backward and divided, lacking a strong central state with established administrative, legislative, and legal institutions; a middle class growing in political importance; and an emerging secular culture.

THE RISE OF PRUSSIA

The second major effort at unifying Germany began in a distant eastern territory on the Baltic Sea—the province of Brandenburg in 1701 proclaimed the Kingdom of Prussia. Ruled by the Hohenzollern dynasty, Prussia began a territorial expansion at the expense of its Slavic neighbors while other German states were the helpless pawns of the far stronger nation-states of France, Sweden, England, and Spain. Although a relatively poor and backward area, Prussia under the Hohenzollerns did have a series of skillful monarchs, beginning with Frederick William (1640–1688) through Frederick the Great (1744–1786), who through wars and diplomatic coups transformed Prussia into one of Europe's Great Powers. Lacking wealth or natural resources, the Hohenzollerns demanded discipline, hard work, and sacrifice from their subjects. It was the first German state with a bureaucracy and army comparable to those of the major powers of Western Europe. This style of politics worked, but there was little room in the Prussian system for the values of political liberalism, which together with nationalism were sweeping Western Europe in the wake of the French Revolution. The Prussian approach to politics was also disliked and feared by many smaller German states and free cities, who, although admiring Prussian successes, were less enthusiastic about the emphasis on authoritarian discipline and territorial expansion through military conquest.

The misgivings of the various German states about Prussia soon gave way, however, to a far greater concern with revolutionary France under Napoleon. Beginning in 1806 Napoleon invaded and dissolved most of the small German principalities, consolidating them into larger units and in effect preparing the way for the third major effort at unification. By invading Germany, the French also brought the ideologies of nationalism and liberalism, which found considerable support among the small but growing urban middle classes, especially in the western German states.

Following Napoleon's defeat and the Congress of Vienna in 1815, the number of German political units was reduced to thirty-eight, and only two of them—Prussia under the Hohenzollerns and Austria under the Habsburgs—had the size and resources to create a single unified German nation-state. Between 1815 and 1866 these thirty-eight states formed a German confederation within which the struggle for supremacy in Germany between Prussia and Austria took place. But Austria, with its multinational empire, was far less enthusiastic about German nationalism and unity than Prussia or the liberals in the other states. The Habsburgs preferred a weak confederation and defended the autonomy of the constituent units. Most German liberals, although still distrustful of Prussia, were also committed to national unity.

In 1848 liberal uprisings in Berlin, Vienna, Frankfurt, and elsewhere culminated in a parliament convened in Frankfurt to draft a liberal constitution for a unified German state that was to include a constitutional monarch. These German liberals of 1848, predominantly middle-class intellectuals and professionals, were at least a generation behind their British counterparts in political finesse and expertise. They were unable to agree whether a Prussian or an Austrian should become emperor, and their own disunity allowed the various rulers in the constituent states to regain power. When the parliament finally offered the crown to the Prussian king, he scornfully rejected it, and the Revolution of 1848 was soon crushed by Prussian and Austrian troops loyal to the monarchs. If Germany was to have a second Reich, it would not be via political liberalism.

After 1848 the Prussian and Austrian rivalry continued within the confederation, but the combination of Prussian military superiority and the skillful diplomacy and leadership of the Prussian prime minister, Otto von Bismarck, overwhelmed the larger but internally divided Austria. Prussia under Bismarck fought successfully against Denmark (1864), Austria (1866), and France (1870) and established its hegemony in most of the northern German states. These military successes dazzled the political liberals and won most of them over to the rather illiberal empire. In 1871, after some last minute bargaining with the reluctant southern Germans, Bismarck could inform the Prussian king that all the German princes and free cities such as Hamburg, Bremen, and Lübeck wanted him to accept the imperial crown. Thus at Versailles, the temporary headquarters of the army after the victorious war against France, Wilhelm I became the *Kaiser* (emperor) of the Second Reich.

THE EMPIRE (1871–1918)

The Second Reich was largely Bismarck's creation, and he dominated German and European politics for almost the next two decades. His constitution for the empire was a complex creation that ensured Prussian hegemony behind a liberal and federal facade. The emperor, who was also the Prussian king, appointed the chancellor (head of government), who was responsible to him and not the parliament. The chancellor then appointed his cabinet ministers. Moreover, the key policy areas of defense and foreign affairs were largely the domains of the emperor and chancellor. Parliament had only indirect control over these matters through its power of appropriations. But in the event of a deadlock between chancellor and parliament, the constitution gave sweeping emergency powers to the emperor.

The imperial parliament was bicameral. A lower house (*Reichstag*) was directly elected on the basis of universal male suffrage, but important legislation required upper-house (*Bundesrat,* or federal council) approval as well and was dominated by Prussia. This upper house was composed of delegates sent by the governments of the constituent states; its members were thus not directly elected by the people. Prussia, as the largest state (*Land*), had seventeen of the chamber's fifty-eight members and could in fact veto most legislation. The Prussian government, which sent and instructed these delegates, was led by the omnipresent Bismarck, who was both premier of Prussia and chancellor of the Reich. To complete the picture, Bismarck headed the Prussian delegation to the Bundesrat and, as leader of the largest state, was president of the upper house. Bismarck's power within Prussia was based not only on his relationship to the king but also on a voting system used for elections to the Prussian parliament, which was heavily weighted in favor of conservative, nationalist, and upper-status groups. Thus Bismarck, who brought the empire into being, also dominated its politics.

This complex system, although strongly biased in favor of Prussian executive power, was nonetheless far from being a totalitarian or even dictatorial state. The lower house was directly elected and did have considerable authority over appropriations. There were also some genuine federal elements in the system. The states (*Länder*) had major responsibilities for education, domestic order and security (police), and cultural affairs.

Bismarck's success in creating the empire and his resultant prestige and heroic stature combined with his unquestioned political skill enabled him, for the most part, to control both parliament and the states. In addition to the conservatives, the middle-class liberals were especially fascinated by his foreign policy successes. In retrospect, they should have known better and worked to increase the power of parliament instead of generally supporting the continued dominance of traditional Prussian elites—the nationalistic nobility and military.

WORLD WAR I AND THE COLLAPSE OF THE SECOND REICH

As long as Bismarck led the Prussian and Reich governments, this complex and potentially unstable system could survive and indeed prosper. After 1871 the new Reich was unquestionably the strongest military power in continental Europe and was rivaled in the world only by Great Britain with its still superior fleet. A rapid industrialization and urbanization after 1871 brought relative economic prosperity as well. But in forging the Second Reich, Bismarck and the Prussians had made many enemies in Europe. Chief among them was France, humiliated in the 1870 Franco-Prussian War and deprived of the provinces of Alsace and Lorraine. Russia was also fearful of further German expansion, and although Bismarck was able to avoid a French-Russian alliance, his successors were not. Neither were they able to contain the further growth of imperialist sentiment, which was manifested in the German effort at the turn of the century to expand its fleet in order to match or exceed that of Great Britain and to acquire, like Britain and France, an extensive overseas empire. Indeed, one of the most romantic nationalists in Germany at this time was Kaiser Wilhelm II.

While the political power of the middle classes in Britain and France grew and generally exerted a moderating influence on policy, in the Prussian-dominated Second Reich the old feudal classes—nobility, military, large land-owners—maintained and expanded their domestic hegemony and pursued defense and foreign policies designed to unify a divided society and maintain their position of power. Germany between 1871 and 1914 was a society that was rapidly modernizing yet was still ruled by traditional elites. The German middle class, expanding in size because of this modernization, did not assume and, for the most part, did not seek political power and influence commensurate with its socioeconomic importance.

This faulted social and political order could not survive a lengthy war, and World War I exposed its fatal weaknesses. After the failure of the initial German offensive in the West, designed to produce a quick victory, the prospect of a protracted conflict began to make manifest the latent tensions and contradictions in the social and political structure of the Second Reich. The Liberal, Socialist, and Catholic political parties in the parliament became less enthusiastic about supporting a war against countries such as Britain and the United States, whose level of constitutional democracy they hoped some day to achieve in Germany. Indeed, victory would strengthen the authoritarian regime. Food and raw materials became scarcer as imports, which had accounted for one-third of prewar supplies, dwindled under the pressure of the Allied blockade. Strikes, officially forbidden, broke out in various industries as workers reacted to mounting casualty lists and severe wartime rationing. A virtual military dictatorship emerged by 1917 as the army, intent on achieving maximum production and mobilization, began to make key political, social, and economic decisions. When, however, the army could not deliver victory, the generals, chief among them Erich Ludendorff, advised the Kaiser to abdicate and the parliamentary leadership to proclaim a republic and negotiate peace with their "fellow democrats" in the Western powers.

THE WEIMAR REPUBLIC (1919–1933)

The departure of the Kaiser and the proclamation of a republic in the wake of Germany's surrender took place in an atmosphere of increasing revolutionary fervor. Mindful of the Bolshevik success in Russia, some German Marxists split from the moderate Social Democratic party (SPD) and formed a Spartakus

League, which later became the Communist party (KPD). Workers' and soldiers' councils were formed in major cities on the Bolshevik model. In Bavaria a short-lived Soviet socialist republic was proclaimed. Germany seemed for a time to be on the verge of a communist revolution.

Conservatives and middle-class liberals combined with the moderate Social Democrats to crush the communist uprising with military and paramilitary units. Conservatives and nationalists, shocked at the prospect of a communist revolution, were willing to accept, at least in the short run, a parliamentary republic. In the small town of Weimar in 1919, a constitution was prepared and later ratified by a constituent assembly; Germany's first attempt at liberal democracy had begun.

The Weimar Constitution, drafted by learned constitutional and legal scholars, was widely acclaimed as one of the most democratic in the world. It featured universal adult suffrage, proportional representation, extensive provisions for popular referenda, petition and recall, and an extensive catalogue of civil liberties. The constitution created a dual executive: a chancellor as head of government appointed by the president but enjoying the confidence of the lower house, and a directly elected president as chief of state. The president under Article 48 also had the power to issue decrees in lieu of legislation if there was a state of emergency. Many historians and political scientists cite this latter provision as a major defect of the document.

The Weimar Republic could hardly have been started under less favorable circumstances. Defeat and national humiliation, widespread political violence, severe economic and social dislocation, and a political leadership with no real executive policymaking experience were major birth defects that the new state never really surmounted. The World War I peace settlement alone saddled Germany with a huge war debt, deprived it of 15 percent of its arable land, 10 percent of the country's population, the loss of all foreign colonies and investments, and much of the military and merchant fleet together with the railway stock. Conservatives and nationalists, soon forgetting the help of liberals and Social Democrats in defeating the communists, openly opposed the "system." The military, whose antirepublican officer corps was never purged, fostered the myth that Germany in World War I had been "stabbed in the back" by liberal, socialist, and Marxist civilian politicians. For some, the entire Weimar Republic was a "Jewish, liberal conspiracy," a "system" devised by "criminals." The bureaucracy and especially the judiciary also harbored many avowed opponents of democracy who were never removed from their positions. Likewise, on the Left, communists and some socialists viewed Weimar only as a brief prelude to the socialist revolution that, in their view, had been only delayed by the failure of the radical revolutionaries in 1918.

Shortly after its inauspicious beginning, the Weimar Republic had to confront an attempted military coup (Kapp *Putsch,* 1920), a disastrous inflation that virtually wiped out the savings of the middle class (1922–1923), an attempted communist revolution in the state of Saxony (1923), Hitler's unsuccessful Putsch in Munich (1923), and the French occupation of the Rhineland because of Weimar's inability to pay the huge war debts imposed by the victorious Allies at Versailles.

For an all too brief period in the mid-1920s Weimar, nonetheless, appeared to have stabilized itself. Long-term American loans and less stringent payment plans eased the war debt problem and aided in economic recovery. Conservatives appeared to be slowly accepting the system as legitimate, and the election of the World War I hero Paul von Hindenburg as president in 1925 brought still more conservatives and nationalists into a position of at least tacit acceptance of the Weimar Republic. The worldwide depression, however, touched off by the collapse of the American stock market in 1929 was a further blow from which Weimar never rallied. By 1931 about half of all German families were directly affected by unemployment. Voters began to desert the republican parties. Between 1919 and 1932 the proportion of the electorate supporting the Social Democrats, the Liberals, and the Catholic centrists declined from 64 percent to only 30 percent. The big gainers were the Nazis on the Right and the Communists on the Left. Between 1930 and 1933 no government could secure majority support in the lower house of parliament (the Reichstag). Indeed, by 1932 the two antisystem parties, the Nazis and Communists who both in their own way determined to overthrow the institution they belonged to, had a majority of seats. The president, the now aging von Hindenburg, who had ambivalent attitudes toward parliamentary democracy, in fact governed by the decree-granting powers given him in Article 48 of the constitution.

By 1932 the Nazis had become the strongest party in the Reichstag. Conservatives and nationalists wanted them in a conservative right-wing government but refused to accept the demand of their leader, Adolf Hitler, that he lead such a government. Support for the liberal, prodemocratic parties had dwindled to the point where they had little influence. German politics were polarized between a growing antisystem Right, headed by the Nazis, and an increasingly radical Left, composed of Communists and splinter socialist groups. The democratic middle, caught between these extremes and plagued by internal divisions, was unable to act decisively to save the system. After an extensive behind-the-scenes intrigue, some conservatives persuaded the now almost senile von Hindenburg that Hitler and the Nazis could be "handled" by traditional authoritarian conservatives and asked him to make Hitler the chancellor of a new conservative-nationalist government. Von Hindenburg agreed, and on January 30, 1933, Hitler became chancellor. By March 1933, Hitler had eliminated all significant opposition in parliament, when the Nazis pushed through an Enabling Act that granted him essentially dictatorial powers. The Third Reich, which was to have lasted a thousand years, had begun.

Why did the Weimar Republic fail? What happened to make a highly developed modern society turn to the primitive racist and nationalist appeals of the Nazis? Certainly there is no more important question confronting the student of modern German history. Some historians view Hitler's triumph as an abnormal, unique event not related to previous German historical and political development. They emphasize the specific set of circumstances in interwar Germany and Europe, and the defects in the Weimar Constitution, especially proportional representation. which worked to the benefit of small splinter parties and increased the difficulty of forming stable majorities in parliament. Thus with at times only 3 percent of the vote, the Nazis were still represented in the Reichstag as a very noisy minority. The dual executive of the Weimar system, which created a strong president independent of parliament, has also been cited by numerous analysts. The mediocre leadership of the democratic parties, the absence of any strong commitment to the system among some of its supporters, the behavior of key personalities such as von Hindenburg, and the effects of the foreign policies of the victorious Western powers are other factors that produced the Nazi dictatorship.[2] If one or more of these factors had been different, the Nazi seizure of power could have been avoided. According to this view, there was nothing inevitable about Nazism; it represented a clear break from Germany's course of political development.

Many non-German historians, especially from the United States and Britain, have taken a different approach to the origins of the Third Reich. Nazism is viewed more as the logical, if not predictable, outcome of German historical development and political culture. They point to the absence of a liberal middle-class revolution such as took place in France or Britain, and the later unification of the Reich, not through constitutional procedures, but through the "blood and iron" policies of Bismarck. The emphasis in the culture on authoritarian values—deference and obedience to superiors, reverence for order and discipline, and the hierarchical character of child rearing in the family and school are also cited. The German tradition of political philosophy and particularly its stress on *statism,* the treatment of the state as an organization superior to other social organizations, collectivism, and the absence of a strong tradition of liberal individualism in political theory have also been singled out as precursors of Nazism.

Other scholars emphasize the disunity and "internal contradictions" within the German middle class as a major factor in the collapse of the Weimar system. The capitalist class was, according to this view, divided between heavy industry, export industry, and the *Mittelstand* (lower-middle class of shopkeepers, artisans, and some salaried employees). Each of these groups had a somewhat different view of what kind of Republic it wanted and, above all, on the extent it was willing to cooperate with Germany's manual workers and their major political party, the Social Democrats. This internal disunity plagued the capitalist camp throughout the Republic and left it with no viable alternative to the Nazis after 1930, when further cooperation with the Social Democrats became impossible for all capitalist groups; that is, when none was willing to support (finance) the social welfare programs that were an indispensable condition of any continuation of a coalition with the Socialists. According to this view, Nazism or fascism was not the inevitable result of the capitalist economic system but, rather, the consequence of the German middle class's inability to develop an alternative solution (a presidential dictatorship, a corporatist system) to the post-1930 economic and political crisis.[3]

A fourth category of explanation stresses the relationship between socio-economic structure and Nazism. Specifically, the success of the Nazis is explained by the support of the German upper and middle classes that, fearing a socialist revolution and their loss of status more than fascism, gave Hitler and the Nazis key political and financial support. Other analysts have argued that fascism is a phase in the development of "late" capitalist societies. Hitler and the Nazis simply exploited this conservative aversion to the democratization of German political, social, and economic life, which the Weimar Republic would eventually have achieved had it not been for the "conservative counterrevolution." As we discuss in Chapter 2, some critics of the Bonn Republic have argued that is represents a "restoration," following the Nazi defeat, of the same capitalist institutions and processes that produced fascism in 1933.

THE NAZI THIRD REICH AND WORLD WAR II

The Nazi, or National Socialist German Workers party (NSDAP), was only one of numerous radical nationalist and *voelkisch* (racialist) parties and movements that sprang up in the chaotic atmosphere of postwar Germany. Founded in 1919 in Munich, it probably would have remained insignificant and eventually have disappeared had it not been for the extraordinary leadership ability of Adolf Hitler. Hitler, the son of a low-level Austrian civil servant, had fought in World War I as a volunteer for the German army. Before the war he was a sometime art student in Vienna, where he absorbed the pan-German nationalism, anti-Semitism, and anti-Marxism characteristic of right-wing circles in the Austrian capital. A powerful orator, he quickly assumed leadership of the National Socialists, and by the early 1920s the party became the most prominent of the radical right-wing groups in Munich. In 1923 the Nazis, allied with other nationalist groups including one led by World War I hero Ludendorff, made an amateurish attempt to overthrow the Bavarian government and begin a revolution throughout Germany. The Putsch failed, and Hitler was arrested and tried for treason; although convicted, he was treated very leniently by sympathetic Bavarian authorities.

Imprisoned or, rather, detained for two years, Hitler used the time to outline his future political plans in his book *Mein Kampf* ("My Struggle") which appeared in 1928 and became the oft-cited but seldom read "bible" of the Nazi movement. The Munich fiasco convinced Hitler that to succeed the party would have to come to power legally. A legal seizure of power would ensure the Nazis the support of most of the bureaucracy, the judiciary, and the army. With a program that promised a national renewal, rearmament, the revision of the hated Versailles treaty, together with social and economic reform for the working classes, the Nazis attempted to appeal to all members of the "racialist community" (*Volksgemeinschaft*). The party was particularly attractive for the marginal groups in German society: the small shopkeepers and artisans caught between big labor and big business, the small farmer losing out to larger enterprises and middlemen, the unemployed university graduates or university dropouts blaming the "system" for their condition. Yet, in spite of its program and a well-developed propaganda apparatus, the party remained a negligible factor until the Great Depression. It was not until the economic crisis of 1929 that the Nazis could break through and become the strongest force in the antirepublican camp.

After the appointment of Hitler as chancellor and the March 1933 Enabling Act, which suspended the parliament and constitution and essentially gave the Nazis carte blanche, the process of consolidating totalitarian one-party rule began in earnest. What Hitler and the Nazis sought was the *Gleichschaltung,* or coordination of all areas of German life to the Nazi pattern. By the end of 1934 this work was largely accomplished; all major social, economic, and political institutions were brought under the control of the party with their pattern of organization corresponding to its hierarchic, centralized structure. The "leadership principle," unquestioning obedience and acceptance of the *Führer's* (leader's) will as the highest law and authority, was the overriding organizational criterion.

Most Nazi coordination efforts took place under the pretext of legality. The burning of the Reichstag in February 1933 was used to secure a presidential emergency decree outlawing the Communist party and also allowing the Nazis to destroy the independence of the Reich's constituent states. Even the murder of hundreds of "counterrevolutionary" SA (storm troop) leaders and other "enemies" in June 1934 was later legalized by the puppet parliament. This pattern of lawlessness or the flagrant manipulation of the law lasted until the collapse of the system through military defeat. There was little qualitative difference between the June 1934 murders, the liquidation of other political and "racial enemies" in the concentration camps, and the later extermination of six million Jews.

Rule by a racially "superior" elite, the manipulation of the racially acceptable but "stupid" masses, and the extermination of Jews and other "inferior" peoples was, according to one authority, "the only genuine kernel of Hitler's ideology."[4] The "socialist" aspect of National Socialism and Hitler's professed opposition to plutocracy were designed to generate mass support for the leader. Regardless of the party's rhetoric or the views of its "left" wing, whose leaders were liquidated or had fled by 1934, "a strong state and the leadership principle, not economic and social reform, were the ideas guiding Hitler's policies on capitalism and socialism, organizations and group interests, reform and revolution. . . ."[5]

As Hitler promised in *Mein Kampf* and the Nazi party program, the elimination of the Jews as the greatest threat to the German *Volk* (race) began shortly after the seizure of power. On April 1, 1933, the Nazis initiated a boycott of Jewish shops in Berlin. In succeeding months Jews were dismissed from political positions and limited in their economic activities. In 1935 the Nuremberg Laws deprived Germany's half-million Jews of all political and civil liberties. Terror and violence were used on a mass scale beginning in November 1938 when the Nazis used the assassination of a German diplomat in Paris by a young Jew to loot and burn Jewish shops and synagogues throughout the Reich. Moreover, the remaining Jews were forced to pay for the damages caused by the Nazi mobs. By 1939 about 400,000 German and Austrian Jews had emigrated. Most of the remaining 300,000 were eventually to suffer the same fate as the rest of European Jewry: mass extermination.

There can be little doubt that the Nazi regime, at least until the start of World War II, enjoyed considerable mass support. Even in 1951, 42 percent of adult West Germans and 53 percent of those over thirty-five still stated that the prewar years of the Third Reich (1933–1939) were the "best" that Germany had experienced in this century. Those were, of course, years of economic growth and at least a surface prosperity. Unemployment was virtually eliminated; inflation was checked; and the economy, fueled by expenditures for rearmament and public works, boomed. That during these "good years" thousands of Germans were imprisoned, tortured, and murdered in concentration camps, and hundreds of thousands of German Jews systematically persecuted, was apparently of minor importance to most citizens in comparison with the economic and policy successes of the regime. The suppression of civil liberties and all political opposition and the *Gleichschaltung* of the churches, schools, universities, the press, and trade unions were accepted with little overt opposition. In a sense most Germans, at least between 1933 and 1939, were willing to give up the democratic political order and the liberal society and accept the regime's racism and persecution of political opponents in exchange for economic prosperity, social stability, and a resurgence of national pride.

Yet, sizable segments of German society remained relatively immune to the Nazis even after Hitler's assumption of the chancellorship in January 1933. The Nazis never, for example, received an absolute majority of votes in any free election during the Weimar Republic. Even at the last election in March 1933 (about five weeks after Hitler took power), which because of Nazi agitation and terror tactics against opposing parties was less free than preceding polls, the party received only 44 percent of the vote, and in some electoral districts its support was as low as 10 or 20 percent. German Catholics and Socialists with strong ties to the highly developed secondary organizations of the church and party, such as youth, labor, and women's groups, were especially resistant to Nazi appeals.

From the beginning, the Nazi system was directed at the total mobilization of Germany for aggressive war. Military expansion was not only to secure *Lebensraum* (living space) for the superior German race but also to justify one-party dictatorship and unify the racial community. Capitalizing on the internal weaknesses and division among the major European democracies (Britain and France), the isolationist United States, and a suspicious Soviet Union, Hitler marched from success to success from 1938 (annexation of Austria) until late 1942 when Soviet troops finally turned the tide at Stalingrad. Each military and foreign political success strengthened the Nazi system at home and made the small and scattered opposition groups unable to mount any serious challenge to the regime.

It was not until July 1944, less than a year before the end of the war, that a group of military officers and civilian opponents made a desperate attempt at a coup d'état. The key element in the plan, the assassination of Hitler, failed, and the entire opposition movement was soon crushed by large-scale arrests and executions.

In the territories conquered by the German armies, the full horror of Nazism was experienced. To establish Hitler's "New Order," millions of European civilians and prisoners of war—men, women, and children—were systematically murdered by special Nazi extermination units. In the name of the German people, "useless human material"—the mentally retarded in hospitals and asylums and Europe's gypsies—were dispatched. Also marked for extermination were actual or potential political opponents—the Polish intelligentsia, the political commissars in the Soviet army, the resistance fighters. Finally, military conquest meant the "final solution" of the "Jewish problem." At large camps serviced by special railway lines and selected Nazi personnel, six million European Jews were murdered.

The existence of the extermination camps was kept secret; most Germans had little if any knowledge of what the Nazis were doing to civilians in the occupied territories. Yet few probably made any effort to find out. Caught up in the demands of war, subjected to incessant propaganda, and fearful of the regime's extensive domestic terror apparatus, which included the secret police (*Gestapo*) and informers among the civilian population, most Germans remained passive until the end.

The Third Reich finally collapsed in May 1945 as American, Russian, British, French, and other Allied forces totally defeated the German armies and occupied the Reich. This time, unlike 1918, there could be no stab-in-the-back legend. The defeat and destruction of the Nazi system brought military occupation and massive uncertainty about the future of Germany as a national community, much less a political system. Point Zero, the absolute bottom, had been reached.

FOREIGN OCCUPATION AND NATIONAL DIVISION

Between 1945 and 1949, Germany's conquerors reduced the size of its territory, divided the remainder into four zones of military occupation, and finally established two new states from these zones: the Federal Republic of Germany (British, French, and American zones) and the German Democratic Republic (Russian zone). All territories annexed by the Nazis between 1938 and 1940 were returned to their former Austrian, Czechoslovakian (the Sudetenland), or French (Alsace-Lorraine) owners. Moreover, consistent with the Allied agreement at Yalta, those German areas east of the Oder and Neisse rivers (the

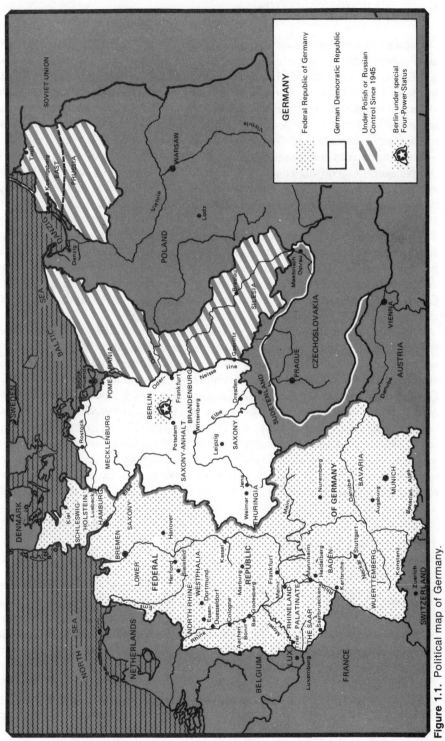

Figure 1.1. Political map of Germany.

Oder-Neisse line), including East Prussia and Silesia, were put under "temporary" Soviet or Polish administration. The ultimate fate of these eastern territories was to be decided by a final peace treaty between Germany and the wartime Allies. Such a treaty, however, has never been signed; in 1972 the Federal Republic, by ratifying treaties with the Soviet Union and Poland, in fact recognized their loss as permanent. Most German nationals living in these regions were expelled by Soviet and Polish forces after 1945 and forced to resettle in the remaining German territory. Deprived of their property without compensation, these expellees had to build new lives in what was left of a war-ravaged country. The integration of these 10 million refugees into postwar West German society was a major task confronting the new Federal Republic in 1949.

The rest of the prewar Reich was divided into British, French, American, and Russian zones of occupation. The former capital of Berlin, lying within the Russian zone, was given special status and also divided into four sectors. Each military commander exercised authority in his respective zone, and an Allied Control Council, composed of the four commanders, was jointly and unanimously to make decisions affecting Germany as a whole.

During the war the Allies had agreed on the general lines of postwar policy toward Germany. First, Germany was to be *denazified;* all vestiges of the Nazi system were to be removed, top Nazi and government officials tried as war criminals, and lesser party activists punished by fines and imprisonment. Second, Germany was to be *demilitarized,* its capability to wage aggressive war permanently removed. Third, postwar Germany was to be a *democratic* society. To this end, extensive programs of political education were to be planned and implemented in the postwar period. A complete reform of the German education system was included under this democratization program. Finally, the former Reich was to be *decentralized,* with important political responsibilities delegated to states (*Länder*) and local governments.

THE FORMATION OF THE FEDERAL REPUBLIC

The wartime consensus that produced these policy plans quickly disappeared after 1945 as differences between the three Western powers and the Soviet Union made any common occupation policy impossible. In the Soviet zone of occupation, local governments controlled by communists or pro-Soviet elements were quickly established. Whole plants were dismantled and shipped to the Soviet Union; the remaining industry was nationalized and agriculture collectivized.

These actions, basically designed to turn at least the Soviet zone, if not all of Germany, into a communist state and society, were both politically and ideologically unacceptable to the Western powers already alarmed by similar Russian actions in Poland and Hungary. By 1948 it was apparent that no all-German political or economic cooperation was possible. In the face of what was perceived by Western policymakers as a growing Soviet threat, the Western Allies began to envision a postwar German state without the Soviet zone of occupation—a West German entity composed of the American, British, and French zones. The French, however, were reluctant at first to agree to the establishment of even a centralized West German state, which could become a power rivaling France on the European continent. By 1948, however, French fear of the Soviet Union exceeded its fear of Germany, and the three Western Allies announced a common economic policy and issued a common currency in their zones. The Soviet Union responded with an attempt to deny the Western powers access to Berlin (the Berlin blockade) and began the construction of another separate German state in its zone, the German Democratic Republic (GDR) with its capital in East Berlin.

By the late 1940s it was thus clear that neither the United States nor the Soviet Union would allow "their" Germans to pursue policies that they could not control and that could possibly be directed against their interests. Both super-powers wanted a single German state only on their terms: a liberal, pluralistic democratic state for the United States; a communist, worker, or peasant state for the Soviet Union. Unable to achieve such a unified state without military conflict, the two superpowers settled for two states each having the social, economic, and political characteristics of their respective protector. Ironically, however, the division of Germany enabled both states within a relatively short time to achieve a status within their respective power bloc that a single German state could never have attained.

These fateful developments, which sealed the division and dismemberment of the prewar Reich, took place with little direct German participation. German governments, however, had existed at the local and state levels since 1946. The initial intent of Western and especially American occupiers was to democratize Germany in gradual stages, beginning at the local level where stronger traditions of democratic self-government existed. Thus local and state institutions *preceded* the creation of central institutions for West Germany.

Most Germans were not concerned with the future of the nation or their own responsibility or guilt for Nazism, much less politics. Their immediate problem was physical survival: food, clothing, and shelter. According to surveys, six out of every ten Germans stated that they "suffered greatly" from hunger in the postwar years. The average caloric intake during the period from 1945 to 1947 was less than 70 percent of that deemed adequate.[6] Almost half of all families suffered partial or total loss of their household through bombing raids. After physical survival came the problem of putting their personal lives back together again: returning to school, resuming a career, starting the business again, finding a job, raising a fatherless family. Thus the events and decisions between 1945 and 1949 that were so crucial to the birth of the Federal Republic were made within a context of mass indifference to politics. Germans in the immediate postwar years had reduced their sphere of social concern to the most basic level: the self and the immediate family.

On July 1, 1948, in Frankfurt, the three Western Allied military governors met with the *Ministerpräsidenten,* or governors, of the various states and "recommended" (i.e., ordered) the calling of a constituent assembly by September 1, 1948, which was to draft a constitution for the three Western zones. This constitution was then to be placed before the electorate for approval. None of the state leaders was enthusiastic about establishing a separate West German state. They felt that the constituent assembly and the resultant constitution would seal the division of Germany. Meeting before the assembly, with the heads of the two major political parties, the state leaders decided to term the document they were to draft a "Basic Law" rather than a constitution and to stress in it the provisional character of the new entity. After a long delay, the states finally convened a constituent assembly to draft the document. Nine months later, in May 1949, their work was completed. But again, wanting to avoid the appearance of permanence, they asked for ratification by the state parliaments rather than through popular referendum. This was acceptable to the Allied authorities. Thus the West German Constitution was never directly approved by the citizens of West Germany.

The declaration of ratification hardly evoked any celebration. One influential news magazine termed the document a "bastard of a constitution" produced in nine months through pressure by the military occupation.[7] In a national survey conducted at the time, 40 percent of the adult population stated that they were indifferent to the constitution, 33 percent were "moderately interested," and only 21 percent were "very interested." Only 51 percent, in another survey conducted in 1949, favored the creation of the Federal Republic; the remainder of the sample were either against it (23 percent), indifferent (13 percent), or undecided (13 percent).[8]

Like it or not, however, Germans in the Western-occupied zones of the former Reich had a new constitution and political system on May 23, 1949. Shortly after in the Soviet zone, a second German state, the German Democratic Republic, was proclaimed in East Berlin.

As we discuss throughout the remainder of this book, by most standards of how political systems are judged—stability, effectiveness, and legitimacy—and especially in comparison to past German regimes, the institutions of the Bonn Republic have performed well. The reluctant drafters of the constitution produced a document that, unlike the constitution of the Weimar Republic, has survived to structure meaningfully the behavior of West Germans and their political decisionmakers. To be successful, political institutions must operate within a socioeconomic and attitudinal or cultural context supportive of these abstract legal structures. The tragic experience of Weimar underscores this requisite for political success. The most carefully constructed constitution is, in the long run, of little value if the society and culture are not supportive of its key principles and norms. Hence two important questions in our survey of the West

German polity must be: To what extent have German socioeconomic conditions and political values changed in the postwar period, and do these changes relate to the stability, effectiveness, and legitimacy of the Bonn system? The following two chapters, which examine contemporary socioeconomic patterns and political values, seek to answer these questions.

NOTES

1. Donald S. Detweiler, *Germany: A Short History* (Carbondale: Southern Illinois University Press, 1976), pp. 46 ff.
2. Karl Dietrich Bracher, *The German Dictatorship* (New York: Praeger, 1970).
3. David Abraham, "Intra-Class Conflict and the Formulation of Ruling Class Consensus in Late Weimar Germany" (Ph.D. dissertation, Department of History, University of Chicago, 1977).
4. Bracher, *The German Dictatorship*, p. 181.
5. Ibid.
6. In some urban areas in the Rhine-Ruhr region, daily food rations in the winter of 1946–1947 dropped to 800 calories per person. By the end of 1946, per capita industrial production had declined to the level of 1865. Günter J. Trittel, "Die westlichen Besatzungsmächte und der Kampf gegen den Mangel, 1945–1949", *Aus Politik und Zeitgeschichte*, no. 22 (May 31, 1986): 20–21.
7. *Der Spiegel* commentary cited in Karl-Heinz Janssen, "Das dauerhafte Provisorium," *Die Zeit* (24 May 1974), p. 10.
8. Institut für Demoskopie, *Jahrbuch der öffentlichen Meinung 1947–1955* (Allensbach: Verlag für Demoskopie, 1956), 1:161.

CHAPTER 2

The Social and Economic Setting

Neither people nor states function in a vacuum. The historical, geographical, and socioeconomic contexts influence political attitudes and behavior as well as policymaking institutions. This is especially true of the Federal Republic, where important postwar geographic, social, and economic changes have created a setting for politics quite different from that experienced by past regimes. This chapter surveys these contextual changes as they relate to modern German politics.

AREA AND POPULATION

The Federal Republic, with an area of approximately 96,000 square miles, roughly the size of Oregon, comprises about 60 percent of the pre-World War II territory of the Reich. As we discuss later, this loss had several important consequences for postwar German politics. The Republic now extends 530 miles from the Danish border in the north to the Bavarian Alps in the south (See Figure 1–1). Its east-west dimensions are much smaller; it is only 270 miles from the Austrian border in the southeast to the border with France in the southwest and only 140 miles from the border with East Germany in the northeast to the border with the Netherlands in the northwest.

In 1939 the present area of the Federal Republic had a population of 43 million; by 1949 this had grown to 49.6 million, with almost all of this increase due to the influx of 6.4 million refugees from German territories annexed or occupied by Poland and the Soviet Union in 1945. Throughout the 1950s and 1960s, the population continued to grow because of the rising birthrate that accompanied economic prosperity, an additional three million refugees mainly (until 1961) from East Germany, and approximately 4 million foreign workers and their families.

Since 1974, however, the population of the Federal Republic has steadily declined. There were 62.1 million people in 1973, but by 1984 the total population had dropped to 61.4 million, 56.9 million of whom were native Germans. West Germany in 1984 had the lowest birth rate in the world (10.1 live births per 1,000 inhabitants). If this trend continues, the native population will drop to 54.9 million in the year 2000 and only 42.6 million by 2030. Over one-half of the Republic's 23 million families are without children, and about half of the remaining families have only one child. Thus less than one family in four has two or more children. Modern contraceptive techniques, liberalized abortion laws, and the growing number of women opting for the work force instead of the traditional *Hausfrau* role are the major reasons for this decline.[1]

URBANIZATION AND INDUSTRIALIZATION

West Germany, with 245 inhabitants per square kilometer, is one of the most densely populated nation-states in Europe. It is also a heavily urbanized society, with half of its population living on less than 10 percent of the land. The large urban areas, however, are distributed throughout the country and make for considerable diversity. The largest of these, with 10.9 million inhabitants, is the Rhine-Ruhr region between Düsseldorf and Dortmund. Six other industrial-urban regions each has a population of more than a million: the Rhine-Main area (Frankfurt), West Berlin, Stuttgart, Hamburg, Munich, and the Rhine-Neckar region. Another six urban areas have a population exceeding 500,000: Nuremberg, Hanover, Bremen, the Saar, Aachen, and Bielefeld and Herford.

Much of this urbanization took place during the last quarter of the nineteenth century when Germany within a generation became one of the world's leading industrial powers. Today the Federal Republic, after the United States and Japan, is the third-largest industrial power in the noncommunist world and the largest in Western Europe.

An Export-Oriented Economy

Lacking self-sufficiency in food and raw materials, Germany's economic well-being, like that of England and Japan, is heavily dependent on successful competition in the international economic arena. In essence, Germany must import food and raw materials and pay for them by the export of manufactured goods. About 85 percent of German exports are manufactured goods—automobiles, chemicals, heavy machinery—sent in 1986, for example, to fellow Common Market members (51 percent); other West European countries (19 percent); North America (11 percent); the developing countries of Asia, Africa, and Latin America (11 percent); and the communist bloc countries (8 percent). Two-thirds of West Germany's imports, on the other hand, consist of food supplies, raw materials, and semifinished products.[2] Success in this exchange depends on the ability of German industry to sell its manufactured goods at a price greater than the costs of raw materials and production. Successful production is in turn strongly related to an adequate supply of skilled, disciplined industrial labor, management expertise, and scientific know-how.

The Germans have been very successful in the business of international trade. Until the late 1970s, the Federal Republic had an annual trade surplus averaging almost $5 billion, and between 1967 and 1978 the surplus averaged about $10 billion per year. Even the skyrocketing price of oil, which by 1974 produced deficits in the balance of payments for most industrial nations, did not deter the West German economy from a balance of payment surplus in 1974 of over $10 billion. In 1987 the German balance of payments surplus was a record $70 billion. Starting with practically no foreign currency reserved in 1949, the Federal Republic by 1987 had accumulated $77 billion in reserves as compared to $35.7 billion for the United States and $40.7 billion for Great Britain. German industry overall receives about 25 to 30 percent of its gross sales from exports. In some industries—automobiles, steel, chemicals, machine tools—almost half of total sales come from the foreign market. By 1986 West Germany was the world's top exporting nation.

Like the United States, the Federal Republic, however, has in recent years lost significant portions of its shipbuilding, electronics, and even automobile market to foreign imports, especially from Japan, Taiwan, Yugoslavia, and other countries where labor costs are lower. To meet this challenge and reduce labor costs, German industry has turned to increased automation, which has, at least in the short run, aggravated the unemployment problem.

In spite of these difficulties, the overall performance of postwar West Germany in foreign trade cannot be equaled by any other advanced industrial society during this period with the possible exception of Japan. Little wonder that the *die Wirtschaft* (the economy) and its representatives are an important power factor in German politics and policymaking. German industrial and business interests have a record of accomplishment that ensures them respectful consideration by any government.

THE RURAL SECTOR

The significance of agricultural production for the West German economy has rapidly declined in the postwar period. The loss of the predominantly agrarian eastern territories reduced the amount of arable land, but even within West Germany the percentage of the gross national product contributed by agriculture and the size of the agricultural work force has also steadily dropped. Between 1950 and 1981 the proportion working in agriculture declined from 25 percent to 5 percent; agricultural production contributed only 12 percent of the gross national product in 1949; and by 1985 this had dropped even further to less than 2 percent.[3]

For the most part, West German agriculture has been inefficient in the use of land, labor, and capital. Although the number of farms of less than four acres in size had dropped by almost a million between 1950 and 1981, 42 percent of German farms in 1981 as compared to 80 percent in 1949 were still in this size category. Germany's farms are on average the smallest of any non-Mediterannean country of the European Community. This small size means a high labor input and an uneconomical use of modern machinery. Since the early 1950s, the policies of West German governments have been directed toward the restructuring of German agriculture through land consolidation (fewer but larger farms) and the improvement of farm buildings, roads, land, and drainage. A succession of "green plans" between 1956 and 1968 pumped roughly $10 billion into these projects. Yet German agriculture remains in a poor competitive position with its more agrarian-oriented neighbors such as France and Italy.

Governmental subsidies have continued, however. In addition to those paid to the farmer under the green plan, new agricultural subsidy laws have been passed in recent years that continue many green plan programs in addition to new measures to aid the farmer in the adaptation to the changed Common Market situation. These subsidies are largely a tribute to the political effectiveness of West German agricultural interests. They also reflect, however, a romantic attachment to the land that persists in spite of the industrialized and urbanized character of the society. Little wonder, then, that the official name of the agriculture ministry, The Ministry for Nourishment and Agriculture, is referred to by Bonn wags as The Ministry for the Nourishment of Agriculture.

In spite of their continued marginal character, farmers and their interest organizations, unlike agrarian interests during the Weimar Republic, have not shown any inclination to support antisystem parties. This is due in part to the integration of agrarian interests into the democratic political parties, but it also reflects the changed structure of rural interests. During the empire and the Weimar Republic, the Prussian landowners (*Junker*) with their large estates had major influence on agricultural policy and often conflicted with the policy claims of small and medium-sized farmers. In contrast, the structure of West German agriculture is more homogeneous, and the interests of farmers can be more easily integrated into party and government programs.

REGIONALISM

The enormous postwar migration of refugees, Europe's largest since the sixth century; the division of the prewar Reich; the loss of the eastern territories to the Soviet Union and Poland; and the general modernization of German society have greatly reduced regional differences in lifestyles, including political behavior and values. Regional dialects and customs remain, of course, but the economic, social, and political characteristics of the Federal Republic show less of the regional variation common before 1933. Germans today read national newspapers, listen to national radio networks, and watch national television programs. The extensive geographical mobility of postwar Germans has also reduced regionalism in the sense of Germany's comprising separate, distinct subcultures.

Although West Germany is a federal system with ten states (eleven, including West Berlin), or *Länder,* having considerable authority in areas such as education, police, and urban development, the geographical boundaries of these states, with the exception of Bavaria and the city-states of Hamburg and Bremen, have few if any historical roots and were created in most cases by the edicts of military government. By forcing regions together into states to form a federal system, the Western Allies ironically further reduced regional differences in the Federal Republic. Moreover, all states administer the same national legal codes and procedures; administrative practices are also quite uniform throughout the Republic.

The development of particularistic and regional sentiments is further inhibited by constitutional provisions (Article 107) requiring a "Unity of Living Standards" throughout all Länder. This equalization takes place through both federal redistribution to poorer states of a proportion of the states' share of certain taxes (vertical equalization) and through direct payments by the richer states to the poorer ones (horizontal integration).[4] In 1986, for example, the "rich" states of Baden-Württemberg, Hesse, and Hamburg paid about $1.4 billion to the poorer states of Bavaria, Lower Saxony, the Rhineland-Palatinate, Schleswig-Holstein, the Saar, and Bremen. Through these procedures a Land such as Schleswig-Holstein, whose per capita income is only 80 percent of that of Hesse, has a per capita tax income amounting to about 95 percent of that enjoyed by its richer neighbor.

OCCUPATIONAL AND CLASS STRUCTURE

As a highly developed industrial society, the occupational structure of the Federal Republic is similar to that of other advanced industrial societies. The largest single occupational group (48 percent in 1986) is composed of those in white-collar and service occupations. Like manual workers, people in these occupations are employees—that is, they are dependent on wages and salaries— but unlike manual workers, they have had on the average more extensive academic training and enjoy a considerably higher social status and, in many cases, income than manual workers. The next largest group (39 percent) is made up of manual workers, most of whom are skilled, having completed extensive vocational training. The third-largest occupational group is composed of those in "independent" nonmanual positions (owners and directors of enterprises, doctors, lawyers, small businessmen, independent artisans). Finally about 4 percent of the work force is employed in agricultural, forestry, and fishing occupations.

The present occupational structure is largely the result of an extensive industrialization and modernization process begun during the last quarter of the nineteenth century, intensified by the demands of the war, and continuing to the present day. The main characteristics of these changes are common to all advanced industrial societies:

1. A steady decline in the proportion employed in the "primary sphere" of the economy: agriculture and independent nonmanuals. At the turn of the century, 36 percent of the work force was still in these occupations, but as Table 2.1 shows, by 1986 they comprised only 13 percent of the work force.

2. A relative stagnation or even slow decline in the proportion employed in the secondary or production sphere of the economy (industrial manual occupations). Its relative position declined from 57 percent in 1882 to 39 percent by 1986.

3. Rapid growth among those in the tertiary sphere: the white-collar and service occupations. The size of this group has more than doubled over the last three decades (21 percent to 48 percent). The tertiary sector overtook manual workers by the late 1970s. The United States reached this point by the mid-1950s.[5]

These structural changes have brought increasing social mobility to West Germany, although by American standards the rate of *upward* mobility is still limited, especially among the offspring of manual workers. According to an extensive social-mobility study conducted in 1970, upward social mobility increased from 25 percent among the oldest age group in the sample (sixty-five and older) to almost 35 percent among respondents under forty-five years of age. Downward social mobility increased slightly from about 17 percent among the oldest age group to 20 percent for the younger members of the sample. Thus, those West Germans entering the labor market in the postwar period (those born since 1926) have experienced more social mobility than earlier generations.[6] Yet the same study found that among *manual workers* "the upward mobility rates and opportunities have not improved during the last fifty years."[7] Upper-class and status occupations requiring extensive academic training still remain relatively closed to the children of manual workers.

TABLE 2.1. OCCUPATIONAL COMPOSITION OF THE WORK FORCE, 1882–1986 (in percentages)

Occupational Category	1882	1925	Year 1950	1974	1986
Agriculture and self-employed	36	33	28	14	13
Manual workers	57	50	51	45	39
Salaried nonmanual (white-collar and service)	7	17	21	41	48

SOURCE: *Statistiches Jahrbuch für die Bundesrepublik Deutschland, 1971, 1975.* (Stuttgart: Kohlhammer Verlag); for 1986: Emil Hübner and Horst-Hennek Rohlfs, *Jahrbuch der Bundesrepublik Deutschland 1987/88.* Munich: Deutscher Taschenbuch Verlag, 1987, p. 11.

THE ECONOMY

Postwar Germany has become one of the world's most prosperous nations. The industrial economy manned by a highly skilled work force has made the Federal Republic a mass consumption society in a relatively short time. A 1983 study, conducted during the midst of the worst postwar recession, still found that two-thirds of all households had combined assets (property, savings, cars, insurance, stocks) exceeding DM100,000 (about $50,000); over a fourth of all households had assets worth more than DM500,000 ($250,000). Finally, one out of every twenty-five households had assets of over DM1 million ($500,000).[8]

The country was not spared, however, two recessions—from 1974 to 1976 and again from 1981 to 1983. The latter was by far the most severe. By February 1983 almost 10 percent of the work force was unemployed, the highest level in over 30 years. From the end of 1980 to 1983 the number of unemployed increased from less than 1 million to almost 2.5 million. In 1981 and 1982 there was virtually no growth in the economy; business failures rose to record levels, and the government was forced to borrow heavily to finance social and welfare expenditures. In spite of record unemployment, however, the extensive system of social insurance and welfare, which links compensation to actual earnings, meant that few Germans suffered a devastating loss in their standard of living.

As Table 2.2 shows, the postwar German economy has gone through four rather distinct stages. The first stage occurred during the 1950s, the years of reconstruction and the "economic miracle," and it paved the way for later decades. Economic growth averaged almost a phenomenal 8 percent per year. Inflation, which averaged less than 2 percent during the 1950s, was among the lowest in the industrialized world. During this reconstruction phase, unemployment was substantial especially during the early 1950s. The ten-year average of 1.2 million still represented less than 5 percent of the work force.

The heavy investment in capital equipment during reconstruction bore fruit in the second stage: the "golden 1960s." Economic growth averaged a healthy 5 percent; inflation remained nominal at only 2.4 percent, and more important, unemployment practically disappeared, dropping to less than 1 percent. In fact,

TABLE 2.2. GERMAN ECONOMIC TRENDS, 1950–1987

Period	Economic Growth %[a]	Inflation, %	Unemployment (average)[b]
1950–1959	7.9	1.9	1.2 million
1960–1969	5.0	2.4	223,000
1970–1979	3.2	4.9	647,000
1980–1987	1.8	3.2	2.1 million

[a] Adjusted for inflation (real growth).
[b] Average annual level.
SOURCE: Federal Statistical Office, Federal Bank.

Germany during the 1960s had a labor shortage that necessitated importing almost 2 million foreign workers. This impressive performance throughout the 1960s also took place in spite of the 1966–1967 economic slump, the first in the Republic's history.

The sharp increase in oil prices during the 1970s and the resultant worldwide recession heavily affected the German economy. These were the "difficult years." Yet the economy remained very strong relative to the other Western European nations and the United States. Economic growth averaged 3.2 percent annually throughout the period, a very respectable performance especially in light of the 1974–1976 recession. Inflation, however, jumped sharply to almost 5 percent, a high figure by German standards. Finally, unemployment became a serious problem for the first time since the early 1950s. From the mid-1970s to the end of the decade, between 800,000 and 1 million Germans were out of work. Some of this unemployment was due to the general worldwide recession, but much of it was also structural. Certain German industries were no longer competitive: textiles, shipping, consumer electronics, and even cameras were lost to the Japanese and other low-wage exporting countries.

Since 1980 the economy has been in a critical period. Economic growth has averaged less than 2 percent. Capital investment has declined. Business failures in 1982–1983 reached record levels. Unemployment has remained high at about 8 to 10 percent. One of the few bright spots has been the low inflation level, which because of the strong mark and falling oil prices dropped to only about 2 percent in 1988. This poor economic performance was a major reason for the collapse of the Schmidt government in 1982. Unemployment, for example, was considered to be an important issue by 88 percent of the voters in the 1983 election. The belief or hope that the Christian Democrats could do a better job than the Social Democrats was a decisive factor in the party's victory.

The lackluster record of the German economy in recent years and especially the high unemployment level has been the result of a variety of factors. First, many economists contend that there is too much regulation and inflexibility throughout the economy. Government monopolies in the postal and telecommunications fields, for example, inhibit innovation or expansion in these areas, which in countries such as the United States have been the source of high growth rates and many new jobs. A second problem contributing to low economic growth is the shortage of venture capital. The German capital market is dominated by large banks that work well with established industries but have been slow to fund innovative, high-risk projects. Third, Germany's labor laws and regulations make it difficult to lay off employees even if the companies are losing money. Even in periods of expansion, many firms increase overtime or hire temporary workers instead of adding to the regular work force. Fourth, long-term subsidies to declining industries such as coal, steel, and shipbuilding as well as agriculture have had a negative impact on growth. These funds could be better spent in funding new, high-tech projects with growth potential. Finally, the service sectors of the German economy could grow at a faster rate were it not for trade-union opposition and rigid government regulations. German retail shops, for example, must by law close at 6:30 P.M. from Monday through Friday and at 2:00 P.M. on most Saturdays.

Allowing these stores to remain open longer would reduce unemployment and provide more convenience for the shopping public. The retail workers' trade unions, however, have threatened to strike over this issue, and the government has thus far sought to avoid a confrontation. Economists estimate that removing these various regulations and restrictions would increase the growth rate by about 2 percent and cut unemployment by 25 percent. Many Germans, however, are more concerned about the inflation that increased growth may bring than they are about sluggish growth rates.

Income Structure

Although almost all gainfully employed West Germans have a relatively high standard of living, there remain persistent and in some cases growing gaps in income and capital resources between different occupational and class groups. Modern Germany is still a stratified society. The average monthly net income of different occupational groups is presented in Table 2.3. At the top is the group referred to by German sociologists as "independents" or "employers" (the owners and directors of enterprises, farmers with their own land holdings, and free professionals: doctors, lawyers, small businessmen), which constitutes about 12 percent of the work force. In 1984 its members had average incomes about 2.5 times greater than those of employees (white-collar or manual). White-collar employees, who constitute 48 percent of the work force, had take-home incomes of more than $2,000 monthly in 1984, whereas manual workers (39 percent of the work force) had net monthly incomes of about $1,600. At the bottom are retired persons, with average incomes of about $900 per month. Given this pattern of income distribution, the differences in the savings and other capital resources of these respective groups are considerable.

TABLE 2.3. INCOME BY OCCUPATION, 1984

Occupational Group	Average Net Monthly Income, in $[a]
Independents (owners, directors of enterprises, free professionals, and farmers)	5,375
White collar, civil servant	2,125
Manual worker	1,620

[a] DM2.00 equals $1.
SOURCE: Federal Statistical Office data cited in Hübner and Rohlfs, Jahrbuch, 1987,88, p. 22.

Capital Resources

Ownership of private property in the form of family homes, for example, will not be experienced by the majority of German manual workers. In 1980, although manual workers made up more than 40 percent of the work force, only about 20 percent of all new homes built had a manual worker as buyer.[9] Independent nonmanuals, only about a tenth of the work force, bought almost 40 percent of all new homes. Thus the well-fed, well-traveled, and motorized German worker will not be likely to own land in his lifetime. He will, however, live in a comfortably furnished apartment (three to four rooms in addition to kitchen), paying about 20 percent of his monthly take-home pay for rent.

The disparity between manual workers and white-collar employees, and especially between these two groups and employers, is most evident in the area of *productive* capital resources (savings, stocks, securities). As Table 2.4 shows, in 1973, the latest date for which these figures are available, white-collar workers had 1.8 times as much "capital" ($7,500) as manual workers ($4,150), and civil servants with $23,000 in capital had about 550 percent more than workers. But even these white-collar employees and civil servants seem impoverished when compared to owners, directors, and free professionals (employers), who had per capita resources of $172,000 in 1973. Indeed, by 1976, 10 percent of the adult population controlled about 50 percent of the nation's productive capital.[10] Little wonder that the problem of the distribution of capital resources has become a major policy issue in modern West German politics.

This economic inequality, which is also reinforced by the education system, is largely the result of postwar governmental economic policy, which gave a free

TABLE 2.4. CAPITAL RESOURCES BY OCCUPATION[a]

Occupation	Percentage of Total Households	Percentage of Capital Resources	Per Capita Capital Resources in $[b]
Independents, (owners, directors of enterprises, free professionals, and farmers)	10.2	44.1	172,000
Civil servants	6.3	4.4	23,000
White-collar employees	20.1	14.8	7,500
Manual workers	28.2	15.8	4,150
Nonemployed (retired, housewives, students, etc.)	35.2	20.9	3,510

[a] Capital resources include land, stocks, bonds, securities, savings, and life insurance.
[b] DM2.00 equals $1.
SOURCE: Horst Mierheim and Lutz Wicke, Die personelle Vermögensverteilung in der Bundesrepublik Deutschland (Tübingen: J. C. B. Mohr Verlag, 1978), cited in Michael Jungblut, "Die heimlichen Reichen," Die Zeit, no. 46 (10 November 1978), p. 25.

hand to market forces and created a very favorable atmosphere for investment capital. The 1948 currency reforms, for example, which abolished the Reichsmark and installed the now-famous Deutsche Mark (DM), to a large extent wiped out the savings of lower- and middle-income groups, who received only about 1 new mark for every 7 old Reichsmarks. Landowners and holders of stocks, securities, and capital in foreign countries lost nothing, however. Indeed, they gained. Moderate tax rates on profits and income from investments, generous subsidies for new plant and equipment, and lucrative tax write-offs also helped to prime the investment pump.

The major economic structures of prewar Germany—business, banking, and industrial firms—were not destroyed by the war or the military occupation but survived fairly intact to provide institutional leadership and support for economic reconstruction.[11] But these institutions of capitalist economic development could perform only if political leadership, both German and Allied, decided to take the free market rather than the socialist path to economic reconstruction. The desire to rebuild as quickly as possible in the face of a perceived Soviet threat meant a decision in favor of the capitalist market economy.

The general success of this system during the past forty years has been described. Its long-run consequences, particularly in producing and sustaining inequality and rigid social stratification, are just now being grappled with in the political arena. The potential that this issue of inequality has in politics can be seen in a 1984 study in which 62 percent of the adult population stated that economic rewards are not justly distributed in the Federal Republic.[12]

West Germany's New Left has been sharply critical of this postwar decision to restore a capitalist system, which had proven so helpless in the face of the Nazi onslaught. They argue that between 1945 and 1949 Germany missed the opportunity of laying the foundations for a true socialist society by not expropriating and socializing industry, banks, and other commercial institutions and creating a state-controlled planned economy. According to this view, there is a close connection between capitalism and the Hitler dictatorship, and by restoring capitalism the Western Allies and postwar German leaders also restored the fascist potential.

It is difficult to evaluate this interpretation of postwar German development. There is little doubt that for the sake of rapid economic reconstruction a conscious decision was made to use established economic resources rather than to build a new economic order from scratch. There is also little doubt that the free market or capitalist approach was, at least in the short run, extraordinarily successful. The West German economy is, however, hardly a "pure" capitalist system. As in other advanced Western countries, government, through subsidies, regulation, and in some cases capital investment, plays a major economic role.[13] In 1988, for example, the federal government paid out over $18 billion in subsidies to groups such as farmers, home builders and owners, the aerospace industry, shipbuilders, coal and steel companies, and the city of West Berlin. The federal government and the *Land* (state) of Lower Saxony are also major

stockholders in the Volkswagen automobile firm. National and state governments are also heavily involved in the coal and iron industries, as well as in
housing and transportation. There is a considerable mix of public and private
components in the economy.

Moreover, Germany's postwar economic elites have assumed a more active
political role than at any other time in German history. But this role has been
distinctly supportive of the liberal Republic. Business and industrial elites, once
subordinate to traditional Prussian and then to radical Nazi political leadership,
finally found political responsibility thrust on them in the Bonn Republic. And
like their counterparts in other advanced industrial societies, they have been
concerned above all with stable political conditions and have supported, indeed
have helped to create, the pragmatic, middle-of-the-road policies the Republic
has thus far pursued. In this sense Germany's economic elites did after 1945 what
they should have done in 1871—assumed their share of responsibility for the
conduct of politics instead of deferring to the traditional Prussian elites in
political matters. Thus far in the Bonn Republic, the economic elites have shown
no inclination to support or be associated with any extremist political movement
or philosophy.

RELIGIOUS COMPOSITION

At birth almost all Germans become members of either the Roman Catholic or
the Protestant church. This division, an aftermath of the Reformation, follows
regional lines: North and East Germany are predominantly Protestant, whereas
in the South and West adherents of the Roman Catholic faith are in the majority.
In the prewar Reich, Protestants outnumbered Catholics by about a 2 : 1 ratio.
The loss of the heavily Protestant (80 percent) eastern territories and the postwar
division of the remaining (also Protestant) territory meant that both confessions
now have about equal strength in the Federal Republic.

Religious parity and the formation of the West German state brought
Roman Catholicism out of its minority status and ended Protestant preeminence
among German political elites. Nonetheless, Catholics still remain underrepresented among business, cultural, and educational elite groups.

The importance of religion in the lives of West Germans and their
attachment to the respective churches, as measured by church attendance, is at
best moderate. About one of five West Germans over the age of sixteen attends
church services "regularly" (at least twice a month). Only about 8 percent of
Protestants are in this category, as compared to 31 percent of Catholics.[14] Church
attendance also varies strongly by age and sex; women and older persons are far
more likely to attend regularly than are men and younger age groups. The
strength and character of religious beliefs also vary significantly by confession.
For example, only 33 percent of Protestants believe in life after death, as
compared to 52 percent of Catholics who accept this rather basic tenet of
Christianity.[15]

Interconfessional hostility appears minimal; about 71 percent of Catholics and 60 percent of Protestants would favor some sort of union between the two churches.[16] The presence of subcultural "in group" values within the two confessions appears to be declining. In 1901, 91 percent of all marriages were between couples of the same faith; in 1938, this had declined to 81 percent; and by 1988, only 53 percent of newly married couples belonged to the same church.[17] A 1982 survey found that only 14 percent of the adult population perceived any significant conflict between Catholics and Protestants. Religious conflict was less salient to West Germans than economic differences (70 percent), or even generational conflict (53 percent).[18] The appearance of biconfessional political parties and labor unions in the postwar period had also reduced interconfessional conflict and hastened the social and political integration of German Catholics.

Although religion may not play a prominent role in the lives of most Germans, the two churches, as social institutions, are closely involved in politics. Unlike the United States, Germany has no strong tradition of church-state separation. Since the Reformation, the religious and regional division of the country has meant that the dominant church in any given area was dependent on existing state authority, that is, on the respective princes, who acted as protectors of the faith in their kingdoms. This dependence on state authority made both churches, but especially Protestantism with no international ties, essentially conservative institutions oriented to the status quo. In exchange for their support, the princes also granted a variety of special privileges to the churches (tax-free land, bishops' residences, salaries), many of which are still in effect.

Certainly the most important privilege and one that makes German churches among the most affluent in the world, is the church tax, which is computed as a percentage (about 10 percent) of an employee's income tax, automatically withheld from paychecks (free of charge to the churches), and then transferred to their coffers. The tax assures churches of a steady, inflation-proof flow of funds because it is tied to the income tax, which rises with wage and salary increases.

To avoid payment of this tax, a citizen must officially "contract out" of his or her church by filing the appropriate documents with state officials. By so doing, however, the citizen will probably have a difficult time securing the services of a clergyman for baptisms, weddings, and funerals, as well as gaining admission to church-run homes for the aged or securing help from the churches' charities.

As one of the few social institutions to survive Nazism and the war with its reputation fairly intact, the church actually increased its political influence after the war in spite of the largely secular, materialist character of West German society. Because the churches were regarded by military occupiers as untainted by Nazism, the best way to get permission during the occupation period for opening or reopening a business or starting a newspaper or a political party was to have ample references from, or some affiliation with, one or both churches. According to one authority: "The immediate postwar years saw the German churches at their most influential since the Reformation."[19] As we discuss in Chapter 4, both churches have since made extensive use of this influence.

AGE AND FAMILY STRUCTURE

The frequent and sudden changes in modern German political history have affected the present age distribution of the population. As Figure 2.1 shows, exceptionally low birthrates occurred during and at the end of the two world wars and during the economic depression of the 1930s. These low birthrates affected the distribution of both men and women, and by the 1980s meant that the 30–40, 45–50, and 60–65 age groups were all underrepresented in the population relative to other groups.

Casualties from the two world wars also produced a shortage of males, which was especially noticeable among those over forty-five. In the immediate postwar period, the combined effect of war losses and low birthrates produced an underrepresentation and shortage of younger males in the work force, hence the need to import foreign workers to alleviate a severe labor shortage. In 1946–

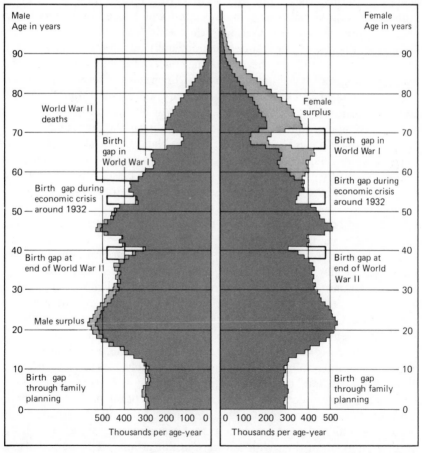

Figure 2.1. Age structure of the population. (*From* Federal Press and Information Office, *Tatsachen über Deutschland,* Gütersloh: Bertelsmann Lexikon Verlag, 1987, p. 19).

1947, for example, in the 20–25-year-old age bracket there were 171 women for every 100 men. Between 1939 and 1946 the proportion of males between the ages of 15 and 40 dropped from 59 percent to 49 percent.[20] In the 1980s these "missing generations" are in middle age and find their underrepresentation increased through the push of higher birthrates in the 1950s and 1960s. A constant feature of German age structure throughout the postwar period, then, has been a shortage of males in the economically productive stages of the life cycle and a surplus in the "dependent" age groups. The low birth rates of the past ten years have further increased the dependent proportion of the population.

Until recently, major generational differences in political attitudes and behavior have not been noticeable. The various generations, according to most analyses, exhibited a high degree of agreement on major political and social topics during at least the first two decades of the Republic's history.[21]

This was due in large part to the familial solidarity and almost exclusive concentration on material reconstruction that characterized the postwar period. This meant that little political communication and hence conflict took place between generations. For most Germans, the family "came to be regarded as the last stable focus in a world of vast destruction, and vital interests returned to the sphere of the family."[22] Given this overriding concern for the maintenance of the nuclear family, politics as a subject of possible disagreement between parents and children and hence a threat to familial solidarity was a taboo topic.[23] Also the concern for economic betterment extended across all age groups and left little room for discussions about politics, much less political participation.

The confrontation and "overcoming" of the National Socialist past, urged by Western occupiers and German intellectuals and a seemingly obvious topic for intergenerational discussion and debate, hardly took place. Student and youth unrest that began in the late 1960s never focused on this topic, in part because it was no longer relevant. Less than a fifth of the West German population in 1988 experienced the Nazi period as adults; the remainder were either too young to remember or not yet born.

Generational differences, however, did become apparent by the late 1960s. Younger age groups, generally those under thirty, were far more likely to support the Brandt government's innovative foreign policies than older age groups. Attitudes toward major domestic reform issues such as codetermination in industry (see Chapter 4) and education were also divided significantly along age lines. Differences in more basic political dispositions such as liberalism and conservatism have been found by researchers. For example, a 1970 survey found Germans under thirty almost three times more likely to describe their basic political position as "left" than do their fellow citizens over sixty.[24] In a 1971 poll of parents and their children over sixteen, 34 percent of the parent group ranked high on measures of authoritarianism as compared to only 8 percent of their children. And while 24 percent of the parent group were classified as politically "liberal," 41 percent of their children were in this group.[25] This period also saw the reduction of the voting age to eighteen and an increasing tendency for younger voters to prefer the Socialist (SPD) and Liberal (FDP) parties over the

Christian Democrats (CDU). At the 1983 and 1987 federal elections young voters provided the new Green political party with the majority of its support. The age structure of the society will be a factor of greater importance in the future than it was during the early decades of the Federal Republic.

In addition, the general withdrawal from politics and the retreat to the primary sphere, so prevalent in the immediate postwar period, did not continue into the third decade of the Republic's existence. This is one important conclusion that can be drawn from a variety of studies conducted since the mid-1960s that examined the extent to which Germans identify with the postwar parties and the degree to which these identifications are transferred across generations. In 1966 and 1969 about half of German young people had the same party preference as their parents.[26] A 1967 study found an even higher rate of intergenerational transmission of the two major parties, the Christian Democrats and the Social Democrats. About three-fourths of children aged 14–16 growing up in homes where both parents supported the Social Democrats adopted their parents' party preference, and over 80 percent of youngsters in "pure" Christian Democratic homes supported the party of their parents. Although there is evidence that such parent-offspring agreement breaks down when attitudes toward specific age-related issues such as child discipline are investigated, in the area of party preference, at least, considerable communication between parents and children is apparently taking place. Indeed, these studies suggest that children from strong supporters of the CDU in the 1960s were receiving an "ideological package" of conservative, traditional, and religious values, of which support for the CDU was an essential part. In the Social Democratic homes, the values associated with the socioeconomic class of the parents facilitate the transmission of loyalties to the children.[27] These types of intergenerational transmissions of partisan loyalties suggest that the present system is socially and ideologically well rooted and institutionalized among postwar generations.

Family Structure

The postwar period witnessed an increase in the importance of the family as a social institution and a change in authority relations within the family. As we have discussed, most Germans after 1945, in the face of the widespread collapse of traditional beliefs and values, withdrew to the family, "the last outpost of social security."[28] Yet this was a different, less authoritarian family structure than had existed earlier in German political history. Parental and especially paternal authority had suffered a decline through National Socialism and the war. In some parts of postwar Germany, up to a third of all children were being raised in fatherless homes. If the fathers did return from war and imprisonment, they were in many cases

> . . . largely dispirited and unable to orient themselves in the post-defeat conditions, thus further impairing their prestige. . . . Men having been indoctrinated to feel as "supermen" were, in varying degrees, unable to deal in a dignified

manner with the occupation forces in the role of subordinates, often discrediting themselves in the eyes of their wives through awkward obsequiousness.[29]

These postwar changes may be important. Wartime and postwar research on the German family, especially that conducted by American social scientists, contended that the typical German family was father-dominated and had not changed significantly since the Industrial Revolution.[30] Father domination and authoritarianism were then linked to the success of the Nazi movement and the apparently strong emotional support that Hitler enjoyed until almost the last months of the war.

Postwar research on the German family has challenged this argument, as well as the assumption that there is any clear-cut relationship between the power structure within the family and the support or nonsupport of particular political systems. In a 1959 comparative study of five nations, about 30 percent of the German respondents reported that their parents' home was "father-dominated" while only 17 percent judged their own families to be so governed. The percentage of "partnership families" increased between generations from 39 percent to 63 percent.[31] The same study found fewer father-dominated families in West Germany than in either Mexico or Italy. An analysis of these five-nation data showed that among respondents growing up before 1917, only 29 percent recalled having had "some influence" in family decisions, while 65 percent of those who grew up, that is, who reached their sixteenth birthday between 1948 and 1953, reported that they had influence in family decisions.[32] A 1971 study of young people aged 14–24 also discovered a consensual style of decisionmaking to be the most frequent in German families (66 percent); only about a fourth were father-dominated, and about a tenth were "mother-dominated."[33] Moreover, from 80 to 90 percent of young people stated that they "got along well" with both parents, and two-thirds felt free to discuss any problem with them.[34]

As Table 2.5 shows, public opinion on the topic of "who should run the marriage" has also changed significantly since the 1950s. In 1954 only 40 percent of males and 54 percent of females felt that both husband and wife should have "equal rights" in a marriage, while 42 percent of the men questioned and 28 percent of the women thought that the "man should have more say." By 1979,

TABLE 2.5. EQUALITY IN MARRIAGE 1954–1979

Question: Do you feel that both husband and wife should have equal rights in a marriage, or do you feel the man should have more to say?

	1954		1979	
	Males	**Females**	**Males**	**Females**
Equal rights	40	54	67	74
Man should have more to say	42	28	10	6
Undecided; "it depends"	18	18	23	20

SOURCE: Institut für Demoskopie, Allensbach Report, June 1979, p. 6.

however, two-thirds of the males and almost three-fourths of the females took the "equal rights" position. The "male chauvinist" proportion had dropped to 10 percent among men and only 6 percent for the women in the survey. Thus the general climate of opinion on this topic has changed markedly over the past quarter-century.

This steady increase in a partnership decisionmaking style, which has apparently been taking place since the turn of the century in spite of rapid and sudden changes in political systems (empire, Weimar Republic, Nazi dictatorship, Bonn Republic), suggests that there is no direct relationship between familial authority relations and the specific structure of the political system. The "authoritarian-father thesis" cannot explain Nazism. Most students of family authority relations attribute the partnership style not to any political system or policy but to the effects of industrialization and modernization—specifically, the entrance of the married woman into the labor force and the larger socioeconomic environment, which, it is argued, increases her power within the family. Thus the present style of decisionmaking is a further indication of the modernization of postwar social structure.

THE EDUCATIONAL SYSTEM

The stratified character of German society is in part the result of an educational system that historically has given a basic education to all but advanced academic training to only a few. The German academic high school (*Gymnasium*) and the universities were designed to educate a small elite for leadership positions with the rest of the population being given only a general education sufficient to enable them to perform satisfactorily at lower levels of the society and economy. This traditional system and the manner in which children are selected for attendance at the higher schools has had the effect of reflecting and perpetuating the existing class structure.

Basic Structure

Most German education still operates on the traditional three-track pattern once common to many European societies. After four years (ages 6 to 10) of compulsory primary school, the 10-year-old child continues on one of three tracks:

1. Five to six more years in a general school (*Hauptschule*) followed by three to four years of both part-time vocational training and actual employment. Between the ages of 18 and 19 this group then enters the work force on a full-time basis. They cease full-time education at the age of 15 or 16.
2. Attendance for up to six years at a general high school (*Realschule*), which combines academic and technical training. Depending on the student's aptitude and course of study, Realschule graduates can transfer to the Gymnasium and the university.

3. Entrance into a Gymnasium for nine years of university preparatory education culminating in the *Abitur* (a degree roughly comparable to an American junior college diploma) and the right to attend a university.

The first two years in any track are considered an orientation period; transfers between various tracks are possible. Until the late 1970s, only about 25 percent of German children pursued tracks two or three, and less than 15 percent ever reached the university. Thus for most children full-time schooling ceased after only nine to ten years of school. The early school-leaving age meant that a career decision had to be made relatively early in life. Many working-class children, who had to make such a decision at the age of fifteen or sixteen, had few options and probably contributed little input into the decision. By the 1980s, however, the proportion of the youngest age cohort in tracks 2 and 3 had risen to over 50 percent as the various reform policies of the state and national governments began to have an impact.

There has been a strong class bias in the entire system. Both the Gymnasium and the university have been largely preserves of the middle class. According to one study, working-class children had only an 8 percent chance of attending a Gymnasium, as compared to a 67 percent chance for the offspring of middle-class parents. Moreover, even the working-class child who did reach the Gymnasium had only about a 12 percent chance of reaching the university, as compared to a 50 percent chance for middle-class children.[35] Thus even in the Gymnasium the children of working-class parents are far less likely to complete the course of study and gain entrance to the university. Even in the 1982–1983 school year, only 20 percent of Gymnasium graduates were the children of working-class parents, one of the lowest levels among industrial societies.[36] It should thus not be surprising when surveys reveal that about three-fourths of German manual workers are the sons of manual workers and that only about one out of every four holders of nonmanual occupations (white-collar, civil servant, self-employed, free professional) comes from a working-class family.

In the immediate postwar years, the Allied occupiers, together with reform-minded Germans, planned extensive changes in this system through the introduction of comprehensive secondary schools, which were to provide greater educational opportunity. For a variety of reasons, not the least of which was the cold war and American endeavors to avoid radical social and economic changes that could possibly hinder German economic reconstruction and rearmament, traditionalist, antireform forces prevailed, and the movement for change dissipated. Antireform elements also saw a relationship between the planned comprehensive school and the Unity School introduced in the Soviet zone (East Germany).

By the mid-1960s public concern with the quality and performance of the educational system rose to unprecedented levels. International comparisons of student achievement and educational quality presented the German system in a very poor light. The federal government, which was, according to the constitution, clearly subordinate to the states in the field of education, began to seek a larger role in educational policy. The result was a 1969 constitutional amendment that assigns to the national government considerable responsibilities for overall educational planning and innovation—from kindergarten to the university. (Ironically, in the country that gave the institution of the *Kindergarten* to the world, there is sufficient space and personnel for only two out of every three *Kinder* [children].)

The key component of plans for restructuring and reforming the system has been the merger of the three-tracked secondary system into a single comprehensive school (*Gesamtschule*). All children, regardless of social background, would attend this school until at least the age of sixteen. At that point, those children with a more vocational orientation would graduate with a first-level Abitur and would then proceed to vocational training and full-time occupations. The second-level (upper secondary) of the Gesamtschule would consist of three more years of academic study and would culminate with a higher-level Abitur, followed by university attendance or full-time employment. Thus the tracking of students would be avoided until at least the age of sixteen rather than the present age of ten. The purpose, of course, is more equality of educational opportunity and hence more social mobility. This relationship between education and equality of opportunity makes the comprehensive school issue more politically controversial than the reform of preschool education, vocational training, or university education. Conservatives (including many Gymnasium teachers), fearing "unmitigated egalitarianism" and valuing a more stratified, hierarchically ordered society, have opposed most reform plans. Most Christian Democrats have essentially taken the conservative position on this issue. The Social Democrats, however, are generally supporters of the comprehensive school and overall education reform.[37]

Since 1969 the comprehensive school has been introduced on an experimental basis in all states. By 1987 there were about 440 integrated comprehensive schools with about 80 percent of them in states governed by the SPD. Only Lower Saxony, among the CDU/CSU-controlled states, had more than ten comprehensive schools. But even in SPD states, West Berlin and Hamburg were the only states that had made the comprehensive school a permanent feature of their school systems. This, then, is a policy issue that has divided the political parties. The general trend in all states is toward more flexibility between the tracks and greater opportunity, however. Since 1950 the proportion of all Germans with some educational experience beyond the basic level has increased from 18 percent to 41 percent. More students, regardless of their social background, are now offered a wider variety of programs and schools as West Germany adapts its educational system to the needs of an advanced industrial society.

MASS MEDIA

As a highly developed industrial society, West Germany has an extensive mass media structure that has made West Germans among the most politically informed people in the world.[38] About 66 percent of the adult population views the half-hour evening newscasts of the two major networks. Political news comprises about a third of these telecasts. Also, political reports in daily newspapers are read by about 60 percent of the adult population.[39] But an increasing concentration of newspaper and magazine ownership and a certain bureaucratic blandness, induced by the structure of public control, in radio and television's political reporting have become problems in the media's relationship to the political system.

The Press

West Germany has about 400 daily newspapers with a combined daily circulation of over 21 million. However, only a third of these have their own complete editorial staff. The remainder have local staff and advertising facilities and rely on wire-service reports or reports from other papers in their chains for state, national, and international news. Moreover, almost 60 percent of daily readers consume the journalistic products offered by the Springer publishing company. Until his death in 1985, Axel Springer used his press empire to oppose left-wing foreign and domestic politics especially as they affected business interests and the possibility of German reunification. During the Socialist-Liberal coalition (1969–1982), his papers were very critical of the government's policies.

In terms of national newspapers, West Germany is limited to one mass-oriented tabloid, the *Bild-Zeitung* (literally "Picture Newspaper"), and several quality, "elite" papers. *Bild,* the flagship of the Springer chain, with a daily circulation of 5.5 million and an estimated daily readership of over 12 million (27 percent of the adult population), is a skillfully edited blend of sensational sex, crime, and conservative-nationalist politics. Claiming to speak for Germany's little man in advocating "commonsense" politics, the paper treated the conciliatory approach to the Soviet Union and Eastern Europe of the Socialist-Liberal coalition as a sellout of German interests and at times imputed traitorous behavior to government policymakers in this area.

Another favorite target has been "radicals and leftists" in the schools, universities, and political parties. The paper, and indeed the entire Springer firm, was the focus of student demonstrations during the late 1960s. The Springer press portrayed the students as the irresponsible, spoiled offspring of an overly tolerant middle class playing into the hands of the communists. The students and many intellectuals have in turn charged *Bild* and the Springer chain with deliberate distortion of the news in a way that contributes to the apolitical tendencies of some citizens.

The major national "elite" daily newspapers, all with circulations between 275,000 and 350,000, are the liberal to middle-of-the-road *Frankfurter All-*

gemeine Zeitung, the more reformist *Süddeutsche Zeitung* (published in Munich), the avowedly left-liberal *Frankfurter Rundschau,* and the one "quality" paper in the Springer chain, *Die Welt,* which was once a highly respected publication until Springer began his active involvement in politics. Although differing in their editorial orientations, these papers present a generally high level of reporting with strong coverage given to politics as well as business and financial news. In recent years a new national daily, *Die Tageszeitung,* or simply *TAZ,* has become the major voice of the alternative media. Its editorial position is close to the Greens and the environmentalist and peace movements.

The best-known political periodical is the weekly newsmagazine *Der Spiegel* ("The Mirror"), with a circulation of about a million. Similar to *Time* magazine in appearance, *Der Spiegel,* however, prides itself on a crusading, critical, iconoclastic style. Its founder and publisher, Rudolf Augstein, the liberal counterpart to Axel Springer, has been active in politics as a parliamentary candidate. In recent years the magazine has become the leading practitioner of investigative reporting in the Federal Republic. Both the *Neue Heimat* scandal (see p. 107) involving the trade unions and the Flick affair (see p. 124) dealing with the finances of the major political parties began with extensive exposés in *Der Spiegel.*

Television and Radio

Mindful of the Nazis' abuses of the airwaves, the Basic Law assigns sole responsibility for radio and television to the constituent states. Both media are administered by state-based, nonprofit public corporations and are for the most part independent of direct political influence. These corporations, however, are supervised by boards of control on which representatives of major "social, economic, cultural, and political forces," including political parties and interest groups, are represented.

There are currently eight such broadcasting corporations, representing the eleven (including West Berlin) Länder. These form the Association of Public Broadcasting Corporations in the Federal Republic (ARD) and constitute the First Network of West German television and also produce cooperative radio programs. A second television network (ZDF) was established in 1962. Both radio and television are financed largely through monthly fees for each household.

The political parties exert considerable influence on the radio and television broadcasting corporations through the presence of their representatives on the stations' governing councils. Some of the regional corporations are clearly identified as either "red" (SPD), such as Bremen or Hesse, or "black" (CDU/CSU), such as the Saar, the Southwest Corporation (Baden-Württemberg), and Bavaria. Proportional CDU-SPD-FDP influence characterizes the North German Broadcasting Corporation (NDR). The Second National Television Network (ZDF) generally tends toward a pro-CDU position. Thus far only the West German Corporation (WDR), financed largely by the state of North Rhine-Westphalia, has remained relatively free of significant party influence.

All these corporations, with the exception of the Second Network, are responsible for producing a common national program. The contribution of each regional corporation to the program is determined by its size and income. This at times leads to considerable conflict, especially when one of the "black" or "red" stations broadcasts programs with a relative partisan bias. The NDR's "Panorama" news program (somewhat comparable to its British namesake or the American "60 Minutes") has at numerous times been very critical of the Bavarian CSU leader and 1980 chancellor candidate, Franz-Josef Strauss, and has attempted to link the CDU/CSU with radical-right groups. This has naturally provoked the wrath of the CDU members of the station's council. The CDU/CSU stations, or commentators close to it on other programs, returned the favor by focusing on communist or radical-left influences in the Social Democratic party or by implying that certain SPD leaders were "soft" or sympathetic to communist countries and made up a "Moscow faction" within the SPD.

In 1983 the new Christian Democratic government of Chancellor Helmut Kohl introduced a variety of proposals for private radio and television stations. In addition, the Christian Democrats now advocate a nationwide cable television system. In 1985 a private channel, SAT−1, which is partly owned by the Springer company, began cable and satellite telecasts to some 250,000 subscription viewers. Its main output was light entertainment and feature films, with some news material. A few months later a second private station, RTL-plus, began its programs. The public networks also plan cable-satellite programs. By 1988 about 3 million households could receive the new stations. The Social Democrats have generally opposed private radio and television networks, fearing an excessive commercialization of the media. The notion that the mass media have a responsibility for educating citizens and elevating the cultural level of the nation, rather than merely providing entertainment, is still supported by many Social Democrats.[40]

SUMMARY AND CONCLUSION

The Federal Republic of Germany today is a more socioeconomically modern, integrated society than was the Germany of the empire, the Weimar Republic, or the Nazi dictatorship. The postwar division of the nation and loss of territory in the east to the Soviet Union and Poland also meant the loss of several major headaches that had plagued political systems in the past: the dominance of Prussia; regional conflicts; an inner-directed Catholic subculture; an antidemocratic, militaristic landed nobility; and Great Power pretensions in foreign policy. Wartime destruction and postwar refugee migration meant a new, modern postwar economic plant manned by an abundant supply of proficient labor, in many cases composed of refugees from the "lost territories." Economic success and prosperity brought an easing of class tensions and the end of working-class social isolation. Ironically and albeit at a frightful cost, the Nazis left German society in a condition more favorable to liberal democracy than they had found it.

These changed socioeconomic conditions now constitute an environment that is more conducive to the growth of support for the Bonn Republic than was the case during Germany's first attempt at political democracy, the Weimar Republic. The dominance of achievement-oriented, materialistic, and individualistic values may make intellectuals dismiss Bonn as provincial and philistine, but they may have made Germany more governable as a political democracy.

As we discuss in the next chapter, a consensus on the key values and norms of political democracy, not present in 1949, has developed in the Federal Republic during the past forty years. As a result of this concensus, the leaders and those who are led in the 1990s and beyond may be ready for more policy innovation than was the case during the earlier decades of the Republic. There are clear signs that West Germany, now a stable democratic society, is fast becoming a dynamic, democratic society as well, as it confronts the whole constellation of social and economic policy problems common to other advanced industrial societies.

NOTES

1. German political leaders have generally avoided addressing this problem, fearful of reviving memories of the Third Reich when Hitler encouraged large families as part of his racist program. During the 1987 election campaign, Chancellor Helmut Kohl alluded to the birth rate problem by encouraging Germans to adopt a positive attitude toward children and large families.
2. West Germany is self-sufficient in grain, sugar, beef and milk. Fruits, vegetables, poultry, eggs, and pork are its major food imports. Friedrich Golter, "Aufgaben der Landwirtschaft in einer modernen Industriegesellschaft," *Aus Politik und Zeitgeschichte,* no. 42 (October 18, 1986): 30.
3. *Statistisches Jahrbuch der Bundesrepublik Deutschland, 1980* (Stuttgart: Kohlhammer Verlag, 1980), p. 510; and Organization for Economic Cooperation and Development, *Economic Surveys: Germany* (Paris, 1987), p. 48.
4. Arnold J. Heidenheimer, *The Governments of Germany* (New York: Thomas Y. Crowell, 1971), pp. 197–198.
5. Daniel Bell, *The Coming of Post-Industrial Society* (New York: Basic Books, 1973), p. 17.
6. Computed from Gerhard Kleining, "Die Veränderungen der Mobilitätschancen in der Bundesrepublik Deutschland," *Kölner Zeitschrift für Soziologie und Sozialpsychologie* 23 (December 1971): 793.
7. Gerhard Kleining, "Struktur und Prestigemobilität in der Bundesrepublik Deutschland," *Kölner Zeitschrift für Soziologie und Sozialpsychologie* 23 (March 1971): 29.
8. Bonn Institute for Social and Economic Policy study cited in *Die Zeit,* no. 18 (13 May 1983), p. 8.
9. Presse- und Informationsamt der Bundesregierung, *Gesellschaftliche Daten 1982* (Bonn 1984), p. 271. Home ownership in the Federal Republic stands at only 38 percent of all households in comparison to 64 percent in the United States. The German level is also below that of any other major West European country. Federal Statistical Office study cited in *Die Zeit,* no. 4 (28 January 1983), p. 14; comparative

data from *Gesellschaft für Wohnungs- und Siedlungswesen* survey cited in *Der Bürger im Staat* 33, no. 1 (February 1983): 55.

10. Federal Savings Bank Association data cited in *Köllner Stadt Anzeiger,* August 25, 1987, p. 2.

11. Karl W. Roskamp, *Capital Formation in West Germany* (Detroit: Wayne State University Press, 1965), pp. 53 ff.

12. General Social Survey, 1984, *Codebook,* p. 51.

13. German governments have also played an active role in organizing rescue operations for industries and major corporations facing a severe economic crisis. Although such bail-outs are a relatively recent development in the United States (e.g., the Lockheed and Chrysler loan guarantees), German national and state governments since the early 1960s have come to the aid of the coal and steel industry, shipbuilding, automobile companies, and major electronic firms. Governments have used devices such as loan guarantees, tax write-offs, subsidies, and even direct grants to major industries in order to save the companies and the jobs they provide. In some cases political officials together with business, labor, and banking leaders have formed a "crisis cartel" to fashion comprehensive, long-term solutions to the problems of key industries such as shipbuilding and electronics. For an analysis of several recent corporate crises in West Germany see Kenneth Dyson, "The Politics of Corporate Crises in West Germany," *West European Politics* 7, no. 1 (January 1984): 24–46.

14. Elisabeth Noelle-Neumann, ed., *The Germans: Public Opinion Polls, 1967–1980* (Westport, CT, and London: Greenwood Press, 1981), p. 235.

15. Noelle-Neumann, *The Germans,* p. 231.

16. Institut für Demoskopie, *Jahrbuch der öffentlichen Meinung 1965–1967* (Allensbach: Verlag für Demoskopie, 1967), 4, p. 38

17. M. Rainer Lepsius, "Sozialstruktur und soziale Schichtung in der Bundesrepublik Deutschland," in *Die Zweite Republik,* ed. Richard Löwenthal and Hans-Peter Schwarz (Stuttgart: Seewald Verlag, 1974), p. 264; and John Ardagh, *Germany and the Germans* (New York: Harper & Row, 1987), p. 231.

18. General Social Survey (Zentralarchiv für empirische Sozialforschung, Cologne University, 1982).

19. Frederic Spotts, *The Churches and Politics in Germany* (Middletown, CT: Wesleyan University Press, 1973), p. x.

20. O. Jean Brandes, "The Effect of War on the German Family," *Social Forces* 29 (1950): 165.

21. Elisabeth Noelle-Neumann and Erich Peter Neumann, *The Germans: Public Opinion Polls, 1947–1966* (Allensbach: Verlag für Demoskopie, 1967), pp. 34 ff.

22. Eugen Lupri, "The West German Family Today and Yesterday: A Study in Changing Family Authority Patterns" (Ph.D. dissertation, University of Wisconsin—Madison, 1967), p. 37.

23. Friedrich H. Tenbruck, "Alltagsnormen und Lebensgefühle in der Bundesrepublik," in Löwenthal and Schwarz, *Die Zweite Republik,* pp. 289–310.

24. Institut für Demoskopie, Study No. 2060.

25. Manfred Koch, *Die Deutschen und ihr Staat* (Hamburg: Hoffmann and Campe, 1972), p. 45.

26. Jack Dennis and Donald J. McCrone, "Preadult Development of Political Party Identification in Western Democracies," *Comparative Political Studies* 3, no. 2 (July 1970): 252 ff.

27. Kendall L. Baker, "The Acquisition of Partisanship in Germany," *American Journal of Political Science* 18, no. 3 (August 1974): 580 ff.
28. Helmut Schelsky, "The Family in Germany," *Marriage and Family Living* 16, no. 4 (November 1954): 332.
29. Brandes, "The Effect of War on the German Family," p. 165.
30. See, for example, Bertram Schaffner, *Fatherland: A Study of Authoritarianism in the German Family* (New York: Columbia University Press, 1949), pp. 15 ff; David Rodnick, *Postwar Germans: An Anthropologists Account* (New Haven: Yale University Press, 1948), pp. 123 ff; David Abrahamsen, *Men, Mind and Power* (New York: Harper, 1947), pp. 154 ff.
31. Lupri, "The West German Family Today and Yesterday," pp. 41–46.
32. Ibid.
33. Koch, *Die Deutschen und ihr Staat,* p. 104.
34. Ibid., pp. 121 ff.
35. Hans W. Weiler, "The Politics of Education Innovation: Recent Developments in West German School Reform" (Report to the National Academy of Education, October 1973), pp. 43 ff.
36. Der Bundesminister für Wissenschaft und Bildung, *Strukturdaten, 1986/87,* Bad Godesberg, 1986, p. 62.
37. Hayo Matthiesen, "Die Parteien und die Schule," *Die Zeit,* no. 16 (21 April 1972), p. 14. The West German public appears to have a "wait and see" attitude on the issue. Only 18 percent of a national sample in 1980 was against the comprehensive school, but an even lower proportion, 9 percent, wanted it as a permanent part of the school system. The remainder preferred the schools as a supplemental offering (31 percent) or wanted it continued on an experimental basis (39 percent). *Der Spiegel,* 7 April 1980, p. 66.
38. Gabriel A. Almond and Sidney Verba, *The Civic Culture* (Princeton: Princeton University Press, 1963), pp. 89–90.
39. Horst Holzer, "Massenkommunikation und Demokratie in der Bundesrepublik Deutschland" in *Deutsche Gesellschaft im Wandel,* ed. Hans-Martin Bolte et. al. (Opladen: Westdeutscher Verlag, 1974), 2:312 ff. Surveys generally find that about 60 to 70 percent of the adult population regularly read the political news in the daily papers and watch the news programs on television. In the case of newspaper reading, the German level of 61 percent in 1983 is considerably above the European average of 43 percent. The Germans' overall degree of exposure to the information media (television, radio, and newspapers) was in 1983 well above the European average. Survey data cited in *Euro-barometre,* no. 19 (Brussels: Commission of the European Communities, June 1983), p. 47.
40. Former Chancellor Helmut Schmidt (1974–1982) was especially critical of private, commercial television. In 1979 he attempted to halt the installation of an experimental cable television network and the broadcast of German language television programs from Radio Luxembourg's satellite. Schmidt contended that a "flood" of commercial television programs would be damaging to German family life and "change the structure of our democratic society." His antitelevision campaign also included a proposal that Germans abstain one day each week from watching television. There was little interest in his plan. *New York Times,* October 15, 1979, p. 1.

CHAPTER 3

Political Culture, Participation, and Civil Liberties

According to many historians, Germany's first experiment with political democracy at a national level, the Weimar Republic, failed because it was a "republic without republicans." The formal structures of political democracy—representative institutions, free elections, constitutional guarantees of civil liberties—were present, but the political attitudes and values of Germans were not supportive of these structures. Most Germans during Weimar, according to this view, longed for either a restoration of the monarchy or a similarly strong authoritarian system, which would return Germany to economic prosperity and Great Power status. As we discussed in Chapter 1, the founding of the Bonn Republic likewise met with little popular enthusiasm. Hence some German and foreign political leaders, as well as scholars, were uncertain in 1949 about the prospects of the Bonn system. Once again, as during Weimar, the constitutional structures of democracy were present, but what about the political attitudes that lay behind the constitution? Would Germans through their attitudes and behavior accept and support this new system, or would they remain indifferent or even embrace antisystem ideologies and movements?

The present chapter explores this question by examining the development of West German political culture—that is, German attitudes and values toward politics and German political behavior since the founding of the Bonn Republic. We will seek to determine how Germans think and feel about the Republic and how they have acted or behaved toward the new system since 1949. Of particular importance in this latter area are the support and maintenance of civil liberties and human rights as well as the treatment of minority groups in the postwar system.

POLITICAL VALUES

National Identity

As a linguistic, ethnic, and cultural unit, the German nation is one of Europe's oldest. Yet, unlike Britain, France, and other European states, which resolved the question of the political and geographical boundaries as well as the criteria for membership in the national community by the late eighteenth century, the question of what Germany is and who the Germans are has never been resolved in a political sense. A single German state incorporating all people who identify with the German nation has never really existed, with one possible exception: Hitler's short-lived and ill-fated *Grossdeutsches Reich* established after Nazi annexations of Austria and the Sudetenland. Even the much-heralded unification and establishment of a Second Reich under Prussian leadership in 1871, which brought twenty-five German political entities into one federation, united most, but by no means all, German-speaking peoples in Europe. The successors to this Second Reich, the Weimar Republic and the Nazi Third Reich, maintained the territory of this unified nation-state, and in the Nazi case briefly extended its borders. Yet by 1945, after only seventy-five years as a unified nation-state, with albeit three different types of political systems, the problem of national identity and the future of the German nation as a political unit had to be resolved once again.

National identity, the sense of belonging to a particular national community, usually sharing a common physical territory, language, history, and cultural values, has been present among Germans at least as long as it has among many other European nations. This general national identification has not been linked, however, with a stable unified state and political system. Thus, to ensure its own stability, each succeeding German political system has unsuccessfully sought to broaden the scope of national identification to include a commitment to the given state. The absence of a shared attachment to a particular state and political system has thus been the missing component in the German sense of national identity. As Devine has pointed out, national identification in the American case includes identification with and support for certain political symbols (the Constitution, flag, national anthem) and ideals (individual liberty, property, equality). To be an American has also meant support for a particular state form and political system: a liberal, democratic republic. Socialism, communism, monarchy—all other possible political forms—are not a legitimate part of the American national identity.[1] Such a linkage between national identity and specific state form has never been present in Germany.

The Republic proclaimed in 1949 was, like its predecessors, faced with the problem of creating and fusing a commitment to a particular political form with an already existent national identity. The presence of a competing German state (East Germany) within the same territory as that of the prewar Reich, and its capital in the communist part of the historic center of the Reich, complicated the task. West German leadership at first also compounded the problem by officially encouraging support for the values of the liberal democratic constitution but not for the specific West German state. Thus in effect West German leadership until recently was urging citizens to become democrats but not to develop too strong an attachment to the Federal Republic because it was only "provisional," until all Germans were reunited within a single democratic state with Berlin as its capital. Until that time, however, this provisional West German state also claimed to be both the sole legitimate successor to the Reich and, by virtue of free elections, the only legitimate representative for all members of the German nation within or outside its borders. Needless to say, this viewpoint was not shared by the leaders of East Germany.

The official West German position was ambivalent and confusing and did little to develop a specific West German sense of national identity linked to support for the postwar democratic state. As we shall see, it was for all practical purposes abandoned during the mid-1960s, when the emerging East-West détente, the stability and prosperity of East Germany, and Bonn's own efforts at normalized relations with the Soviet Union and Eastern Europe made it hardly tenable any longer.

In spite of the official position, to what extent has a national identity with a political component developed in the last quarter-century? Do the inhabitants of the Federal Republic think of themselves as West Germans or "Federal Republicans"? In the immediate postwar period, for understandable reasons, many wanted to forget about being German. A few enthusiastically embraced the "European idea," a politically united Europe with no national borders, or gladly submitted to the "Americanization" so apparent in popular culture. Most simply reduced their scope of allegiance to the self, the family, and perhaps the local community. This mass withdrawal to the primary sphere, or *privatization,* as some social scientists have termed it, gave German leaders considerable freedom of action but also imposed limits on the intensity of commitment or identification they could demand from citizens.

This condition could not last indefinitely, and there are signs that West Germans are "coming out" and rediscovering the larger national community and at the same time developing a specific identification with the Federal Republic.[2] Public opinion data, for example, show a growing tendency on the part of West Germans to differentiate themselves from citizens of East Germany and a steady decline in concern with the reunification question. A 1971 study tapped West German perceptions of state and society in the Federal Republic in comparison to East Germany and found a great divergence in the image West Germans had of the two German states. The Federal Republic was seen above all as a state and society that allows much "personal freedom" (88 percent), is "progressive" (80 percent), and has "good social welfare and health programs" (78 percent). East Germany, however, was seen as a state that "exerts excessive influence on personal liberty" (81 percent), is "militaristic" (81 percent), and is a society "in which people are distrustful of one another" (78 percent). When asked what they understood to be "our national interests," over two-thirds of the respondents referred only to the Federal Republic and did not include East Germany in the "nation."[3]

Although unification was ranked by West Germans throughout the 1950s as either the "most important problem" or at least as one of the major problems facing the Federal Republic, by 1982 less than 5 percent of the adult population held either view. West German perceptions of the other German state have over the past quarter-century, changed from "our brothers and sisters in the Soviet occupation zone" to that of a separate entity, albeit related to the Federal Republic through language and cultural ties.[4] Moreover, public support for specific West German symbols has also increased since 1949. A positive identification with the Republic's flag, for example, is now present among a majority of the adult population.[5]

Recent foreign policies of the West German state, particularly *Ostpolitik* (eastern policies), evidence a growing sense of political independence and identity consistent with public opinion on national and reunification matters. The normalization of relations through treaties with Poland, Czechoslovakia, and the Soviet Union in which the Federal Republic recognized the 1945 Soviet and Polish annexations of former German territories east of the Oder-Neisse line and accepted the present West German-Czech border, represented initiatives unthinkable during the early history of the state. The de facto recognition of East Germany in 1972 meant the acceptance of the territorial status quo in Europe as well as the division of the prewar Reich.

West Germany has also shown a greater willingness to assert its political power within the European Community, especially in those areas where West German economic strength inclines other European states to listen to German proposals and, in some cases, to follow the German lead. A $2 billion loan to Italy in 1974, for example, was made only after the Italian government committed itself to anti-inflationary policies required by West Germany as a condition for the loan.

Finally, recent West German opinion has become increasingly critical of the United States, the once protective "Big Brother" who could do no wrong. This began during the Vietnam war when criticisms of American foreign policy became, for German conditions, quite vocal, even reaching the point where the then finance minister and later chancellor, Helmut Schmidt, while in the United States, publicly criticized the 1971 American bombings of Hanoi. Differences over policies in the Middle East have also become apparent as West Germany, far more dependent on Arab oil than the United States, has attempted to maintain a posture of strict neutrality. A similar pattern can be seen in West German reaction to American policies following the Soviet invasion of Afghanistan in December 1979. The Schmidt government did not unconditionally support Washington's request for sanctions against the Soviets, including a boycott of the Olympic games. Instead, it warned against "overreaction," "alarmism," and a "backslide" into a cold war. A Social Democratic newspaper, edited by a leading figure in the party organization, even contended that Bonn "should risk a limited political conflict with the United States, if the alternative is a return of cold war conditions because of Afghanistan."[6] Bonn clearly felt slighted and not properly consulted before many decisions of the Carter administration. The widespread opposition in the early 1980s to the stationing of new NATO intermediate range missiles in Germany was also an expression of this emerging national identity. According to one observer, "the rejection of 'American missiles'—even missiles originally urged by a West German government and ratified by NATO . . . is seen [by the missile protestors] as an assertion of national self-reliance against an unreliable American tutelage."[7]

The question of national identity and German-American relations was also involved in the 1985 controversy surrounding the visit of President Reagan to a German military cemetery in the small town of Bitburg. The presidential visit, forty years after the end of World War II, had been proposed by Chancellor Kohl as a symbolic gesture of German-American reconciliation. After it was discovered that the cemetery also contained the remains of forty-nine SS troops, President Reagan came under heavy pressure from American Jewish and veterans groups to cancel the visit. Reagan, however, citing his commitment to Chancellor Kohl and the strong support this "noble gesture" had in the Federal Republic, refused. Kohl, who was privately pressed by the White House to propose an alternative to the cemetery visit, rejected any changes in the presidential itinerary.

In Germany almost three-fourths of the adult population supported the Bitburg visit. Significantly, only the Green political party called for its cancellation. Although the Social Democrats, the major opposition party, sharply criticized the manner in which the Reagan visit was organized, they did not advocate the abandonment of the presidential gesture to Germany's war dead. Generally, Germans were surprised at the intensity of the American reaction. For many Germans born since 1945, the Third Reich and World War II belong to a dark past that should no longer have any influence on West Germany's present international stature and prestige. According to this view, West Germany in the past forty years has earned the right to be accepted as an equal within the Western community of nations.

In recent years several conservative intellectuals and political figures, some with ties to the Kohl government, have argued that the Federal Republic is hindered in its dealings with other nations by its lack of a national identity and pride comparable to those found in other European countries.[8] The major obstacle, they contend, to the development of such an identity is an excessive focus on the Third Reich by historians, educators, and the media, which burdens younger generations with an unjustified sense of guilt. The conservatives stress that German history is long and complex and that even during the period from 1933 to 1945 there were phenomena other than National Socialism. A country that is obsessed with guilt, they argue, will be incapable of dealing with the challenges of the future. To counteract this, conservatives want to create and stress common positive historical memories and traditions. This concern for the whole of German history and the need for a stronger sense of national identity prompted the Kohl government to sponsor the construction in the late 1980s of two new historical museums: one in Berlin dealing with all of German history and the second in Bonn, which will focus on the postwar Federal Republic.

Many liberal and socialist intellectuals have been critical of what they believe is an attempt by conservatives to gloss over, or to relativize, the singularity of the Nazi experience and especially the Holocaust. The debate has been particularly intense among several leading historians and social scientists. This *Historikerstreit* (historians' dispute) attracted national attention in 1986 when a leading social philosopher, Jürgen Habermas, accused two historians of seeking to trivialize the Nazi period. He linked their efforts to a larger movement among conservative historians to create a new view of the past that would "limit the damage" done by the Third Reich and give Germans confidence and pride.

Although he did not deny the need for national identity, Habermas urged Germans to focus their patriotism and pride on the open, democratic society that has been created since 1945:

> The creation of such a society was the greatest achievement of the postwar generation, for it opened Germany unconditionally to the political culture of the West. . . . The only patriotism that will not alienate us from the West is constitutional patriotism. Unfortunately, a tie to universal constitutional principles that is based on conviction has only been possible in Germany since, and because of Auschwitz. Anyone who wants to drive the blush of shame over that deed from our cheeks by using meaningless phrases like "obession with guilt," anyone who wants to call Germans back to a conventional kind of identity, destroys the only reliable basis of our tie to the West.[9]

Habermas's charges were sharply denied by the historians, and the debate continued for several months in the pages of West Germany's leading newspapers and periodicals. This *Historikerstreit* and the Bitburg incident illustrate how difficult and sensitive the question of national identity has become in the Federal Republic.

West Germans do have the lowest level of national pride in Europe. As Table 3.1 shows, only 62 percent of the adult population in 1985 felt "proud" to be German as compared to 88 percent of the British, 82 percent of the French, and 87 percent of the Italian respondents. The twelve-nation European average of 80 percent was also above the German. This low level of national pride reflects the relative newness of the Federal Republic in comparison with its neighbors, but probably more important, it is a residual effect of the Nazi period. The Third Reich and World War II still make some Germans reluctant to display such national feelings. Significantly, the 1985 survey found national pride to be especially low among those respondents who were born just after World War I (between 1921 and 1925) and who thus experienced the Third Reich as young adults.[10]

TABLE 3.1. FEELINGS OF NATIONAL PRIDE IN MAJOR EUROPEAN COUNTRIES, 1985

Question: Would you say you are very proud, quite proud, not very proud, or not at all proud to be German (British, French, etc.)?

| | Percentage of Respondents, by Country | | | | |
National Pride	Germany	France	Britain	Italy	European Community[a]
Strong ("very" or "quite" proud)	62	82	88	87	80
Moderate ("not very" proud)	21	12	9	18	13
Weak ("not at all" proud)	11	3	2	3	4
Don't know/no reply	6	3	1	2	3

[a] Twelve-nation weighted average.
SOURCE: *Euro-barometre*, no. 24 (December 1985), p. 21.

Legitimacy

Like many new states, the Federal Republic was also confronted with the problem of acquiring legitimacy. Would the inhabitants of the Western occupation zones accept and obey the authority of the new state? Would the policy output of the new state be consistent with what most citizens regard as right and wrong? In spite of national division and a constitution (Basic Law) never subjected to direct popular approval, there has been no serious internal challenge to the authority of the Bonn state. The overwhelming majority of West Germans consider the institutions and processes of the Federal Republic as legitimate. Support for this statement can be found in part in the high levels of voting turnout and the concentration of electoral support in the parties committed to the Republic. Extremist, antisystem sentiment is confined to minuscule percentages of the electorate. Direct challenges to the Republic's authority have been limited to the Communist and neo-Nazi parties and to the small but extremely active urban terrorist groups that have plagued police and courts since the late 1960s and that are discussed in greater detail later in this chapter.

The legitimacy of the Bonn system, especially in the early years of the Republic, was based in part on the absence of any credible alternative. After experiences in this century with monarchy, the Weimar Republic, and Nazism, postwar Germans had no historically successful alternative to put forward. They were quite willing to take, in essence, what the Allies offered (a liberal, parliamentary system in only part of the former Reich). However, this decline in support for past political systems and the resultant increase in support for the present regime were part of a developmental process affected by both the passage of time and the performance of the new system.

Through opinion surveys in which West Germans were periodically questioned about their attitudes toward two of the past political systems, monarchy and the Hitler dictatorship, and their support for key principles of the present regime, we can examine the character and sources of this process. In Table 3.2, responses to questions about monarchy and the Hitler dictatorship are presented. In 1951, thirty-three years after the collapse of the Hohenzollern dynasty, almost a third of the adult population favored its restoration. Nevertheless, fourteen years later, support for monarchy had dropped to only 11 percent. Much of this decline, according to one analysis, was due to the simple passage of time; those with living memories of the Hohenzollerns constituted an ever-smaller segment of the population.[11] Some of this decline, however, was related to the policy successes of the Bonn system.

This is even more apparent in the case of attitudes toward Hitler and the Nazi party. When asked whether Hitler would have been one of the greatest German statesmen, had it not been for the war, almost one-half of the adult population in 1955 answered affirmatively; by 1967 this had dropped to less than one-third, with a majority flatly rejecting the proposition. Age is an important factor in explaining this change. Each age group socialized since 1949 was progressively less likely to support the Hitler dictatorship than older generations who grew up under earlier regimes.[12]

Also, when national samples on nine different occasions between 1953 and 1977 were asked how they would react if a new Nazi party attempted to come to power, a similar trend was apparent. Potential support for neo-Nazism dropped from 16 percent in 1953 to only 7 percent in 1977. The percentage of respondents who would actively or passively oppose such a party increased from 62 percent to 79 percent over the same time period, and perhaps more important, by 1977 almost 60 percent of the adult population stated it would do "everything possible" to see that a new Nazi party would not come to power. In addition to age, the steady drop in support for a neo-Nazi party was a result of economic prosperity and other policy successes of the first chancellor, Konrad Adenauer, such as German acceptance into the European community, NATO, and the integration of 10 million postwar refugees. The effects of political education in the schools were apparently also a factor in producing this decline. In short, there was some support for past regimes in the early 1950s, which diminished over time with the growing effectiveness of the Bonn system. By the 1960s, the Republic, originally legitimated by Allied occupation, could now stand on its own by virtue of its performance.

Thus far we have accounted for the legitimacy of the postwar system through (1) the total absence of a credible alternative to what the Western Allied occupiers established in 1949; and (2) the performance of the postwar system, above all economic prosperity, effective executive leadership, and policy successes. What, however, would happen if for some reason its performance would falter? Does the present regime now have some reserve of citizen goodwill it could fall back on in crisis situations? Is there some support for this regime that is not specific or output-oriented? Have Germans over the past forty years developed a more affective, if not emotional, commitment to this regime, that

TABLE 3.2. CHANGES IN ATTITUDES TOWARD PREVIOUS REGIMES (MONARCHY AND DICTATORSHIP) AND KEY VALUES OF THE BONN REPUBLIC (POLITICAL COMPETITION AND REPRESENTATION), 1950–1978 (in percentages)

Questions	1950	1951	1952	1953	1954	1955	1956	1957	1958	1959	1960	1961	1962	1963	1964	1965	1966	1967	1968	1971	1977	1978
Restore monarchy?																						
Yes	—	32	—	—	22	—	—	16	—	—	—	—	—	—	—	11	—	—	—	—	—	—
No	—	36	—	—	51	—	—	60	—	—	—	—	—	—	—	66	—	—	—	—	—	—
Don't know	—	32	—	—	27	—	—	24	—	—	—	—	—	—	—	23	—	—	—	—	—	—
Hitler, one of Germany's greatest statesmen?																						
Yes	—	—	—	—	—	48	43	—	—	42	34	30	37	35	29	—	—	32	—	—	—	31
No	—	—	—	—	—	36	37	—	—	41	43	43	44	44	44	—	—	52	—	—	—	56
Don't know	—	—	—	—	—	16	20	—	—	17	23	27	19	21	27	—	—	16	—	—	—	13
A new Nazi party?																						
Support	—	—	—	16	—	—	15	11	11	11	—	—	8	—	—	—	7	6	—	7	—	—
Oppose	—	—	—	62	—	—	61	66	64	62	—	—	71	—	—	—	74	78	—	79	—	—
Indifferent	—	—	—	22	—	—	24	23	25	27	—	—	21	—	—	—	19	16	—	14	—	—
Political competition. It is better for a country to have:																						
One party	25	23	21	20	19	15	11	12	12	12	11	11	—	—	—	—	—	8	7	6	—	5
Several parties	53	60	68	66	69	74	76	77	77	76	79	73	—	—	—	—	—	82	81	90	—	92
Undecided, other, no answer	22	17	11	14	12	11	13	11	11	12	10	16	—	—	—	—	—	10	12	4	—	3
Do members of parliament represent:																						
Personal interests	—	32	26	—	17	—	—	—	17	—	—	—	—	—	11	—	—	—	—	—	—	15
Party interests	—	14	14	—	10	—	—	—	8	—	—	—	—	—	7	—	—	—	—	—	—	3
General interest	—	25	33	—	39	—	—	—	41	—	—	—	—	—	51	—	—	—	—	—	—	55
Other, no answer	—	29	27	—	34	—	—	—	34	—	—	—	—	—	31	—	—	—	—	—	—	27

SOURCE: Institut für Demoskopie, Allensbach, West Germany. These and all other public opinion polls cited in this study were obtained from the Institut. Sole responsibility for the presentation, analysis, and interpretation of these data rests with the author.

52

could see it through hard times? In short, is there *diffuse support,* that is, general support not related to specific system performance, a reserve of citizen goodwill toward the basic levels of the political system?[13] These are hypothetical questions and hence difficult to answer. Nevertheless, the available evidence suggests that this diffuse support is developing and that the Bonn system is more than just a "fair weather" democracy. Our evidence for this assertion comes from two general sources: (1) the ever-present public opinion poll and (2) the actual behavior of Germans at both elite and mass levels during political crises of the recent past.

Democratic Values, Processes, and Institutions

The decline in popular support for past political regimes has indeed been paralleled by a steady increase in support for the values, processes, and institutions of the Bonn democracy. The essentially passive acceptance of the postwar system for a basically negative reason—because everything else had failed—was being displaced by a more active, positive orientation to the new Republic. Moreover, by the late 1960s, levels of popular support had become sufficiently high and diffuse so that some observers were describing the Bonn system as "institutionalized" and "established."[14]

This process can also be illustrated through public opinion trend data covering two key values of liberal democracy—freedom of political conflict and competition—and its central institution and process—representation of the popular will via a legislative assembly.

Conflict and Competition. The inability of liberal democracy to take root in Germany in the first half of the twentieth century has been explained by many scholars as the result of an absence of popular understanding of the role of conflict and competition in democratic politics. Germans, it has been said, long for conflictless solutions to social and political problems. Unlike citizens in the "classical" democracies such as the United States and Britain, Germans do not, according to the West German sociologist Ralf Dahrendorf, recognize that differences of opinion and interest in politics are inevitable. They have thus concentrated not on managing conflict through the creation of institutions that guarantee its expression, nor on the development of rules of the game acceptable to conflicting parties, but have instead sought to eliminate the *causes* of conflict by searching for "absolute solutions" to social and political problems without ever considering whether such solutions actually exist.[15] This aversion to conflict has made Germans at both elite and mass levels unable to accept the necessity of opposition parties or extensive bargaining within and between parties in parliament. It has instead made them "expert-oriented," "legalistic," with an administrative conception of politics.[16]

Available evidence suggests, however, that if aversion to political conflict and competition was characteristic of German attitudes in the past, this aversion has diminished greatly over the past forty years. In a 1968 study of social, economic, cultural, religious, and political elites, over 70 percent of the sample agreed that "progress in modern society comes about through social conflict." Almost 90 percent agreed that "the common good can only be achieved through open conflicts between differing interests and their resolution by mutually acceptable compromises," and 97 percent replied affirmatively to the statement: "Democracy lives from constant public criticism of political events and from a steady effective parliamentary opposition to the government in power."[17] A 1970 study of high-level civil servants found a general acceptance of conflict as a normal part of the political process. Only 13 percent of this German sample thought that parties "uselessly exacerbate political conflicts," as contrasted to 22 percent of the British bureaucrats and 65 percent of the Italian sample. Only 9 percent of the German respondents, as compared to 4 percent of the British and 48 percent of the Italians, thought that conflicting interest groups endanger "the general welfare of the country."[18] The study concluded that "top level civil servants in Germany in 1970 displayed great sensitivity to and support for the imperatives of politics in democracy."[19] Moreover, these patterns were especially noticeable among younger civil servants. At least on the basis of these studies of elites, there is little of the aversion to conflict and competition that Dahrendorf thinks impeded democratic political development in the past.

There is a similar pattern among the general public. National samples of adult West Germans were asked on sixteen separate occasions between 1950 and 1978 whether "it is better for a country to have several parties, so that a variety of different opinions can be represented, or only one party, so that as much unity as possible exists." The proportion of the adult population supporting political competition was only 53 percent in 1950; attitudes toward this key value of liberal democracy were thus still mixed and ambivalent. By 1978, however, 92 percent of adult West Germans supported the principle of party competition. Moreover, explicit support for a one-party system dropped from about one-fourth of the population in the early 1950s to less than one-tenth by the early 1970s.[20] These trends suggest that at both the elite and the mass levels, then, the value of political competition continues to be a widely held belief in the West German political culture of the 1980s.

Representation and Parliament. According to most theories of democracy, the central institution for political democracy in large societies is the legislative assembly in which the various interests and opinions are represented. Do Germans feel they are represented in parliament? Do they support, in theory at least, this important institution? Once again, available data show steady gains in popular support for this key process and institution. In 1951 about half of the adult population stated frankly that if they sent their representative a letter, it would not be read or perhaps might not even reach him. Twenty-one years later, only about a fifth of the population held this view. By the mid- to late 1960s most Germans felt that their communications with representatives would be read and acted on.[21] When asked in surveys conducted between 1951 and 1965: "What do you think of the Bundestag in Bonn as our representative assembly?" the proportion evaluating it as "excellent," "basically good," or "fair" increased from 66 percent in 1951 to 86 percent by 1965.[22]

As Table 3.2 indicates, the belief that parliamentary deputies are primarily concerned with the "general interest," rather than their personal interests or those of their party, has steadily increased over the past thirty-five years. In 1951 only a fourth of the adult population felt that the Bundestag deputies in Bonn were concerned above all for the interests of the population as a whole. By 1978 this had more than doubled, increasing to 55 percent. The proportion of the electorate that attributed a primary concern with either personal or party interests to the parliamentary deputies dropped during this period from 46 to 18 percent.

Thus, support for key political values, a central political process (representation), and the major republican institution (parliament) had by the late 1960s reached levels where it was indeed possible to speak of a consensus on liberal democracy in modern West Germany. And although the increase in support for the present system and the decline in positive feelings for past regimes have been the result of both generational changes and the performance of the Bonn system, the important point for our purposes is that by the end of the period covered in these surveys all major social, economic, and political groups ranked high in their support for political competition, their sense of representation, and their support of the parliament. Support, at least for the liberal Republic established in 1949, has become *diffuse*, not significantly related to any particular group or policy of the government. These principles and processes have become accepted norms for the conduct of politics in the Federal Republic. The major unknowns about West German politics no longer revolve around the possible reversion to an authoritarian or even a fascist past but, rather, to the future scope of democracy as not only a political but also a social and economic way of life.

POLITICAL INTEREST AND INVOLVEMENT

The General Pattern

The formal, legal rules of the Bonn system have thus far placed few participatory requirements upon citizens beyond periodic voting. This leaves major responsibility for system maintenance, policy innovation, and development to political elites. Most Germans in 1949 probably did not want it any other way. The immediate postwar period witnessed a widespread withdrawal from public and political matters and an almost exclusive concern with private and familial affairs and above all with material acquisition. Many Germans had their first political experiences during the Weimar and Nazi periods, and these experiences were for the most part not pleasant. The common man, caught up with the initial enthusiasm for National Socialism and Hitler, who joined the party after 1933 may well have found himself after 1945 unemployed and his bank account and other assets frozen during denazification, in addition to the myriad other calamities suffered by all Germans in the immediate postwar years. In short, many "little people," political innocents, got burned by politics and were very reluctant to try again. Hence, beyond the limited and hardly taxing act of voting, there have been relatively low rates of participation in activities such as party organizations, election campaigns, and public causes.

Formal participation in elections, however, is high by both European and American standards. Turnout in national elections has ranged from 79 percent in 1949 to 91 percent in 1976, averaging 87 percent over eleven elections. Turnout in state and local elections has averaged around 60 to 70 percent, also much higher than for corresponding subnational elections in other advanced industrial societies. Yet participation in elections, although high in frequency, has been low in intensity. Survey research conducted in the 1950s and 1960s found that most Germans traditionally go to the polls more out of a sense of duty or because "it is the usual thing to do" than from a belief that they are in fact helping to decide the personnel and policies of government.[23] Moreover, most studies of West German political behavior have found that those citizens who are interested in politics and discuss political issues with any frequency restrict such activity to their family and very close friends.[24] The overall pattern has thus been one of privatization, with little involvement beyond voting.

There is growing evidence, however, that this traditional pattern is changing. Economic prosperity and rising educational levels have given more people the resources of knowledge, conceptual ability, and time necessary to participate in politics. Data over time on a variety of items—interest in politics, "talking politics," and an inclination to join a party—show a steady increase in the politicization of German citizens.

Political Interest. At various times between 1952 and 1983, one West German polling organization asked national voter samples: "Generally speaking, are you interested in politics?" As the responses presented in Figure 3.1 show, there has been a general rise in the proportion expressing an interest in politics, from 27 percent in 1952 to 57 percent by 1983.

"Talking Politics." When asked, "Do you discuss politics with others?" in eight national surveys conducted between 1955 and 1973, the proportion reporting frequent political conversations increased from 15 percent in 1955 to 28 percent by 1973. Those "occasionally" talking politics increased during the same period from 41 percent to 50 percent, and the proportion reporting that they never discuss politics dropped from 44 percent to 22 percent during this period.[25] In a 1983 survey conducted in the nations of the European Community, German respondents reported the highest frequency (84 percent) of political discussions. Whereas 44 percent of Italian respondents, 36 percent of the British sample, and

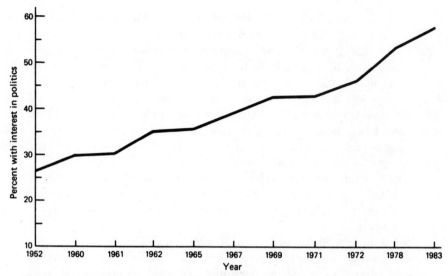

Figure 3.1. Levels of interest in politics, 1952–1983. (*From* Institut für Demoskopie, Survey No. 3061, *Jahrbuch der öffentlichen Meinung* 5:213 and 8:339.)

30 percent of the French reported that they "never" talked politics, only 16 percent of the West Germans were in this category.

Party Membership. The proportion of Germans holding active memberships in political parties has increased from about 4 percent of the electorate in the early 1970s to over 8 percent by 1983.[26] In addition, those contemplating party membership increased from only 7 percent in 1952 to 15 percent by 1975.[27] Thus almost a fourth of the electorate now either is in a political party or is considering joining one. The actual and potential body of activists has more than doubled since the 1950s.

New Forms of Political Participation: Citizen Initiative Groups

The emergence of widespread citizen initiative and action groups outside the existing party system is another phenomenon indicative of growing mass confidence in the citizen role. Some of these groups were in evidence as early as the 1965 election, but they were only *voter* initiative groups in support of particular parties and candidates, and in some cases their spontaneity and freedom from the existing parties was in question. In 1972 there were more than 300 voter initiative groups supporting the SPD. The movement was led by nationally prominent writers, artists, and personalities such as Günter Grass and Heinrich Böll—hardly your average concerned citizen.

Of greater interest for our purposes are the local initiative groups organized by citizens to protest and remedy a particular local problem: arbitrary increases in mass transit fares; inadequate children's playgrounds, kindergartens, schools; air and water pollution. These groups are indicative of new patterns of political participation that contradict the traditional characterization of Germans as politically passive, relying only on intermittent, indirect participation through voting or formal contact with the state bureaucracy. It is difficult at present to ascertain the scope and the size of the citizen initiative movement, but available evidence suggests that it is more than just a passing phenomenon restricted to a few middle-class activists in large cosmopolitan, metropolitan areas. One study by a Hamburg social scientist found about a thousand parents' groups working in the Federal Republic for the establishment of progressive kindergartens.[28] In 200 cities, youth groups, urging the construction of recreation centers, are active. Environmental protection groups have been formed, according to one estimate, in 350 localities.[29] Various problems of city planning are another concern of local initiative groups.

Most of these groups concentrate on one issue area and tend to be free from any encompassing ideology. Nevertheless, they reflect the inability of the established party system and the institutions of local government to meet key needs of the citizenry. Petitions, demonstrations, protest marches, and political "happenings" are all part of their tactical arsenal.

These groups had their precedent in the widespread demonstrations that took place in the late 1960s over the Emergency Laws,[30] the Vietnam war, and university reform; they are to some extent the adult version of the student protest movement.[31] In recent years the focus has shifted to the local level, the one least penetrated by the national political parties, where the problems of outmoded school systems, environmental decay, inadequate zoning, and land use regulations exceed the capacities of most local governments and officials. In early 1977, however, a massive citizen initiative protest over the construction of nuclear power plants was organized successfully on a national level. The emergence of the Greens, discussed in Chapter 4, is also closely related to the movement. Recently, many environmentalist initiative groups have campaigned extensively against the proposed deployment of new, middle-range nuclear missiles in Western Europe. Some elements of this movement also call for West Germany's withdrawal from NATO, complete military disarmament, and the development of nonviolent forms of defense. In 1981 to 1983 the movement was able to organize several large demonstrations against the NATO missile plan.

The success of citizen initiative groups together with the increases in the more traditional forms of political participation already described seem to indicate that West Germans are ready for a more direct democracy than that envisioned in the Basic Law. Proposals have indeed been made for more citizen involvement and influence especially at the local level through referenda, petitions, the right to recall public officials, and even state financial support for citizen groups. Surveys have found that most West Germans disagree with the drafters of the Basic Law and the constitutional scholars. When asked to choose between a system in which parties and political leaders made the important decisions with popular influence limited to voting (that is, the present one or one in which "important political questions should not be left to parties and political leaders, but to citizens in referenda"), 63 percent of a national sample preferred the "direct democracy" alternative, and only 22 percent opted for the present "elitist" system; the remainder were undecided.[32] Whether the existing policy-making institutions can adjust to this new situation will be a major problem in the future.

CIVIL LIBERTIES AND HUMAN RIGHTS

Unlike the United States, Britain, or France, Germany does not have a strong civil libertarian tradition. German political and legal theory has for the most part emphasized the duties of the individual vis-à-vis the state rather than state responsibilities toward the protection of individual liberties. Indeed, as Leonard Krieger has pointed out, German political thinkers defined liberty largely in collectivist terms.[33] That is, the individual was "free" only within the confines of the collectivity or state, and obedience to its rules and regulations ensured his freedom and personal development. To be sure, this state, according to the German political tradition, was to be a *Rechtsstaat,* a state based on the rule of law, and great attention was given to the detailed legal codes that defined individual rights and duties and delimited state authority. The interpretation of these laws and their social and political effect traditionally restricted, rather than enlarged, individual freedom, however. This Rechtsstaat tradition also produced an excessive legalism, which resulted in many unjust statutes that were steadfastly adhered to in the name of the rule of law. The Nazi seizure of power, the persecution of Jews, and many other acts of the Nazi dictatorship were all "legal." During the extensive student demonstrations of the late 1960s, for example, courts used the old provisions of the penal code against disturbance of the public order to punish protesters who were exercising rights of free expression guaranteed in the Basic Law. The postwar prosecution of war criminals was consistently delayed and complicated by the retention of laws and regulations passed before and during the Nazi era, laws that protected judicial and bureaucratic wrongdoers. There is no German version of the American Civil Liberties Union, no culturally ingrained sympathy for the underdog. The German humanistic tradition is above all abstract, philosophical, and not pragmatic.

Evidence also suggests that the rule of law is less likely to apply to lower-status, disadvantaged groups in German society than to the more established, prosperous segments of the community. Foreign workers, the very young, the elderly—in short, the weak in this society—have been subjected to various subtle forms of discrimination and neglect in spite of the welfare state. The upper-middle class character of the judiciary creates a situation, especially in criminal cases, in which one class in effect sits in judgment on another class about whose lifestyle it knows or understands relatively little.[34] In a 1978 survey almost half of a representative sample of the adult population stated that people from lower social classes receive poorer treatment from the courts; among manual workers almost 60 percent took this position.[35] Many manual workers and lower-level white-collar employees (the bulk of the working population) are, according to one authority, "estranged from the courts," lacking basic knowledge about how the judicial system can meet their needs.[36] The procedures, rules, jargon, and bureaucratic red tape of the criminal justice system are beyond the comprehension of many citizens. When asked in surveys whether "rich people" received better treatment from the police, 83 percent of the *police officers* questioned replied that they did; only 11 percent of the police thought that the system gave equal treatment to all groups and classes.[37]

Nevertheless, public awareness of and sensitivity to the importance of civil liberties has become substantial in the Federal Republic. In surveys in 1968 and 1982 more than 90 percent of the adult population agreed that "every person should have the right to express his opinion regardless of what the majority thinks."[38] When asked what freedoms they would give up in exchange for reunification with East Germany, only 2 percent would consider forfeiting freedom of speech and only 3 percent would sacrifice free elections and competing parties; 10 percent, however, would consider abandoning freedom of assembly in exchange for reunification.[39]

The constitution, or the Basic Law, in its first twenty articles, lists an impressive array of fundamental and inalienable rights and liberties. Equality before the law, the prohibition of any discrimination based on sex, race, language, national origin, religion, or political persuasion, is guaranteed in Article 3. Freedom of religion (broadly defined to include any belief system) and the right to refuse military service for reasons of conscience are granted in Article 4. Civil rights connected with the freedom of expression and information via speech, writing, pictures, broadcasts, and films are enumerated in Article 5. Censorship is rejected, although "general laws" dealing with the protection of youth (obscenity) and "personal honor" (slander and libel) limit this freedom. Explicit academic freedom (teaching), conditional on loyalty to the constitution, is granted in Article 5 (paragraph 3). Article 5 also clearly guarantees freedom of assembly, association, and movement, the privacy of mail and telephone messages, and the right to petition.

Finally in an extraordinary departure from German constitutional tradition, Article 20, as amended in 1968, declares that "all Germans shall have the right to resist any person or persons seeking to abolish the constitutional order, should no other remedy be possible." In a 1974 speech commemorating the July 20, 1944, plot to assassinate Hitler, Chancellor Helmut Schmidt specifically referred to this article as one that would legalize armed resistance against any authority that violated the individual liberties enumerated in the basic rights of the constitution.

Although major controversies involving alleged violations of these basic liberties have thus far occurred infrequently, they are illustrative of how civil rights matters are treated by the political system. The most publicized and dramatic civil rights case during the past forty years involved a government raid in 1962 on the offices of the newsmagazine *Der Spiegel* and the arrest of its two major editors. The government charged that the magazine had illegally procured and published secret defense documents and planned to publish more; hence the police raid and arrests. The minister of defense responsible for the police action, Franz-Josef Strauss, had been (and still is) a frequent target of the magazine. Perhaps not coincidentally, the magazine had also begun an exposé of alleged corruption involving Strauss in connection with aircraft purchases and government-sponsored military housing projects in his native Bavaria.

The government argued that its strong suspicion of treason justified extreme measures. The German press, the opposition party in parliament, and sizable segments of the governing coalition felt otherwise. The minister of justice, who had not been informed of the action, resigned; and his party, the Free Democrats (FDP), threatened to leave the coalition if Strauss did not leave the government. His subsequent resignation and the squashing of the government indictment by the Federal Appeals Court closed the case for all practical purposes. The near-unanimous opposition of the press and the response of some, but not all, elements of public opinion were indicative of considerable support for freedom of the press, or at least opposition to overt, heavy-handed attempts at censorship reminiscent of an earlier era. Clearly, after this incident, any government would be more reluctant to use such tactics against a critical press.

THE "RADICALS" IN PUBLIC SERVICE CONTROVERSY

A more recent civil liberties controversy involves the employment of "political radicals" by the state. Can a communist, neo-Nazi, or any other "radical" be a civil servant (including teachers, who at all levels also have civil service status)? This issue became political when New Left groups within the Social Democratic party supported the radicals' position and successfully opposed the party establishment's hard line in this area. This enabled the conservative Christian Democrats to charge that Socialists were allowing left-wing, radical teachers and bureaucrats to flood the civil service and ultimately undermine the constitutional order.

Most cases have involved allegedly radical teachers in elementary and secondary schools. In one Hessian community, for example, four school teachers taught communist "popular front" slogans to their pupils. When more than 500 parents refused to send their children to school, two teachers were immediately dismissed, and the other two suspended.[40] In a high school geography class in Bremen, the teacher, in order to illustrate the class structure of the community, sent his pupils into various neighborhoods to photograph homes and apartments and interview their occupants about their lifestyles, finances, and sociopolitical attitudes. Irate homeowners in the city's more affluent sections protested the "Nazi-like tactics," and the instructor was suspended. Many of these young teachers attended universities during the salad days of student protest and New

Left influence. Now active as teachers and administrators, they are, in their own way, on the "long march through the institutions."

In 1972 the federal government and the Ministerpräsidenten of the ten state governments issued an executive decree that was supposed to establish unified national policy in this area until formal legislation could be passed by the parliament. Although each case was to be examined and resolved separately, some general guidelines were given. An applicant for public employment who was engaged in "anticonstitutional" activity was not to be hired. If an applicant was a member of any organization that was anticonstitutional, that alone was to be grounds for doubting whether he or she would support the "free democratic order." Thus any member of such a group, usually the Communist party or the radical-right NPD (National Democratic party) would normally have his or her employment application rejected. For those already in the public service, membership in such organizations could be grounds for dismissal. For manual workers and white-collar employees in public service, without civil service status, the relevant sections of trade union contracts would apply.

This decision represented a hard line approach to the question of political extremists in the civil service. It also reflected the fears of the Social Democrats of being portrayed by the opposition as "soft on radicalism." Critics charged that the decree could be interpreted to mean that even ordinary or nominal membership in groups such as the communists or the NPD would mean a denial of or dismissal from employment. Furthermore, "anticonstitutional" activity could mean everything from participating in street demonstrations to blowing up the capitol. The whole decree, it was argued, would encourage denunciations and petty spying of civil servants on one another reminiscent of the Nazi era. Critics also charged that the degree violated Article 3 of the Basic Law, which prohibits discrimination on the basis of political views and grants equal access to public jobs. In spite of these objections, a 1975 decision of the federal constitutional court (see pp. 192–195 for a description of this court) essentially upheld this policy, although the court emphasized that membership in radical groups would have to be substantiated by other "anticonstitutional" activity to justify dismissal from public service.[41]

In practice, this "unified" statement has been differentially applied in the various states. In those governed by the Social Democrats, no civil servants have been dismissed for mere membership in radical organizations, although a leadership or officeholding function has been grounds for removal. In states governed by the Christian Democrats, on the other hand, membership alone has been sufficient for dismissal. One of these states, the Rhineland-Palatinate, has advocated a nationwide system of security checks. Another, Bavaria, maintains dossiers on teachers and college professors. One teaching intern in the Bavarian city of Augsburg was dismissed because he took part in a demonstration during which "communist slogans" were shouted, and as a student, had been a member of the SDS (Socialist German Student League). Between 1972 and 1975 only about 300 citizens had been denied public employment, and only about fifty out of almost 3.7 million public employees had been removed from public service because of "radical" political activities.

In 1975 the federal government submitted legislation that would have created guidelines consistent with the court's ruling—that is, that mere membership in a radical organization would not be grounds for dismissal from public service. The government bill was vetoed by the upper house of parliament. In May 1976 the federal government then issued new guidelines similar to those in the defeated legislation. These guidelines, however, apply only to federal employees and not to those working for state or local governments.

By the late 1970s an increasing number of party and government officials at all levels became convinced that the 1972 decree was a mistake and that the existing security clearance practices were unfair and in need of major revision. The SPD mayor of Hamburg in late 1978 announced that Hamburg, like its sister city-state of Bremen, would no longer routinely request that the Office for the Protection of the Constitution provide information on all candidates. Several months earlier the SPD minister of education in Berlin declared that the 1972 decision of his party to support the decree was wrong and that Berlin would change its procedures. In January 1979 the SPD-FDP coalition in Bonn also abolished the practice of automatically checking each application with security agencies. A month later the Saar became the first CDU-governed state to eliminate the routine check. Clearly, a combination of experience with the policy, the reaction of public opinion, especially among the younger, educated segment of the population, and foreign criticism of the Federal Republic had produced a trend away from the policy. On balance, however, the entire controversy probably inhibited the expression of unpopular ideas and the support of "different," unpopular causes.[42]

CIVIL LIBERTIES AND THE CENSUS

In the early 1980s a planned national census became another major civil liberties issue. The last complete census was taken in 1970. For budgetary reasons a new census, planned for 1980, was postponed until 1983. A 1982 law authorizing the census was unanimously passed by the parliament with little debate or controversy. But citizen initiative groups and the new Green political party (see Chapter 4, pp. 99–101) began a campaign against the census, which they regarded as an unnecessary intrusion by the state into the private lives of German citizens. Specifically, the anticensus groups were critical of provisions in the law that would allow officials, including police and security agencies, to compare the new data with domicile registration information already collected by local and regional authorities. In short, information given by individuals to the census takers could be shared with the police and other public bodies.

The anticensus movement was denounced by the Interior Minister as "a minority of extremists seeking to undermine the system."[43] But in April 1983 the federal constitutional court, responding to a petition by census opponents, issued an injunction halting the census, which had been scheduled to begin that same month. Finally, in December 1983 the court in a major decision unanimously struck down many of the provisions of the 1982 law. The court objected to the open-ended character of the law's language, which it ruled did not set sufficient limits on the state's authority to question its citizens. The court also ruled unconstitutional the law's provision for the sharing of data between government agencies. In addition, the introduction of a single identification number for each citizen, which could be used to retrieve personal data from a variety of files, was rejected by the court. The government and parliament had to draft a new law that satisfied the constitutional standards set by the court. Most civil libertarians and constitutional lawyers praised the decision as an important advance for civil liberties in the Federal Republic.[44]

In 1985 a revised law, which met the objections of the court, was passed by the parliament and the census finally took place in 1987. Some Green leaders still opposed the new law and the called for citizens to boycott the census.[45] The Greens contended that citizens could not be certain that the personal data obtained in the census would remain confidential. The other parliamentary parties, including the Social Democrats, strongly criticized the Green boycott as a clear violation of the law.

Generally, the West German public is still not particularly sensitive to the rights of politically deviant or fringe groups that advocate unpopular ideas. As Table 3.3 shows, many citizens perceive limits to the constitutional guarantees of free speech and expression.

Criticism of major public officials, the chancellor, and the federal president is seen as guaranteed in the constitution by about 90 percent of the adult population, although only about two-thirds are "absolutely" sure that criticism of these officials is allowed. But when asked whether these guarantees also apply to

TABLE 3.3. PUBLIC OPINION AND THE LIMITS OF FREE EXPRESSION

Question: Does the constitutional right of freedom of expression mean that anyone has the right to publicly:

	% "Yes, absolutely"	% "Yes, apparently"	% No/ undecided
Criticize the chancellor?	68	20	12
Criticize the federal president?	62	22	16
Oppose religion, Christianity?	55	23	22
Advocate the abolition of the army?	50	20	30
Advocate communism and the world communist revolution?	33	18	49
Advocate the founding of a new Nazi party?	26	16	58

SOURCE: *Jahrbuch der öffentlichen Meinung* 5:226.

public criticism of Christianity or the advocacy of the abolition of the army, West Germans are less certain about free speech. Finally, only about half of the adult population is fairly certain that the constitution protects those who advocate a world communist revolution or a new Nazi party. Public understanding of individual liberties is greatest when the terms of reference are within the existing liberal parliamentary framework; the population is less clear about whether or not the constitution protects the advocacy of extremist political opinions or the criticism of major, established social values.

THE STATUS AND ROLE OF MINORITY GROUPS

Foreign Workers

The most significant and conspicuous minority group in the Federal Republic are foreign workers. Germany's fabled postwar economic boom was due in part to a large labor supply created by the forced migration of almost 10 million refugees from territories annexed by the Soviet Union and Poland, together with the influx of almost 3 million additional refugees from East Germany that continued until the Berlin Wall was put up in August 1961. These additions to the labor supply initially compensated for the loss of manpower through the war. Yet, by the early 1960s, the economy's need for labor could no longer be met internally, and workers from Europe's poorer regions were recruited extensively by business with government assistance.

The number of foreign workers, or "guest workers" (*Gastarbeiter*) as they are euphemistically termed, increased from about 110,000 in 1957 to more than 2.5 million by 1973. Although the recessions of 1974–1976 and 1981–1983 reduced their number to about 1.7 million, foreign workers still account for about 8 percent of the total work force and roughly 15 percent of the total *manual* work force. In 1988 the three largest "exporting" countries were Turkey (23 percent), Yugoslavia (21 percent), and Italy (17 percent). Spain and Greece also sent sizable contingents.

In many large West German cities, such as Frankfurt, Munich, Stuttgart, and Hamburg, foreign workers constitute from 15 to 20 percent of the total work force and probably 30 to 40 percent of the manual workers. They have usually been assigned tasks that Germans are no longer willing to perform: street cleaning, common labor, grave digging. About 50 percent of Frankfurt's and 80 percent of Munich's garbagemen are foreign workers. Although those in major industries receive the same pay as German workers, wage discrimination in smaller firms is not uncommon.

Even in large firms, foreign workers are invariably in the lowest-paid manual occupations. This is due partly to their, by German standards, poor vocational training and language difficulties, and also to discrimination on the part of German employers. Nonetheless, most foreign workers are covered by governmental health, security, and pension programs and, where applicable, are unionized. Thus, although in low-paying jobs, they do not constitute a subculture of poverty in the Federal Republic.

It is in the area of social integration that the foreign workers pose a particularly difficult policy problem. Generally, West German society has tolerated foreign workers more than it has accepted them. Opinion surveys of native citizens have found considerable latent prejudice: two-thirds of the German population, according to one poll, regard foreign workers as "terribly loud and boisterous," about half think "they are after our women," 35 percent see foreigners as a "necessary evil," and 14 percent think "they are dumb and vulgar."

When the guest worker, after a year or so of employment, brings his family into West Germany, his problems are compounded. The education of his children has been particularly difficult. Should the children be educated and socialized completely as Germans, or should special school classes with native teachers be established at least in language and social studies? In many cases the parents themselves are not able to indicate their preferences or future plans, much less those of their children. Many of these children have spent most or all of their lives in Germany. Yet their parents cling to the goal of someday returning to their home country and thus want their children to retain its language and values. The result is that the children grow up in a sort of twilight zone—they master neither their parents' culture and language nor the German. They invariably drop out of school and, urged on by their parents, attempt to secure some kind of employment to augment the family's finances and hasten its "return" to the homeland. But in recent years the tightened job market has made it difficult for half-literate, untrained, foreign young people to find employment. The result is a growing body of unemployed adolescents, especially in the large cities, involved in petty crime and, increasingly, the drug trade.

In spite of the declining number of foreign workers in recent years, their higher birthrate and the influx of family members have actually increased the total number of foreign residents. By 1988 there were about 4.7 million foreign residents, with only 1.7 million in the work force. The number of foreign dependents has grown from 1.4 million in 1973 to almost 3 million by 1983. In some large cities such as Frankfurt, up to half of all newborn children are from families of foreign workers. Thus there are now two and even three generations of foreign residents.

The ambiguity of the foreign workers' future plans complicates the whole issue. Many still insist that their goal is to someday return to their home country. They are in Germany just to earn as much money in as short a period as they can and are thus not interested in becoming politically involved. For some, this "return to the homeland" has become a myth or illusion that enables them to endure the discrimination and deprivation they experience.[46] By the second and third generation, however, it becomes less viable, and the frustration of their children increases. The potential for social unrest that exists in this situation should be obvious, especially to British and American readers.

Several proposals have been made to improve the status of the guest workers and their families. One involves giving the franchise to foreign workers for local elections. This would, it is argued, make local officials more responsive to their needs, especially in housing and education. Some students of the problem have advocated that all children of foreign workers that are born in the Federal Republic should automatically become German citizens when they reach the age of eighteen. It would thus become simpler for the second and third generations to identify with the Federal Republic and reject the "return to the homeland" myth. Finally, it has been suggested that the naturalization laws be liberalized so that foreign workers could have a viable option to their present condition.[47] Thus far, however, there is little significant support for any of these proposed changes. In a practical sense, German churches, labor unions (by requiring equal pay for equal work), and charitable organizations have in many cases done more to alleviate their problems than the government.

In the early 1980s popular pressure to reduce the number of foreigners increased. Between 1978 and 1982 the proportion of the population who agreed with the statement "Foreigners should go home" increased from 39 percent to 68 percent. This change was in part due to the poor economy, but it also reflected a fear of some Germans that their lifestyle would be fundamentally altered if the influx of foreigners, especially those from non-European countries, continued.

Other studies, however, have found a growing tolerance among West Germans of foreign workers' life styles and increased understanding for their particular housing and educational problems.[48] These trends are especially pronounced among younger Germans. Another possible indicator of increased sensitivity to the problem was the extraordinary success in 1986 of a book *Ganz Unten* ("At the Very Bottom") by a German journalist who disguised himself as a Turkish worker and spent several months in various towns and cities working at low-level jobs. His chronicle of discrimination, humiliation, and the indifference of authorities and institutions, including the churches, to his plight was read by a broad cross section of the public, including many working-class Germans who seldom buy or read books. *Ganz Unten* has sold over 3 million copies, making it the biggest bestseller of the postwar period.

Women

Politics in Germany, as elsewhere, has traditionally been a man's business. German women are less likely to participate in all political activities—voting, "talking politics," party membership, campaigning, candidacy—than are men. They are less likely to have opinions on or interest in political issues. The classic functions assigned to women in German society, neatly summarized by the three Ks—*Kinder* (children), *Kirche* (church), and *Küche* (kitchen)—have been slow to change and leave little room for explicit political roles. The traditionally subordinate status of women in politics is also shown in surveys that have found most women stating that they would have more confidence in a man as the representative of their political interests than in a fellow woman. Only about 30 percent of a national sample in 1975 felt that women could represent women's political interests better than men; among university-trained women, however, this proportion is higher.[49] A 1976 survey found that 56 percent of female respondents attributed better political judgment to their husbands, as compared to only 4 percent of men who felt the same way about their wives.[50]

A 1983 study among the nations of the European Community found German respondents to be more likely to take a male chauvinist position on the question of women in politics than citizens in other major West European countries. As the data presented in Table 3.4 show, 38 percent of the German sample agreed with the statement "Politics should be left to men" as compared to 25 percent for the Italian respondents, 23 percent for the British, 22 percent for the Dutch, and only 21 percent of the French sample. Germans were also less likely to express strong disagreement with the idea that politics is a man's business.

Yet, since the late 1960s a greater awareness and visibility of women in politics has become apparent. The elections of 1972 and 1976 showed that the Christian Democrats could no longer count on receiving lopsided majorities from female voters. It was especially among Catholic women that the Socialists were able to make exceptional gains. Public attitudes toward women in politics also show significant change; between 1965 and 1979 the proportion of men who "liked the idea" of a woman becoming politically involved rose from 27 to 64 percent. Although women are underrepresented among the membership of the political parties, there is a trend of increased female participation. From 1971 to 1985 the number of women active as members in the political parties increased from about 200,000 to 440,000. By 1985 about a fourth of all SPD members were female and more than a fifth of CDU/CSU members were women. In the smaller parties women made up over a third of the Green membership and about a fourth of FDP members. In the 1987 election, 80 women (15 percent of the total) were elected to the parliament, the highest number in the history of the Federal Republic.[51] The Green party is especially committed to a greater

TABLE 3.4. "POLITICS SHOULD BE LEFT TO MEN." MAJOR WEST EUROPEAN COUNTRIES, 1983 (in percentages)

	Germany	Italy	Britain	Netherlands	France
Strongly Agree; agree	38	25	23	22	21
Disagree	30	21	21	16	23
Strongly Disagree	32	54	56	62	56
Total	100	100	100	100	100

SOURCE: Euro-Barometer surveys, April 1983. I am grateful to Jacque-René Rabier and the Inter-University Consortium for Political and Social Research for making these data available.

leadership role for women. Almost 60 percent of the Greens' parliamentary delegation are female, and one, Jutta Ditfurth, is a very visible national party leader.

Also in recent years a woman was elected president of the German parliament; a second woman member was added to the cabinet; a woman was elected national chairman of the Young Socialists; and in one German state, a 33-year-old housewife and teacher became minister of labor. In 1988 the Social Democrats, at their national congress, adopted new party rules that will require that at least 40 percent of party officials and office holders be female by 1994. This quota system will apply at all levels—local, state, and national—of the party organization.

There was, to be sure, some element of tokenism in these developments. There has been a woman member in all but one of the fifteen national governments, and women deputies have been in all parliaments since 1949. But most of these traditional female activists came to politics from prominence in women's organizations, church groups, and similar female activities. They had rarely studied at a university and were given political positions in such "women's fields" as health and family policy. The new breed of female political activist is different; she has, above all, university training and has already established solid credentials in business, party, or government work.[52]

Income differences, however, between men and women remain substantial. White-collar males in industry earned in 1988 about 50 percent more than females. Differences among male and female manual workers were also considerable; male manual workers earned about 30 percent more than their female counterparts. These incomes differences are largely the result of the high proportion of women in lower-paying jobs. Only 6 percent, for example, of women in manual occupations were skilled workers in 1986 as compared to 59 percent of male blue-collar workers. Among white-collar employees, 7 percent of females are in supervisory positions as compared to 39 percent of men.[53]

A 1980 study of working women in the nine countries of the European Community found that feelings of discrimination in finding employment, training, salary, fringe benefits, and promotion were most widespread in the Federal Republic (Table 3.5). German women were about three times more likely to report discrimination on the job in the form of lower salaries and penalties for pregnancy or absences caused by children than their counterparts in France, Great Britain, Italy, the Netherlands, or Belgium. A major source of this discrimination, according to the survey, is the male-dominated authority structure in the workplace.[54]

Legal discrimination against women has also hindered the progress of the women's movement, West German style. The nineteenth-century civil legal code put married women especially in a subordinate position. According to the "marriage and family law," a husband could divorce his wife if she took employment without his permission, and a woman could not legally retain her

TABLE 3.5. DISCRIMINATION EXPERIENCED BY WORKING WOMEN: MAJOR WEST EUROPEAN COUNTRIES, 1980 (in percentages)

Country	Lower Salary	Refused Employment or Transferred Because of Pregnancy	Reprimanded for Absence Caused by Children	Asked if Pregnant at Job Interview	Sexual Harassment (Blackmail)
			Discrimination		
West Germany	28	32	30	28	4
France	8	5	13	9	8
Great Britain	5	3	6	13	7
Italy	6	6	13	12	6
Netherlands	10	8	7	20	4
Belgium	5	7	8	6	3

SOURCE: *European Women in Paid Employment* (Brussels: Commission of the European Communities, December 1980), p. 59.

maiden name after marriage. Not until 1974 were these provisions repealed. A liberalized abortion law passed by the parliament in 1974 with strong support from women's rights groups was, in a 6–2 decision, declared unconstitutional by the federal constitutional court in 1975. The court's decision touched off protest demonstrations, especially in large cities, and a bomb exploded in the court's building in Karlsruhe. Nonetheless, the attempted reforms in the legal status of women, noticeable since 1969, are indicative of a greater sense of political awareness among women and a capacity of the system to respond, although with mixed success, to their needs.

Youth

The postwar baby boom, which, unlike that in the United States, did not begin until after 1948, and a relatively high birthrate during the 1960s has resulted in 36 percent of the population being under thirty years of age. The traumatic experiences of depression, war, defeat, and foreign military occupation are to young Germans events to be studied in history classes and not living memories. The postwar generation has grown up in a politically stable and economically prosperous society that, however, has never been "youth oriented" and for the most part has been ill-prepared for the youth culture that has emerged. Nowhere is this more evident than in education—from preschool to university—where discontent and pressure for change are greater than in any other policy area. The lifestyles of West German youth in the 1970s, even in their most superficial aspects, were apparently not appreciated by their elders. When adults were asked in a 1970 survey "what they complain about the most," "long-haired, lazy young people" came in second place, right after high prices, in the opinion of a national adult sample. "Radical students" ranked fifth, ahead of the "government in Bonn" or even "crowded streets."[55] Clearly, for many West Germans, the long hair, beards, and unusual dress of young people, together with the assumed political radicalism of students, were a "red flag."

But, like their counterparts in other Western societies and their older fellow citizens, young people are not a hyperpoliticized, ideologically radical element in a staid, middle-class society. Their rate of participation in elections is below that of older age groups; the youth organizations of the political parties— Young Socialists (SPD), Young Democrats (FDP), and the Young Union (CDU/CSU)—count only about 5 percent of the 18–29 age group within their ranks. Less than 10 percent of all university students are affiliated with "radical" student groups; and less than 10 percent of college and university professors reported that their classes had ever been disturbed by radical students.[56] Surveys of young people have shown them to be concerned above all with the quality of their education, vocational training, employment prospects, individual happiness, and a sense of fulfillment—goals with which their elders could hardly disagree.

While not particularly involved in political matters, much less radical causes, German young people are more likely to have opinions supportive of liberal democratic values and innovative reform policies than older age groups. In recent years, young people have also been more likely to vote for the Socialist and, above all, Green political parties rather than for the more conservative Christian Democrats.

Official concern about youth questions and the organization of young people has been strong among all West German governments since 1949. This is expressed by the presence of a Youth and Family Ministry (since 1972 merged with Health), several major white papers on youth, and a variety of legislative programs relating to the activities and problems of young people (vocational education, mental health, scholarship programs, child labor laws). For the West German state, "youth" is a bureaucratic category, a "group" like the elderly, refugees, farmers, or labor. Most traditional solutions to problems of drug abuse, juvenile delinquency, school truancy, and unemployment among young people that are proposed by various governments tend to revolve around the organization of youth in a wide variety of cultural, religious, recreational, labor, and educational associations all subsidized by the state. About 40 percent of young Germans aged 15–24 belong to at least one of these organizations. Attempts at "political education" designed to create a "critical, active citizen" are characteristic of most of these groups; indeed, some political educational program is usually required to receive state subsidies for their other activities. Whether this extensive state concern with young people is effective has yet to be determined. Given the reported increases in drug abuse, alcoholism, juvenile delinquency, and crime, these traditional official youth programs appear to be insufficient.

In the 1980s the weak economy produced record high unemployment levels among young people. The government and the private sector have attempted to increase the number of apprenticeship positions, and in 1983 Chancellor Kohl even made a personal commitment to secure a training position for every applicant. However, neither he nor his government was able to deliver the necessary openings. The very high level of support given by young people to the Greens in 1987 (67 percent of Green support came from voters under 35) was in part their reaction to this economic situation. In addition to the missile and peace issues, there was an economic component of youth support for the Greens.[57]

Refugees

About 22 percent (13.7 million) of the West German population is officially classified as refugees or expellees from either the eastern territories lost to the Soviet Union and Poland after World War II, other parts of Eastern Europe, or East Germany. The absorption of this mass of homeless, hungry, and in most cases impoverished people was a major problem for the young West German state, already overcrowded and unable to feed and house its pre-1945 population adequately. Within two decades, this group has become integrated into West German society—a major accomplishment of the postwar system. Today they represent neither a social nor an economic problem, and hence, as refugees, they have little political relevance. There is no longer a refugee political party, and other parties make no special appeals for the refugee vote. Neither are there longer any significant differences between refugees and the rest of the population in terms of voting behavior, political attitudes, or ideologies.[58] Generally they have been just as supportive of the government's policy of reconciliation with Eastern Europe and the Soviet Union as the rest of the population.[59]

Political Radicals and Extremists

The legitimacy threshold for extremist movements has been higher in the Federal Republic than in other West European societies. Citing the Weimar, Nazi, and East German experiences for support, both West Germany's postwar occupiers and the political elites of the Federal Republic have had a relatively low tolerance level for any individual, group, or movement that advocated radical changes in the basic structure of the political, social, or economic order. In short, it has been difficult to be an extremist in West Germany and, in comparison to France, Italy, and Britain, relatively easy to be labeled as such by the established parties, courts, and other institutions.

The framers of the Basic Law in 1948–1949 gave the Federal Constitutional Court the power to ban any political party whose program or policies in the judgment of the Court threatened the basic structure of the Republic. Under this provision, the Court in the 1950s did outlaw a right-wing party and the German Communist party. Thus the Basic Law does not leave the fate of allegedly extremist parties to the electorate but, rather, to the courts.

In addition to constitutional prohibitions against extremism (defined as opposition to the "basic free democratic order"), West Germany and its constituent states have established offices for the Protection of the Constitution (*Verfassungsschutz*), which are charged with investigating individuals and groups suspected of undermining the system. The national office is under the Interior Ministry. It publishes an annual report to the parliament that catalogues extremist activity (political parties, members, acts of political violence) and assesses any trends. At times critics have charged that the government has misused the office for political purposes.

The Radical Right. Between 1949 and 1969 a variety of right-wing parties and organizations, many of which were led by former Nazis or people with close ties to former Nazis, came and departed from the political scene. Most of these groups were very small in numbers, but they could be very noisy, and given Germany's past, they drew considerable attention, especially from foreign observers.

At the 1969 election, one of these organizations, the National Democratic party (NPD), made a strong effort to gain representation in the national parliament. But with 4.3 percent of the vote, it failed to clear the 5 percent hurdle necessary for entrance into the legislature. After 1969 the party quickly faded; at the 1976 election it received less than 1 percent of the vote, and between 1970 and 1974 it lost all its seats in several state parliaments. Various other nationalist and right-wing organizations did mount protests against the government's policy of détente with the Soviet Union, East Germany, and Eastern Europe, but little has been heard from them since the ratification of the treaties. By the late 1980s, the total membership of these organizations was less than 25,000; they have become almost dormant, restricting themselves to occasional meetings and rallies, and the publication of newsletters, pamphlets, and a few limited-circulation newspapers.

With the virtual disappearance of radical right political groups, most media and official attention has recently focused on a few paramilitary right-wing organizations, some of which have apparently engaged in terrorist activity. Shortly before the 1980 election, a member of one such group (the *Wehrsportgruppe Hoffmann*) placed a bomb at one of the entrance gates to the *Oktoberfest* in Munich. Several people, including the terrorist, were killed in the explosion; the Hoffmann group, however, denied that it had any connection with the terrorist.

Although the prospects of a resurgent Nazi movement still stimulate the imaginations of novelists and screenwriters, no right-wing, much less neo-Nazi, organization has ever emerged in sufficient strength to seriously challenge the legitimacy of the Republic. Although the Republic's record in its early years of removing ex-Nazis from key public positions or preventing their reemployment was checkered, the simple fact is that by the 1980s such individuals were either dead, were very old and retired, or had by their subsequent behavior repudiated their past affiliations.

The Radical Left. The focus of media and public attention shifted in the 1970s from right-wing, neo-Nazi movements to the various radical terrorist organizations and revolutionary Marxist groups that emerged.

In the immediate postwar period, the remnants of what had been Germany's ideological left wing during the Weimar Republic—old-guard socialists, radical intellectuals, pacifists, and socially committed churchmen (especially on the Protestant side)—were frustrated as the anticipated moral regeneration and drastic change in the structure of society, economy, and polity did not take place. Original hopes for a "humanistic socialism" were thwarted as a middle-class, materialist, and elitist ethos came to dominate the politics of the new Republic. The radical dissenter became isolated, an oddball in the affluent society.

This postwar rejection of the ideological Left and its identification in the minds of many West Germans with Stalinism and the GDR (East German) dictatorship contributed to the rigid, uncompromising opposition of the New Left, which emerged in the mid-1960s, to the parliamentary system of the Bonn Republic.[60]

Isolated, its ideology spurned by all major parties and leaders, the New Left developed a socialist theory that rejected and denied legitimacy to the liberalism embodied in the Bonn system. The cold war, West German rearmament,

Vietnam, the Social Democrats' (SPD) acceptance of the market economy, and Adenauer's foreign policy all intensified the Left's total opposition to the parliamentary system. The SPD's entrance into a grand coalition with its long-time adversary, the Christian Democrats, in 1966 was thus the last straw and marked the beginning of intense, visible radical left activity.

After 1966, greatly strengthened by new recruits from the universities, the Left adopted various direct action tactics: demonstrations, mass meetings, clashes with police, seizures of university buildings, and attacks on the Springer press concern (the alleged center of media "manipulation of the masses").

In addition to classic Marxism-Leninism, the movement derived intellectual sustenance from several sources: social philosophers at the universities in Berlin, Marburg, and Frankfurt; French and Belgian socialist thinkers such as André Gorz and Ernst Mandel; and probably most important, the German-born American philosopher Herbert Marcuse. It was Marcuse, according to one authority, who in his evaluation of bourgeois liberal parliamentary politics as an inevitable forerunner of fascism, "provided [the West German New Left with] justification for the rejection of the game of parliamentary politics based on respect for the market place of ideas and rules of liberal discussion."[61]

By 1969 internal divisions over ideology and tactics, the massive indifference if not opposition of the West German "proletariat," and the increasing tendency to violence among factions of the movement greatly weakened the New Left. The Socialist-Liberal election victory of 1969 and the end of the Grand Coalition also took the wind out of the radical argument that the Republic was on the verge of a fascist takeover. Nonetheless, the New Left in its own way contributed to the increased politicization of West German citizens evident since the late 1960s. The new emphasis on "discussions" rather than speeches by political leaders, the increased readiness of a traditionally passive citizenry to use the rights of free expression to protest unpopular governmental action and seek redress and reform, so evident in the citizen initiative movement already discussed, all were to some extent influenced by the innovative and often audacious tactics of the "extraparliamentary opposition."

Where have all the radicals gone? Like their American counterparts, many have taken teaching and research positions at colleges and universities, and some are active in the Social Democratic party, the Greens, the trade unions, churches, journalism, and other middle-class occupations.[62] Several splinter groups from the movement, however, have resorted to guerrilla-type violence in an apparent attempt to bring down the state. Terrorist activities began in the 1970s with bank robberies, kidnappings, and murders. By June 1972, with the capture of the hard core of the so-called Baader-Meinhof band (named after two leading figures in the movement), terrorist activity subsided. In 1974, however, the death in prison of one of the terrorists through the consequences of a hunger strike, touched off the murder of a West Berlin judge. In 1975 another splinter group kidnapped the leader of the Christian Democrats in West Berlin shortly before the city elections and as ransom demanded the release of several terrorists from West German jails.

In 1977 terrorist activities assumed new dimensions when, within a five-month period, a series of well-planned attacks upon major government and business leaders took place. The chief federal prosecutor (equivalent to the American solicitor general) and the head of a major bank were assassinated, and in September the director of the Federation of German Industry was kidnapped and later murdered. The scope of these actions clearly indicates that terrorist groups had acquired new recruits and had achieved a degree of organizational and tactical sophistication exceeding that of earlier organizations. The terrorists had the support of many sympathizers who provided them with falsified identification papers, escape automobiles, conspiratorial hideouts, and other logistical support. Money was secured largely through periodic bank robberies.

The terrorists and their sympathizers constitute a significant challenge to the Republic's internal security. By the late 1980s the Red Army Faction (RAF) had about 20 hard-core or commando-level members living underground. Officials estimate that they are supported by about 200 militants and roughly 400 sympathizers who distribute propaganda and provide logistical support. In 1986 the RAF claimed responsibility for the car-bombing death of a leading executive of the Siemens electronics company and the assassination in Bonn of a senior official in the Foreign Ministry. In recent years another radical group, the Revolutionary Cells, has also engaged in terrorist activity mainly in the Rhine-Main area and in West Berlin. The Revolutionary Cells have a total membership of about 200 organized into five- to eight-member cells. They appear to act independently without contacts with the RAF or foreign terrorist groups.[63]

The Communist Party. West Germany's Communist party, not represented in the parliament since 1953 and declared unconstitutional, or "anticonstitutional," in 1956 by the federal constitutional court, reemerged in 1968–1969 with a slightly changed name (German Communist Party, instead of Communist Party of Germany). By 1979 the party had about 30,000 members, or about half as many as did the old KPD before its demise. However, most of these members are under forty, and the average age of delegates to the party's annual conventions had been about thirty-five. Although receiving only a tiny 0.1 percent of the popular vote in the 1987 federal election, the Communists have secured about 8 percent of the vote from young electors (under the age of thirty) at local elections in a few predominantly working-class communities.

The party's major efforts have been directed not at contesting elections but, rather, at organizing workers in industrial factories and university students. Within the factories, its members have the reputation of being very efficient, hard-working, and dedicated. The party supports at least for the time being the mainstream labor organization and seeks a common front with the Social Democrats. The party also supported the Socialist-Liberal governments of Willy Brandt and Helmut Schmidt, and although opposed to proposed policies such as workers' participation and profit sharing in industry as mere devices to prop up a "decadent" capitalist order, it has so far refrained from attacking the Socialist position on these issues. The party's strategy has clearly been to seek a broad popular front with all progressive forces to the left of the Christian Democrats. This strategy is also designed to avoid any prosecution of the party as anti-constitutional.

SUMMARY AND CONCLUSION

The much-discussed postwar political stability of the Federal Republic is now rooted in a solid attitudinal consensus on the values, processes, and institutions of liberal democracy. Bonn, in contrast to Weimar, is not a Republic without republicans. Moreover, since the mid-1960s there has been an increasingly closer fit between citizen attitudes and values and actual behavior. Germans at elite and general public levels are becoming more interested in politics and more inclined to use politics as a means of social change and personal development. Consider the following: Since 1966, two alternations of government and opposition have taken place without straining the system; widespread citizen initiative groups have emerged to campaign for social and political issues especially at the local level (housing, education, the environment); election campaigns have seen extensive citizen participation and involvement; the party system has become more polarized and conflictual, within the rules of the game; the intensity of political debate, both inside and outside of parliament, has increased as major innovations in foreign and domestic policies were attempted. Finally, neither the 1974–1976 nor the 1981–1983 economic recessions, the most severe since the Great Depression, which brought down the Weimar Republic, produced any noticeable increase in antisystem sentiment or movements. In short, the institutions and processes of liberal democracy are being used extensively without any perceptible stress on the basic structure of the political system. The stability of the West German political system has been supplemented by a vitality in political life not apparent during the Republic's early years.

NOTES

1. Donald J. Devine, *The Political Culture of the United States* (Boston: Little, Brown, 1972), pp. 347 ff.
2. This takes several forms. There has been, for example, a renewed interest among historians and the media in Prussia and its influence on German history. The immediate post-World War II period, during which the "switches were set" (*Weichenstellung*) for the formation and evolution of the Federal Republic, has also attracted the serious attention of historians in recent years. See Wolfgang Mommsen, "Wandlungen der nationalen Identität," in *Die Identität der Deutschen,* ed. Werner Weidenfeld (Bonn: Bundeszentrale für politische Bildung, 1983), pp. 170–192, and Heinrich August Winkler, ed., *Politische Weichenstellungen im Nachkriegsdeutschland, 1945–1953,* (Göttingen: Vandenhoeck und Ruprecht, 1979).

3. Erich Kitzmüller, Heinz Kuby, and Lutz Niethammer, "Der Wandel der nationalen Frage in der Bundesrepublik Deutschland," *Aus Politik und Zeitgeschichte,* 25 August 1973, p. 24.

4. Between 1966 and 1980 the proportion of West Germans who used the official, "legitimate" term GDR (German Democratic Republic) when speaking of East Germany, instead of the less legitimate or derogatory Eastern Zone or Zone, increased from 11 percent to 61 percent. Elisabeth Noelle-Neumann, *The Germans: Public Opinion Polls, 1967–1980* (Westport, CT, and London: Greenwood Press, 1981), p. 125. The terms "Eastern Zone" or "Zone" were those used by many West German political leaders throughout the 1950s and 1960s. They ascribe to East Germany, of course, an inferior status.

5. Elisabeth Noelle-Neumann and Edgar Piel, eds., *Allensbacher Jahrbuch der Demoskopie, 1978–1983* (Munich and New York: K. G. Saur, 1983), p. 187.

6. *Vorwärts,* January 24, 1980.

7. James M. Markham, "German Missile Protests: Mixed Signals for Kohl," *New York Times,* 24 October 1983, p. A3.

8. English-language analyses of this debate can be found in *German Politics and Society,* no. 13 (February 1988), Cambridge, MA: The Center for European Studies, Harvard University, and in Gordon Craig, "The War of the German Historians," *The New York Review of Books,* January 15, 1987.

9. Jürgen Habermas, "Eine Art Schadensabwicklung", *Die Zeit,* July 11, 1986, reprinted in *Historikerstreit,* Munich: Piper Verlag, 1987, pp. 75–76.

10. *Euro-barometre,* no. 21 (December 1985), p. 24.

11. G. Robert Boynton and Gerhard Loewenberg, "The Decay of Support for Monarchy and the Hitler Regime in the Federal Republic of Germany," *British Journal of Political Science* 4 (October 1974): 488.

12. Ibid., p. 485.

13. David Easton, *A Framework for Political Analysis* (Englewood Cliffs, NJ: Prentice-Hall, 1965).

14. Lewis J. Edinger, "Political Change in Germany," *Comparative Politics* 2, no. 4 (July 1970): 549–578.

15. Ralf Dahrendorf, *Society and Democracy in Germany* (New York: Doubleday, Anchor Books, 1969), pp. 137–138.

16. Ibid.

17. Rudolf Wildenmann, "Eliten in der Bundesrepublik" (Mannheim University, August 1968), pp. 49, 51.

18. Robert D. Putnam, "The Political Attitudes of Senior Civil Servants in Western Europe: A Preliminary Report," *British Journal of Political Science* 3 (January 1974): 270, 281–282.

19. Ibid., pp. 281–282.

20. David P. Conradt, "West Germany: A Remade Political Culture?" *Comparative Political Studies* 7 (July 1974): 222–238.

21. *Jahrbuch der öffentlichen Meinung, 1965–1967* (Allensbach: Verlag für Demoskopie, 1968), 4:182.

22. Cited in Gerhard Loewenberg, *Parliament in the German Political System* (Ithaca: Cornell University Press, 1967), p. 429.

23. Sidney Verba, "Germany: The Remaking of Political Culture," in *Political Culture and Political Development,* ed. L. W. Pye and S. Verba (Princeton: Princeton University Press, 1965), pp. 130–170.

24. Erwin K. Scheuch, "Die Sichtbarkeit politischer Einstellungen im alltäglichen Verhalten," *Kölner Zeitschrift für Soziologie und Sozialpsychologie, Sonderheft* No. 9 (1965): 169–214.

25. *Jahrbuch*, 4:214.

26. *Euro-barometre*, no. 19.

27. *Jahrbuch*, 6:64.

28. *Der Spiegel*, 21 November 1972, pp. 54 ff.

29. Ibid.

30. In 1968, after years of discussion and debate, the parliament passed a series of laws and constitutional amendments prescribing the conduct of government in emergency situations. Mindful of how the conservative nationalists and later the Nazis had abused the emergency provisions of the Weimar Constitution after 1930, various groups such as trade unions, student organizations, and some intellectuals mounted a vigorous opposition to the proposed legislation. Strong criticism was also levied against the Social Democrats, who, while in the parliamentary opposition, had opposed previous proposals for emergency provisions, but who in 1968, as a governing party, supported the laws.

31. Horst Zillessen, "Bürgerinitiativen im repräsentativen Regierungssystem," *Aus Politik und zeitgeschichte*, no. 12 (23 March 1974), p. 6.

32. Martin Müller, "Repräsentativerhebung: Einfügung plebiszitärer Elemente in die Verfassungsordnung der Bundesrepublik?" *Zeitschrift für Parlamentsfragen* 5, no. 2 (July 1974): 144. Since 1983 the new Green political party has taken this issue into the parliament. The Greens wanted a "consultative referendum" on the issue of whether the new NATO missiles should be stationed in West Germany. Their resolution was defeated, but it marked the first time that a national level debate on the question had taken place.

33. Leonard Krieger, *The German Idea of Freedom* (Chicago and London: University of Chicago Press, 1957).

34. Theo Rasehorn, *Recht und Klassen—Zur Klassenjustiz in der Bundesrepublik* (Darmstadt: Luchterhand Verlag, 1973).

35. Cited in Martin and Silvia Greiffenhagen, *Das schwierige Vaterland* (Munich: List Verlag, 1979), p. 205.

36. Rudolf Wasserman, "Wer arm ist, bekommt weniger Recht," *Die Zeit*, no. 45 (2 November 1973), p. 65.

37. Ibid.

38. Data for 1968 cited in Max Kaase, "Demokratische Einstellungen in der Bundesrepublik Deutschland," in Rudolf Wildenmann (ed.), *Sozialwissenschaftliches Jahrbuch für Politik*, Vol. 2, Munich-Vienna: Gunter Olzog Verlag (1971), pp. 225–26; for 1982, General Social Survey Codebook, *Zentralarchiv fur empirische Sozialforschung,* Cologne University, p. 82.

39. Institut für Demoskopie, *Jahrbuch der öffentlichen Meinung, 1968–1973* (Allensbach: Verlag für Demoskopie, 1975), 5:227.

40. *Der Spiegel*, 9 April 1973; *Die Zeit,* 27 September 1974, p. 18.

41. *Der Spiegel*, 28 July 1975, pp. 28–29.

42. K. H. F. Dyson, "Left-Wing Political Extremism and the Problem of Tolerance in Western Germany," *Government and Opposition*, no. 2 (Spring 1975), p. 308.

43. Interior Minister Zimmermann, quoted in *Die Zeit*, 30 December 1983, p. 5.

44. Hans Schüler, "Der Staat darf nicht alles wissen," *Die Zeit,* 30 December 1983, p. 5. The court's decision and strong opposition from civil libertarians also caused the

government to reconsider the proposed introduction of a computerized identification system for all citizens. Under the plan each adult would receive a coded plastic card containing a variety of personal data that could be read out by any authority with the appropriate computer terminal. Opponents argued that the identification system, like the census data, could be easily abused by police and security forces.

45. Some of the early census boycott supporters linked the issue to the NATO missile question instead of civil liberties (i.e., they called for a boycott as a protest against the government's plan to deploy the missiles). Barbara Pfetsch, "Volkszählung '83: Ein Beispiel für die Thematisierung eines politischen Issues in den Massenmedian," in *Wahlen und politischer Prozess,* eds. Hans-Dieter Klingemann and Max Kaase (Opladen: Westdeutscher Verlag, 1986), p. 21.

46. Ray C. Rist, *Guestworkers in Germany: The Prospects for Pluralism* (New York and London: Praeger, 1978).

47. To become a naturalized German citizen requires ten years of residency, a steady job, no criminal record, the passing of a difficult language test, which may include the local dialect, and the payment of a $1,000 fee. West Germany also does not allow dual citizenship. Not surprisingly, the Federal Republic has one of the lowest levels of naturalization of any West European country. Only about three-tenths of 1 percent of all resident foreigners become citizens each year as compared to 1.2 percent for France, 2 percent for Britain, and 5.2 percent in Sweden. Since 1945, only 100,000 foreign residents have become naturalized. Also, children born in Germany to foreign residents do not automatically have the right to become German citizens as in the United States. Naturalization is less difficult if one of the parents, especially the father, is a German national. Proposals to liberalize these naturalization laws have thus far met with strong opposition, particularly from conservatives in the Christian Democratic Union. John Ardagh, *Germany and the Germans* (New York: Harper & Row, 1987), pp. 250–51.

48. Annekatrin Gehring and Ferdinand Boeltken, "Einstellungen zu Gastarbeitern 1980 and 1984: Ein Vergleich," *Information* (Zentralarchiv fuer empirische Sozialforschung), no. 17 (November 1985): 23–33.

49. *Die Zeit* (7 February 1975), p. 2.

50. Institut für Demoskopie, *The Allensbacher Report,* June 1979, p. 8.

51. Beate Hoecker, "Politik: Noch immer kein Beruf für Frauen," *Aus Politik und Zeitgeschichte,* nos. 9–10 (February 28, 1987): 5, and *Das Parlament,* no. 32 (August 10, 1985): 11.

52. Nina Grunenberg, "Viele reden nicht, sie gucken nur," *Die Zeit,* 4 June 1983, p. 2.

53. *Der Buger im Staat* 37, no. 2 (June 1987): 29.

54. *European Women in Paid Employment* (Brussels, Commission of the European Communities, December 1980), pp. 32, 46, 59.

55. Institut für Demoskopie, Study No. 2066, November 1970.

56. Cited in *Der Spiegel,* 6 January 1975, p. 50.

57. David P. Conradt and Russell J. Dalton, "The West German Electorate and the Party System: Continuity and Change in the 1980s," *Review of Politics* 50, no. 1 (January 1988), pp. 3–29.

58. Dietrich Strothmann, "Die Vertriebenen," in *Nach 25 Jahren, Eine Deutschland Bilanz,* ed. Karl Dietrich Bracher (München: Kindler Verlag, 1979), pp. 300–321.

59. Bernd Buchhofer, Jürgen Friedrichs, and Hartmut Lüdtke, "Junge Vertriebene: Abschied vom politischen Erbe," *Aus Politik und Zeitgeschichte* 8 (April 1972): 30–38.

60. Kurt Shell, "Extraparliamentary Opposition in Postwar Germany," *Comparative Politics* 2, no. 4 (July 1970): 659.
61. Ibid., p. 663.
62. Michael Neumann and Wolfgang Kunz, "Katzenjammer und Karrieren," *Zeit Magazin,* 13 April 1973, pp. 2 ff.
63. Hans-Josef Horchem, "Fünfzehn Jahre Terrorismus in der Bundesrepublik Deutschland," *Aus Politik und Zeitgeschichte,* no. 5 (January 31, 1987): 3–15.

CHAPTER 4

The Party System and the Representation of Interests

The postwar party system differs in structure and in function from that of the empire and the Weimar Republic. Structurally, the number of political parties seriously contending for parliamentary representation has dropped to only four, in contrast to the twelve to twenty-five parties represented at various times in the Reichstag between 1871 and 1933. The extremist, regional, and small special-interest parties that made stable coalition government so difficult during the Weimar Republic either did not reappear in 1949 or were absorbed by the major parties by the elections of 1953 and 1957. Functionally, postwar German parties have become key carriers of the Bonn state and have assumed an importance and status unprecedented in German political history. Before the Bonn Republic, democratic political parties, fragmented and narrowly based, were not for the most part major forces in political life. Most of the important decisions were made by the executive, the bureaucracy, the military, and the economic elites—not by the democratic political parties. Frustrated and thwarted in their quest for governmental and specifically executive power, German parties concentrated more on ideological differentiation and the construction of their extraparliamentary organizations than on the more practical matter of organizing government. The presentation of meaningful alternatives to the electorate, the ability to translate party policy into governmental programs, and the control of governmental leaders were functions rarely performed by German parties.

THE PARTY STATE

The Bonn Republic, on the other hand, has been termed a "party state." The German political scientist Kurt Sontheimer, provides a clear definition of this term: ". . . all political decisions in the Federal Republic are made by the parties and their representatives. There are no political decisions of importance in the German democracy which have not been brought to the parties, prepared by them and finally taken by them."[1] Political parties in the Bonn Republic finally became agencies that made nominations and fought elections with the goal of controlling the personnel and policies of government. They no longer stood on the sidelines.

The Bonn system parties antedated the Republic. Indeed, they created it and they have penetrated key institutions as never before in German history. Relatively untainted by Nazism (they were all outlawed in 1933), the parties began work early, and between 1945 and 1950, with considerable amounts of patronage at their disposal, they ensured that not only parliament but the bureaucracy, the judiciary, the educational system, the media, and later even the military were led directly or indirectly by their supporters. Even today, few German generals or diplomats would dare attempt to "go public" with criticism in any controversial area without the protection of a party/political figure. Moreover, these democratic parties were distrustful of what an American would term "independents." In Germany, to be independent has historically meant to be "above the parties," and those "above the parties" have usually sided with the authoritarian-statist tradition. Hence the parties opposed the efforts of American occupiers to establish a Federal Personnel Office along the lines of the nonpartisan American Civil Service Commission to staff, especially the upper levels of the bureaucracy, with "independents." To postwar German party leaders, a nonpartisan civil service meant at best a bureaucracy indifferent to the democratic system, and at worst one opposed to it. Hence today, after forty years of democratic politics, the highest positions in the state bureaucracy, the educational system, and even the radio and television networks are mainly given to people who are active party members.[2]

The constitutional source of this strong position held by the parties is found in Article 21 of the Basic Law, which states that "the political parties shall take part in forming the political will of the people. They may be freely established. Their internal organization must conform to democratic principles. They must publicly account for the sources of their funds." It is rare for any democratic constitution to mention political parties in such detail, much less assign them a function. Article 21 goes on in paragraph 2, however, to grant the federal constitutional court the right to *prohibit* any party that does not accept the constitution: "Parties which by reason of their aims or the behavior of their adherents, seek to impair or abolish the free democratic basic order or to endanger the existence of the Federal Republic of Germany, shall be unconstitutional. The Federal Constitutional Court shall decide on the question of unconstitutionality." In other words, a political organization exercising the rights of free speech and freedom of assembly that opposes the constitutional order may be outlawed. Indeed, in the 1950s two political parties—the Communists and an allegedly neo-Nazi party—were banned by the court under this provision. Many constitutional scholars and political scientists questioned the wisdom of this action, arguing that the ballot box is the best place to defeat extremist groups in a democracy, but its inclusion in the constitution indicates the determination of the leaders of Germany's democratic parties to avoid a recurrence of Weimar conditions and to close the system to all extremist movements. However, the reluctance of any government since the mid-1950s to use the constitution to outlaw later radical movements, such as the right-wing National Democratic party or the new version of the Communist party that emerged on a very modest scale in the late 1960s, indicates the greater confidence of German political elites in not only the viability of the Republic's institutions but also the judgment of its electorate.

The constitutional recognition given to the parties is the major rationale for the extensive state financial support they receive especially for election campaigns (see Chapter 5). Each of the major parties also has a quasi-official foundation that sponsors extensive domestic political education projects and engages in "political developmental" work in several less developed countries. The overall thrust of the foundations' overseas work tends to be directed toward establishing goodwill for the Federal Republic in the Third World by supporting the training and development of native democratic parties and interest groups. Political education in the sense of training party and interest-group officials and functionaries is also included in this overseas work. The SPD's Friedrich Ebert Foundation has supported the Social Democratic parties of Spain and Portugal while those countries were still under dictatorial control. The training and support of trade unionists in developing countries is another area of activity for the foundation. Similar projects, in some cases oriented to more center or conservative political movements, are sponsored by the CDU's Konrad Adenauer Foundation, the CSU's Hans Seidel Foundation, and the FDP's Friedrich Naumann Foundation. The Adenauer Foundation has close ties to the Turkish Center party and has provided much of the impetus for the developmental aid package that the European Community countries offered to Turkey in 1979. Almost all funds for these party foundations come from the state. In 1986 the four parties received about $95 million for these activities.

The achievement of the Bonn "system" parties (SPD, CDU/CSU, FDP[3]), and more specifically their elites, is all the more remarkable when one considers the general indifference of the vast majority of West Germans during the postwar period to politics and parties, as well as the antiparty attitudes of traditional statists. What postwar German party elites have succeeded in doing is to all but erase the image many Germans had of parties as ineffective, unreliable, and incapable of meeting key citizen demands. As Wilhelm Hennis has pointed out, German party leaders after 1945 did not agonize over questions of collective guilt, overcoming the past, or the Weimar tradition, but got right to work on building the new state.[4]

This system of strong parties, or the "party state," is not without its shortcomings or critics. It is, for example, difficult for new interests, parties, and movements to gain a political foothold. The influence of the grass roots is also limited by the parties' hierarchical structure. The emergence in the 1970s of a significant citizen initiative movement outside the boundaries of this party system illustrates the extent to which some important issues, such as nuclear power, housing, and urban planning, are not being dealt with by the parties to the satisfaction of large groups of involved West Germans.

There is also increasing evidence that the established parties have abused and manipulated the laws governing their financing. In 1983 the minister of economics, Count Lambsdorff, and other officials from the FDP were indicted for illegally receiving campaign funds. In 1981 all major parties prepared a law that would have legalized many of their past excesses in the financial area. Only the ensuing public uproar caused the proposed law to be withdrawn. In 1984 a similar effort, this time by the FDP and the CDU/CSU, to grant an amnesty to individuals and firms under investigation for illegal political contributions, failed when the Free Democrats, reacting to intense media and voter criticism, withdrew their support.

By the late 1980s, public subsidies to the political parties accounted for about half of their total income. No other democracy is so generous in its support of parties through public funds as the Federal Republic. Because the parties control both the state and national parliaments that allocate these funds, there are few means to independently control their ever-increasing demand for taxpayer support.

In addition, the parties' permeation of the bureaucracy brings with it the problem of civil servant loyalty to a new government or the relative importance of values such as merit and professionalism. Finally, there is the question of the independence of the judiciary and the balance between political, executive, and legislative responsibilities. Some critics tend to identify democratization with still more control by party elites and are hence skeptical about its prospects in the Federal Republic.[5]

The Party System

THE CHRISTIAN DEMOCRATS

For the first twenty years of its existence, the Federal Republic was governed by a political party that, like the Republic itself, was a distinctly postwar creation. The Christian Democratic Union (CDU) and its Bavarian affiliate, the Christian Social Union (CSU), represented the efforts of widely divergent groups and interests to seek a new beginning following the Nazi catastrophe and postwar occupation.

Between 1945 and 1948, small groups of political activists made up of former Weimer Center, Liberal, and Socialist party members, together with Catholic and Protestant laymen, organized throughout Germany. The dominant theme in the motivations of these disparate interests was the need for a new party based in part on the application of general Christian principles to politics. It was felt that the traditional differences between Catholics and Protestants must be bridged, at least at the political level, to create a new movement that could be a powerful integrating force in the new political system. Also, by stressing its ties to the churches, this new party linked itself to the one pre-Nazi social institution that survived the war with some authority, legitimacy, and organizational strength.

In its early years, the CDU, particularly in the British zone, was programmatically committed to wide-ranging socioeconomic reform. The major statement of the party, the Ahlen Program of 1947, indeed called for the nationalization of large industries and rejected the restoration of many prewar capitalistic structures in the Federal Republic. In addition, Article 15 of the Basic Law, which permits, with proper compensation, the socialization of land, natural resources, and the means of production, was supported by most CDU/CSU delegates to the Parliamentary Council.

By 1949, however, the Socialist and Catholic labor wing of the party had been superseded by the proponents of a capitalist, free market economic system centered on the policies of the economics minister in the American zone, Ludwig Erhard, whose views were now also supported by the chairman in the British zone and future chancellor, Konrad Adenauer.

What happened between 1947 and 1949? Essentially the success of Erhard's currency reform of 1948, which ended postwar inflation and the black market; the end of Allied dismantling of German industry; American opposition to "socialist policies"; and the realization that the Christian Democrats, given the presence and strength of the Socialists, had little freedom of maneuver on the left of the political spectrum made the CDU change to a more center-right than center-left position. In short, there was by 1949 room for a middle-of-the-road, center party with a conservative economic policy, a major party to the *right* of the SPD, but not for another center-left party. The performance of the party at the first federal election in September 1949, the economic boom that began with the Korean War in 1950, and the foreign policy successes of Chancellor Adenauer solidified the more conservative course.

Nonetheless, the party remained remarkably open to a wide variety of political viewpoints. Apart from a general commitment to the "social free market economy" (a sort of capitalism with a heart) and a pro-Western, anticommunist foreign policy, the Christian Democrats avoided any specific policy orientation, much less ideology. To its critics, this was opportunism; to supporters, however, the Union's pragmatic, bargaining approach to politics represented a welcome relief from the ideological rigidity that had characterized many Weimar parties. It thus provided a political home for liberals, socialists, conservatives, Catholics and Protestants, north and south Germans, rural, urban, industrial, and labor interests, all held together by, above all, the electoral successes of Chancellor Adenauer. The CDU became a prototype for what Otto Kirchheimer termed a "catchall party," a broadly based, programmatically vague movement that capitalized on the mass economic prosperity of postwar Europe.[6]

The stunning victories of the party in the 1953 and 1957 elections were essentially personal triumphs for Adenauer. The CDU's dependence on the popularity of the chancellor was to prove a short-run advantage but a long-run liability. In riding the crest of his personal popularity, the Union did not take the necessary steps to strengthen its organization and depersonalize its appeals to retain its position after Adenauer's inevitable departure. At the 1961 election, Adenauer's age (eighty-five), thirteen years of governmental responsibility, and a "new look" SPD began to erode the party's electoral base. The Christian Democrats lost their absolute majority, and as a condition for a coalition with the Free Democrats, Adenauer had to agree to step down by 1963. His successor, Ludwig Erhard, had never been a party leader and had little real political power within the Union. Indeed, he first toyed with the idea of joining the FDP and was a rather late convert to the CDU. But as the architect of postwar economic prosperity, he did possess an electoral appeal that the Union gratefully employed at the 1965 election. With the 1966 recession, however, his status as an "electoral locomotive" declined and with that his position in the party and his chancellorship.

With no strong, electorally successful chancellor to hold it together, the party's numerous factions and wings began to struggle among themselves for control of the organization. Taking the SPD into the government in 1966 (the Grand Coalition) kept the party in power until 1969 but failed to halt the steady decline in its image among many voters as the only party capable of governing Germany at the national level. For the first time in its history, the CDU/CSU in 1969 found itself without a leader, without a program, and, above all, without power.

Yet the closeness of the CDU/CSU defeat in 1969 (the party fell only thirteen seats short of an absolute majority) provided the Union with sufficient reasons *not* to prepare for its new role as the parliamentary opposition. Although its percentage of the vote declined, the CDU in 1969 remained the largest single party. However, given the prior announced intention of the SPD and FDP to form a government, the 1969 results clearly justified the Socialist-Liberal alignment. But the Union's leadership insisted that, as the largest party, it was entitled to form the government, a privilege denied them by the "manipulations" of a "desperate" FDP and SPD. Thus, the party concentrated much of its effort between 1969 and 1972 on short-range tactical maneuvers designed to split the coalition parties or at least gain enough support from discontented government deputies to erase the coalition's twelve-seat majority and return the Union to power without new elections. Instead of concentrating on the development of its organization, program, and leadership, the party sought to topple the government and take a shortcut back to political power.

After the decisive SPD-FDP victory in the 1972 election, however, the CDU/CSU could no longer deny the necessity of accepting its role as the opposition party. Yet the Union in opposition lacked leadership, policy, and organizational consensus. After three years of intraparty maneuvering, Helmut Kohl, the young Ministerpräsident of the state of the Rhineland-Palatinate, emerged in 1975 as the party's new leader and chancellor candidate. In the October 1976 election the CDU/CSU made impressive gains but nonetheless narrowly missed returning to power (see Chapter 5). This 1976 electoral performance was interpreted as a defeat by Kohl's foremost challenger in the party, the leader of the Bavarian CSU, Franz-Josef Strauss. Barely six weeks after the election, Strauss attempted to separate the CSU from the Union and make it a new national party. Pressure from party members in Bavaria and Kohl's threat to campaign *against* the CSU in Bavaria if it did not return to the Union finally forced Strauss to abandon his plans shortly before the start of the new legislative term. This Kohl-Strauss conflict overshadowed the important improvements the CDU had made in its organization and its sophisticated and effective 1976 election campaign.

After the 1976 election, Kohl did not retain his position in the Rhineland-Palatinate but decided to become the opposition leader in the national parliament in Bonn. His inexperience in parliamentary politics at this level in comparison to his rival, Helmut Schmidt, his inability to lure the Free Democrats away from their coalition with the Social Democrats, and the continued criticism of his leadership ability by Strauss and the CSU took their toll, and by early 1979 he was forced to abandon any plans for a second try at the chancellorship in 1980. Strauss in the meantime had left Bonn to become minister-president of Bavaria. With the CSU solidly behind him, Strauss was able to convince the more conservative elements within the CDU, especially in states like Baden-Württemberg and Hesse, that he deserved a chance as chancellor candidate and could indeed win. Many CDU activists, ideologically opposed to the Bavarian, nonetheless also began to accept the idea of a Strauss candidacy. They reasoned that given the high popularity of Chancellor Helmut Schmidt and the solid record of his government, the CDU/CSU, regardless of its candidate, was bound to lose in 1980. Why not let Strauss have his chance and thus, after his inevitable defeat, be rid of this source of so much tension and division within the Union? This argument was quite persuasive for a sufficient number of moderate and liberal parliamentarians to give Strauss a majority. In July 1979 after several days of intense debate, the CDU/CSU members of parliament elected Strauss as the party's 1980 chancellor candidate.

The Union's decisive defeat in 1980 was absorbed at the leadership level with relatively little intraparty rancor. Strauss returned to Bavaria, and Kohl retained his position as national chairman of the CDU and parliamentary floor leader. His loyal support of Strauss in the campaign increased his stature within the CSU and among CDU conservatives. Kohl's performance as opposition leader in the Bundestag also improved.

The postelection difficulties of the Schmidt government provided the Union with ample reason to quietly absorb the 1980 defeat and regroup. By early 1982 it was apparent that the Socialist-Liberal coalition would not last until the next scheduled election in 1984. Helmut Kohl, now the unchallenged leader of the party in Bonn, carefully maintained his good relations with the Free Democrats and especially their leader, Hans-Dietrich Genscher. In September 1982 the Free Democrats left the Schmidt cabinet. Shortly thereafter they joined with the CDU and removed Schmidt, replacing him with Kohl. After thirteen years in opposition, the Christian Democrats returned to power in Bonn.

Six months later at the March 1983 election, the CDU/CSU had all the advantages of incumbency without any of its disadvantages. From the chancellor's office, Kohl could campaign against the thirteen years of Socialist rule and optimistically point to the new beginnings that his government now wanted to make if the electorate would give it the opportunity. Although the economy continued to decline after October 1982, the Union disclaimed any responsibility, dismissing even the record high unemployment level for February 1983 (2.5 million) as its *Erblast,* the burden inherited from the Socialists. The Greens, a political party formed in the late 1970s, were portrayed as Luddites who would destroy rather than create jobs. An "ungovernable" SPD-Green coalition would thus mean economic disaster. The CDU/CSU promised a better future through its policies of reduced spending, increased consumer taxes, and tax incentives for business.

The party's most difficult task following its return to power in 1983 was to deliver on its promise of economic recovery. In other policy areas it has pursued its traditional pragmatic course: the innovations of the Socialist-Liberal years in foreign policy (such as Ostpolitik) have been consolidated and even extended; the commitment of the Schmidt government to station new missiles was accepted and carried out by the Kohl government.

The CDU and the 1987 Federal Election

In the 1987 election the Christian Democrats campaigned on the record of the Kohl government. The party emphasized that it had brought Germany back to economic prosperity, reduced the federal deficit, cut taxes, and restored the Federal Republic's status as a dependable ally of the United States and a major force in the European Community.

The CDU in 1987 pursued a two-camp electoral strategy. West Germany was portrayed as divided between two irreconcilable groups—the Christian Democrats and the Free Democrats in one camp, the "Reds" (SPD) and the Greens in the other. Although conceding that there were well-meaning and reasonable people in the SPD, the CDU stessed that moderate Social Democrats could come to power only with the support of the extremist Greens and the left wing of the SPD. The Union thus attempted to dominate the center of the political spectrum and play on the strong German aversion to extreme or radical change.

With 44.3 percent of the vote, the CDU/CSU dropped to its lowest level since 1949. Intracamp switching to the FDP, low turnout among farmers protesting the government's agricultural policies, and overconfidence among its activists were the major factors cited by the party's leadership in explaining the outcome. The Union also lost votes to the SPD because of the still high unemployment level among manual workers. Kohl's supporters in the CDU also blamed Strauss and the Bavarians for their campaign attacks on the Free Democrats, which caused some moderate government supporters to vote for the party. Strauss in turn attributed the decline to Kohl's relatively low popularity.

Conflicts between the conservative Bavarian wing of the Union and the more moderate elements of the party continued after the 1987 election. The conservatives in the Union opposed the Kohl government's support of the "double zero" missile option, which eventually became the cornerstone for the Soviet-American treaty signed at the Washington summit in late 1987. They contended that the treaty would leave Germany vulnerable to superior Warsaw Pact conventional forces. The Kohl government, after some delay, accepted the American position that even after double zero the West would still have enough nuclear punch in battlefield weapons, bombers, and intercontinental missiles to deter a Soviet attack.

THE SOCIAL DEMOCRATS

The only major Weimar political party to reemerge in the Federal Republic was the Social Democratic Party of Germany (SPD). The SPD maintained an executive committee in exile throughout the Nazi period, and together with members who had survived within Germany, it was able to reestablish its national organization in relatively short order after 1945.

In view of the party's unequivocal opposition to National Socialism (the SPD was the only party to vote against Hitler's Enabling Act in March 1933) and its strong organization, it appeared that the SPD would soon become Germany's natural governing party with the resumption of democratic politics at the national level. These expectations were not fulfilled, because the party at the first parliamentary election in 1949 fell far short of an absolute majority and by 1953 was clearly subordinate to the enormously successful CDU under Adenauer.

Why did the SPD fail in the immediate postwar period to become Germany's major governing party? Most analyses attribute this to (1) the party's leadership and specifically its national chairman after 1945, Kurt Schumacher, (2) its incorrect reading of German public opinion on key foreign and domestic policy issues, and (3) the unexpected appeal of Adenauer and the free market economic policies of Economics Minister Ludwig Erhard.

Following the disastrous 1953 and 1957 federal elections, at which the party fell below the 30 percent mark, major changes in policy, leadership, and strategy were advocated by an increasing number of SPD state leaders, particularly in Hamburg, Frankfurt, and Berlin. The major leaders of this reform movement were Herbert Wehner, Willy Brandt, Karl Schiller, and Helmut Schmidt. The movement to transform the SPD into a non-Marxist, broadly based party of reform began in earnest. The reformers flatly argued that the party would be permanently consigned to the "30% ghetto" unless it made major changes. The analysis of the election defeats and public opinion polls showed that the SPD had several major electoral barriers to surmount.

First, large segments of the electorate had doubts about the SPD's foreign policy and specifically its commitment to NATO and the pro-Western, anticommunist policy initiated by Adenauer, which was so strongly supported by the electorate during the 1950s. By 1960 the great majority of West Germans accepted the Western orientation of the Bonn Republic, and the reformers were convinced that the SPD must commit itself to NATO and the Western alliance. Second, there were doubts about the patriotism of the Socialists. Were they really "German" enough or still "wanderers without a country," as Kaiser Wilhelm had once termed them? Third, the party's working-class image, its formal commitment to Marxism, and its generally proletarian style made it difficult for middle-class electors to identify with it. Fourth, the SPD's commitment to the "social free-market economy" was still questioned by large segments of the electorate who feared that the party would experiment with the highly successful economic system and thus endanger prosperity. Finally, the party's anticlerical past remained a significant obstacle among Catholic voters with a strong attachment to the church. The SPD's stress on integrating its members via numerous suborganizations—youth, women, adult education, mutual assistance, sports, newspapers, magazines—made it appear to many as an ersatz religion, a whole way of life competing with the churches for the hearts and minds of the working class. The reformers clearly wanted to deemphasize this dimension of the SPD's public image.

At its 1959 convention in Bad Godesberg, the SPD formally abandoned many of the policies and procedures that hindered its support among Catholic and middle-class electors. Its commitment to the Western alliance and strong anticommunist policies, seen in the behavior of Berlin Lord Mayor Willy Brandt, who was elected national chairman a year later, were underscored at this convention. Moreover, the party at Bad Godesberg dropped those parts of its program calling for the nationalization of the means of production and compulsory national economic planning. Finally, at Bad Godesberg, the party repeated its 1954 statement on Christianity and socialism, in which it was argued that Christianity together with classical and humanistic philosophy were the intellectual and moral roots of socialist thought. In short, the SPD now saw no contradiction between socialism and Christianity; the party was firmly committed to the constitutional guarantees respecting the freedom of religion as well as state support for religious institutions. Visits of SPD leaders to the Vatican during the 1950s also expressed this SPD desire for a new relationship with Catholicism.

The SPD's new look was rewarded by the electorate with increased support in 1961 and 1965. But, while gaining on the Christian Democrats, the Socialists remained well behind the Christian Democrats and had no national political power or responsibility. The SPD during the 1960s was concerned above all with "embracing the middle," that is, appealing for middle-class support by stressing its allegiance to the free market economy and the Western alliance. Major policy differences with the Christian Democrats and other middle-class parties were avoided. Instead of policy, the SPD focused on its leader, Willy Brandt. Much younger than Konrad Adenauer, Brandt was projected as a dynamic, reform-oriented, yet reliable personality who would build on the accomplishments of the (aging) postwar leadership. Yet, although Brandt's considerable popular appeal—together with the extensive employment of modern advertising and public relations designed to "sell" the "new" Social Democrats to the traditionally conservative middle-class segments of the electorate—brought electoral gains, national political responsibility came only after the collapse of the Erhard government in 1966 and the subsequent Grand Coalition with the Christian Democrats.

The Return to Power

By entering into a coalition with its long-time opponent, the Socialists propped up a severely divided and leaderless Christian Democratic Union. The pact with the CDU, in which the Union still retained the chancellorship, was opposed by a sizable proportion (about 40 percent) of the SPD's membership and some top leaders, among them Willy Brandt. The main strategist of the party during these years and the key architect of the Grand Coalition, Herbert Wehner, successfully argued that such a coalition would finally give the party the opportunity to show its critics that it could govern West Germany efficiently and responsibly, indeed better than the Christian Democrats. Moreover, successful performance in the coalition could set the stage for the assumption of sole political responsibility after the elections of 1969 or 1973.

These arguments prevailed, and the Social Democrats in 1966 assumed national political responsibility for the first time since 1930. The party used its opportunity well. Almost all the SPD ministers in the coalition performed successfully; one of them, Economics Minister Karl Schiller, had spectacular policy successes that even surpassed those of Brandt, who had assumed the foreign ministry.

It was Schiller who received major credit in the minds of the electorate for leading the economy out of the 1966–1967 recession.[7] Applying essentially Keynesian policies of increased governmental spending, tax reductions, and lower interest rates, Schiller by 1969 had restored the economy to full health. Mainly through these efforts, for the first time in German history, economic prosperity and the Social Democrats were closely associated by large segments of the electorate.

Complementing Schiller's successes in economic policy, Foreign Minister Brandt began what was to become after 1969 his *Ostpolitik*, the normalization of relations by West Germany with Eastern Europe and the Soviet Union. Social Democratic ministers in justice and social welfare also got high marks for their performance.

The party was rewarded in 1969 with a further 3.5 percent increase in its share of the popular vote. Much of this increase came from middle-class electors supporting the Socialists for the first time in their lives. The 1969 gains enabled the party to become the dominant partner in a "small coalition" with the Free Democrats under the chancellorship of Willy Brandt.

With their foreign policy successes after 1969, the strong personal appeal of Brandt, and continued economic growth and prosperity, the Social Democrats in 1972 became the strongest German political party and, together with the Free Democrats, increased their parliamentary majority from twelve to almost fifty seats. The long march from the "30% ghetto" of the 1950s was over. Political power and responsibility, however, brought new tensions.

Electoral success and governmental power had come largely through the party's conscious move into the center of the political spectrum, where, as we shall see in Chapter 5, "the votes are." But success also brought increased criticism from both young and old socialists that the SPD had sold its ideological or Marxist soul for political power. Dormant since the Bad Godesberg reforms, the SPD's left, composed of Young Socialists (about 180,000 members), "old" Marxists largely from the trade union movement, and some intellectuals, had sprung to life in 1966 over the coalition with the bourgeois CDU. The left argued that the party, instead of trying to persuade the electorate of the need for an extensive restructuring of the economy and society along Marxist lines, had taken the easy route to political power by being content simply to represent diverse social groupings and classes without changing the power relationships between them. In short, the party had been opportunistic and not much better than the Christian Democrats.

The SPD and Federal Elections, 1976–1987

In October 1976 the SPD suffered its first decline in support at a national election since 1957. The 1974–1976 recession, the disillusionment with the slow pace of détente with Eastern Europe and the Soviet Union, together with the party's internal organizational and programmatic disputes, had a negative impact on the party's electoral fortunes. With the prospects of a return to the opposition looming larger, the SPD leadership attempted to unite the party behind the Schmidt government, whose parliamentary majority was reduced to only ten seats. The key integrating figure in the party became its national chairman, Willy Brandt, who retained this post after his resignation as chancellor in 1974. In addition to the improvement of its organization, Brandt sought some form of intraparty consensus on policy.

The Social Democrats were disappointed with the results of the 1980 election. In spite of the high personal popularity of SPD Chancellor Schmidt, the party gained less than 1 percent over its 1976 total. It was the small coalition partner, the Free Democrats, who profited the most from Schmidt's popularity.

Soon after the election, intraparty conflicts flared up over the issues of defense spending, the sale of arms to Saudi Arabia, nuclear power, and the deployment of new middle-range missiles in Western Europe. The SPD left sharply criticized the Schmidt government for cutting social programs but raising defense expenditures in the new budget. The left also attacked compromises the party had made with the Free Democrats over the reform of the pension system and fiscal policy. Even Willy Brandt publicly criticized the government for its lack of a clear-cut policy toward East Germany.

In January 1981 the collapse of the scandal-ridden SPD-FDP coalition government in West Berlin provoked new speculation over the long-run stability of the Bonn coalition. In public opinion polls the CDU/CSU had by early 1981 jumped ahead of the coalition as voters reacted negatively to the conflicts within the SPD. By the spring of 1981 the electorate's dissatisfaction with the party had spread to Chancellor Schmidt as his popularity level (the proportion of the electorate satisfied with his performance) dropped to its lowest point since he assumed office and was even below that of Willy Brandt before his resignation in 1974. Finally, in May 1981 Schmidt threatened to resign unless the left factions within the SPD ceased undermining the NATO plan for the deployment of new middle-range nuclear missiles.

In September 1982 the SDP-FDP coalition government of Helmut Schmidt collapsed, and the Social Democrats, after almost sixteen years as a governing party, went into opposition. This was followed five months later, in the 1983 election, by the party's worst electoral performance (38.2 percent) in almost twenty years. In 1983 the SPD campaigned for the first time since 1965 as an opposition party and was led by a chancellor candidate, Hans-Jochen Vogel, who had less than six months to prepare for the role. The party's leadership responsible for the campaign, Willy Brandt and General Secretary Peter Glotz, held to the belief that there was a majority "to the left of the CDU." By emphasizing the "new politics" issues of the environment, nuclear power, and the NATO decision to station new intermediate-range nuclear missiles on German soil, they believed that sufficient support could be attracted from Green voters and new voters, which would make an SPD-Green alignment numerically if not politically possible. But by moving to the left to attract Green support, the SPD lost important segments of its traditional core electorate: skilled workers and lower- and middle-level white collar and technical employees.

The SPD Left and the Missiles

Although the party during the 1983 campaign questioned the missile decision, it still agreed to support the deployment if the negotiations between the United States and the Soviet Union in Geneva were unsuccessful. After the March election and as the date for deployment of the first missiles approached, one regional SPD organization after another passed resolutions opposing the decision and any deployment of missiles on German soil regardless of the outcome of the

Geneva negotiations. This position was not shared by most party leaders at the national level, but they had little influence over these local and regional activists, many of whom were well to the left of the party's Bonn establishment. Some SPD activists (and a few state leaders) also questioned the role of West Germany in NATO and called for a reassessment of Germany's position in the Atlantic Alliance. Finally, in November 1983 a special national party convention in Cologne formally voted against the 1979 decision and rejected any deployment of Pershing 2 missiles. The convention stopped short, however, of proposing a change in Germany's NATO membership or relationship to the United States.

The SPD left, which was relegated to a minor role when the party was in power, has thus become more visible and influential in opposition. The more moderate elements, centered in the trade unions, generally opposed the left on the questions of the missiles and Germany's role in NATO, but it also recognized the left's importance in the party's organization. The students, young teachers, "new middle-class" civil servants, and white-collar workers who constitute the bulk of the left are the party's most enthusiastic workers and organizers at the grass roots. During the 1970s the SPD lost many of these activists to the Greens, and the party could ill afford further defections. In the 1983 election these developments did not bring the party any increased support from the crucial center of the electorate.

The 1987 Federal Election

Following the 1983 defeat, the SPD made little progress toward resolving its internal divisions or raising its level of popular support. Throughout 1984 the party's standing in public opinion polls averaged only 39 percent, well below the Union's average of 46 percent. Moreover, for many voters the Greens and not the Social Democrats had become the more effective opposition party.

The party's fortunes improved in 1985 when it won decisive victories in two state elections. In the Saar the SPD for the first time in its history won an absolute majority. Shortly thereafter, at the state election in North Rhine–Westphalia, Germany's largest state with almost a third of the electorate, the Social Democrats also received an absolute majority of the votes. In both cases the Greens failed to secure representation in the state parliament. The twin victories also brought two new leaders into national prominence. These new political figures were Oskar LaFontaine in the Saar and Johannes Rau from North Rhine–Westphalia. On the strength of his victory, Rau was named the SPD's Chancellor candidate for 1987.

As a state leader, Rau had never been involved as a major participant in the SPD's numerous internal conflicts. Party leaders apparently hoped that his consensual image would unite the party and win back voters from the center of the electorate. His state campaign became the model for the party's 1987 effort. Rau's personal qualities were emphasized while issues and conflicts with the opposing parties were downplayed. The party's main slogans: "Reconciliation instead of Division" and "Germany Needs a Chancellor Again" summarized the essence of the original SPD campaign plan.

The Rau candidacy meant that the SPD would seek an absolute majority of the national vote, thereby avoiding the question of a coalition with the Greens. Rau also pledged that he would not allow himself "to be elected Chancellor with the votes of the Greens" in the event that the party fell short of the absolute majority. Both of these decisions lacked credibility for most voters. Surveys found that less than a third of the electorate believed that the SPD could win an absolute majority and that only about 40 percent agreed that Rau would indeed reject Green support if needed after the election.

The absolute majority strategy depended on Rau's high personal popularity and the extension of the successful 1985 campaign in North Rhine–Westphalia to the rest of the Republic. It also represented an attempt to bridge the deep divisions within the SPD over policy and the party's relationship to the Greens. The SPD was divided almost equally between strong supporters and equally strong opponents of any alignment with the Greens. If voters on the left who were leaning toward the Greens could be convinced that the SPD had a realistic chance of achieving a majority and replacing the Kohl government, they would have enough incentive to remain loyal to the SPD and not defect to the Greens.

This strategy failed in part because many voters doubted that the SPD could achieve an absolute majority but also because the party's left wing undercut Rau's centrist approach. At the pre-election party congress, the left called for the cancellation of West Germany's agreement with the United States for cooperation on Star Wars research and the withdrawal of NATO's American-made medium-range missiles. The left also passed resolutions repudiating the party's earlier support for nuclear energy and pledged to shut down the Federal Republic's nuclear plants within ten years. Shortly after this conference, the SPD suffered major defeats at state elections in Bavaria and Hamburg. Rau's candidacy collapsed. The party's vote at the 1987 election dropped to 37 percent, its lowest level since 1961. For the second time in the 1980s, the party was returned to opposition where it must still rebuild its organization, develop a viable program, and find new leadership.

THE FREE DEMOCRATS

Located ideologically somewhere between the two major parties is the only small party to survive the steady reduction in the number of serious contenders for parliamentary representation: the Free Democratic Party (FDP). The Free Democrats have never received more than 13 percent of the party vote in any federal election, and they have not sent a representative to parliament in a direct, district winner-take-all contest with the CDU and SPD since 1957. The party's survival is due, above all, to the electoral system that gives parliamentary representation on a proportional basis to any party that secures at least 5 percent of the popular vote.

The FDP has played a role in the German political system far out of proportion to the size of its electorate. It has participated in thirteen of the sixteen cabinets formed at the national level since 1949. From 1949 to 1956 and from 1961 to 1966, it was the junior coalition partner of the CDU/CSU; between 1969 and 1982 the Free Democrats were in a coalition with the SPD, and since 1982 the party has been again aligned with the Christian Democrats. Thus the FDP has been in power for thirty-three of the Federal Republic's first forty years. Moreover, two of the six presidents of the Republic have been Free Democrats.

This extraordinary success of the FDP is a result of its position as the needed "pivot" party in the parliament. Simply put, the FDP has held the balance of power in the Bundestag following most federal elections. Because both major parties have with one exception (the CDU in 1957) failed to win an absolute majority of seats, they are faced with three alternatives in the postelection coalition negotiations: a coalition with the FDP, a "Grand Coalition" with the other major party, or opposition. Obviously, the first of these has been far more preferable to the latter two. This gives the FDP an enviable bargaining position, assuming that the party is willing to consider a coalition with either major party and that the major parties have roughly the same number of parliamentary seats.

The party regards itself as the legitimate heir to the tragic German liberal tradition. Historically, German liberals have been divided between a conservative, nationalist wing, one with strong ties to large industrial interests and an ambivalent commitment to parliamentary democracy, and a progressive, or left, wing centered in the southwest and the Hanseatic cities (Hamburg, Bremen), whose support for parliamentary government took precedence over nationalism and the authoritarian imperial system. Thus, unlike liberals in Britain or France, German liberals were as a whole not staunch supporters of parliamentary government and the liberal state. During the turbulent last years of the Weimar Republic, the vast majority of the liberal parties' supporters defected to the right-wing parties including, above all, the Nazis. The small band of liberal deputies remaining in the Reichstag after the last free election in March 1933 voted for Hitler's Enabling Act.

It was not until the formation of the FDP in 1948 that the two tendencies in German liberalism were united within one organization, and unity in terms of policy has still been a rare commodity in the party's postwar history. The nationalist, or right, wing held the upper hand during the 1950s when, in coalition with the CDU/CSU, the party—especially in economic policies—was to the right of the Union. Even at this time, however, its opposition to Catholic church influence in the CDU/CSU and Adenauer's pro-Western orientation, which the Free Democrats claimed neglected if not abandoned reunification, differentiated the party from its much larger partner.

The FDP's drift to the center-left and hence toward the SPD in the mid-1960s was made as much for tactical as for policy reasons. As a junior coalition partner, it always ran the risk of suffering a fate similar to that of the other small parties: absorption by the CDU/CSU. Thus, it had to seek to retain its identity vis-à-vis the CDU/CSU by either pulling out of the coalition, as it did in 1956 and 1966, or stressing, especially prior to elections, its differences with the major partner.

Following the Grand Coalition between the SPD and CDU/CSU in December 1966, the FDP became the sole opposition party for the first time in its history. Key party leaders at this time, such as Walter Scheel, from 1974–1979 federal president, and Hans-Dietrich Genscher, foreign minister, sought to demonstrate through a series of policy and leadership changes that the party was not a mere satellite of the CDU/CSU. Their purpose was not only to gain votes from SPD and CDU/CSU supporters discontented with the Grand Coalition but also to demonstrate to the Social Democrats that it could at some future time be an acceptable and reliable coalition partner. The party's positions on foreign-policy issues, such as the normalization of relations with Eastern Europe, and educational and legal reform became increasingly consistent with those of the Social Democrats. Then in March 1969 the FDP's delegation gave nearly unanimous support to the Socialists' candidate for the presidency. This exceptional display of unity by the FDP was an unmistakable signal to the SPD and set off a wave of speculation about a possible SPD-FDP coalition after the September 1969 election. It was also accompanied by widespread defections of old, pro-CDU, FDP supporters to the Union. These defections continued through the 1969 elections and coalition negotiations. By this time, the old FDP electorate had changed from a rural, small-town, middle-class clientele to one composed largely of younger, middle-class voters living in large metropolitan areas who clearly wanted an end to two decades of CDU/CSU rule.

After the 1980 election, the Free Democrats agreed to a renewal of their coalition with the SPD. Soon after, however, it became apparent that the FDP was attempting to loosen its ties with the Socialists in preparation for another switch in coalition partners—this time back to its old ally from the 1950s and 1960s, the Christian Democrats. The FDP and the Socialists were unable to agree on the type of economic policies needed to deal with the recession that hit the Federal Republic after 1980. The SPD supported a variety of pump-priming measures—tax cuts, public works projects—while the Free Democrats wanted to reduce state spending, especially on welfare programs, and stimulate private sector investment through tax concessions to business. Conflicts between the coalition partners continued throughout 1981 and into 1982 over this issue.

The Free Democrats also had political reasons for leaving the coalition. Divisions within the SPD and the rise of the Greens convinced many FDP leaders that the Socialists would not be strong enough after the next election to form another coalition. In state elections after 1980 the FDP in several cases failed to secure the 5 percent of the vote necessary to be represented in a state parliament. The Greens in some states pushed the Free Democrats into fourth place. The Social Democrats also lost heavily, and FDP leaders feared that if the trend continued, their party would be eliminated at the next federal election. In short, the SPD had become a sinking ship, and the FDP had no desire to go down with their larger partner. What for the Socialists was a political setback meant political extinction for the much smaller FDP.

The formal break took place in October 1982, but the party was by no means united in dropping the SPD and joining the Christian Democrats. About a third of the Free Democrats' parliamentary delegation and a corresponding proportion of party members and voters opposed the switch. The party was accused of "betraying" Helmut Schmidt, and in state elections held in late 1982 the FDP dropped to only about 3 percent of the vote. By 1983, however, support from CDU/CSU voters via ticket splitting and the return of some of its old clientele from the 1950s and 1960s enabled the party to secure 7 percent of the vote and return to parliament.

Following the 1983 vote, the FDP was able to further stabilize its position through gains from its former middle-class clientele of the 1950s and 1960s. At state elections where the party was seen by the voters as a necessary coalition partner of the Christian Democrats—that is, where the CDU could be expected to fall short of an absolute majority—the FDP surmounted the 5 percent hurdle. By 1986 in most polls the party was well above this minimum. Hans-Dietrich Genscher, who had resigned as party chairman in 1985, remained foreign minister and was ranked among the most popular leaders in the Federal Republic.[8] Most Christian Democratic voters now felt that their party needed the FDP in order to deal more effectively with problems such as unemployment, the environment, arms control, and economic growth.

The Free Democrats in the 1987 election emphasized their role as a liberal corrective to the conservatism of certain CDU/CSU factions. The party's stress on continuity in foreign policy, especially in Bonn's relations with the Soviet Union and Eastern Europe and Genscher's criticism of Bonn's participation in the Star Wars program, enhanced the FDP's position among government supporters who wanted an alternative to the hard-line anticommunism and uncritical pro-Americanism of some Christian Democrats. The FDP also used the specter of a Red (SPD)-Green coalition to appeal for votes. Since the CDU/CSU would not receive an absolute majority, the Free Democrats argued, the only way for the government to remain in power was through a coalition with the FDP. With 9.1 percent of the vote in 1987, the Free Democrats achieved their best result since 1980 and successfully completed the transition from being the partner of the Social Democrats to the partner of the Christian Democrats.

THE GREENS

In 1983 for the first time since the 1950s a new political party—the Greens—secured representation in the parliament. The party began as the political arm of the citizen initiative group movement discussed in Chapter 3. In the late 1970s those groups concerned with the environment and especially the danger of nuclear power plants established a national political party. In 1979 and 1980 the

Greens entered two state parliaments but fared poorly in the national election, securing less than 2 percent of the vote. After 1980, however, the Greens' cause was greatly aided by the emergence of the NATO missile question, the planned deployment of new middle-range ballistic missiles in the Federal Republic. The nationwide peace movement, which arose in response to the missile deployment plan, was a major source of new support for the party. The peace movement also brought the Greens additional activists, many of whom had had extensive political experience in the Social Democratic party, the student protest movement of the 1960s, and various left-wing splinter groups. These new supporters, who came to the Greens less out of a concern with the environment and more because of the arms race and various socioeconomic problems such as inner-city housing and education, gave the movement badly needed organizational and tactical expertise. The Greens entered state parliaments in Berlin (1981), Lower Saxony (1982), Hamburg (1982), and Hesse (1982). With the addition of these new supporters, generally termed the "alternative" movement, the Greens were in a position to seriously challenge the system parties at the national level. At times during 1982 and 1983 their support in public opinion polls was close to 10 percent. Although the SPD made a major effort to capture the Green vote after the SPD fell from power in 1982, the new party managed to enter the parliament with 5.6 percent of the vote.

With the twin issues of the environment and the NATO missile or "peace" question, the party in 1983 made significant inroads into traditionally SPD voter groups as well as receiving impressive support, almost 25 percent, among young voters with some college or university background. Throughout 1984 the party continued to gain voters at local and state elections as the Greens' emphasis on environmental protection and disarmament struck a responsive chord among voters dissatisfied with the established parties.

In 1985, however, the Greens' string of successes was snapped as the SPD kept the party below the 5 percent minimum in two state elections. The internal divisions within the movement now became an issue. The critical problem was the party's relationship to the Social Democrats. Should the Greens seek power through a coalition with the SPD, or should they remain a protest movement uncontaminated by any association with the old, established parties? Most Green voters supported an alignment with the SPD. The party's activists and leaders, however, were divided. One group, the Fundamentalists (*Fundis*), reject any cooperation with the established parties, whereas a second wing, the Realists (*Realos*) are willing to form coalitions with the SPD at state and national levels in order to achieve Green goals if only in piecemeal fashion. In late 1985 the Realists appeared to have the upper hand as the Greens in the state of Hesse formed a coalition with the SPD and took over the Environmental Affairs ministry.

The 1986 nuclear accident at Chernobyl in the Soviet Union brought the Fundamentalists back in control of the party. At their convention that year, the Greens passed resolutions calling for West Germany's immediate withdrawal from NATO, unilateral demilitarization, and the dismantling of all nuclear power stations in the country. The Greens also refused to distance themselves from the violent demonstrations that took place at nuclear power plants and reprocessing facilities following the accident.

In the wake of the Chernobyl disaster, support for the Greens in public opinion polls doubled to over 12 percent. For a time it appeared that if the Greens decided to coalesce with the SPD, the two parties would have an absolute majority after the 1987 election. By mid-1986, however, the effects of Chernobyl began to wane, and the potential Green-SPD vote dropped from 53 percent to 43 percent. Although the Greens clearly gained support because of the Russian accident, they also lost voters because of their radical positions on foreign policy, defense, and domestic issues.

In spite of these problems the Greens were able to increase their share of the vote at the 1987 election from 5.6 percent to 8.3 percent and the size of their parliamentary delegation from 27 to 42 deputies. Moreover, the proportion of Germans who think it is good that the Greens are in parliament rose from 28 percent in 1983 to 54 percent at the time of the 1987 elections. Thus most Germans now seem to accept the party as a legitimate political force.

The Representation of Interests

EXTENT OF INTEREST GROUPS

West Germany is a densely organized society. Germans are used to organizations and accustomed to working with them for the satisfaction of individual needs. The Almond-Verba five-nation study, for example, found German respondents much more likely to use interest groups as a means of influencing government than were Americans, Englishmen, Italians, or Mexicans.[9] Ellwein has estimated that there are three or four voluntary associations for every 1,000 inhabitants of the Federal Republic, or about 200,000 in all.[10] This includes, however, thousands of local sports clubs and singing societies, whose explicit political activity is very limited and restricted to the local level. There are also various politically latent interests, such as those of consumers and foreign workers, that are poorly organized and represented.

IMPORTANCE AND STYLE
OF INTEREST REPRESENTATION

German political tradition and values, the new political parties with their consensual style, and the structure of the Bonn Republic have all combined to make interest groups a vital factor in the policymaking process. Germany had interest groups long before the formation of the Reich, indeed before the formation of any independent sovereign political entity on German soil. A variety of associational groups representing occupations and economic interests can trace their origins to the corporate guilds of the Middle Ages. Composed of practitioners of a particular trade or craft (carpenters, bakers, cabinetmakers, butchers), these groups still perform regulatory functions for the state such as licensing and the supervision of training, and membership is compulsory for those desiring to practice the occupation legally. Almost all skilled artisans, in addition to the practitioners of the "free" professions (law and medicine), belong to these chambers, which also determine and enforce standards for the craft and control the recruitment of new members. Their legal responsibility for membership recruitment and conduct gives the chambers important political as well as economic power. They are all organized hierarchically from the local to national level. Thus their national spokesmen have considerable authority in dealing with the ministerial bureaucracy. The highly structured, hierarchical, quasi-governmental character of these associations clearly makes the individual member dependent on the group's leadership for the furtherance of his or her interests. The centralized national-level leadership becomes part of a larger elite structure within which informal bargaining plays a key role.

Most of the major occupational chambers also have members in the parliament, mainly in the delegations of the CDU/CSU and FDP. The Christian Democrats, for example, have a parliamentary group composed of about forty deputies, most of whom have direct affiliations with one or several of the chambers. Loewenberg estimates that about a third of the parliament's 500 members "represent their occupations in politics."[11] Either they are professional interest-group employees assigned to represent their groups, or they are associated with certain trade, occupational, or professional interests on a part-time basis. The influence of interest groups in the recruitment of parliamentary candidates is to a great extent the result of the parties' dependence on groups for financial and electoral support. The electoral system, as we discuss in Chapter 5, also facilitates the nomination and election of these interested parliamentary deputies. Their efforts are particularly noticeable in committee work.

Perhaps more important than their role in the recruitment of parliamentary deputies is the access of interest groups to the ministerial bureaucracy. Such access allows them to influence the design of legislation. Major interest organizations are consulted, as a matter of administrative procedure, in the drafting of laws affecting them. This practice dates back to the early nineteenth century and reflects the strain of corporate or group, instead of individual, representation in the German political tradition, as well as the government's interest in the expertise of these groups and their cooperation in the implementation of policy.[12] In the Weimar Republic, access to the ministries was limited to nationally organized interest groups. This practice was also adopted in the administrative rules of the Bonn ministries. It tends to accentuate the hierarchical character of German interest groups and the formal, quasi-legal character of interest group activity.

This pattern of strong government/interest group/political party integration became more institutionalized during the late 1960s when the top representatives of government, business, and labor met in a Concerted Action, a regular conference at which general economic conditions were discussed and guidelines for wages, prices, and economic growth were set. At these meetings business, labor, and the national government sought to reach a consensus on (1) what a reasonable wage increase would be for various industrial workers, (2) the acceptable level of price increases, and (3) the amount of government spending and taxation necessary to ensure stable economic conditions and moderate—that is, noninflationary—economic growth. Although the Concerted Action disbanded in the late 1970s, as labor interests became dissatisfied with what they felt were the unreasonable sacrifices they were called on to make, informal labor/business/government contacts continued, and the Concerted Action may well be revived in the near future.

The Concerted Action and the other less formal interest-group and government contacts have prompted some observers to term Bonn a "neo-corporatist" state.[13] *Corporatism* is an old term in social and political thought, referring to the organization of interests into a limited number of compulsory, hierarchically structured associations recognized by the state and given a monopoly of representation within their respective areas. These associations become in effect quasi-governmental groups, training, licensing, and even exercising discipline over their members with state approval. The power of these associations is not determined by a group's numerical size alone but also by the importance of its function for the state and community.

In addition to the parliamentary recruitment and the extensive consultations between government and interest groups, the practice of appointing group representatives to the many permanent ministerial advisory commissions and councils affords the interest groups still more input into the policymaking process. Finally, the highly developed system of semipublic institutions and administrative courts, discussed in Chapter 7, offers to interest associations additional opportunity to influence the policy process.

MAJOR INTEREST ALIGNMENTS

Business and Industrial Interests

In a society in which the stability and legitimation of new political institutions are closely connected with economic prosperity, business and industrial interest groups enjoy considerable cultural support when they enter the political arena and make policy demands on the system. Regardless of which party or parties form the government, the interests and claims of German business will receive a thorough hearing. Indeed, a frequent charge of the Left is that even the Social Democrats, when in office, are too receptive and accommodating to the interests of business.

The numerous local and state employer organizations, in addition to their own national offices, are represented by three umbrella organizations with extensive facilities and staffs in the capital: the Federation of German Industry (*Bundesverband der Deutschen Industrie* [*BDI*]), the Federation of German Employer Associations (*Bundesvereinigung Deutscher Arbeitgeberverbände* [*BDA*]), and the German Industrial and Trade Conference (*Deutscher Industrie- und Handelstag* [*DIHT*]). The BDA tends to specialize in wage policies, whereas the Industrial and Trade Conference concentrates most of its efforts on maintaining the economic viability of small independent businessmen and craftsmen. Thus neither organization is as politically active or visible on as broad a front as the Federation of German Industry, which focuses its activities on the government's national and international economic policies and is clearly the most influential and effective voice of business in national politics.

The BDI is a federation made up of thirty-nine individual industrial associations, which together have a membership of more than 90,000 firms. During the two decades of Christian Democratic rule, it had very close ties to the government and in competition with trade unions for political advantage tended to get the edge. Yet, given the commitment of all major parties to the capitalist market economy, the BDI has under the Social Democrats had little difficulty in putting its proposals to the government.

Apart from its general support of German industry, the BDI evaluates all proposed legislation in any way related to business during all stages of policymaking, from ministerial drafting through parliamentary debate and even administrative implementation. In addition to sympathetic parliamentary deputies and general cultural support by virtue of its accomplishments, business interests command considerable financial resources, and their support or nonsupport— especially of the middle-class parties, the CDU and FDP—gives them added weight in electoral politics.

From 1969 to 1982, when the Social Democrats were in power, the BDI and other business groups concentrated most of their efforts on opposing government plans for parity codetermination in industry (equal workers representation on a firm's board of control), *Vermögensbildung* (the building of capital resources among the general public involving some redistribution through compulsory profit sharing), and tax reform. The BDI has also generally opposed upward revaluations of the deutsch mark because of their effect on exports. It also consistently resists extensions of the social welfare system that would increase employer contributions, and like its counterparts in the United States (the chamber of commerce and the National Association of Manufacturers), it constantly implores the government to "hold the line" on spending. The BDI, as expected, has been very critical of labor unions, Young Socialists, intellectuals, and any other "radical" group that would weaken industry's position in West German society or undermine the market economy.

The collapse of the SPD-FDP government in 1982 and the return to power of the Christian Democrats were strongly supported by the BDI. The plans of the

Kohl government to encourage private sector investment and cut social programs were very consistent with BDI policy. The BDI's major problem in recent years, however, has been the unions' demands for a thirty-five-hour week as a means of reducing unemployment. The BDI, with the strong backing of the Kohl government, took a hard line on this question, which has increased the level of labor-management conflict.

Most BDI activity takes place in direct, small-group consultations with ministerial officials, parliamentary deputies, and governmental leaders. It has an extensive research department that supplies information to its member associations, the media, schools, and universities. Only rarely has it engaged in advertising campaigns to influence large groups of voters. It did, however, help sponsor some of the massive advertising campaigns that selected business interests mounted against the Socialist-Liberal government in 1972. Nevertheless, most observers, including the CDU/CSU and some of the campaign's sponsors, found such activities to be counterproductive.

Labor

The major West German labor organization, the German Federation of Labor (*Deutscher Gewerkschaftsbund* [*DGB*]) is also a postwar creation. Previously, the German labor movement had been closely tied to political parties and their respective ideologies. In the Weimar Republic, Socialist, Communist, Liberal, and Catholic unions all vied for the support of workers, thus politicizing and fragmenting the labor movement. Western Allied occupiers, particularly in the American zone, strongly urged the separation of the unions from the political parties and the establishment of a single, unified trade union federation that would emphasize the basic economic objectives of wages and working conditions rather than radical social and economic change. Many German labor leaders also wanted an organization less attached to parties, and in 1949 the DGB was founded. The DGB is composed of seventeen separate unions with a combined membership of almost 8 million; the largest unit of the federation is the metalworkers' union (steel, automobiles, machinery), with about a third of the total membership.

Although the DGB's initial programmatic statements in 1949 had a decidedly Marxist tone (socialization of key industries, central economic planning), which reflected the majority position held in the new organization by former leaders of the Weimar socialist unions, the major emphasis in the union movement's work soon shifted to more pragmatic goals of a shorter work week and higher wages. In 1963, in its new basic program, Marxist elements for all practical purposes were abandoned. Like its American counterpart, the AFL-CIO, the DGB now emphasizes collective bargaining to improve the economic status of the worker gradually within the existing social, economic, and political framework. Unlike American business unionism, the DGB has given strong backing to workers' representation and input into the decisionmaking of the industrial firm through codetermination, according to which workers would be represented on a company's board of control in equal proportion to the representatives of management and capital (stockholders).

This change in DGB policy, from a general support for Marxist-oriented policies to collective bargaining and workers' participation within the context of the market economy, is consistent with the general decline in socialist programs that followed the success of the liberal economic policies of the first Adenauer governments during the early 1950s. A similar transformation, as we have seen, also took place in the CDU/CSU after 1948 and in the SPD by 1959.

Labor is represented in the parliamentary delegations of both major parties, but its influence and sympathies lie far more with the Social Democrats than the CDU. Most (about 70 percent) SPD members eligible to join labor unions are members of the DGB-affiliated groups, and the unions indirectly account for a large portion of SPD income. About 35 to 40 percent of the SPD's parliamentary party have strong ties to the labor movement.[14] Two cabinet members during the Brandt governments (1969–1974) and five members of Helmut Schmidt's first government (1974–1976) also had close labor connections. Generally the labor unions have supported Social Democratic policies, although at times they have been impatient with the slow pace of the party's domestic reform programs. The DGB was especially disenchanted with the Brandt government's proposed codetermination and profit sharing bills introduced in early 1974. Nonetheless, union criticism of the SPD has generally been moderate. On balance, the DGB's relationship to the SPD is probably not as close as that of British unions to the British Labour party, yet closer than the AFL-CIO's relationship to the Democratic party.

Although there is a labor wing in the Christian Democratic Union, led by deputies from the Rhine-Ruhr region, there is little or no labor influence in the Bavarian affiliate of the Union, the CSU, and since 1969 the power of the labor wing has declined in the Union's internal councils. It is possible, however, that the CDU's efforts to regain the once strong position it had in the center of the electorate may mean an increase in the role of its labor wing. The DGB also goes to considerable lengths to maintain its independent, nonpartisan posture and points to its representation in the CDU as evidence of its willingness to support any party that will work to implement its programs.

The labor movement has come under increasing criticism in recent years from left-wing intellectuals for its alleged conservatism and allegiance to the status quo. Certainly it has been a disappointment to orthodox Marxists, who envision it as a key force for revolutionary change. The movement has also disappointed liberal and socialist reformers by its relative indifference to change in areas such as education and civil rights (reform of the criminal code, liberalized abortion, for example).

Yet unions in the Federal Republic are faced with the necessity of branching out into new areas of activity if they are to continue as a major force in West German social, economic, and political life. The more than 8 million organized workers in the Federal Republic represent only about 36 percent of the total employed work force. This degree of organization represents a considerable decline from the 45 percent level of the early 1950s. Indeed, the level of organization has remained almost constant since 1961.[15] Because the constitution (Article 9, Section 3) prohibits the closed shop, membership and recruitment must depend on the ability of the unions to offer concrete benefits that are acquired only through union affiliation. Many benefits, however, such as unemployment compensation, health, disability, accident, and pension programs, once private goods that could be obtained only through union membership, are now the province of the state and as public goods, are available to all without affiliation with the union. Support during strikes is still provided by the unions, but given the low strike rate in West Germany, this is a marginal benefit. Unions must thus seek new ways to provide their members with programs that are not public goods. This is one factor behind their strong drive for codetermination, under which *union* members would sit on the board of directors as the major representatives of workers, as well as their interest in assuming some responsibility for vocational education and the administration of labor and social welfare laws.

In 1982 the trade union movement was shaken by revelations of a major scandal involving its housing construction company, *Neue Heimat,* the largest in Europe. Several leaders in the company, which is wholly owned and at least formally controlled by the trade unions, had for years established companies which supplied Neue Heimat with land, building supplies, heating fuel, and even television antenna service. The Neue Heimat executives had hidden their involvement through a system of complicated corporate structures. They were charged with having used their positions for personal enrichment at the expense of the parent company, the trade union movement, and millions of tenants. The major figures in the scandal were quickly dismissed, but many of the DGB's rank and file still wonder why the union leadership had allowed these practices to continue for over twenty years.[16]

Since the late 1970s the relations between labor and management in the Federal Republic have become more conflictual.[17] Higher unemployment levels, reduced rates of economic growth, and the weaker competitive position of German goods in export markets have all contributed to this development. Significantly, many of these recent labor conflicts have been over the issue of automation, with the unions giving job security a higher priority than direct wage increases. As unemployment reached record levels during the early 1980s, the unions began a major drive for a thirty-five-hour workweek as one means to provide more jobs. In 1984 a strike of metal workers over this issue shut down the German automobile industry and caused large-scale layoffs at other plants throughout the Federal Republic and Western Europe. The conflict level has also been heightened by the German employers' extensive use of the lockout in strike situations. This practice, legal in the Federal Republic but strongly opposed by the unions, means that many employees not directly affected by the strike are barred from working. This makes it difficult for the unions to strike only selected firms and compels them to strike by geographical region.

In 1986 the Kohl government passed legislation that limited the right of workers idled by strikes to receive unemployment compensation. The law was strongly opposed by the trade unions, which claimed that it was designed to restrict their constitutional right to strike and thus to reduce their power *vis-à-vis* employers. The legislation was prompted by the 1984 strike in the metal industry that has been previously mentioned. In this strike the unions employed a "mini-max" strategy: Only about 13,000 workers in key plants went on strike and were supported by the unions' strike funds, but over 300,000 additional workers were idled and most of these received unemployment compensation from the state. The new legislation, sections of which were drafted in consultation with business groups, denies unemployment compensation to workers who are outside of the geographical region being struck but in the same industry and with contract demands similar to those of the striking union. For example, if a strike of Mercedes workers in Stuttgart also shuts down the nonstriking Mercedes plant in Bremen, and if the union demands in Bremen are similar to those in Stuttgart, the idled Bremen workers would not be entitled to unemployment compensation. This law makes it more difficult for the unions to employ their mini-max strategy. They now view the Kohl government as blatantly antibusiness and are challenging the legislation in the courts.

Agriculture

As analysts of interest groups have long known, the effectiveness of a group's efforts is closely related to its internal cohesiveness and unity of purpose. The experiences of West German agrarian interests, the so-called Green Front (not to be confused with the Green political party discussed earlier in this chapter), substantiates this thesis. The vast majority of the Republic's 2.4 million farmers are organized into three organizations that constitute the Front: the German Farmer's League (*Deutscher Bauernverband*), the Association of Agricultural Chambers (*Verband der Landwirtschaftskammern*), and the *Raiffeisenverband*, a cooperative association involved in banking, mortgage loans, and retailing. In part because of their steadily dwindling number and increasing social isolation, agrarian interests are closely integrated and, unlike American rural interests, do not for the most part pursue conflicting aims. This united Green Front constitutes, according to many observers, Bonn's best-organized lobby. In addition, there are about thirty-five parliamentary deputies (most of whom are in the CDU/CSU) who form a relatively cohesive farm group within the legislature and dominate the parliament's agriculture committee.[18]

Mindful of past agrarian support for right-wing radical groups, including the Nazis, all parties have made major efforts to placate agriculture and meet its demands. Indeed the influence of farm organizations probably increased under Socialist-Liberal governments (1969–1982). In an effort to secure the support of the FDP's right wing, the post of agriculture minister in 1969 was given to a

Bavarian conservative. Fearful of a break in the coalition, the Social Democrats, with little if any rural support themselves, were very generous and conciliatory to their strange bedfellow. During this period an SPD minister was more likely to have his budget cut than the FDP agriculture minister.

But after a quarter-century of large subsidies and structural change, German agriculture remains a major problem child of the economy. In comparison to France, Italy, and the Netherlands, it is in a poor competitive position. The focus of farm interests has thus been on the protection and maintenance of the farm market through price supports and direct subsidies. Germany's farmers want above all the continuation of the European Community's Common Agricultural Policy (CAP).[19] The program, begun in 1967, ensures them high prices in a protected market. This is good news for the farmers but bad news for consumers. Germans and other West Europeans spend about 10 percent more of their income for food and tobacco than do North Americans. Most of this difference is due to the price support program.[20] In countries with large sectors of the work force in agriculture, such as France and Italy, support for CAP is strong. But why in the Federal Republic, which must import much of its food, does this policy encounter no significant opposition? Indeed the high food prices caused by this policy have never been a major item on the German political agenda.[21] There are two major reasons for this paradox: (1) the highly organized agricultural interests in the Federal Republic, whose members constitute a critical voting bloc in many districts, and (2) the overall net gains to the Federal Republic from membership in the European Community. The Green Front has been a significant force in the parliamentary delegations of both the Christian Democrats and the Free Democrats. There has never been a time in the history of the Federal Republic when at least one of these parties did not hold national political power. Generally, German policymakers, regardless of party, accept the CAP because the losses to agriculture have been more than compensated for by profits from industrial exports to other Common Market countries.

The Churches

By law and custom, the Catholic and Protestant churches occupy a privileged position in German society, which affords them extensive opportunities to exert influence in a wide range of public policy areas. In addition to the church tax, discussed in Chapter 2, church officials appointed by the state, such as military and hospital chaplains, are considered civil servants. (The sixty-eight Jewish congregations, with a total membership of about 28,000, also derive support from state funds.) Various kindergartens, hospitals, and children's and nursing homes run by the two churches are subsidized in part by state funds in addition to those received through the church tax. Charitable work among foreign workers and foreign missionary activity also benefit from state subsidies. All church-owned properties are tax-free. Both churches are by law represented on the boards of control of radio and television networks. In Bavaria, church leaders even sit as appointed members in the upper house of the state parliament. Representatives of the churches are also found on numerous advisory commissions at both federal and state levels. Finally, both church bodies maintain offices in Bonn, headed by a commissioner charged with maintaining contacts with party and governmental leaders and presenting the churches' position.

Although sharing this common legal and political status, the two churches have differed sharply in their approach to public policy. The German Catholic church has traditionally been more active in pursuing specific policy aims than Protestants. Well organized with extensive lay organizations with over 3 million members and a press with 25 million readers, German Catholicism has sought output from the political system consistent with its goal or claim that the church has a right to intervene in certain political, social, and spiritual matters.

From the 1940s to the mid-1970s the Catholic Church made a major effort to secure state financial support for separate Catholic and Protestant school systems. The church insisted that parents had the right to send their children to a state-funded Catholic school. Unable to get a clear statement supporting separate schools for Catholics and Protestants in the Basic Law, the Catholic hierarchy relied on the 1933 *Reichskonkordat* (treaty) between the Vatican and the Nazi government, which guaranteed a state-supported religious school system. Most Protestant states, however, exercising their newly restored rights in the education field, established biconfessional public schools after the war, in some cases abolishing previously separate Catholic systems.[22] A 1957 decision of the federal constitutional court upheld the relevant states' rights provisions of the Basic Law in this area, thus making the *Konkordat* unenforceable on state governments.

Separate school systems were established in heavily Catholic areas such as Bavaria, Baden-Württemberg, the Rhineland-Palatinate, the Saar, and parts of North Rhine–Westphalia. But by the late 1960s, the inefficiency and in many cases inferiority of this "separate but equal" school structure became apparent to most Catholic parents as well as German education reformers. The Catholic hierarchy nonetheless insisted on the status quo but found itself increasingly isolated from its laity and younger clergy. By 1974, both Baden-Württemberg and Bavaria had abandoned the dual school system, and North Rhine–Westphalia had separate schools only in Catholic areas for the first four grades. Nationally, the percentage of children attending separate schools had dropped from 57 percent in 1961 to only 18 percent by 1974. The Catholic Church lost the battle not because of the strength of the opposition but through massive desertions by its own troops, Catholic parents.

In addition to confessional schools, the Catholic church has actively sought extensive state support and recognition of the family, stiffer divorce laws, strict control over "obscenity" in films and magazines, and the continued prohibition of abortion for all but the most pressing medical reasons. As in the case of the church school issue, it has been losing the battle in all these areas. The Ministry of Family Affairs (a pet project of the church since 1949) was abolished in 1969 and became part of the Health and Youth Affairs Ministry. During the Grand

Coalition, criminal penalties for homosexual relations between consenting adults, blasphemy, and adultery were removed. And since 1969, the Socialist-Liberal government, over strong and vocal Catholic opposition, has liberalized the laws dealing with divorce, abortion, and pornography. A growing gap between the attitudes of the Catholic laity and the hierarchy, seen in increased Catholic support for the SPD during the 1970s, meant that the church leadership was unable to mobilize its membership in these policy areas. Moreover, the strong commitment and association the church has had with the Christian Democrats left it in the Socialist-Liberal years (1969–1982) without any major direct influence on policy to the extent it enjoyed during two decades of CDU rule.

In every election, with the exception of 1969, the Catholic hierarchy has made clear its preference for the CDU and in varying degrees has regarded being a good Catholic and a good Socialist or Liberal as a contradiction, a position obviously not shared by a growing number of its members. Shortly before the 1980 election, the Catholic leadership issued a pastoral letter sharply critical of the Socialist-Liberal government. The letter included references to the growing public debt, a favorite campaign theme of the CDU/CSU, as well as to more traditional church concerns such as divorce and abortion. The incident had little apparent effect on the outcome of the election and was probably an expression of the frustration of some Catholic leaders over the impending SPD-FDP victory.

In contrast to Roman Catholicism, German Protestantism—or more specifically its political arm, the Evangelical Church in Germany (EKD)—has placed greater emphasis on the support of the basic political values of the Bonn Republic than on matters directly affecting the immediate interests of the church. Its major policy concerns, which it pursues less intensely than does the Catholic church, have been with reunification, a nonconfessional labor movement, codetermination in industry, East-West détente, civil liberties, and education reform. Traditionally conservative on social-economic policies, the postwar leadership of German Protestantism, if not its members, has changed almost 180 degrees and now has the reputation of being a center-left progressive movement in domestic policies. Unlike the Catholic leadership, however, the Protestant hierarchy has been unwilling to make any of its policy pronouncements binding on its members and has kept lines of communication open to all parties.

Both churches today find their traditional relationship to state and society in flux. The historically close relationship between the churches and state bodies, which has its roots in the aftermath of the Reformation, has made most Germans accept the traditional character of church-state relationships as legitimate. Criticism of state financial support and the advocacy of a clear separation of church and state have been restricted to small groups of liberal intellectuals centered in the larger metropolitan areas such as Hamburg and Berlin. Nonetheless, the sentiment that at least the church tax must be reduced or eliminated is growing. Given the growing secularization of German society and the recent unsuccessful efforts especially by the Catholic church to block liberal reforms in areas such as pornography and abortion, the restructuring of church-state relations will clearly be a subject of continued and increased debate in West German politics.

SUMMARY AND CONCLUSION

The traditional, established interest groups in German society have for the most part adapted well to the postwar Republic and "party state." They have all become less attached to and dependent on specific parties and now tend to concentrate on policy goals directly related to their major area of concern. Hence, the ending of two decades of Christian Democratic rule and the assumption of political power by the Social Democrats in 1969 did not result in any intense protest or opposition by any major group. As we have seen, business interests discovered that they could flourish under a Socialist government as they did under Christian Democratic rule. Agricultural interests, more pragmatic than during the Weimar Republic, saw the subsidies and protectionist policies so vital to their survival continued under Socialist and Christian Democratic governments. In short, there has been a high degree of consensus and cooperation between major interest alignments and all three system parties.

But what of those interests not accommodated by the existing structures? And to what extent is the institutionalized, hierarchical character of German interest groups, parties, and—as we discuss in Chapter 7—the bureaucracy a help or hindrance to the development of popular attitudes favorable to participation and involvement in the political process? The emergence and success of citizen initiative groups and the Greens, discussed in Chapter 3, is testimony to the presence of demands that neither established parties nor interest groups have met. The interests of foreign workers, consumers, and working women have also been inadequately represented by existing structures. Because membership in many occupational and professional groups is compulsory, or automatic, the constitutional provisions for intragroup democracy should be, but have not been, enforced. The same absence of democratic procedures also applies to decisionmaking within the political parties.

These are by no means uniquely German problems. To some extent they are the result of a constitutional order that puts little confidence (with some historical justification) in the ability of the common man to meet the participatory requirements of political democracy. If established parties and interests have adapted well to this constitutional system, so cautious and conservative in its approach to popular participation, their next task may well be to respond and adapt to new demands from a citizenry no longer in its democratic political infancy.

NOTES

1. Kurt Sontheimer, *The Government and Politics of West Germany* (New York: Praeger, 1973), p. 95.
2. Is a 1981 survey of elites, 68 percent of high-level civil servants were party members;

the corresponding figure for the general population was about 4 percent. Data cited in Ursula Hoffmann-Lange. "Eliten zwischen Alter und Neuer Politik," in H. D. Klingemann and Max Kaase (eds.), *Wahlen und politischer Prozess*, (Opladen: Westdeutscher Verlag, 1986), p. 113.

3. CDU = Christian Democratic Union (in Bavaria, CSU = Christian Social Union); SPD = Social Democratic party; FDP = Free Democratic party.

4. Wilhelm Hennis, "Die Rolle des Parlaments und die Parteiendemokratie," in *Die Zweite Republik*, ed. Richard Löwenthal and Hans-Peter Schwarz (Stuttgart: Seewald Verlag, 1974), pp. 203–243.

5. Kenneth H. F. Dyson, *Party, State and Bureaucracy in Western Germany* (Beverly Hills and London: Sage Publications, 1977), p. 56.

6. Otto Kirchheimer, "Germany: The Vanishing Opposition," in *Political Opposition in Western Democracies*, ed. Robert A. Dahl (New Haven: Yale University Press, 1966), pp. 237–259.

7. David P. Conradt, *The West German Party System* (Beverly Hills and London: Sage Publications, 1972), pp. 18–21.

8. Genscher was the principal architect of the 1982 collapse of the Schmidt government. He was also involved in the 1984 plan to give amnesty to those individuals and business firms under investigation for violating the party finance laws. Because of their smaller membership base, the Free Democrats are more dependent on larger contributions (and contributors) than the other parties. In 1985, for example, 28 percent of the FDP's reported income came from its 80,000 members, as compared to 49 percent for the Social Democrats and about 44 percent for the Christian Democrats. Emil Hübner and Horst-Hennek Rohlfs, *Jahrbuch der Bundesrepublik Deutschland, 1987–88,* (Munich: C. H. Beck Verlag, 1987), p. 347.

9. Gabriel A. Almond and Sidney Verba, *The Civic Culture* (Princeton: Princeton University Press, 1963), p. 218.

10. Thomas Ellwein, *Das Regierungssystem der Bundesrepublik Deutschland* (Opladen: Westdeutscher Verlag, 1973), p. 151.

11. Gerhard Loewenberg, *Parliament in the German Political System* (Ithaca and London: Cornell University Press, 1966), p. 113.

12. Ibid., pp. 285–286.

13. Gerhard Lehmbruch, "Liberal Corporatism and Party Government," in *Trends toward Corporatist Intermediation,* ed. Philippe C. Schmitter and Gerhard Lehmbruch (Beverly Hills and London: Sage Publications, 1979), pp. 147–188; and Helmut Willke, "Zur Integrationsfunktion des Staates. Die Konzertierte Aktion als Paradigma in der neuen Staatstheoretischen Diskussion," *Politische Vierteljahresschrift* 20 (September 1979): 221.

14. A 1982 survey of West German elites found that 81 percent of all leading labor officials supported the Social Democrats while only 13 percent preferred the CDU/CSU. Ursula Hoffman-Lange, "Eliteforschung in der Bundesrepublik Deutschland," *Aus Politik und Zeitgeschichte,* no. 47 (26 November 1983), p. 18.

15. Norbert Eickhof, "Mitgliedschaft bei Gewerkschaften," in *Hamburger Jahrbuch für Wirtschafts- und Gesellschaftspolitik,* ed. Heinz Dietrich Ortlieb, Bruno Molitor, and Werner Krone (Tübingen: J. C. B. Mohr, 1973), p. 176.

16. The scandal did not help the firm's financial condition. By 1985 it had to sell many of its properties to meet loan obligations of almost $5 billion. In 1986 the DGB sold the entire company to a Berlin bakery magnate for the symbolic price of 1 mark. Unable

to gain the confidence of banks or receive government loans or subsidies to keep the company afloat, the new owner eventually sold the firm back to the union for the same price.

17. Andrei S. Markovits and Christopher S. Allen, "Power and Dissent: The Trade Unions in the Federal Republic of Germany Re-Examined," *West European Politics* 3, no. 1 (January 1980): 68–86. A long and bitter labor dispute occurred in the steel industry from November 1978 to January 1979. Almost 100,000 steelworkers, mainly in the Rhine-Ruhr region, walked out, not for more wages but on the issue of a thirty-five-hour week, which the union regarded as one means to secure existing jobs from the threat of automation. The thirty-five-hour week, it was felt, would force industry to add an extra shift. The steel industry responded with an offer of an annual six-week paid vacation for all employees, another long-time goal of the union. The final settlement did not include a thirty-five-hour week but did give the steelworkers a wage increase and greatly increased paid leave time over the three-year contract period, especially for older workers. The settlement was just barely approved by the union membership, which was very critical of the union's leadership for failing to achieve the thirty-five-hour week. See Andrei S. Markovits and Christopher S. Allen, "The 1978–79 Steel Strike: German Unions at a Crossroad" (unpublished manuscript, Wesleyan University, 1980). In 1984 the same issue was at the center of the largest strike in the Federal Republic since the 1950s. In May more than 300,000 metal workers left their jobs after management refused to consider their demand for a thirty-five-hour week with no loss of pay.

18. Jörg Foshag, "Ein Machtfaktor, mit dem man rechnen muss," *Das Parlament,* no. 34 (25 August 1973), p. 3.

19. The CAP was originally conceived when Western Europe still had to import food. European farmers were encouraged to produce by fixed prices and guarantees from the Community to purchase whatever the free market could not absorb. Once Europe became self-sufficient in food, however, the program was not modified but continued under the original assumption of a dependency on imported food.

20. Erich Andrlik, "The Farmers and the State: Agricultural Interests in West German Politics," *West European Politics* 4, no. 1 (January 1983): 104.

21. Andrlik, p. 108.

22. In biconfessional or community schools, children of both confessions attend the same school but are given separate religious instruction (usually two to three hours per week) by representatives of the two faiths.

CHAPTER 5

Elections and Voting Behavior

The most common and extensive form of political participation in West Germany, as in other industrialized societies, is voting. Indeed, in the absence of any significant plebiscitary components in the Bonn Constitution, voting affords the West German citizen the major formal means of influence in the policymaking process. Elections were held at the local and state levels as early as 1946 in the British and American zones, and the first national election in 1949 was regarded as a quasi-referendum on the constitution. Subsequent Bonn claims to be the sole legitimate representative of the German nation (East and West Germany) were based on the freely elected character of West German governments. Thus the results of early local, state, and national elections were viewed primarily as indicators of system support and legitimacy. How many citizens would actually vote? And how many would support the democratic parties? The high turnout and the general rejection of neo-Nazi, Communist, and other extremist parties evidenced in these early elections were seen as securing the legitimation of the postwar system.

The other major functions that elections have for a political system—providing succession in leadership, influencing and controlling the policy decisions of government—were of lesser importance in the early years of the Republic. The elections of the 1950s and even the 1961 poll were largely referenda on Adenauer's leadership; the policy and personnel alternatives of the opposition parties played a subordinate role in these campaigns. Since the mid-1960s, however, the policy, leadership succession, and control functions of elections have become more prominent at both the national and the state levels.

In 1969, for example, the electorate effected the first alternation of government and opposition in the history of the Republic, ending twenty years of Christian Democratic rule. The near-miss of the Christian Democrats in 1976 and the Schmidt-Strauss "duel" in 1980 continued this pattern of hard-fought election campaigns the outcome of which can directly influence the policies and personnel of government. In 1983 the electorate strongly endorsed the Christian Democratic-Free Democratic coalition that had taken office six months earlier when the government of Chancellor Schmidt collapsed. German voters in 1983 also brought the first new party since 1957 into the parliament, the Greens. In 1987 for the first time in the history of the Republic both major parties lost support at the same election. Voters returned the coalition government of Helmut Kohl but with a reduced majority.

ELECTORAL MECHANICS

Elections to the national legislature must be held at least every four years but can be held sooner if the government loses its majority and requests the federal president to dissolve parliament and call new elections. This has occurred twice: in 1972, when the Brandt government, through the defection of several FDP and SPD deputies, lost its majority, and the opposition was unable to secure a majority for a new government; and in 1982, when the new Kohl government called for elections to legitimize the parliamentary developments that ended thirteen years of Socialist-Liberal rule. Elections to the various Länder parliaments are held every four or five years, but special elections can be called earlier. Usually state elections are held in off-years, a procedure especially favored by the opposition party at the national level to mitigate "coattail" effects.

For elections to the national parliament, the Republic is divided into 248 constituencies with an average size of about 250,000 residents and 170,000 registered voters. This does not include West Berlin, which is represented by 22 deputies elected by the city's parliament (*Senat*); these Berlin deputies have no legal voting power. Each district must be a contiguous whole, while respecting state (*Land*) and, if possible, county (*Kreis*) boundaries. The size of each district must not deviate by more than one-fourth from the national average. There is thus considerable variation in district size. In 1976, following an extensive apportionment, the smallest district had about 130,000 registered voters, the largest about 210,000 electors.

The Basic Law, as amended in 1970, grants universal suffrage and the right to hold public office to Germans eighteen years of age or above. West Germany has automatic registration based on residence records maintained by local authorities. If a citizen has officially reported his or her residence in the constituency (it is required by law to do so), he or she will automatically be placed on the electoral register, provided that the age requirement is met. Before election day, the citizen will then be notified of registration and polling place.

THE ELECTORAL SYSTEM

The procedures by which popular votes are converted into parliamentary seats, a country's electoral system, are more than just a technical problem best left to constitutional lawyers. Most political scientists and political leaders assume that the electoral law will affect the character and structure of its party system and hence its politics. Generally, there are two basic types of electoral systems: a plurality system, usually with single-member districts, as in the United States and Britain, according to which the party or candidate securing the most votes takes all; and a proportional electoral system, by which a party's share of parliamentary mandates is proportional to its percentage of the popular vote. Most political scientists have argued that a plurality system encourages a concentration of popular support among a small number of parties and enables clear decisions to emerge from an election, thus making postelection coalition negotiations unnecessary. The proportional system, on the other hand, is said to produce a fractionalization of the party vote and hence a multiparty system in which no single party secures a majority of the parliamentary seats, and government by coalition must result.

The assumption that a certain type of electoral law is related to a particular type of party system and hence favors some parties more than others makes the electoral law question a partisan political issue. Small parties generally favor a proportional system because it would guarantee them some parliamentary representation even if their percentage of the popular vote was far less than a plurality. Large parties tend to support a winner-take-all system, confident of their ability to mobilize the marginal voter.

The present West German system has been termed a "personalized proportional law" with half of the 496 parliamentary deputies elected by plurality vote in single-member districts and the other half by proportional representation from Land (state) party lists. Each voter casts two ballots—one for a district candidate and the other for a party. The party vote is more important because it is used to determine the final percentage of parliamentary mandates a party will receive. The seats won in the district contests are then *deducted* from this total. Thus, the more district mandates a party wins, the fewer list seats it will receive.

An example from the 1987 election clarifies this procedure. As Table 5.1 shows, the CDU/CSU in 1987 with 44.3 percent of the second ballot vote was entitled to 222 seats. It had won 169 district contests, however, so it received only 53 mandates from its state lists, and it received an additional seat because in one of the states it won one more district mandate than it would be entitled to under proportional representation. The SPD, on the basis of its second ballot percentage, was entitled to 186 seats, but because it won 79 district elections, it received 107 mandates from the state lists. Finally, the Free Democrats and the Greens won no district contests but did receive 9.1 and 8.3 percent respectively of the second ballot vote, which entitled the FDP to 46 seats and the Greens to 42 parliamentary mandates.

TABLE 5.1. SEAT DISTRIBUTION IN THE 1987 FEDERAL ELECTION

Party	% 1st Ballot	% 2d Ballot	No. of Seats Entitled to under Proportional Representation	No. District Contests Won (1st Ballot)	No. List Candidates Elected
CDU/CSU	52.1	4.3	222	169	54
SPD	40.4	37.0	186	79	107
FDP	2.8	9.1	46	0	46
Greens	4.1	8.3	42	0	42
Minor parties	0.6	1.3	0	0	0
Total	100.0	100.0	496	248	249[a]

[a] The CDU received one extra deputy because it won an additional district contest.

In practice, then, this is a proportional representation system with two important exceptions to "pure" proportionality: (1) A party must receive at least 5 percent of the vote or win three district contests in order to be proportionally represented in the parliament; hence the minor parties in our example with about 1.0 percent of the vote received no seats, and the six or seven mandates they would have been allotted in a pure proportional system were given to the parties that secured parliamentary representation; (2) if a party wins more direct mandates than it would be entitled to under proportional representation, it would retain these extra seats, and the size of the parliament would be increased accordingly. Let us assume, for example, that the CDU in 1987 had won all 248 district contests but had received only 40 percent of the second ballot vote. In a pure proportional system, it would be entitled to only 198 seats. According to the existing law, however, it would retain all 248 district seats but receive no mandates from the proportional lists, and the total size of the Bundestag would be increased from 496 to 546. An enlargment of the parliament to this extent has never occurred. Indeed, the greatest number of extra seats ever won was five in 1961. In 1987, the CDU received one additional seat because of this rule.

This electoral system, through its provisions for two ballots and the extra seats in the event a party wins more direct district contests than it would be entitled to under proportional representation, could also facilitate a great deal of ticket splitting, or "lending" of votes by supporters of two coalition or prospective coalition partners. Supporters of one party could cast their first ballot vote for its coalition partner, thus ensuring it a high number of district victories; voters of the second party could return the favor by casting their second ballot for the coalition partner, thus increasing its share of mandates from the state lists. In recent years ticket splitting of this type has become fairly widespread. In state elections in 1970 and in the federal election in 1972, many SPD voters (1.5 million at the 1972 election), fearing that their junior coalition partner in Bonn, the Free Democrats, would not surmount the 5 percent clause, "lent" their second-ballot vote to the FDP. Because the FDP's district candidate has little chance for direct election (the FDP has not won a direct mandate since 1957), Free Democratic voters in turn "lent" their first-ballot votes to the SPD. Such ticket splitting by supporters of the SPD-FDP coalition was especially evident in 1972 in major metropolitan areas (Hamburg, Cologne, Frankfurt). In 1987 the proportion of German voters splitting their ballots rose to a record 14 percent. In the 1983 and 1987 elections, ballot splitting was a key factor for both the Free Democrats and the Greens. Most voters who supported the Free Democrats on the second part of the ballot gave their first ballot vote to the Christian Democrats. For the Greens, support from first-ballot Social Democratic voters made up about 40 percent of their second-ballot vote. It is quite possible that without ticket splitting neither the Greens nor the Free Democrats would have entered the parliament.

Proposals for the change of this electoral system have usually been toward a plurality system of the Anglo-American type, that is, plurality elections in single-member districts. Such a system, it is argued, would eliminate the necessity for coalition governments by creating clear winners (and losers) and thereby increase the electorate's role in the selection of a governing party; it would also eliminate the possibility of antisystem parties, even those securing above 5 percent, from gaining parliamentary representation with only a small percentage of the vote.

These proposals have been opposed most intensely by the Free Democrats, whose survival as a serious political force is dependent on the retention of the present proportional system. Thus, before the party enters into any coalition with one of the major parties, it secures a pledge from its potential partner that the electoral law will not be tampered with. The Greens would also oppose any major change in this system.

NOMINATION AND CANDIDATE SELECTION

The electoral system is also an important structural factor influencing the recruitment and nomination of candidates to the parliament. The party list section of the ballot allows parties to bring into the parliament, through a high position on the list, representatives of interest groups and experts with specialized knowledge who would for various reasons (personality, background) have a difficult time winning a grass roots campaign. A district campaign, on the other hand, affords candidates an opportunity to establish their personal vote-getting appeal and can provide a second chance for personalities left off the state list or given a hopelessly low position. Moreover, a strong district following gives an incumbent a measure of independence from the state or national party organization.

Yet, in spite of one-on-one district contests (the personalized part of the electoral system), most Germans vote for a party label rather than a personality. In 1987, for example, about 60 percent of a representative sample of the electorate stated that the most important factor in their vote was their attachment to a party "whose basic policies I agree with." An additional 20 percent stated that their vote was based on particular issues, rather than on any general attachment to a party. Only 13 percent mentioned the candidates of the parties as the determining factor in their vote.[1]

Constituency candidates, by law, must be nominated after a secret-ballot election either by all party members in the district or by a district selection committee that has itself been elected by the vote of the entire membership. This nomination must be made not more than one year before the election. The official nomination papers must also contain minutes of the selection meeting together with attendance records and voting results. The enforcement of these legal provisions, however, has thus far been left to the parties.

The selection of candidates for state lists takes place at party conventions held from six to eight weeks before election day. The construction of these lists is usually a controversial matter in which the various factions struggle and bargain to receive positions high enough to ensure election or, in most cases, reelection. There is a tendency for even those candidates running in supposed safe districts to seek the safety net provided by a high list position.

At the district level, the entire process of candidate selection is, according to most observers, a relatively decentralized procedure in which local party oligarchies and issues play a more important role than does the construction of state lists. The grass roots organizations are very sensitive to pressure from above and jealously seek to maintain their power. Indeed, there are reports that, especially at recent elections, national "prominents," seeking a district nomination feel themselves handicapped by the so-called local matadors and under pressure to prove themselves sufficiently in touch with the base. Moreover, the district selection process is becoming more conflict-laden. This development reflects the influence of new members in the local party organizations and the emergence of contending ideological factions at the grass roots level, especially in the SPD between Young Socialists and the established oligarchies.

Criteria for Selection

How does an aspiring German politico become a candidate for parliament? Because most nominees are incumbents, the most obvious qualifications are previous experience and performance. In the absence of national experience, however, a good record in some local or Land office is an important qualification. About half of all district candidates have held local office, and about a fourth have had some experience at the state level. The reputation as a good party man, that is, being a loyal, hard-working partisan, especially in local party work, will further enhance the aspirant's prospects. The political culture values expertise, so occupational and educational experience is a further qualification. Finally, the degree of interest group support for a particular candidate and the character of the expected opposition are also at work in the local nomination process.

A good position on the state list (second part of the ballot) usually requires one or more of the following: state or national prominence, the support of top leaders of interest groups vital to the party (especially important in the CDU/CSU), leadership positions at the state or national level in auxiliary organizations of the party (youth, women, farmers), and the support of important ideological groupings within the organization. Because the top three names on each party's state list will be printed on the ballot, most state party organizations will try to have the most prominent national or state leaders possible in these slots to aid in voter recognition. The use by some district candidates of the list as a safety net, and the ability to do so, usually also requires senior leadership status in the party. In some cases, a candidate in a hopeless district, who has nonetheless done a good job of campaigning in the area over several elections, will be rewarded eventually with a good list position.

This process of candidate selection for state party lists can be illustrated by the data presented in Table 5.2, where the list of the Christian Democratic Union in the largest Land, North Rhine–Westphalia, is analyzed according to some of the criteria just mentioned. In this election, the first fifty list positions were regarded as good prospects for election because some candidates in this group also were running in "safe" district constituencies. The first five positions were taken by party and governmental prominents; the Catholic labor wing (important in the CDU organization in this state) received six good list positions; industrial interests were assigned four slots; various middle-class groups and women's organizations were given three positions each; and youth, Protestant, agrarian, and civil service/military interests each received two choice list positions. The minimal importance of agriculture in this Land is underscored by the absence of any good position for this interest, although some farmers may have been included in the middle-class organization category.

Proposals for the reform of the nomination system have focused on the introduction of American-type primary elections, the stricter enforcement of the provisions of the party law governing the selection process at both district and

TABLE 5.2. GROUP AFFILIATION OF THE TOP FIFTY CANDIDATES ON THE CHRISTIAN DEMOCRATIC LIST FOR NORTH RHINE–WESTPHALIA

Positions	Group
1–5	Party leadership
26, 32, 36, 42	Industry
8, 12, 48	Middle-class groups
6, 14, 20, 34, 40, 46	Catholic labor groups
24, 28	Civil service/military
30, 38	Agriculture
10, 16, 50	Women's organizations
18, 22	Protestant groups
22,[a] 44	Youth organization

[a] Double membership.

state levels (secret ballots, public announcement of meetings), and the establishment of nationwide candidate lists at the parties' national conventions. Given the
recent growth in grass roots participation in party affairs, reform proposals are
likely to gain increasing support.

ELECTORAL POLITICS
AND CAMPAIGN STYLES

As in other advanced Western societies, the style of election campaigns in West
Germany has become strongly influenced by professional advertising and public
relations techniques. All major parties contract with ad agencies for the design of
the campaign appeals: slogans, posters, television spots, and newspaper and
magazine advertisements are all pretested to achieve, if possible, the desired
effect on the target group of voters.[2] Nonetheless, it would be erroneous to
assume that the West German version of Madison Avenue is a behind-the-scenes
power in West German politics. The message, or main themes, of a campaign are
the decision for the most part of the parties, with the public relations and
advertising managers largely determining the manner in which these themes are
presented.

The extensive, well-developed media structure and the close, well-financed
relationship between major interest groups and the parties ensure that the
German voter will be subjected to a massive barrage of electoral propaganda. In
addition to daily press, radio, and television news coverage, parties are given free
time for political spots on radio and television. Special election previews, with
commentary and analysis, are standard fare during the final four to six weeks
before the election. Televised debates between the leaders of the parties
represented in the parliament have also been held since 1969. During the 1987
campaign, a three-hour debate among Chancellor Helmut Kohl (CDU), Franz-
Josef Strauss (CSU), and Vice-Chancellor and Foreign Minister Hans-Dietrich
Genscher (FDP), representing the government, Johannes Rau (SPD) and Jutta
Ditfurth (Greens) for the opposition, was viewed by an estimated 60 percent of
the electorate. Mass mailings, posters, and advertisements are also extensively
employed. As in other political areas, the West German voter was well informed
about the candidates, parties, and issues.

A new feature of German electoral politics, especially apparent since the
1970s, is a sharp increase in public involvement during the campaign. Traditionally, German voters have been rather passive and reticent during campaigns,
dutifully absorbing information channeled to them by the media and party
organizations. Discussions among family and friends, attendance at election
meetings, and the public display of partisan preferences were restricted to only a
part of the electorate. Since 1972, however, public interest and involvement in
the elections have taken on new forms and reached higher levels than during
previous campaigns. The proportion of voters reporting that they discussed the
elections with family or friends almost tripled between 1969 and 1976. Atten-

dance at election rallies has also increased during this period. New forms of public involvement included widespread voter initiative groups and the public display of partisan preferences through lapel buttons and bumper stickers.[3] Voter initiative groups were organized by the novelist Günter Grass on behalf of the SPD on a small scale in the elections of 1965 and 1969, and they were in evidence in some local and state elections between 1969 and 1972. In the federal election in 1972, citizen groups were working for all parties, although most of them tended to favor the Socialist-Liberal government.[4] These groups organized rallies, manned information booths in downtown shopping areas, sponsored advertisements, distributed literature and campaign buttons, and generally attempted to stimulate voter interest and activity in the campaign. These various signs of interest, popular concern, and involvement may indicate that Germans have acquired a fuller understanding of the citizen role and of the potential for political change available through political participation.

CAMPAIGN AND PARTY FINANCE

As in the United States, election campaigns in the Federal Republic have become very expensive. Unlike those in most other modern democracies, however, German political parties are the recipients of extensive governmental subsidies with which they finance a large part of their organizational and campaign work. In 1983, for example, public subsidies constituted about a third of the total income reported by the parties represented in parliament and over 60 percent of that received by the smaller, splinter parties that failed to gain parliamentary representation.

State subsidies began in 1959 with a modest annual allotment of about $2 million (DM4 million) to the three parties. By 1965 the allotment had grown to $20 million (DM40 million), including the addition of subsidies from some states. In 1967, a new law provided a public subsidy of about a dollar for each vote received by any party gaining at least 2.5 percent of the popular vote at the preceding (1965) election. Thus, by 1976 the federal government alone paid out over $60 million (DM120 million) to the parties contesting the federal election. The 1967 law also required the parties to file annual statements of their finances and to disclose the names of all individuals contributing more than $10,000 (about DM20,000) in any one year, as well as all corporations contributing more than $100,000 (about DM200,000). The federal constitutional court (see Chapter 7) later ruled that the law was unconstitutional in a number of ways. It ordered the minimum percentage needed for a party to receive subsidies dropped to 0.5 percent (about 175,000 votes) and also required that the disclosure ceilings be lowered. The reduction of the minimal percentage means that public subsidies are a major source of funds for small parties such as the Greens.

The costs of the expensive West German election campaigns and party bureaucracies, however, are far from covered by state funds and membership dues. The parties seek to meet these expenses through large, tax-deductible contributions from business and other interest groups. As in the United States, there is a real danger that political favors will be anticipated or actually promised by the parties in exchange for financial support. In 1982 and 1983 a series of reports in a major newsmagazine, *Der Spiegel,* revealed that the giant Flick business group had contributed large sums of money to all the major parties with the expectation that the company would receive a favorable ruling from the economics ministry in a tax case.[5] At stake was about $175 million in taxes that the Flick company sought to avoid paying. The economics minister had indeed interpreted the tax laws to Flick's advantage. In late 1983 both the economics minister and his predecessor were indicted on charges of misusing their office by accepting financial contributions for their party (the FDP) from Flick. Several months later the economics minister, Count Lambsdorff, resigned. Charges were brought against only the Free Democratic officeholders and Flick employees involved with the tax decision, but investigators also found that the Flick company had made many large contributions over the years to the Social Democrats and the Christian Democrats in order to create the "proper environ-ment" in Bonn for a favorable decision.[6]

THE PATTERN OF FEDERAL ELECTIONS 1949–1987

The results of the eleven national elections held since 1949, presented in Table 5.3, indicate four major characteristics of West German voting behavior:

1. The hegemonic position of the CDU/CSU in the party system from 1953 to 1965, due above all to the party's spectacular electoral victories in 1953 and 1957.
2. The steady increase in support for the SPD between 1957 and 1972, averaging about 3 percent in each election.
3. The gradual decline of smaller parties, whose percentage of the poll had dropped from 28 percent in 1949 to about 1 percent in 1987.
4. The competitive and less predictable character of elections since 1972; long-term trends such as those above have been replaced by short-term fluctuations from election to election.

TABLE 5.3. PARTY VOTE IN FEDERAL ELECTIONS, 1949–1987, SECOND BALLOT (in percentages)

Year	1949	1953	1957	1961	1965	1969	1972	1976	1980	1983	1987
Turnout, %	79	86	88	88	87	87	87	91	91	89	84
CDU/CSU	31	45	50	45	47	46	45	49	44.0	49.0	44.3
SPD	29	29	32	36	39	43	46	42	43.0	38.0	37.0
FDP	12	9	8	13	10	6	8	8	11.0	7.0	9.1
Greens	—	—	—	—	—	—	—	—	1.5	5.6	8.3
Others	28	17	10	6	4	5	1	1	0.5	0.4	1.3

In the first federal election in 1949, fifteen parties secured parliamentary representation, but only two—the CDU/CSU and the SPD—received more than 25 percent of the popular vote. The CDU/CSU campaigned on the twin issues of the Republic's integration into the Western alliance abroad and the market economy at home. "We don't want any socialism in Germany" was its major slogan. With the exception of the Communist party, which secured 5.7 percent of the vote and fifteen parliamentary seats, all other smaller parties generally agreed with these two basic Christian Democratic positions. The differences between them and the Union were far less than between them and the Social Democrats. If one combines the CDU/CSU's 1949 vote and that of the smaller, nonleftist parties in that first election, the total—44.3 percent—is similar to that achieved by the Union alone in the elections of 1953 and 1957.

The elections of 1953 and 1957, which brought the Christian Democrats to the pinnacle of their electoral success, represented the continuation of the 1949 pattern. By this time, however, the policy successes of the Adenauer-led government began to take their toll on the small, regional, special-interest parties, whose support steadily dwindled. The CDU gains resulted above all from its absorption of these smaller parties rather than from gains from the SPD. The SPD's policy alternatives—neutralism in foreign policy and a socialist planned economy at home—were decidedly rejected by the majority of the electorate. By absorbing the smaller parties, the CDU/CSU greatly simplified the party system and reduced the possibility of a reversion back to the unstable multiparty system of the Weimar Republic.

The early successes of the Christian Democrats provided the impetus for the SPD's transformation from a narrowly based, ideologically committed socialist movement to a heterogeneous, pragmatic, center-left party of reform. This process, described in Chapter 4, produced steady electoral gains after 1957 and by 1972 gave the SPD a larger share of the popular vote than the CDU. Most of the SPD gains over these years, however, came from Christian Democratic voters and new voters, not from the ranks of the minor parties. The SPD, unlike the CDU, had no small parties on the left of the spectrum to absorb. Until 1972, the CDU was able to compensate for losses to the SPD by gains from minor parties. Had it not been for this reservoir, the Union's decline between 1965 and 1972 would have been even more apparent.

The tenacity of the FDP and its ability so far to avoid the fate of other "third' parties is largely the result of its function as an alternative for CDU/CSU and SPD voters temporarily dissatisfied with their party. During the FDP's coalitions with the Union from 1949 to 1956, and again from 1961 to 1966, there was considerable movement between the electorates of these two parties. Essentially, those CDU/CSU voters who were somewhat dissatisfied with their party would vote for the FDP as a means of sending the big party a message without leaving the middle-class camp and going all the way over to the opposition, the SPD. During its coalition with the Socialists (1969–1982), the FDP sought the support of the SPD voters who were unhappy with their party but did not want to remove it from power. The FDP has thus acted as a type of opposition party within the coalition, a "corrective" to the major partner.

The 1976 federal election saw the return of the Socialist-Liberal coalition that has governed Germany since 1969, but with a majority of only ten seats, down sharply from the forty-six-seat advantage held after the November 1972 poll. The opposition Christian Democrats not only regained their status as Germany's largest single party but also achieved their highest proportion of the party vote since 1957 and reversed the steady gains the Social Democrats had achieved at every election since 1957.

In addition, the CDU/CSU in 1976 won an absolute majority (54 percent) of *direct mandates* for the first time since 1965. The SPD, which captured 61 percent of the single-member district contests in 1972, lost thirty-nine direct mandates and dropped to 46 percent of the total. Thus, under an Anglo-American electoral system, the Christian Democrats would have won an absolute majority of Bundestag seats in 1976.

In the 1980 federal election the SPD-FDP coalition, but especially the liberal Free Democrats, won a decisive victory over the Christian Democrats led by the controversial Franz-Josef Strauss. The SPD-FDP majority increased from ten to forty-six seats, due mainly to a rise in the FDP proportion of the vote from 7.9 to 10.6 percent. The electorate decisively rejected the Strauss candidacy but did not endorse the Social Democrats, preferring instead to return a stronger "liberal corrective" to the SPD. The CDU/CSU, in spite of a 4.1 percent drop in its vote, remained the strongest party.

The 1980 defeat actually left the CDU/CSU in a more consolidated condition than it was after the losses in 1969, 1972, and 1976. By giving Strauss and the party's right wing a chance, the CDU had rid itself of the persistent argument that the electorate would respond to a hard-line, conservative national-ist appeal. The Strauss candidacy, however, clearly hurt the Union and enabled the Free Democrats to make considerable gains among dissatisfied CDU/CSU voters. In spite of the almost 2 : 1 advantage Chancellor Schmidt enjoyed over Strauss, his party made only marginal gains. Had it not been for the strong support of new voters in 1980, the SPD would have suffered a small decline. The "floating" segment of the electorate in 1980 was more likely to express its preference for a continuation of the Schmidt-led coalition by voting for the FDP than for the Social Democrats.

In 1980 the three established parties also had to contend with a nationwide environmentalist political party. In the late 1970s a variety of environmentalist groups, with a common opposition to the government's plan for the expansion of nuclear energy plants, banded together into the Green political party.

In October 1979 the Green party gained entrance into the parliament of the city-state of Bremen, and in March 1980 it surmounted the 5 percent hurdle in the relatively large state of Baden-Württemberg. The Greens have a strong protest component to their image, and this helped them skim votes from all the established parties but especially the SPD and FDP in state and local elections. In

1980 they were unable, however, to overcome the charge of being simply a single-issue protest movement with no capability to assume or share responsibility for all the myriad tasks and problems of government. The established parties also stole some of the Greens' thunder by adding stronger environmental protection sections to their 1980 election programs. Persistent intraparty conflicts between left or neo-Marxist Greens and the more middle-class Friends of Nature faction further added to the party's problems. In spite of a strong national effort, the Greens secured less than 2 percent of the national vote in 1980.

The poor performance of the Greens in 1980 did not result in their disappearance from the party political landscape. Almost a third of the electorate still agreed that the party was a needed force in West German politics.[7] The issues of nuclear power and the environment remained of major concern to sizable numbers of voters. But after the 1980 election the NATO missile question and the resultant nationwide peace movement gave the party new momentum and put the Greens into three more state parliaments by 1982.

In the March 1983 elections, the Greens with 5.6 percent of the party vote became the first new political party to enter the parliament since the 1950s. Their electoral success in 1983 was due above all to the strong support they received from younger voters, especially those with college or university educational backgrounds. The Green's success in 1983 also indicates that the electoral system does not place insurmountable barriers to new political parties.

In the 1987 election, the eleventh in the Republic's history, the electorate returned the ruling Christian Democratic/Free Democratic coalition but with a reduced majority. For the first time in postwar German electoral history, both major parties lost support in the same election. The combined CDU (44 percent) and SPD (37 percent) share of the vote dropped to 81 percent, the lowest since 1953. The Free Democrats increased their vote to 9 percent, whereas the Greens' proportion of the party vote rose to over 8 percent. Voting turnout, generally among the highest in Western Europe, dropped to 84 percent, the lowest level since the first federal election in 1949.

THE BASIC ORIENTATIONS OF THE ELECTORATE

Ideology

The absence of major electoral support for parties proposing drastic changes in the political and economic order of the Federal Republic and the success enjoyed by the Social Democrats since they moved more to the center of the political spectrum indicate that the West German electorate has thus far had little interest in extremist or ideological parties and politics. The Christian Democrats during the 1950s and 1960s were a middle-of-the-road party par excellence, and they were essentially joined by the Social Democrats in the early 1960s. Survey data on the ideological orientations of the electorate tend to substantiate this

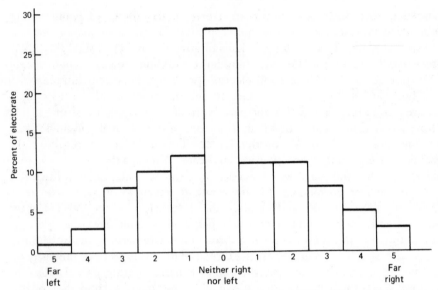

Figure 5.1. Ideological self-estimate of the electorate, 1987. *(From Forschungs-gruppe Wahlen,* March 1987. This study was kindly made available to the author by Dr. Dieter Roth of Mannheim University.)

interpretation. In Figure 5.1, the ideological self-image of the electorate in 1987 is presented. Respondents were asked to rank themselves as "left," "right," or "neither left nor right," and, if left or right, to indicate the intensity of this identification by a scale ranging from 1 (weak identification) to 5 (strong identification); a respondent who identified neither with the right nor the left would score himself as 0. As Figure 5.1 shows, the majority of the German electorate positions itself in the middle of the left-right continuum. Given these orientations, electoral success in the Federal Republic clearly resides in the vital center of the political spectrum.

Party Preference

As Table 5.4 indicates, most Germans tend to vote for the same party from election to election, although the percentage remaining faithful to their party has declined steadily from 73 percent in 1965 to 63 percent at the 1987 election. Thus the dynamic segment of the electorate has expanded from 24 percent to 30 percent over this period.

The consistency of support is roughly similar for the major parties with both managing to retain about 80 percent of their supporters between elections. The FDP, however, has had by far the most unstable electorate; it has generally been able to hold only about 40 percent of its voters from the previous election.

TABLE 5.4. CONTINUITY AND CHANGE IN VOTING BEHAVIOR, 1965–1987
(in percentages)

Respondent	1965–1969	1969–1972	1972–1976	1976–1980	1980–1983	1983–1987
Supported the same party at both elections	73	69	67	66	65	63
Changed party choice between elections	11	14	16	18	20	19
New voters	13	12	10	9	9	11
Nonvoter	3	5	7	7	6	7

SOURCE: for 1965–1969, Hans D. Klingemann and Franz Urban Pappi, "Die Wählerbewegungen bei der Bundestagswahl am 28. September 1969," Politische Vierteljahresschrift 11, no. 1 (1970): 122. For 1972–1987, sample survey data were made available to the author by Professor Werner Kaltefleiter (Kiel University), Dr. Ferdinand Müller-Rommel (University of Hamburg), and Dr. Dieter Roth (Mannheim University).

THE DETERMINANTS OF VOTING BEHAVIOR

Sociodemographic Factors

Social class, usually measured through occupation, and religion are the two most important demographic factors structuring the party vote. The hard core of the Social Democratic electorate is composed of manual workers. In 1987 they preferred the SPD to the middle-class parties by about a 60:40 ratio. The Christian Democratic Union, on the other hand, enjoys a very high level of support (70 percent) among independent nonmanuals (professionals, the self-employed), including farmers. The Free Democrats receive their strongest support from white-collar workers or salaried nonmanuals, sometimes referred to as the "new middle class," in contrast to the CDU's "old middle class."

In terms of the religious factor, the overall relationship is also quite clear: Christian Democratic support is greatest among Catholics, especially those with a strong attachment to the church, usually measured by church attendance. The Socialists and Liberals receive, on the other hand, disproportionate support from Protestants with a moderate or weak attachment to their religion. Because Protestants, as compared to Catholics, are less likely to attend church regularly and are apparently less attached to their church, it may well be more accurate to term SPD and FDP supporters as more *secular* than CDU/CSU voters.

Three other demographic factors of some importance are age, sex, and the voter's place of residence (rural community, metropolitan area). Generally speaking, the younger voters entering the electorate for the first time, especially since 1980, have been more likely to support the SPD or the Greens than the CDU/CSU. In the 1983 election the overall importance of the age factor increased sharply as the Greens made a successful appeal to new and young voters. About one of every five new voters in 1983 supported the Greens; among the rest of the electorate the party received the vote of only about one of every twenty voters. Age, rather than class or religion, was the most important determinant of support for the Greens.

There have been sizable differences in the party vote of men and women at least until 1972. In four elections held between 1957 and 1969, the percentage of women supporting the CDU/CSU exceeded that of males by about ten percentage points. Female support for the SPD, however, was on the average about 6.2 percent below that of males. It is ironic, indeed, that Germany's "left" party, which consistently fought for women's suffrage, was not rewarded at the polls. If the electorate had been composed only of males, the SPD would have become the strongest party by 1965 instead of 1972.

This tendency of disproportionate support for the CDU among females was halted, however, in the 1972 election, as the difference in male-female support for the CDU/CSU dropped from 10 percent in 1969 to only 3 percent. In the case of the SPD, the male-female difference declined from 5.2 percent in 1969 to only 1 percent in 1972 and 1976. In 1980 the Social Democrats for the first time actually received more support from females than males. Female support for the CDU/CSU in 1980 dropped to a record low level of 44 percent. In the 1987 election there was also no significant gender gap in the West German electorate.

Finally, urbanization also structures the party vote. Here the relationship is quite straightforward: The smaller the community in which the voter resides, the greater the likelihood that he or she will support the CDU/CSU. Conversely, SPD support increases with the size of the community. Especially since 1969, the FDP has also received disproportionate support in metropolitan areas. Nevertheless, both social class and religious factors are also at work to produce this relationship.

These demographic variables, then, form the major structural determinants of German voting behavior. Yet by themselves they do little to explain the dynamics of this behavior and specifically the factors that produce social changes in party support between specific elections and over the course of several elections. To explain these aspects of voting behavior, most analysts explore the *dynamic interrelationships between social change and electoral choice,* together with opinions toward *candidates, party policies,* and *issues.* A fuller understanding of voting and its function in the political system must also take these factors into account.

Voter Dynamics

Social Change. As we have seen, most manual workers (59 percent in the 1987 election) support the SPD and most Catholics support the CDU. What, then, of Catholic workers? Or unionized, low-paid white-collar workers? Likewise, SPD support is strongest among younger voters, manual workers, Protestants with marginal attachments to their church, and residents in large metropolitan areas, whereas CDU/CSU support is centered in older age groups, women, middle-class occupations, Catholics with strong attachments to the church, farmers, and voters in small towns. What, then, of young Catholic women living in metropolitan areas? These groups of voters are referred to by social scientists as "cross-pressured"—that is, their socioeconomic positions expose them to conflicting political communications. Their support for any one party tends to be less constant than that of voters with consistent attributes—for example, older Catholic women living in villages or young manual workers with little interest in religion living in metropolitan areas. The size of the cross-pressured component has been estimated at about 30 percent of the electorate. Moreover, it is growing as German social structure becomes more complex.

Another important source of change can be found in the class and religious composition of the electorate. As was discussed in Chapter 2, the size of both the manual-worker segment and old middle-class segment of the work force have declined in the postwar period, while the number of Germans in new middle-class occupations has greatly increased. New middle-class voters are generally more likely to change their vote from election to election than are voters in manual or old middle-class occupations. This development is seen in Table 5.5, which presents the party preferences of the three class groups since 1980. The old middle class remains largely the preserve of the CDU and the FDP with these two parties receiving about 80 percent of the vote. The Christian Democratic decline among this group in 1987 was compensated for somewhat by gains for the Free Democrats. The long-term decline in the size of the old middle class, however, reduces its importance in explaining aggregate change.

The expanding new middle-class part of the electorate has been more volatile in the 1980s than the old middle class or the working class. Between 1980 and 1983, the CDU was able to increase its support among this group from 37 percent to 47 percent. In 1987 the Union, although declining overall, held its share of this voting group. The FDP, after leaving its coalition with the SPD in the early 1980s, lost support among the new middle class. In recent years the Social Democrats have suffered the sharpest decline among this class. Once the

TABLE 5.5. PARTY VOTE BY CLASS, 1980–1987 (in percentages)

Party	Old Middle Class			New Middle Class			Working Class		
	1980	1983	1987	1980	1983	1987	1980	1983	1987
CDU/CSU	70	77	70	37	47	47	30	41	33
SPD	20	15	16	50	43	37	62	55	59
FDP	10	4	8	11	4	6	6	1	2
Greens	0	4	6	2	6	10	2	3	6
Total	100	100	100	100	100	100	100	100	100

SOURCE: INFAS (Institut für angewandte Sozialforschung) Surveys, 1980–1987. Each survey contains 5,000 to 6,000 cases, random samples. Cited in Ursula Feist and Hubert Krieger, "Alte und neue Scheidelinien des politischen Verhaltens," Aus Politik und Zeitgeschichte, no. 12 (March 21, 1987), p. 38.

favorite of the new middle class, the SPD share of the vote has dropped to 37 percent, a thirteen-point decline since 1980. Most of these voters have moved to the Greens, whose support within this stratum has jumped from only 2 percent in 1980 to 10 percent in the January 1987 election.[8]

One of the few bright spots for the SPD in 1987 was its ability to win back some of the blue-collar workers who had defected to the CDU/CSU in 1983. The Christian Democrats increased their vote among manual workers in 1983 from 30 percent to 41 percent, their highest level since 1965.[9] The Union's emphasis on economic issues in 1983 and its ability to link an economic upturn with its return to power in 1982 contrasted with the absence of any convincing economic arguments from the SPD. By 1987, however, the still high level of unemployment and the special efforts of the party and the trade unions to mobilize manual workers bore fruit. Although the total SPD vote dropped 1.2 percent to 37 percent, it increased among working-class voters from 55 percent to 59 percent. The classic, albeit dwindling, electoral base of the SPD was thus somewhat revived in 1987.

The growing secularization of the Federal Republic has also changed the significance of the religious factor in voting behavior. In the 1950s more than 40 percent of the electorate attended church on a weekly basis; by the 1987 election barely 25 percent attended church this regularly. Among German Catholics, regular church attendance has declined from 54 percent in 1953 to 32 percent in 1987.[10] Although church-going Catholics were about as likely to vote for the Christian Democrats in 1987 as they were in the 1950s, their numbers and hence the aggregate impact of religion on the vote have declined.

This trend can be seen in Table 5.6, which presents the support level for the Christian Democrats since 1976 among Catholics and non-Catholics. The majority of German Catholics continue to vote for the CDU/CSU, but the overall importance of religion for the party has dropped. In 1976 the CDU/CSU received almost 30 percent more support among Catholics than among non-Catholics; by 1987 this gap had narrowed to 18 percent. Fewer and fewer voters are exposed to the social and political cues of a religious milieu, and therefore they turn to some other source in making their voting decisions.

Candidates: The Chancellor Bonus. As in other Western societies, the incumbent government has a distinct advantage over the opposition. Its ability to dominate the news, announce new programs such as tax reductions and pension

TABLE 5.6. SUPPORT FOR CDU/CSU BY RELIGION, 1976–1987 (in percentages)

	1976	1980	1983	1987
Catholics	63	56	65	51
Non-Catholics	34	32	40	33
Difference	29	24	25	18

SOURCE: Forschungsgruppe Wahlen, election surveys.

increases, and proclaim foreign policy successes—all timed to the campaign and election—are tactics well known to Americans that are also practiced in Germany. The announcement of new policies, subsidies to various interest groups, trips to the United States for special conferences (and lots of photographs) with the president are standard preelection procedures for any German chancellor.

In Germany, however, the government also benefits from certain features of the political culture. The concept and role of a loyal opposition, for example, is still poorly understood by some Germans who have an administrative, expert-oriented conception of politics in which there are only "correct" answers to political problems. Opposition, in the sense of an institutionalized function of criticism, is still regarded by some voters as at best superfluous and at worst damaging to the efficient functioning of the state. Germans like to perceive their government as strong and decisive, as something certain in a world of uncertainty, something they can count on to protect and maintain the social order. These statist orientations provide a powerful advantage for any incumbent government, and any chancellor—even a Social Democrat—quickly learns to tap these cultural supports to his authority.

When Brandt attempted to challenge Adenauer for the chancellorship in 1961, the electorate, according to public opinion surveys, preferred the incumbent, Konrad Adenauer, over the young Berlin mayor by a 3 : 2 margin. When running against the then popular Chancellor Ludwig Erhard in 1965, Brandt fell further behind; Erhard was preferred by a 5 : 2 ratio. Even in 1969, as foreign minister and campaigning against Chancellor Kiesinger, Brandt could not overcome the handicap of opposition; Kiesinger was the electorate's favorite as chancellor by about a 2 : 1 margin. In 1972, however, Brandt, as the incumbent, enjoyed a similar advantage over his Christian Democratic rival, Rainer Barzel.[11] From 1949 to 1969, it was the CDU/CSU that benefited from this bonus, whereas from 1972 to 1980 the SPD and its chancellor candidates Willy Brandt and Helmut Schmidt were the beneficiaries.

Party Policies. The policies and programs of a party are another dynamic factor affecting voting behavior. The SPD between 1957 and 1972 made steady gains of about 3 percent in each federal election. Most of this increase came from new voters and from middle-class voters who had previously supported the bourgeois parties. This growth in support was related to changes in SPD policies since the late 1950s. As has been discussed, the party made a major effort to attract middle-class support by abandoning the more radical or Marxist components of its programs (nationalization of industry and banks and national economic planning) and attempted to project itself as a modern, innovative, change-oriented party that nevertheless accepted the basic characteristics of the West German social and economic order. Moreover, when the Social Democrats did come to power at the national level through the 1966 Grand Coalition (discussed in Chapter 4), they assumed the Ministry of Economics and were thus afforded the opportunity to demonstrate to the electorate that the party could outperform the CDU/CSU and were not irresponsible radicals who could not handle money and finances. Thus the policies and behavior of the party, as surveys have shown, reduced the impact of social class and effected change in voting behavior to the net benefit of the SPD. Likewise, the policy changes of the Free Democrats after 1966 also relate to changes in the behavior of the mass electorate. The FDP between 1965 and 1969 lost up to 50 percent of its electorate, mainly to the CDU/CSU.[12] These former FDP voters were responding to what they perceived to be the party's drift to the left, as evidenced by its support for the SPD's presidential candidate in March 1969 and its new progressive foreign and domestic program formulated in 1968. These gains from the FDP enabled the CDU/CSU to compensate for much of its loss to the SPD.

The personnel and strategy decisions of the parties can also influence electoral outcomes. The selection of Franz-Josef Strauss by the CDU/CSU, for example, as its chancellor candidate in 1980 was a major factor in the party's subsequent electoral defeat.[13] The SPD's decision in 1983 to all but ignore the unemployment issue and emphasize noneconomic issues such as the NATO missile decision was another strategic error that cost the party sizable blue-collar support. During the 1987 campaign, both parties made questionable strategy choices. The Christian Democrats underestimated the extent of discontent among Germany's farmers, many of whom stayed home.[14] The SPD's decision to seek an absolute majority with Johannes Rau conducting an American-style campaign lacked credibility in the view of most voters.[15] To compound the problem, the party essentially abandoned this approach about two months before the January 1987 vote.

Issues. In preelection surveys in 1983 and 1987, a national sample of voters was given a list containing policy issues or problems. Each voter was then asked to name those issues that were pesonally "very important" to him or her. In Table 5.7 the issues are ranked according to the percentage of respondents stating that the particular issue area was personally "very important." If 60 percent or more of the sample regarded the issue as very important, its salience was coded as *high*, 40–59 percent as *medium*, and 0–39 percent as *low*.

In 1983 economic issues were the most salient for the majority of voters. Issues of great importance to the Social Democrats such as relations with the United States (the missile question) and Eastern Europe and those emphasized by the Greens—environmental protection, more citizen influence in policymaking—were salient to less than half of the electorate. In 1983 the Christian Democrats, by stressing economic issues, were more in tune with the central concern of the voters than were the SPD and the Greens. Neither of

TABLE 5.7. RANK ORDER OF MAJOR COMPAIGN ISSUES BY SALIENCE TO THE ELECTORATE, 1983 AND 1987

Salience	Issue	
	1983	1987
High (above 60 percent)	Unemployment Security of Pensions	Unemployment Environmental Protection Security of Pensions Disarmament
Medium (40–59 percent)	State deficits Inflation Environmental protection Law and order	Inflation Economic Growth Law and Order
Low (0–39 percent)	Good relations with the United States More citizen influence Improve relations with East Germany	State deficits Improve relations with East Germany Good relations with the United States More citizen influence Advance European integration

SOURCE: David P. Conradt and Russell J. Dalton, "The West German Electorate and the Party System: Continuity and Change in the 1980s." Review of Politics, 50, no. 1 (January 1988): 14. Reprinted with permission.

these parties presented clear alternatives to the Christian Democrats on issues such as unemployment and deficit spending.

In the 1987 federal election, the voters' issue interests were divided between economic and noneconomic questions. On the one hand, economic issues persisted in importance. Inflation rates had declined and reforms had strengthened the pension system, yet public interest in these issues remained strong. With unemployment rates stuck at a high level, most of the electorate (82 percent) still saw this problem as the most pressing political issue. The clear economic advances made during Kohl's first term were not enough to lessen the importance attached to economic issues. On the other hand, a set of noneconomic issues received nearly equal attention from the voters. The nuclear disaster at Chernobyl in 1986 struck West Germany with a special force; citizens were told not to eat certain foods and to keep their children indoors. This crisis was soon followed by a series of chemical spills into the Rhine. The ecological cries of the Greens were now taken seriously by supporters of all political colors; over two-thirds of the electorate in 1987 mentioned environmental protection as an important political issue. Even though the stationing of NATO missiles had been accomplished, concerns about the disarmament and peace issue continued to garner widespread public attention.

SUMMARY AND CONCLUSION

In spite of an electoral law that supposedly encourages a multiparty system, German voters over the past forty years have concentrated their support in two major parties and two small but important "third" parties. After two decades of governments dominated by the Christian Democrats, this electorate in 1969 used the ballot to give the long-time opposition party, the Social Democrats, the major share of political responsibility for the first time. In 1972 the Social Democrats together with their junior partner, the Free Democrats, were retained in office with a greatly increased majority. Throughout the 1950s the center-right parties (the CDU plus small middle-class parties) secured about 70 percent of the popular vote and the center-left SPD only 30 percent, but by 1980 the distribution of preferences had changed to about 55 percent for the center-left and 45 percent for the center-right. Yet in 1983 the electorate gave the Christian Democrats their highest vote total in twenty-six years. The Social Democrats after sixteen years in power were dropped back to their vote level of 1965. Moreover, the SPD monopoly over the center-left of the electorate was broken as the first new party in thirty years, the Greens, gained entrance to the parliament. The West German electorate has thus become increasingly volatile.

These changes in voter behavior have been accompanied by a growing politicization and mobility of the electorate. Interest in elections, knowledge and concern about issues, and the readiness to switch party allegiances have increased. German voters are drifting from their once firm demographic moorings, as the concrete performance of parties, their leadership, and their treatment of policy issues become relatively more important in determining behavior than social class or religion. This is, then, an electorate that is both *stable* in the sense of supporting prosystem parties over time and *in transition* in the sense of becoming more sophisticated about issues and policies and more willing to use the ballot to effect political change and secure the desired policy outputs.

NOTES

1. Institut für angewandte Sozialforschung, *Politogramm. Bundestagswahl 1987,* Bad Godesberg, 1987, p. 75.
2. Gunhild Freese, "Trommeln für die SPD," *Die Zeit,* (23 January 1976), p. 20.
3. Max Kaase, "Die Bundestagswahl 1972: Probleme und Analysen," *Politische Viertel-jahresschrift 14, no. 2 (May 1973):* 158.
4. Institut für Demoskopie, *Jahrbuch der öffentlichen Meinung, 1968–1973* (Allensbach: Verlag für Demoskopie, 1975), 5:337. For corresponding 1976 data, see Elisabeth Noelle-Neumann, "Kampf um die öffentliche Meinung" (ms., Institut für Demoskopie, Allensbach, West Germany, 1977), p. 25.
5. The Flick company had sold its share of Daimler-Benz stock at a large profit. It sought to avoid taxes on this profit by reinvesting the money consistent with the provisions in the tax laws that exempt profits from taxation if they are invested in a way that benefits the German economy. The German Foreign Investment Law also allowed a tax

exemption for funds invested in non-German projects, provided that such investments through technology transfers or the international division of labor helped the German economy. Flick invested most of the Daimler-Benz profits in the American firm, W. R. Grace and Company. In its petition for tax exemption, the Flick firm in 1978 stressed the technical know-how Germany would acquire from the American firm. Flick also emphasized that it would eventually acquire a "dominant" position in the Grace firm. Two years later, however, only three of the thirty-three Grace board members were German.

6. Between 1977 and 1980 the then opposition leader and current chancellor, Helmut Kohl, received about $65,000 from the Flick company for the Christian Democrats. The Social Democrats, largely through their Freidrich Ebert Foundation, received several large contributions during the same period.

7. David P. Conradt, "The Electorate," in *West Germany at the Polls: The 1980 and 1983 Federal Elections,* ed. Karl Cerny (Durham and London: Duke University Press, 1988).

8. Although the Greens have an antitechnology image, which is partially deserved, the party in 1987 did better among white-collar employees in high-tech occupations than it did among those working in low or traditional technology occupations. Among younger new middle-class workers, however, the party's vote (15 percent) did not vary by the level of technology. It was among older members of the new middle class that the level of technology was related to support for the Greens. Elisabeth Noelle-Neumann and Edgar Piel, eds., *Allensbacher Jahrbuch der Demoskopie,* Vol. 8, 1978–1983 (Munich and New York: K. G. Saur Verlag, 1983), pp. 685–687; Ursula Feist and Hubert Krieger, "Alte und neue Scheidelinien des politischen Verhaltens," *Aus Politik und Zeitgeschichte,* no. 12 (March 21 1987): 45, 47.

9. Feist and Krieger, "Alte und neue Scheidelinien," pp. 38–39.

10. Institut für Demoskopie, Survey No. 061; Mannheim Election Panel, 1986–87.

11. Werner Kaltefleiter, *Zwischen Konsens und Krise: Eine Analyse der Bundestagswahl 1972* (Cologne: Carl Heymanns Verlag, 1973).

12. Hans-Dieter Klingemann and Franz-Urban Pappi, "Die Wählerbewegungen bei der Bundestagswahl am 28, September 1969," *Politische Vierteljahresschrift* 2, no. 1 (1970): 120 ff.

13. Jürgen W. Falter and Hans Rattinger, "Parteien, Kandidaten und politische Streitfragen bei der Bundestagswahl 1980" (unpublished manuscript, Bundeswehr Hochschule, Munich, June 1981), p. 85.

14. Institut für angewandte Sozialforschung, *Politogramm: Bundestagswahl 1987* (Bonn-Bad Godesberg:INFAS):114.

15. Surveys cited in *Der Spiegel,* 40, no. 22 (1986): 42, 43.

CHAPTER 6

Policymaking Institutions I: Parliament and Executive

In the preceding chapters we have surveyed the historical, socioeconomic, cultural, organizational, and behavioral contexts in which the West German political process takes place. We now turn to an examination of the process itself and to its outcomes: governmental policies. In comparison to countries such as the United States and Britain, the policymaking institutions of the Federal Republic are still relatively new, and stable patterns are only now emerging. The provisional character of the new state, the traditional weakness of representative institutions in Germany, the particular circumstances of Allied occupation, and the strongly authoritarian character of the first chancellor, Konrad Adenauer, all led to a decisionmaking process in the early years of the Republic that was clearly dominated by the executive. Since Adenauer's departure in 1963, all major institutions of policymaking have been changing, and new relationships between them are developing.

At the outset it must also be kept in mind that West Germany is a less centralized, unitary state than Britain or France, and the eleven states that constitute the Federal Republic play important roles, which are more fully discussed in Chapters 7 and 8. In addition, at the national level, which concerns us in this chapter, the states also have direct influence on policymaking through the *Bundesrat*, or federal council, an institution whose role has undergone considerable change in recent years.

There are three major national decisionmaking structures: (1) the parliament, or *Bundestag*; (2) the Federal Council, or *Bundesrat*; and (3) the federal government, or executive (the chancellor and the cabinet). In addition, a federal president, indirectly elected and with little independent responsibility for policy, serves as the ceremonial head of state. Each of these institutions has some precedent in the German political tradition, and their contemporary roles reflect in part the influence of this tradition.

Legislative Institutions

THE BUNDESTAG

In theory, the center of the policymaking process in the West German political system is the Bundestag (federal diet), or parliament. The Basic Law assigns to it the primary functions of legislation, the election and control of the federal government (chancellor and cabinet), the election of half of the membership of the Federal Constitutional Court, and special responsibilities for the supervision of the bureaucracy and military. Its 496 members are elected at least every four years and are the only directly elected political officials in the constitutional structure.

In practice, however, the present parliament, like its predecessors—the Reichstag of the empire (1871–1918) and the Weimar Republic (1919–1933)—has had a long uphill struggle to realize the lofty authority assigned to it in the constitutional documents. Parliamentary government has both a weak tradition and a poor record of performance in the German political experience. During the empire, the Reichstag was hindered in the performance of its control and legislative functions by a Prussian-dominated upper house and a government whose chancellor was appointed by the monarch. This, together with executive control of the military and bureaucracy, left the parliament with the power of the purse as its main source of influence but with little direct initiative in the policymaking process. The chamber's posture toward the government was defensive and reactive, and although the government had to seek some accommodation with Reichstag opinion, there was little parliamentary control over the government. The policy successes of the legendary Bismarck, particularly in foreign policy, awed even the most antimonarchical deputy and intensified the reputation of the executive as a branch that "acted" while the parliament only "talked."

The Weimar Constitution of 1919 greatly enhanced the power and function of the parliament. The executive (chancellor and cabinet) was now directly responsible to the lower house and could be removed by a vote of no confidence. In what most analysts regard as a major error, however, the framers of the Weimar system also created a strong, directly elected president independent of parliamentary control. This dual executive of president and chancellor, only one of which could be directly controlled by parliament, created the conditions for conflict and competition between the chancellor and parliament on the one hand and the president and state bureaucracy on the other. The former became identified as Republican institutions; the latter, especially after the election of the promonarchical, authoritarian Paul von Hindenburg in 1925 as president, as anti-Republican. This arrangement also put the cabinet somewhere between the chancellor and the president and encouraged both executives to vie for its support. Executive responsibility was thus not clearly fixed.

In addition, the growing polarization of politics during the Weimar period steadily reduced the strength of pro-Republican parties in parliament. After the first parliamentary election in 1919 about three-fourths of the deputies belonged to parties more or less committed to the Republic, but in the last elections in 1933 most deputies belonged to parties (Nazi, Nationalist, and Communist) committed to the destruction in one way or another of the very institution and constitution they were supposed to support. Parliament became increasingly immobile; successive governments in the early 1930s had no parliamentary majority supporting them, yet neither could the parliamentary opposition secure a majority for a new government. The strong president, however, at the request of the chancellor, could and did rule by decree, hardly an ideal situation for a fledgling democracy. Through the incessant attacks of the anti-Republican parties, especially the Nazi and Communist, but also through their own inexperience and ineptness in the ways of democratic politics, the pro-Republican parties together with the parliament itself became identified in the public mind as weak, ineffective, indecisive—a *Quasselbude* (gossip chamber), as the Nazis' propaganda chief, Josef Goebbels, termed it.

The world economic collapse between 1929 and 1930 and the government's feeble response all but ended the parliamentary system. The government, lacking a majority, was unable to act without the crutch of presidential decrees. Government by executive fiat made the legislature superfluous. Finally, by approving Hitler's Enabling Act in March 1933, it ceased to function as a lawmaking body and became merely an occasional forum for the dictator's public pronouncements.

The Bundestag, established in 1949, inherited this tragic parliamentary tradition. Unlike earlier parliaments, however, it had in theory at least no longer to compete with an executive over which it had no direct control. For the first time in German constitutional history, the Basic Law assigned sole control over government and bureaucracy to the parliament. Although during the early years of the Republic this control function of the parliament was undercut by the strong leadership of Chancellor Adenauer, the Bundestag since the 1960s has begun to assume a role in the policymaking process more congruent with its formal/legal position.

Structure and Organization

West German legislators meet in the most unpretentious surroundings of any modern parliament. The chamber itself was built in 1949 as an addition to a former teachers' college. Until 1970 most deputies had to share offices, which were once class rooms, with one or two of their colleagues. The city of Bonn, with 300,000 inhabitants crowded into an area more suitable for 150,000, is by no means a capital city in the classic European sense. There are no grandiose buildings, wide boulevards, or rich cultural life. Most deputies do not maintain homes in Bonn but live in rented rooms or apartments and return to their homes and families on weekends. Bonn is a small, provincial, rather unexciting place that closes down on Friday afternoon. For many deputies, life in Bonn is somewhat similar to their student days, with rented rooms and landladies. Some members even sleep in their offices to save costs!

The key organizing agents of the Bundestag are the parliamentary groups of the political parties, or *Fraktionen* (caucuses). A *Fraktion* is a group of parliamentary members all belonging to the same party. From an organizational and technical standpoint, the parliament is composed of these Fraktionen and not individual deputies. The size of a party's Fraktion determines the size of its representation on committees, the number of committee chairmen it can name, the amount of office space and clerical staff it receives, as well as its representation on the important executive bodies of the chamber, the Council of Elders, and the Presidium. Although there have been independent deputies not formally affiliated with any party, they have invariably had "visting rights" with a Fraktion.

The importance of the political parties in organizing the work of the chamber also extends to the relationship between the leadership of the parties and the individual deputy. As in Britain, party discipline and hence party voting are high in the parliament: about 85 to 90 percent of all votes are straight party votes, with all deputies following the instructions of the Fraktion leadership or the results of a caucus vote on an upcoming bill. Free votes, when the party gives no binding instructions to its deputies, are rare. Nonetheless, the constitution guarantees that a deputy who cannot support his party can leave its Fraktion and join another without losing his mandate, at least for the duration of the legislative period.

The daily agenda of the chamber is determined by the Council of Elders—in essence a steering committee—composed of the Bundestag's president (a member of the largest Fraktion), the three vice-presidents, and twelve to fifteen representatives of all Fraktionen. The Council schedules debates, allots time to each party, and assigns committee chairmanships to each in proportion to its parliamentary strength. A second executive body in the Bundestag is its Presidium, consisting of the president and vice-presidents of the chamber. The Presidium is responsible for the overall administration of the chamber from its furnishings to the recruitment of clerical and research personnel. In theory, partisan factors play a lesser role in the conduct of its business than they do in the Council of Elders.

Committees. Parliamentary committees are more important in West Germany than in Britain or France, yet less important than in the U.S. Congress. The Bundestag has twenty-one standing committees. Both the partisan composition and leadership of these committees are proportional to party strength in the chamber. Thus, unlike the American system, the opposition party or parties have a share of committee chairmanships. In addition, German committees cannot pigeonhole or reject bills but must examine them carefully, take testimony, and propose, if necessary, amendments to the whole house. The activities of committees generally reflect the parliament's self-image as a responsible critic of the government but not a rival force. Committees do not have the large independent staffs of their American counterparts. In meetings, most of which are still secret, the drafts of proposed legislation are frequently explained to the lawmakers by the relevant ministerial officials who wrote the bill. Until recently, parliamentary committees were not aggressive in the use of their investigatory and information-gathering powers. This resulted in part from the chamber's traditional deference to the government and state bureaucracy and in part from the party loyalty of the committee majority to the government. This latter phenomenon is common to parliamentary committees in unitary systems, where support for the government inhibits the independence of the committee and parliamentary majority, especially in the exercise of their control function.

The Members

The members of the Bundestag constitute part of West Germany's political elite. The chancellor, almost all cabinet ministers, and all parliamentary state secretaries (the minister's political assistants) are drawn from its ranks. Thus the social backgrounds of these 496 people reveal something about the quality and characteristics valued by the prevailing elite culture and by that relatively small group of party leaders at national, state, and district levels who, through their control of the nomination process, play a key role in Bundestag recruitment.

The social background of Bundestag deputies has changed dramatically between the first Bundestag in 1949 and the eleventh Bundestag elected in 1987. According to the careful analysis of John D. Nagle, almost half (49 percent) of the first parliament was composed of employees (manual and lower-level white-collar workers) dependent on wages for a livelihood.[1] The value placed on this type of individual declined rapidly after 1949, and by 1961 less than 15 percent of parliamentary deputies came from this relatively modest occupational background. Since 1961 and even after the Social Democratic victories of 1969 and 1972, this proportion has not increased.

Two specific occupational groups that by the 1980s were especially prominent in the chamber were civil servants and interest-group leaders. Together these two occupations now account for over 60 percent of the membership.[2] And civil servants are represented at a rate about ten times greater than their proportion in the population at large.

Unlike the United States or Britain, a West German civil servant can be elected to legislative office (local, state, or national) without resigning from the service. Indeed, the existing civil service regulations encourage standing for public office. A government employee desiring to run receives a six-week leave of absence with full pay during the election campaign. If elected, he or she takes a leave of absence for the duration of the legislative term. Moreover, while on parliamentary leave, the civil servant receives pension credit and normal promotions. The possible conflict of interest between civil servants serving as parliamentary deputies with, among other duties, the responsibility for setting civil service salary scales has as yet not prompted any change in the laws.[3] Little wonder that the civil servant contingent (by 1983, 40 percent of the total membership) is sometimes termed the parliament's "fourth" party.[4]

Apart from these incentives, the strong representation of state officials in parliament is also consistent with the expert, administrative orientation to politics that characterizes German political culture. As Gerhard Loewenberg has pointed out:

> In a society noted for the early development of a modern bureaucracy, government is still widely regarded as a purely administrative matter. From this, it is an easy step to the conclusion that administrators are the best qualified occupants of any governmental position, and that the parliamentary mandate is a type of administrative office.[5]

Interest group leaders and functionaries from business, industry, agriculture, and labor constitute another major part of the chamber's membership. Like civil servants, they have also had extensive experience with bureaucratic structures and procedures. Thus almost 60 percent of the deputies can be said to have essentially bureaucratic backgrounds (as civil servants or interest-group representatives). This leaves workers, housewives, farmers, and even those in business and professional occupations heavily underrepresented in the parliament. Being unable to take temporary leave of job or career, they are at a comparative disadvantage to those in occupations strongly related to the activities of parliament.[6]

In addition to changes in occupational backgrounds, the educational level of the deputies has steadily increased. Between 1949 and 1983, the proportion of deputies with some education beyond the basic eight-year *Volksschule* increased from 70 percent to 95 percent; by 1987, about 30 percent of the members held doctorate degrees. Younger deputies are most likely to enter the chamber with this higher educational background. Moreover, Nagle found that successful reelection was highest among the younger, upper-educated members with managerial or administrative occupational backgrounds.[7] These trends apply to all parties in the chamber. Indeed, in terms of social background, the first Bundestag in 1949 was actually more representative of the total West German population than were succeeding parliaments.[8] And the fact that the members of all parties are becoming more similar also means that interparty conflict arising from differing socialization experiences is also diminishing. Thus, West German parliamentarians have become more of an internally unified professional elite distinct from the general population by social background and training. These developments certainly facilitate a consensual policymaking style at the elite level and are indicative of a certain political maturity. They also relate to the increased assertiveness of the chamber vis-à-vis the executive in recent years. Yet the increasingly closed character of the membership also raises serious questions about democratic representation and the access of especially disadvantaged social groups to the decisionmaking centers of the system.

Electing and Controlling the Government

The Bundestag elects the federal chancellor. Unlike the procedures under the Weimar Constitution, the chamber does not elect specific ministers but only the chancellor, who then appoints the cabinet ministers. Although this election is by secret ballot, it follows strict party lines and has, with the possible exception of the CDU/CSU's unsuccessful positive vote of no confidence in 1972, provided few surprises.

The parliament's efforts to control the government and state bureaucracy is, of course, a far more complex activity than the election of the chancellor. One important control procedure is the question hour, a practice adopted from English parliamentary procedures, in which a deputy questions orally the relevant minister or the minister's representative about a particular problem. These questions vary considerably in tone and content. Many deal with citizen complaints, which a deputy can take for mutually beneficial publicity to the "highest level." Others deal with more fundamental questions about the direction of governmental policy. Since 1949, use of the question hour has increased dramatically. During the first Bundestag—in retrospect, the pinnacle of executive domination—members asked the government only 392 questions over four years. By the fifth Bundestag (1965–1969), this had increased to about 10,500; and during the seventh Bundestag (1972–1976), almost 19,000 questions were put to the government by the deputies.

To supplement the question hour, an *Aktuelle Stunde* (current hour) procedure was added in 1965, according to which a group of deputies (usually from the opposition) can petition the Bundestag leadership and the government for a question period about a particularly pressing problem. Deputies may also submit to the government written questions that can be answered in writing and inserted in the record. If at least twenty-five deputies submit such a petition, it is regarded as a "small inquiry" needing no parliamentary debate; if at least thirty deputies submit a written question, it becomes a "large inquiry," and a plenary debate must be held on the question and the government's reply. Almost 40 percent of all large inquiries were made during the first Bundestag (1949–1953). This was a time of great debates about the fundamental principles and policies of the Republic: the Western alliance, European integration, federalism, rearmament, and the market versus planned economy.

A further control procedure is the chamber's right to investigate governmental activities and its power to demand the appearance of any government or state official. Upon the request of at least one-fourth of the deputies, an investigating committee must be formed, whose partisan composition is proportional to party strength in the whole house. Therein lies one of the major problems of parliamentary investigating committees in a unitary system with disciplined parties. The possibility that its findings may embarrass the government and hence hinder their own political careers is an impediment to the type of more freewheeling investigatory practices found under "separation of power" systems with loose party discipline, as in the United States. Furthermore, there is at best a weak tradition for parliamentary investigations in Germany. The historical relationship of subordination to the executive, the cultural bias in favor of the state bureaucracy, and the relatively inadequate staffing of parliamentary committees have also worked against the effective use of the investigatory function as a means of control.

Finally, the most drastic form of parliamentary control is a formal vote of no confidence in the chancellor and his cabinet. Because of the stable, disciplined parties and the Basic Law's positive vote of no confidence, discussed later in this chapter, this procedure has been used only twice in the chamber's history.

The Parliament in the Post-Adenauer Era

Since the departure of Adenauer in 1963, the chamber has become more assertive and has shown signs of overcoming its historical legacy of inferiority to the government and state bureaucracy. Ironically, many of these changes and the increased independence of parliament first became apparent during the Grand Coalition (1966–1969), when neither of the two major parties wanted to be embarrassed by any back-bench revolt, and the parliament sought to maintain itself against such a powerful government and to prevent any independent opposition in its own ranks. The parliamentary leaders (*Fraktion* chairmen) were part of the Kiesinger-Brandt government's inner circle of decisionmakers and made sure that upcoming legislative proposals were cleared with the parliamentary parties before submission.[9] It was also during the Grand Coalition that the Bundestag finally acquired some control over the controversial "Reptile Fund" in the budget of the chancellor's office (alleged to be a slush fund for securing favorable journalistic and media comment). Even under the laws governing a possible state of emergency in the Republic, finally passed in 1968, the parliament still has an important role and does not yield complete control to the executive in emergency situations.

Since the late 1960s, the Bundestag has also taken a greater role in the prestatutory or planning stage of the policy process. Preliminary drafts of legislation, previously circulated to affected interest groups for comment, but not to the chamber, must now be submitted to parliament as well. According to the provisions of a parliamentary reform bill passed in 1969, the government is required to present the chamber with advance drafts of its annual reports on the economy and state of the nation, as well as defense white papers and lists of organizations and individuals receiving public subsidies. Thus, the parliament now—more than in the past—wants to be informed early and thoroughly about what the government is planning.

The Bundestag's use of its investigative powers and its efforts to increase public knowledge and involvement in its work have become more extensive in recent years. Although public committee hearings (the English word has been adopted) on proposed legislation, for example, have been possible since 1952, little or no use was made of this provision until the mid-1960s. In the fourth Bundestag (1961–1965), only four bills were given public committee hearings, but in the fifth Bundestag (1965–1969) fifty-eight public hearings on proposed legislation were held.[10] The chamber's reference and research facilities have been enlarged; since 1970, each deputy has been provided with a research assistant and in addition, since 1965, the size of the parliament's staff has been increased from about 100 employees to over 750. Since the late 1960s, public debates have become more lively and focused, partly because of increased issue conflict between the parties and the reduction of time limits for speakers. Television coverage of important debates has also enhanced the image of the chamber. Debates can now be scheduled according to policy areas—for example, one week on foreign policy, the next on education. Thus the government can be questioned about a specific complex of problems over an extended period.

Many of these changes in the chamber's procedures are related both to the roughly equal strength of government and opposition after 1969 and to the influx of younger, academically trained deputies. Since 1965 none of the three parties can be certain whether it will be in the government or opposition after the next election; hence all are equally interested in a more effective parliament. Many of the well-trained, newer members of the chamber were impatient with the chamber's outmoded facilities and procedures. Coming from the well-equipped offices of business, industry, and state administration, they would not accept shared quarters, standing in line at the typing pool, or stamping their own correspondence.[11] Unlike their older colleagues, they were not heistant to ask for more clerical and research assistance. For most of these deputies, Bonn is hardly a provisional arrangement anymore.

The overall effect of these changes has been to make the parliament a more independent if not sovereign institution, but they should not be exaggerated. The initiation of legislation is still for the most part the responsibility of the chancellor and the cabinet. Party discipline and the hierarchy within the *Fraktionen* still limit the impact of the lone deputy. Only about 40 percent of bills introduced by individual deputies, most of a "private" and marginal character, are passed, in comparison to 85 percent of those introduced by the government.[12] In addition, the conditions associated with the oft-discussed decline of parliament in other countries—the increasingly technical character of government that requires expertise available only in the executive, the alleged necessity for speedy decisions, and the strict discipline imposed by modern mass parties—are also prevalent in Germany.[13]

In terms of its influence vis-à-vis the executive, the Bundestag now occupies a middle position when compared to the United States Congress and the British Parliament. It is not as independent from the executive as is the American Congress, but neither is it as controlled by the government as the British House of Commons. The Bundestag supplies the government with a working majority, but through a strong committee system and the prevalence of coalition governments it has been able also to maintain some independence from the executive. In the preparation of bills, even government bills, the Bundestag has more influence than the House of Commons. The German chancellor, in contrast to the British prime minister, also has less influence on the day-to-day schedule and agenda of the parliament. The German executive must engage in more informal negotiations with the leadership of the parliamentary parties (*Fraktionen*) than in Great Britain. The Bundestag in committee can make major changes in a government bill without forcing the government to resign; numerous bills submitted by the government have in fact been extensively rewritten by the parliament with both government and opposition parties influencing the bill's final form.[14]

The Bundestag has secured a firm position in the Republic's political life. By the 1980s the great majority of Germans regarded it as a necessary and important political institution.[15] Citizen belief in the responsiveness of the parliament also appears to have grown over the past three decades. When asked in 1951 whether a parliamentary deputy would respond to their letter, almost half (49 percent) of a national sample thought they would get no answer; by 1983 the proportion of the electorate with such a pessimistic assessment of parliamentary responsiveness had dropped to only 19 percent.[16] As the data in Table 6.1 show, the Bonn parliament also fares well in comparison to the legislative assemblies of other major European countries, most of which have stronger democratic and parliamentary traditions than does Germany. Only the British respondents have a higher estimation of the importance of their parliament than do West German citizens.

TABLE 6.1. IMPORTANCE OF PARLIAMENT: MAJOR WEST EUROPEAN COUNTRIES, 1983 (in percentages)

Question: How important, would you say, is our own national parliament in the life of our country nowadays?

	Germany	Britain	Netherlands	Belgium	France	Italy
Very Important	35	56	28	27	25	25
Important	56	33	53	49	53	47
Not very important; not at all important	9	11	19	24	22	28

SOURCE: *Euro-Barometer surveys, April 1983.*

THE BUNDESRAT

The purpose of the Bundesrat, or federal council, is to represent the interests of the *Länder* (constituent states) of the federation. It is the continuation of a tradition that extends back to the Bundesrat of the empire. The unified Reich established in 1871 was possible only after Bismarck and the Prussians had made some concessions to the states—specifically, a strong representation in Berlin and the right of states to implement state-related national policy. In effect, this bargain of 1871 meant that Berlin would rule but that the states would administer these rules. The framers of the Basic Law, many state officials themselves, with strong Allied and especially American encouragement, returned to the federal structure of the empire and Weimar Republic and in some ways gave the *Länder,* now without Prussia, more influence than they had in either of these two earlier regimes.

The states are represented by forty-one delegates sent and instructed by the Länder governments. The delegates from each state must vote as a unit on instructions from their state government. Thus the parliamentary opposition in these states is not represented in the Bundesrat. The members of the Bundesrat are apportioned as follows: Of the four most populous states (North Rhine–Westphalia, Bavaria, Baden-Württemberg, and Lower Saxony), each receives five delegates; of the three middle-sized states (Hesse, the Rhineland-Palatinate, and Schleswig-Holstein), each receives four delegates; and of the three small states (Hamburg, Bremen, and the Saar), each has three delegates.[17] The degree of "malapportionment" in the Bundesrat ranges from one delegate for every 233,000 inhabitants of Bremen to one delegate for every 3.4 million citizens of North Rhine–Westphalia. Thus, although the Bundesrat does not represent the states as equal units (as does the American Senate), the smaller states are still clearly favored in the distribution of delegates.

Functions

According to the Basic Law, the Bundesrat can initiate legislation, and it must approve all legislation directly related to the states' responsibilities such as education, police matters, state and local finance questions, land use, and most transportation issues. In addition, any legislation affecting state boundaries, national emergencies, and proposed constitutional amendments require Bundesrat approval.

In practice, however, the Bundesrat has, at least until 1969, rarely initiated legislation or exercised its veto powers.[18] Its influence in the policymaking process has nevertheless steadily increased since 1969, and especially since 1972 it has become a much more politicized institution. This somewhat paradoxical development is due, above all, to changes in (1) the actual composition of the chamber's membership; (2) the determination of those areas where the Bundesrat has an absolute veto; and (3) the party control of the two houses of parliament, the "divided government" Germany had between 1972 and 1982.

Formal vs. Actual Composition of Membership. In its early years, the Bundesrat was more of an administrative than a policymaking institution, or, as one authority has said, it was "between" politics and administration.[19] Because the states have to administer much of federal law, the Bundesrat has been mainly concerned with examining governmental legislation from the standpoint of how the states would implement the legislation. This function of the institution was related to the types of people who actually did the work of the chamber: state-level civil servants who had been deputized by the formal members, state political officials. Thus, with the exception of the monthly plenary sessions, state-level civil servants far outnumber politicians in the chamber.

Most of these civil servants come from the ministries of the formal Bundesrat members. Originally, the framers of the Basic Law included this deputation provision (contained in Article 51) with the expectation that it would be used only rarely, when regular members could not attend committee and plenary sessions because of state commitments. In practice, however, in the Bundesrat's committees, where most of the work takes palce, bureaucrats from state administrations outnumber politicians (elected officials) by about a 15:1 ratio.[20] When ready for a formal vote, the draft legislation is presented to the plenary session, which usually approves pro forma the result of the committee's work. Thus, in practice, the Bundesrat did not reject bills outright, but early in the policymaking process, after committee study, it would recommend changes in legislation designed to facilitate its implementation at the state level. In most cases, the expert advice of the Bundesrat did produce revisions or withdrawal by the government of the proposed legislation, thus making an outright veto unnecessary but also testifying to the influence of the states, through their governmental administrations, on the national policymaking institutions.

Expansion of Veto Power. Originally, the framers of the Basic Law anticipated that only about 10 percent of all federal legislation would require Bundesrat approval and hence be subject to Bundesrat veto. In practice, however, through bargaining in the legal committees of each house and judicial interpretation, the scope of the Bundesrat's absolute veto power has been enlarged to the point where it can now veto roughly 60 percent of all federal legislation. This unforeseen development occurred largely because many federal laws that refer to matters not subject to Bundesrat veto nonetheless contain provisions that set forth how the states are to administer and implement the legislation. Citing Article 84 of the Basic Law, the states have argued that, because they are instructed as to how the federal legislation is to be administered, the legislation requires Bundesrat approval in both its substantive and procedural aspects. This corresponsibility theory has generally been supported by the courts. Thus, if the law affects the states, even if only in its administrative aspects, the entire law falls under the Bundesrat's veto power. This has also, in most cases, applied to any subsequent extension or amendments to the legislation that the Bundesrat may propose. Administrative decrees and regulations issued by the government require Bundesrat approval under this interpretation.

This enlargement of Bundesrat power, however, has prompted some students of German constitutional politics to propose that the powers of the Länder and federal government be more explicitly stated in the constitution. And in an important decision in September 1974, the federal constitutional court ruled that legislation that amends existing statutes does not need Bundesrat approval if the original legislation had previously passed the chamber.

Divided Parliamentary Control. From 1972 to 1982 the Bundestag and the Bundesrat were controlled by different parties. Although in opposition in the Bundestag, the Christian Democrats held a majority in the Bundesrat. Although it would be without precedent, significant segments of the CDU/CSU argued that the Bundesrat would be an ideal instrument for the party to block, or at least force revisions on, governmental programs.[21] In spite of its slim (one vote) advantage in the upper house, the CDU/CSU delegates voted en bloc against the Brandt government's treaties with the Soviet Union and Poland and its transportation program, as well as its urban finance reform, tax reform, land use, and liberalized divorce and abortion bills. In areas where the Bundesrat had an absolute veto, the CDU/CSU delegation forced major compromises on the government and in some cases, such as the higher education planning law (1974), completely blocked the proposed government bill.[22] The Bundesrat also vetoed several key policies of the Schmidt cabinet, including a proposed tax increase and the government's bill on radicals in public employment.

Although in the majority, however, the CDU/CSU did not attempt to draft and introduce alternative programs to those offered by the government in the Bundestag. Its efforts were concentrated largely on delaying legislation and forcing changes on the government.[23] It would, indeed, be difficult to develop the Bundesrat into a coequal chamber. Neither the structure nor the tradition of the house favors such a development. The strength of each party group, for example, always depends on state-level conditions, which can change rapidly. Because there are ten different state elections every four years, most majorities in the Bundesrat would be very unstable.

For the Bundesrat to become a consistently effective opposition to the government in the Bundestag, the state leaders, who control the delegations, must also be willing to accept directives from the national leadership in Bonn.[24] Generally, where there has been considerable interparty unity at both the state and national levels and a clear partisan division, such as in education (comprehensive school, university reform) or land policy, Bundesrat opposition has been strong and successful. But most issues still do not fall into these categories. The CDU-controlled Bundesrat rejected bills that the CDU in the Bundestag approved, and likewise, the Bundesrat unanimously passed some legislation opposed by the CDU in the Bundestag. Thus the CDU itself must be in agreement if the Bundesrat is to become an effective instrument of opposition.

If, however, the parliamentary (Bundestag) opposition ever achieved a two-thirds majority (twenty-seven delegates) in the Bundesrat, it could at least temporarily wreak havoc on the government's program. In that case, any Bundesrat veto, regardless of whether the proposed legislation is in the states' area of competence, could be overridden by the government only if it could muster a two-thirds majority in the Bundestag. All these develoments and potential future changes make the Bundesrat a much more political institution and thus an object of controversy than it was in the first two decades of the Republic.

Executive Institutions: Chancellor and Cabinet

CHANCELLOR DEMOCRACY

In framing the Basic Law of the Federal Republic, the delegates to the parliamentary council centered executive authority in the chancellor. Unlike under the Weimar Constitution, the chancellor does not share executive power with a strong president, nor do the provisions of the Basic Law make him as vulnerable to shifting parliamentary alignments as were the Weimar chancellors. In some respects, the West German chancellor's constitutional position is similar to that of the chancellor under the Imperial Constitution, although his powers over cabinet ministers and the Länder are not as extensive.

The position of the chancellor as the chief executive of the state is defined in Article 65 of the Basic Law:

> The Chancellor determines and bears responsibility for the general guidelines of governmental policy. Within this policy, each minister conducts the affairs of his department independently and under his own responsibility. The government decides on differences of opinion between ministers. The Chancellor conducts the business of the government in accordance with the rules of procedures adopted by it and approved by the President.

It is the chancellor who also appoints and dismisses cabinet ministers, whose primary political responsibility is to the chancellor's policies and not the parliament. The power of the chancellor to set guidelines and his sole responsibility for the appointment and removal of ministers place him in a stronger position than his Weimar counterparts. Although ministers are not his administrative subordinates, as under the Imperial Constitution, the Bonn chancellor supervises their work and has veto power over their decisions if they contradict his general guidelines. Moreover, unlike the Weimar system, the parliament cannot remove individual ministers but must vote no confidence in the chancellor before the cabinet is also dismissed.[25]

The framers of the Basic Law also made it more difficult for the parliamentary opposition to bring down a chancellor than was the case during the Weimar Republic. A parliamentary majority against him does not suffice; the opposition must also have a majority in favor of a new chancellor before the incumbent chancellor is dismissed. This positive vote of no confidence was added to protect the chancellor from the shifting and unstable parliamentary alignments that brought down many Weimar chancellors.

In practice, as discussed in Chapter 4, the unstable multiparty system of Weimar, which the framers of the Basic Law had in mind when drafting the positive vote of no confidence, has not reemerged. The concentration of electoral support in two large, well-disciplined parties and two smaller parties has assured most chancellors of firm parliamentary majorities. The positive vote of no confidence has been attempted only twice. In April 1972 the Christian Democrats filed a no-confidence motion against Chancellor Brandt and nominated their parliamentary leader as the new chancellor. The CDU's leadership was convinced that it had enough support from its own ranks and from dissatisfied members of the Free Democrats to remove Chancellor Brandt. The motion failed, however, as the parliament in a dramatic secret ballot split 247–247 with two abstentions. Apparently, one or two of the CDU members either abstained or voted for Brandt, In October 1982, however, the Christian Democrats with the help of the Free Democrats did successfully employ the constructive no-confidence vote when an absolute majority of the parliament voted to remove Helmut Schmidt and replace him with Helmut Kohl. About five months later, the electorate gave its stamp of approval to this change as the Kohl government (CDU/CSU-FDP) was returned with a large majority.

The chancellor is constitutionally superior to the cabinet, whose members serve at his pleasure and not that of the parliament. Yet the exact division of responsibility between chancellor and minister is, in theory, difficult to determine. Article 65, after giving the chancellor responsibility for the overall direction of government policy, goes on to state that "within this policy, each minister conducts the affairs of his department independently and under his own responsibility." This has been interpreted to mean that the chancellor cannot interfere in the day-to-day affairs of a department or deal directly with a civil servant within a department, or bypass a minister and issue direct instructions to a department.[26] But he can dismiss a minister or order him directly to rescind or abandon a particular policy or planned policy on the basis of his guideline authority. In addition, in times of war, he assumes supreme command of the armed forces from the defense minister.

The chancellor, however, will rarely give formal instructions to a minister. The communication of chancellor guidelines usually takes place through cabinet discussions, informal face-to-face contacts, and advisory memoranda from the chancellor's office to the ministries. The ministries, in turn, are required to keep the chancellor's office informed of developments in their area, and the chancellor must clear all ministerial statements.

Thus these ministers are constitutionally more than civil servants but less than British cabinet ministers. They do, however, have legal and administrative responsibility and, in practice, through their positions in the party and coalition and through procedures such as the question hour in parliament, they have also acquired political responsibility.

The Chancellor's Office

Consistent with his constitutional position, the chancellor has facilities and staff that exceed those of the British and French prime ministers but are less than those of the American president. The chancellor's office has a staff of about 400 (an increase from about 125 before 1969), headed by either a cabinet minister without portfolio or a high-ranking civil servant. The office is organized into departments, usually directed by senior civil servants, that correspond to the cabinet ministries and act as a liaison between the chancellor and the respective ministry. The chancellor's office has above all a right to information, and its key officials, with daily access to the chancellor, are among the most influential members of the government. The office is also a type of institutional watchdog over the various ministries to ensure that the chancellor's guidelines and cabinet decisions are indeed being carried out.[27]

When one considers the constitutional position of the chancellor and adds to it the strong personality, popular appeal, and authoritarian style of its first incumbent, Konrad Adenauer, the origins of the term "chancellor democracy" become evident. With presidential-like control over the cabinet, the bureaucracy, and his political party, Adenauer was able, in fact, to bypass parliament in many policymaking cases. Adenauer, supported by Article 65, which he interpreted liberally to his benefit, dominated his cabinet and led the government unlike any chancellor during the Weimar Republic. His relationshp to his ministers was not unlike that of an American president to his cabinet members or that of the Imperial chancellor to his state secretaries.

The Cabinet

In forming a cabinet, the chancellor has to consider (1) the commitments made to his coalition partner, (2) the demands of the various factions within his own party, and (3) the objective needs of each position in relation to the qualifications of the various candidates. Most students of German leadership would agree that criteria (1) and (2) have outweighed criterion (3) in the cabinet selection process. The size of West German cabinets has ranged from sixteen during the first Adenauer government (1949–1953) to twenty-two in the Erhard government (1963–1966). Expansion of cabinet size beyond eighteen seems invariably connected to coalition and internal party considerations—that is, some important faction or personality demands to be accommodated. For example, in 1987 the Free Democrats, after increasing their vote from 7.0 to 9.1 percent, requested an additional minister. At other times, an existing ministry may be divided in order to provide still more ministerial posts.

The major ministries, however, have remained relatively intact or have expanded through consolidation. They are foreign affairs, defense, finance (enlarged after 1972 by the addition of many functions previously performed in the economics ministry), interior (internal security, police), justice, labor, economics, agriculture, and transportation. Ministries for refugees and all-German relations have been abolished or consolidated into new ministries. Others, created over the past decade, that have grown in importance are foreign assistance, education, science, health, the environment, and urban affairs.

Generally, the classic ministries—foreign affairs, defense, finance, interior (internal security, policy, civil service), and justice—are the most important cabinet posts. Their incumbents are correspondingly viewed as the strongest cabinet members and the heirs apparent to the chancellor. For example, most observers regard the finance minister in the present CDU-FDP government, Gerhard Stoltenberg, as the strongest member of the cabinet and the most likely to succeed Chancellor Kohl.

Cabinet Ministers. The German cabinet minister, like his counterpart in Britain and France, has usually achieved his rank after an extensive and successful apprenticeship in parliament, a party, or a professional career. An extensive analysis of the social and political backgrounds of all cabinet members who served from 1949 to 1969 identified four pathways to ministerial office:

1. Through a successful rise up the *party* hierarchy and into the circle of ministerial candidates.
2. Through successful *occupational* experience, especially in business, the free professions, or interest-group administration.
3. Through *local and state officeholding* or *civil service* experience, especially in areas such as justice, finance, and economics.
4. Through *expert status* in an important field such a science or education.[28]

Given the number of qualified applicants, achieving ministerial office is in itself a considerable accomplishment and brings a variety of additional political and administrative responsibilities as well as considerable personal power and prestige. A minister inherits the traditionally strong German respect for state authority. Responsible for the "house," as a ministry is commonly termed, he or she receives a substantial salary (about $150,000 annually plus a generous expense allowance) and pension, not to mention a chauffeur-driven Mercedes limousine. Moreover, the minister's power and influence within the party are also usually enhanced by ministerial office. A minister's power within the cabinet depends on political support, relationship to the chancellor, and the nature of the specific issue. Formally, the finance minister is the only member with special power. He or she can veto, with the support of the chancellor, any proposal that deals with public spending. This is a major reason why the finance ministry is consulted early in the drafting of spending bills.

As a cabinet member, the minister belongs to the top governmental elite and is, together with the chancellor and ministerial colleagues, collectively responsible for all acts and policies of the government. Yet in practice the necessity of coalition governments and the heterogeneity of German parties have greatly reduced cabinet solidarity. On numerous occasions, German cabinet ministers have disagreed publicly with their colleagues. It is not unusual for a chancellor, through top aides, to leak criticisms of the ministers to the news media.

The minister is aided by at least two state secretaries, a career civil servant responsible for the administration of the ministry, and another—a parliamentary state secretary (similar to a junior minister in the British system)—who assists in the political and representational tasks of the minister.

Governmental Control of the Military

Through most of German history the military has played a major role in state and society. From the rise of Prussia in the eighteenth century to final military defeat in 1945, "the army rather than the political forces of the society traditionally provided the impetus toward national independence and greatness and thus the army has always been the dominant partner in its relations with civilian authorities."[29] Military values of order, obedience, dedication to duty, and hierarchy were also diffused throughout the rest of society. The army, or at least its leadership, thought of itself as "the school of the nation," an institution uniquely qualified to inculcate the proper values of citizenship and patriotism in succeeding generations of German youth.

Germany's conquerors in 1945 were determined to eliminate the political and social influence of the military and to prevent the reemergence of Germany as a significant military power. By the early 1950s these same wartime Allies, now split into opposing camps, were in the process of rearming their former enemy. The cold war had made Germany too important a territory to remain unarmed or neutral.

In the immediate postwar years, however, there was little public support for an independent army or even one integrated into a supranational European defense force. Rearmament, which began in the mid-1950s, was strongly opposed by opposition parties in the parliament but also by significant elements in the ruling Christian Democratic Union, the churches, labor unions, and many intellectuals. The army, in view of its collaboration with the Nazis, was a discredited institution. Fears of a reemergence of militarism and a new military elite, which would attempt to play an independent political role, were also widespread.

Civilian control of the military was thus of prime importance when the parliament, after long and sometimes bitter debate, finally approved the establishment of a West German army in 1956. During peacetime, supreme command of the armed forces is vested in the defense minister, who is expected to work closely with the defense council, a subcommittee of the cabinet. In wartime, the chancellor becomes commander-in-chief. Parliamentary control operates largely through supervision of the military budget and the Bundestag's commissioner for military affairs, a type of ombudsman, who is empowered to hear the complaints and grievances of soldiers and to protect their constitutional rights. The officer corps, which leads a very modern defense force of more than 500,000 men, has not become a politically powerful elite, and its influence in policy matters has been subordinate to elected political leadership. Most Germans by the 1970s perceived the military as another public service institution with specific functional tasks, somewhat like the railways or post office.[30]

In the 1980s, however, the emergence of a nationwide peace movement and the widespread protests over the deployment of new missiles in the Federal Republic have had an impact on the status of the military in German society. Public induction ceremonies for new recruits have been the scene of sometimes violent demonstrations by peace movement activists. The number of petitions for exemption from military service has also increased. In some areas, teachers and school authorities have denied recruiting officers access to school classes unless peace groups receive equal time. In a 1982 survey, only 35 percent of the German adult population stated that they would be willing to fight for their country in the event of a war. In contrast, almost 70 percent of Americans and over 60 percent of the British respondents would be willing to fight.[31] There has not been a national debate on the question of the military in German society since the rearmament struggle of the 1950s.

Chancellor Democracy under Adenauer

During his thirteen-year tenure, Konrad Adenauer established the procedures and style of chancellor government with which all future incumbents of the office have in some way had to contend. His early successes in dealing with the Western occupation powers, the integration of West Germany into Europe, the reconciliation with France, and the rapid economic recovery that began shortly before his first term and became an economic boom by the mid-1950s, gave him a record of accomplishment that enabled him to dominate parliament on many important matters, especially in foreign policy. Impatient with the delays and indecisiveness of government by committee, he frequently made commitments (for example, to the Allied occupiers on German rearmament) without any prior consultations with his cabinet, much less the parliament. He was also very adept at keeping the various wings and factions of the Christian Democrats in balance and under control, while at the same time discouraging its organizational and programmatic development. For all practical purposes, the party was run from the chancellor's office.

Adenauer was also able to bring the new state bureaucracy under control and make it responsive to his demands. His chief aide in this area was Hans Globke, a former high-ranking official in the Prussian bureaucracy, who played a major role in rebuilding the postwar civil service along traditional lines.[32] Indeed, some observers have argued that Adenauer placed far more confidence in his government's top civil servants than he did in his cabinet ministers, whom he tended to regard as a necessary evil of party politics.[33]

In Adenauer's chancellor democracy, the general public played a minor role. Deeply pessimistic about the capacities of the German people to measure up to the demands of democratic citizenship, he wanted their support but not their involvement. In short, Adenauer wanted to govern and he did not want the parliament, his party, his cabinet ministers, or the public to bother him while he went about his business. His message to the German electorate was, in essence: "Go about your private affairs, rebuild your lives, concentrate on regaining and improving your economic position, and leave the politics to me." Many Germans accepted and indeed welcomed this approach, even though it meant that much of the state building and the resolution of major problems, such as reunification and social reforms, would have to be postponed until after the Adenauer era.[34]

Adenauer, however, did make a major contribution toward the institutionalization of the Federal Republic in that he convinced most citizens that a republic could be strong and effective, that strong state authority and firm leadership could operate within a democratic framework and give West Germans what they desperately wanted in the postwar period: security and economic prosperity. Through his authoritarian, paternalistic style, he sold West Germans on the Second Republic.[35]

The Heirs of Chancellor Democracy

It is unlikely that Adenauer's thirteen-year tenure as chancellor will be equaled or broken in the foreseeable future. As Table 6.2 shows, none of his first three successors lasted more than five years, and the trend toward younger political leaders, the internal divisions within the major parties, and the increased intensity of parliamentary opposition all work against a long incumbency for any future chancellor.

Adenauer's immediate successor was Ludwig Erhard, the father of the economic miracle, who had been a self-designated heir ever since the late 1950s and whom Adenauer ceaselessly criticized publicly and privately as ill-suited for the top job. In retrospect, he was probably correct.

Erhard never had any close contact with his party organization and did not consolidate his position within the CDU/CSU. He was, as one observer put it, a "guest" in the CDU.[36] Proud of his accomplishments as economics minister and aware of his enormous electoral appeal, he regarded the party as secondary to his government and never really attempted to gain the support of its key factions. He attempted to project himself as a *Volkskanzler,* a people's chancellor, above the parties. This posture left him in a very vulnerable position when Germany's first serious postwar recession in 1966 took the luster off his reputation as the guarantor of economic prosperity. After Christian Democratic defeats in key state elections in 1966, the Erhard government fell, ostensibly because of the

TABLE 6.2. WEST GERMAN CHANCELLORS, 1949–1989

Name	Party	Term of Office	Age at Assumption of Office	Age at Nazi Seizure of Power (1933)	Percentage of Adult Life (after 18) under Democratic Regime before Becoming Chancellor[a]
Konrad Adenauer	Christian Democrat	1949–1963	73	57	24
Ludwig Erhard	Christian Democrat	1963–1966	66	36	56
Kurt-Georg Kiesinger	Christian Democrat	1966–1969	62	29	65
Willy Brandt	Social Democrat	1969–1974	56	20	60
Helmut Schmidt	Social Democrat	1974–1982	56	15	63
Helmut Kohl	Christian Democrat	1982–present	52	3	100

[a] Including the Weimar Republic.

departure of the junior coalition partner, the Free Democrats, but more through the internal maneuvering for power within the various factions of the Union. A stunned, disbelieving Erhard, still somewhat of a political innocent, retired to elder statesman status.

The Erhard period, however, did see the faint beginnings of a new policy toward the Soviet Union, Eastern Europe, and East Germany. Long-overdue administrative and tax reforms were also passed during this period, and the beginnings of change in education policy were noticeable. But major innovations in domestic and, above all, foreign policy had to await the Grand Coalition of Christian and Social Democrats and the Socialist-Liberal cabinets that governed Germany from 1969 and 1982.

The chancellorship of Erhard's successor, Kurt-George Kiesinger, was inextricably connected with the rise and fall of the Grand Coalition between the SPD and CDU/CSU. Kiesinger had been a Bundestag deputy from 1949 to 1958, specializing mainly in foreign policy. Finding the road to national prominence too crowded in Bonn, he returned to his native state of Baden-Württemberg and became its chief executive. When the Erhard government collapsed eight years later and the CDU/CSU desperately needed a new chancellor candidate who would also be acceptable to the Social Democrats in the likely event of a Grand Coalition, Kiesinger became the ideal person simply because he had the fewest number of outright opponents in either party. It was a case of absence making the heart grow fonder, or at least of not making it more antagonistic.

As chancellor, Kiesinger had the very difficult task of leading a government in such a way that neither he nor his party nor its partner, the Social Democrats, would be too successful. Partisanship might have caused the strange alignment to break up before 1969, something both parties feared. He became, in the words of the government's press secretary, "a walking mediation committee." This structurally induced, honest broker style of leadership gave some of his cabinet ministers considerable freedom of action, and as discussed in Chapter 4, the Social Democrats in the government took full advantage of the opportunity. After the 1969 election and the SPD-FDP government, Kiesinger became a liability to the Christian Democrats, and after a decent interval he stepped down from the titular leadership of the party. Whether he could have been an effective national leader was never really determined because, given the character of the Grand Coalition, he never had a chance.

The SPD Chancellors: Willy Brandt and Helmut Schmidt

In 1969, Willy Brandt became the fourth chancellor of the Federal Republic. In terms of policy innovation, controversy, foreign stature, and significance for the political system, Brandt ranks as one of Germany's most important postwar leaders. Born in the north German city of Lübeck, he became active in socialist politics as a teenager and was forced to flee Germany for Norway and later Sweden shortly after the Nazi seizure of power. He thus is the only chancellor not to have lived in Germany during the Third Reich. Returning to Germany in 1945 as a Norwegian press attaché in a Norwegian military uniform, he resumed German citizenship and became active in Social Democratic politics in Berlin. Identified with the reformist, pragmatic wing of the party led by Ernst Reuter, Brandt quickly rose in the Berlin organization as Reuter's protégé and became lord mayor of the city in 1957. Soviet pressure against this isolated city intensified in the late 1950s and made it a major source of East-West tension. As its mayor, Brandt acquired a national and international reputation as a young, dynamic, progressive, yet non-Marxist and anticommunist political leader. The image coincided with the SPD's new look after 1959. Brandt was elected national chairman in 1964 and became the party's chancellor candidate in 1961 and again in 1965. His defeats in these two elections, during which he was subjected to numerous personal attacks regarding his illegitimate birth and his wartime activity—which to some Germans made him a traitor—almost caused his retirement from national politics. The collapse of the Erhard government and the Grand Coalition, however, compelled his return to the national scene as foreign minister in the Kiesinger government. Brandt was actually against the Grand Coalition but consented to participate largely out of a sense of party loyalty.

As foreign minister, he laid the foundations for the new relationship that the Federal Republic would develop with the Soviet Union, Poland, East Germany, and other East European states. Although limited somewhat by the demands of coalition politics, Brandt was able to establish himself as a competent, innovative foreign minister and in so doing erased much of the loser image he had acquired in his unsuccessful bids for the chancellorship.

Immediately after the results of the 1969 election, Brandt seized the initiative and formed a coalition government with the Free Democrats in spite of a SPD-FDP majority of only twelve seats. He thus became the first Socialist chancellor since 1930. Between 1969 and 1972, Brandt together with Foreign Minister Walter Scheel effected a major transformation of West German foreign policy through treaties with the Soviet Union, Poland, and East Germany. During this period, some domestic reforms were also made in the criminal legal code, pension system, and social welfare programs. Yet, although promising a government of internal reform, most of the government's domestic program was postponed because of its weak and dwindling parliamentary majority.

Following the 1972 election, which gave the government a solid working majority of almost fifty seats, the unfinished domestic projects, such as codetermination, capital resources reform, urban renewal, education, and tax reform, were placed high on the political agenda.

Yet, to the considerable disappointment of SPD supporters, the government in the first year and a half following the 1972 victory did not use its parliamentary majority to move forward in the domestic field with the same decisiveness it had demonstrated three years earlier in foreign policy. This relative inactivity was explained in part by the government's attempt to curb inflation through ceilings on government expenditures and the postponement of new programs. Personality and party/political factors were also involved. After 1972, it became apparent that neither Brandt nor Scheel had expertise or interest in domestic affairs. Brandt had little knowledge of economics or finance and disliked much of the detail work and bargaining associated with domestic politics. In addition, unlike in foreign policy, there were serious differences between the coalition partners over major domestic issues such as codetermination, tax, and education reform. Even after 1972, these issues were consigned to study commissions and coalition negotiation committees where agreements and recommendations were slow in coming. It was not, for example, until early 1974—five years after they were promised—that the government produced draft legislation for codetermination and profit sharing programs, and even then they were not ready for submission to the Bundestag. After 1972, the middle-class Free Democrats were intent on creating an image and identity as a "liberal corrective" to the Socialists. Politically, this meant they were concerned about holding their essentially middle-class electoral clientele by moderating some of the more extreme SPD policies. In short, the German liberals, like their French counterparts during the Third and Fourth Republics, tended to have their hearts on the left but their wallets on the right. On matters of foreign policy, criminal and legal reform, and state support of religious schools, they had little difficulty supporting the Social Democrats, but when such issues as codetermination and tax reform involved the possible redistribution of economic resources and power, the Free Democrats held relatively firm for the maintenance of special concessions and subsidies to middle-class groups.

The arrest of an East German spy on Brandt's personal staff in April 1974 was the final blow in a series of setbacks since his triumph in November 1972. The East German agent, a resident of the Federal Republic since 1957, had been under suspicion by security agencies for almost a year before the actual arrest. Brandt had been privately informed of this but apparently acceded to the requests of security officials to keep the agent on his staff.

The entire affair was poorly handled by all agencies and officials involved. Initial denials in parliament that the agent had any access to top-secret intelligence materials were later retracted. Mutual recriminations between the agencies and cabinet ministers hardly changed the appearance of a government badly shaken by the affair. Following consultations with the SPD leadership and the Free Democrats, Brandt assumed full responsibility for all errors connected with the affair and resigned as chancellor in May 1974.

Brandt's five-year tenure was distinguished above all by his foreign policy of reconciliation with Eastern Europe and the Soviet Union, for which he was awarded the Nobel Peace Prize in 1971, only the fourth German so honored. As the first chancellor with an impeccable record of uncompromising opposition to Nazism, he contributed greatly to the Republic's image abroad as a society that had finally overcome its totalitarian past. In spite of shortcomings in domestic policies, the Brandt chancellorship was at least one in which many innovations and long-overdue reforms began to be discussed and programs formulated.

Helmut Schmidt

Less than two weeks after Brandt's resignation, Helmut Schmidt became the fifth chancellor of the Republic. Schmidt had been the strongest figure in Brandt's cabinet and was his designated successor. He had been finance minister (1972–1974), defense minister (1969–1972), chairman of the SPD's *Fraktion* (1966–1969), and interior minister in his native Hamburg (1961–1965). In these posts Schmidt acquired the reputation as a very capable, some would say brilliant, political decision maker. He was also criticized for what some regarded as an overbearing, arrogant, cold personal style. He clearly lacked the emotional, warm image of Brandt, yet he is given much higher marks for his concrete performance. Schmidt is identified with the SPD establishment. A pragmatic, problem-solving approach to politics, with a basic acceptance of the main features of the economic and political system, is characteristic of his political philosophy.

Schmidt assumed the chancellorship in the midst of the worldwide economic recession that followed the 1973 Arab oil embargo and subsequent astronomical rise in oil prices. His expertise and experience in national and international economic affairs and his ability to take charge in crisis situations, such as the 1977 terrorist hijacking and commando raid, soon became apparent. Within two years, inflation was brought under control (below 5 percent), and unemployment was reduced from more than 1,000,000 to less than 700,000 (still well above pre-1973 figures). Moreover, the German international balance of payments remained in the black; by 1976 the Federal Republic's sale of manufactured goods to the Middle Eastern oil countries exceeded the value of its petroleum imports.

In addition, the Schmidt governments (1974–1976, 1976–1980, 1980–1982) continued, albeit at a lower key, the Ostpolitik of their predecessors. A 1976 treaty with Poland extended the 1970 pact and provided for the resettlement of German nationals living in Poland but desiring to move to the Federal Republic. A variety of supplemental agreements with East Germany and the Soviet Union were also concluded. During the 1980 Afghanistan crisis, Schmidt consistently warned about losing the benefits achieved through détente.

Unlike Brandt, Schmidt had little patience with the SPD's left. He is a strong supporter of the market economy. While chancellor, he maintained a close relationship with the Federal Republic's economic and industrial elite. Indeed, in 1980 he was seen even by many CDU voters as more capable than the Union's own candidate. Schmidt's electoral and policy successes, however, were not matched in his relationship to his party, the Social Democrats. Specifically, he was unable to overcome and integrate the opposition of the SPD left and especially the Young Socialists. He also underestimated the intensity of opposition within his own party and in the country as a whole to nuclear power as an energy source. Soon after the 1980 election victory Schmidt was once again confronted with opposition to his leadership by segments of the SPD. Budget cuts in social programs, due in large part to the worsening economic situation, the planned deployment of new middle-range nuclear missiles in Western Europe, and arms sales to Saudi Arabia, were issues that prompted sharp criticism from the SPD left. The Schmidt government by 1981 also became a prime target for the peace movement, a loose collection of environmentalists, religious pacifists, and elements of the SPD left, which strongly opposed the NATO missile decision. The movement accused Schmidt of deferring to the alleged American military strategy of attempting to localize at least the first stages of a nuclear conflict to Europe and specifically the Federal Republic. Schmidt rejected this charge, but the peace movement had significant support among SPD activists and became a force that seriously weakened the governing coalition.

On September 17, 1982, Helmut Schmidt lost his parliamentary majority when the Free Democratic party, the junior partner in the governing coalition with the SPD since 1969, left the government. Two weeks later, in the first successful use of the constructive vote of no confidence procedure, Helmut Kohl became West Germany's sixth chancellor.

Chancellor Democracy under Helmut Kohl

Helmut Kohl has been a significant figure on the West German political scene since 1969 when he became chief executive of the state of the Rhineland-Palatinate (Rheinland-Pfalz). His success at the state level coincided with the decline of his party, the CDU, in national politics. After CDU/CSU defeats in 1969 and 1972, Kohl moved from his provincial power base, and in 1973 he assumed the leadership of a divided and weakened CDU. He is credited with initiating a thorough modernization and revitalization of the party's organization. In 1976, as the chancellor candidate of the CDU/CSU, he conducted a well-planned campaign that almost toppled the Schmidt government.

Born in 1930, Kohl is the first chancellor who did not experience the Third Reich and World War II as an adult. Following the completion of his university studies in the early 1950s, he began a political career. Like his predecessor, Helmut Schmidt, Kohl is a political pragmatist. Unlike Schmidt, he does not have the reputation as a crisis manager or innovative political leader.

The most difficult problem confronting the Kohl government has been the economy. Like other West European states, Germany has been slow to recover from the 1981–1983 recession. Cuts in social programs, tax incentives for business investment, and a general tax reform have been the chief means he has used to stimulate the economy. Kohl, however, is generally identified with the moderate or Catholic labor wing of the Chrstian Democrats, which supports the extensive social welfare state.

In foreign affairs Kohl and the Christian Democrats have been more enthusiastic in their support of the United States and the Atlantic Alliance in recent years than the Social Democrats. In spite of widespread protests and the opposition of the Social Democrats and the Greens, the Kohl government in November 1983 secured parliamentary approval for the stationing of new intermediate-range missiles. Kohl's major foreign policy success has been the dramatic improvement in Bonn's relations with East Germany. Since 1983 Bonn has approved almost $2 billion in loan guarantees to East Berlin. In return, the East Germans have eased restrictions on intra-German travel and permitted over 40,000 of its citizens to leave for the Federal Republic, the largest number since the construction of the Berlin Wall. The two German states have also concluded extensive agreements on cultural, scientific, and economic issues.

In 1985 the controversial visit of President Reagan to a German military cemetery, which also contained the remains of SS soldiers, provoked the sharpest sustained ciriticism that Kohl has faced since taking office. The visit was originally proposed by the chancellor as a symbolic gesture of reconciliation between the United States and the Federal Republic. In the United States, Jewish organizations, veterans groups, many members of Congress, and even some of Reagan's strongest supporters opposed the visit and urged Chancellor Kohl to propose an alternative. In Germany Kohl was charged with sloppy planning and insensitivity to the horrors of the Nazi era. But two weeks before the visit Kohl, speaking at the Bergen-Belsen concentration camp, clearly stated that "Germany bears historical responsibility for the crimes of the Nazi tyranny. This responsibility is reflected not least in never-ending shame."

In spite of his party's losses at the 1987 election, Kohl's coalition government retained a solid majority in the parliament. Unlike Helmut Schmidt, Kohl is an active party leader who carefully attends to the tasks of political fence-mending and coalition-building within the diverse Christian Democratic Union. He is portrayed by some segments of the media as a weak leader, prone to mistakes and unable to control several of the strong personalities in his cabinet and party.

Nonetheless, his record shows several notable successes. The 1987 United States–Soviet treaty eliminating middle-range nuclear missiles from Europe vindicated the strong position he took against the peace movement's demand that the missiles not be stationed in the Federal Republic. During his tenure, West Germany has assumed a greater leadership role within the European Community and has deepened its economic and military ties to France, including the creation in 1988 of a joint Franco-German defense council and military brigade. Although the economy remains sluggish, his government has reduced deficit spending, cut taxes, and with the help of the Federal Bank (see Chapter 7) kept inflation low.

The Federal President

The framers of the Basic Law were determined to avoid the problems created by the dual executive of president and chancellor during the Weimar Republic and thus made the office of federal president clearly subordinate to the chancellor and parliament in the policymaking process. In contrast to the Weimar system, the president is not directly elected but is chosen every five years by a federal assembly (*Bundesversammlung*) comprising all Bundestag deputies and an equal number of deputies from the various state parliaments. The president is the ceremonial head of state; he formally proposes the chancellor and his cabinet for election by the Bundestag; he signs all laws and must certify that they were passed in the prescribed manner; and he formally appoints and excuses national civil servants and federal judges. If the federal government and the Bundesrat request, the federal president can declare a state of legislative emergency that would enable the government, but not the president, to rule by decree. In all these functions, however, the president is merely carrying out the will of the government or parliament. The question as to whether the president has the power to refuse to accept the recommendation of a chancellor for a particular cabinet appointment has never been legally resolved. Yet, on those few occasions when the president has in various ways indicated his reservations or objections to a particular candidate, he has seldom been able to block the appointment.

The president does, however, have the right to be consulted and thoroughly informed about planned governmental actions. In the event of a parliamentary crisis, he is expected to be a mediator and conciliator. Thus, in selecting candidates for this position, emphasis has been placed on personalities with a fairly nonpartisan image, who evoke few strong negative feelings among the parties and whose background and personal style would make them appropriate representatives of the new Republic.

The first president, Theodor Heuss (1949–1959), had all these qualities. A former journalist and parliamentary deputy of the left liberals during the Weimar Republic, he had played a major role in the founding of the Free Democratic party and in the drafting of the Basic Law. Heuss carefully avoided any partisanship during his two terms and was an effective symbol of the new, democratic state both at home and abroad. His successor, Heinrich Lübke (1959–1969) had been minister of agriculture in the Adenauer government and generally followed in the traditions established by Heuss. He became, however, a frequent target of press and media criticism for occasional lapses into partisanship and his alleged participation as an architect in the construction of concentration camp buildings during the Third Reich. This latter charge, however, was never substantiated, and Lübke steadfastly denied any involvement. His personal preference for a Grand Coalition between the CDU/CSU and SPD, long before the alignment actually took place, was well known.

The third president of the Republic and the first Social Democrat was Gustav Heinemann, who was elected with the help of the Free Democrats in 1969. Heinemann was also the first president whose general political philosophy was clearly left of center. A CDU minister in the early Adenauer cabinets, he left the party and government in 1950 over Adenauer's decision to rearm and founded a short-lived, small party that advocated neutralism in foreign policy. In 1957, he joined the SPD and quickly rose to a prominent position within the party, and in 1966 he became minister of justice in the Grand Coalition. Unlike his two predecessors, he did not seek reelection in 1974, largely for reasons of age and health. During his tenure, he raised the prestige of the office and distinguished himself by his concern for the underprivileged in German society and his support for the conciliatory foreign policy of the Federal Republic toward its Eastern neighbors.

In 1974, Walter Scheel became the Republic's fourth president and the second Free Democrat to hold the post. When elected, Scheel was also at the height of his career as party leader and foreign minister. As president, Scheel explored briefly the possibilities of enlarging the power of the office. He delayed signing some legislation and refused to sign a few other bills on the grounds of their questionable constitutionality. He also attempted to challenge the authority of some Cabinet ministers to dismiss top ministerial aides.[37] His efforts were firmly blocked by the chancellor and the parliament, and there was little support for Scheel's exploration into the constitutional limits of his office.

The majority in the federal assembly held by the SPD and FDP disappeared after 1974 as the two coalition parties suffered declines in support in various state elections. By mid-1978 it was apparent that Scheel could not be reelected for a second term without the support of at least some Christian Democrats. The CDU (and especially its more liberal wing) was willing to support Scheel's reelection as one way of signaling to the Free Democrats that the CDU was still interested in a possible future coalition, and as a way of avoiding an intraparty conflict over the selection of its own candidate. The coalition and particularly the SPD used the upcoming presidential election as a campaign issue during state elections in 1978 and 1979, urging voters to support the SPD or FDP as a means of keeping the popular Scheel in office in Bonn. The CDU leadership responded to this strategy by announcing that the Union would present its own candidate, who, given the CDU/CSU majority, would be elected.

After a brief period of intraparty maneuvering, the Union finally united behind Dr. Karl Carstens, a former chairman of the Union's *Fraktion* and top-ranking civil servant in the Foreign Ministry and chancellor's office. Although from northern Germany, Carstens's conservative-nationalist image also made him acceptable to the Bavarians. In May 1979 Carstens was elected on a straight party vote by the federal assembly as the fifth president of the Republic. Revelations about his membership in the Nazi party while a young law student provoked strong criticism from some foreign countries, but it was not a significant factor in his election. Some SPD and FDP leaders questioned whether his partisan past would be a hindrance in the office, but after his election he took care to maintain a neutral political stance.

In 1984 Carstens declined to run for a second term. The Christian Democrats, with an absolute majority in the federal assembly, nominated Richard von Weizsäcker as Carstens's successor. Von Weizsäcker, who had been the governing mayor of West Berlin since 1981, was widely regarded as an ideal choice. A lawyer by training, he had been a leading lay figure in the Protestant church and a prominent member of the Christian Democrats' moderate wing. As a sign of his nonpartisan image, the Social Democrats did not nominate their own candidate.

Since his election, one of President von Weizsäcker's most notable achievements was his address on the fortieth anniversary of Nazi Germany's unconditional surrender, May 8, 1985. For the first time a major West German political leader challenged the traditional explanation used by older, "ordinary" Germans that they "knew nothing" about the Holocaust:

> . . . every German was able to experience what his Jewish compatriots had to suffer, ranging from plain apathy and hidden intolerance to outright hatred. Who could remain unsuspecting after the burning of the synagogues, the plundering, the stigmatization with the Star of David, the deprivation of rights, the ceaseless violation of human dignity? Whoever opened his eyes and ears and sought information could not fail to notice that Jews were being deported. . . . When the unspeakable truth of the Holocaust then became known, all too many of us claimed that they had not known anything about it or even suspected anything.[38]

This speech, which attracted worldwide attention, illustrates the capacity of the Federal president to bring important questions that transcend party politics to the attention of the public.

Summary: The Formal Lawmaking Process

PREPARLIAMENTARY STAGE

About three-fourth of all bills submitted to the parliament are conceived and drafted by the government. The impetus for such legislation, however, may come from outside—from interest groups, the governing coalition parties, parliamentary delegations, or programs. In some cases, a proposal from the parliamentary opposition may even find its way into a bill, as was the case with the revision of the pension system passed in 1972. Some idea of the mix between ministerial bureaucracy, party, and parliament can be seen in the replies of two SPD cabinet ministers to the question of where and how policy proposals originate. According to one minister:

> The overwhelming number of bills submitted by me can be traced to my and my ministry's conceptions and preparatory work. In one or another case, the suggestion to prepare a specific bill came from the coalition *Fraktionen,* but was limited to their suggestion for a ministerial initiative. The way in which such initiatives were then considered and formulated was left up to me.[39]

For the other minister:

> The source of bills nearly always goes back to multiple impulses and demands, thus making a rare "monocausal" explanation. Parliamentary decisions, resolutions and electoral programs of parties, discussions among the public about long-range development trends or suddenly emerging problems, preparatory work in the ministries, the chancellor's decision about the government program and, last but not least, the personal interest of a minister produce the most diverse combinations, which often make it impossible subsequently to sort out the decisive factors for the origin of a law.[40]

During the ministerial drafting process, the rules of procedures in German governmental departments, as discussed in Chapter 4, also allow civil servants to consult with the affected interest groups. This is done as a matter of course, and the interest group–state bureaucracy relationship is well established. However, in order to ostensibly simplify the consultation process, ministries are generally required to negotiate only with the leadership or national offices of these interest groups. In practice, this procedure contributes to the centralized, hierarchical character of both governmental and interest-group bureaucracies.

If a policy area is the concern of more than one ministry, such as economics and finance or defense and foreign policy, interministerial negotiations will take place. In cases of conflict due to overlapping responsibilities, the chancellor's office will also be informed and, if necessary, will mediate and resolve the dispute. This is consistent with the chancellor's responsibility for the overall direction of policy. Most bills requiring new or increased appropriations will also be cleared with the finance ministry at the drafting stage. This planning and drafting stage, as Braunthal has found, involves in many cass a "protracted bargaining process among specialists and politicians" within the ministries and governing parties.[41] Repeated revisions are very frequent.

Following ministerial approval, the draft legislation will be presented to the full cabinet for approval before its submission to parliament. Most internal (governmental) opposition to the legislation will have been resolved before formal discussion in the cabinet. Although most cabinets—especially since Adenauer—have pursued a consensual style of decisionmaking, the chancellor has in fact veto power over any ministerial proposal, and likewise the support of the chancellor virtually ensures cabinet approval. This latter situation has rarely occurred, although there is some evidence that Adenauer at various times, especially over questions of foreign policy and rearmament during the 1950s, was in a minority position.

In practice, however, the chancellor's power can be limited by the size of the government's parliamentary majority, his personal interest in the policy area, the demands of the coalition partner, and the internal pressures from his party and the state bureaucracy. Governments with a relatively small majority have had difficulty in getting their proposed legislation through the chamber. The first Brandt government (1969–1972), with a majority of only twelve which dwindled to zero by 1972, was able to pass a relatively low 75 percent of its proposed legislation. After the 1972 election, which gave the SPD-FDP coalition a majority of about fifty seats, the government's success ratio rose to 93 percent, the highest percentage since the third Adenauer government (1957–1961).

Chancellors such as Adenauer and Brandt had little interest in many domestic policy areas and were willing to trade off concessions in this area for support in foreign policy and defense matters. Brandt's indifference or even disdain for issues such as a liberalized abortion law—an issue of considerable importance to elements in the SPD—was a major factor in the long delay before its passage in 1974.

During their coalitions with the Free Democrats, both major parties had to make concessions to their junior partner. The Christian Democrats, especially after Adenauer's departure, were urged by the FDP to pursue a more dynamic foreign policy toward Eastern Europe and to take a less clerical position on issues such as church schools. In collaboration with the CDU's conservative business wing, the Free Democrats were also able to block several social welfare programs advocated by the Union's labor wing. From 1969 to 1982, the Free Democrats played a major role in the delay that plagued the SPD's commitment to internal reform in areas such as codetermination and the reform of vocational education.

PARLIAMENTARY STAGE

After cabinet approval, the draft legislation is presented to the Bundesrat for a first reading. The Bundesrat at this point can either approve, reject, or amend the bill. Regardless of Bundesrat action at this stage, however, the bill will be submitted to the Bundestag; for, even if the Bundesrat rejects a bill, it can still be overriden by the Bundestag. In the Bundestag, the bill will be discussed in the Fraktionen. At this point, party strategy and policy toward the bill will be formally discussed and determined. The bill is then given its first reading during which only introductory formal debate is held, with no amendments allowed. Referral to the appropriate committee follows this first reading.

Because the government parties have a majority in each committee, a bill is rarely returned to the floor with a negative report; committees also cannot pigeonhole a bill. In many cases, however, after consideration of a bill the committee will propose amendments.

After the committee report, a second and more thorough debate takes place in the Bundestag. At this time, amendments to the bill will be considered. House debate will be led by specialists in the policy area who act as spokesmen (*Berichterstatter*) for the committee. If, after the second reading and debate, a bill is approved without amendment, the third and final reading follows immediately. If the bill has been amended and passed in the second reading, a waiting period of at least two days after the distribution of the revised bill to all deputies is observed before the final vote.

Following Bundestag action, the bill returns to the Bundesrat for a second reading. If the policy area involved requires Bundesrat approval and if the Bundesrat has vetoed the policy, the bill is dead. When the policy area is not one affecting the states (defense, for example) a Bundesrat veto can be overriden by a simple Bundestag majority. If the Bundesrat veto was by a majority of two-thirds or more, the veto must be overriden by a majority of two-thirds.

In most cases, as discussed earlier in this chapter, the Bundesrat will object to parts of a bill affecting the states, and these differences will then be refered to a joint conference committee (*Vermittlungsausschuss*) for resolution. In some cases, Bundesrat objections are already incorporated into amendments introduced in the Bundestag. The report of the conference committee is then submitted to both houses for approval. Finally, the bill is examined for constitutionality by the chancellor's office, justice ministry, and president's office before being signed and promulgated by the president.

This entire process has been executive-dominated, and our examination of the state bureaucracy in Chapter 7 should make this even more apparent. Nonetheless, there are instances when the government will meet resistance from its parliamentary delegations after the submission of legislative proposals. In most of these cases, interest groups disappointed in their preparliamentary bargaining with the ministries will attempt to mobilize their parliamentary contacts for one last try at revision. In addition, the increasing politicization of the Bundesrat and the new assertiveness of the Bundestag may be indicative of even more difficulty for chancellor democracy in the future.

NOTES

1. John D. Nagle, "Elite Transformations in a Pluralist Democracy: Occupational and Educational Backgrounds of Bundestag Members, 1949–1972" (manuscript, Syracuse University, 1974).

2. Adalbert Hess, "Berufstatistik der Mitglieder des 10. Deutschen Bundestages, *"Zeitschrift für Parlamentsfragen.* 14, no. 1 (December 1983): 487–489.

3. The Bundestag's committee that deals with most civil service questions (Domestic Affairs) is composed largely (80 percent) of civil servants, and the informal subcommittee that specializes in civil service salaries is made up solely of civil servants.

4. Rolf Zundel, "Ein Parlament der Regierungsräte?" *Die Zeit,* 28 November 1969, p. 12.

5. Gerhard Loewenberg, *Parliament in the German Political System* (Ithaca: Cornell University Press, 1966), p. 46.

6. Ulrich Lohmar, "Das Hohe Haus," *Das Parlament,* no. 42 (19 October 1974), p. 9.

7. Nagle, "Elite Transformations," p. 36.

8. Ibid., p. 37.

9. Rolf Zundel, "Das Parlament hat sich gemausert," *Die Zeit,* 11 July 1969, p. 6.

10. Carl-Christian Kaiser, "Teach-In der Spezialisten oder Forum der Nation?" *Die Zeit,* 9 January 1973, p. 40.

11. Ibid.

12. Gerard Braunthal, *The West German Legislative Process* (Ithaca: Cornell University Press, 1972), p. 246.

13. Gerhard Loewenberg, "Role of Parliaments in Modern Political Systems," in *Modern Parliaments, Change or Decline?* ed. Gerhard Loewenberg (Chicago, New York: Aldine-Atherton, 1971), pp. 15ff.

14. Kurt Sontheimer, *Grundzüge des politischen Systems der Bundesrepublik Deutschland* (Munich: Piper Verlag, 1984), pp. 162–163.

15. Institut für Demoskopie surveys cited in Peter Schindler, ed., *Datenhandbuch zur Geschichte des Deutschen Bundestages,* (Bonn: Presse und Informationszentrum des Deutschen Bundestages, 1983), p. 1048.

16. Institut für Demoskopie surveys, Nos. 0040 and 4036.

17. There are also four members without voting power from West Berlin.

18. Heinz Laufer, "Der Bundesrat," *Aus Politik und Zeitgeschichte,* no. 4 (22 January 1972), pp. 50–52.

19. Karlheinz Neunreither, *Der Bundesrat zwischen Politik und Verwaltung* (Heidelberg: Quelle & Mayer Verlag, 1959), pp. 84–86.

20. Laufer, "Der Bundesrat," p. 52.

21. Norbert Prill and Jochen van Oerssen, "Was wird aus dem Bundesrat?" *Die Zeit,* 23 July 1971, p. 36; and Peter Schindler, "Der Bundesrat in parteipolitischer Auseinandersetzung," *Zeitschrift für Parlamentsfragen* 3, no. 2 (June 1972): 148–149.

22. *Die Zeit,* 28 June 1974: 8.

23. Ingo von Münch, "Der Bundesrat als Gegenregierung?" *Die Zeit,* 5 April 1974, p. 5.

24. Peter Pulzer, "Responsible Party Government and Stable Coalition: The Case of the German Federal Republic." *Political Studies,* 26 (June 1978): 181–208; and Karl Friedrich Fromme, *Gesetzgebung im Wiederstreit: Wer beherrscht den Bundesrat? Die Kontroverse 1969–1976* (Stuttgart: Bonn Aktuell Verlag, 1976).

25. This has not prevented opposition parties, however, from attempting to dismiss individual cabinet ministers through no-confidence resolutions. Such resolutions have been introduced at various times since 1949. They have all been either rejected, tabled, or withdrawn. This is a political tactic designed to embarrass the chancellor and the cabinet member. Even if a resolution against an individual minister passed, it would have no legal effect. For a listing of these resolutions from 1949–1982 and a

discussion of their constitutionality see Peter Schindler, ed., *Datenhandbuch zur Geschichte des Deutschen Bundestages 1949 bis 1982* (Bonn: Presse und Informationszentrum des Deutschen Bundestages, 1983), pp. 418–421.

26. F. F. Ridley, "Chancellor Government as a Political System and the German Constitution," *Parliamentary Affairs* 19, no. 4 (February 1966): 446–461; Kenneth Dyson, "The German Federal Chancellor's Office," *Political Quarterly* 45, no., 3 (July-September 1974): 364–371.

27. Braunthal, *West German Legislative Process*.

28. Rolf-Peter Lange, "Auslesestrukturen bei der Besetzung von Regierungsämtern," in *Parteiensystem in der Legitimationskrise,* ed. Jürgen Dittberner and Rolf Ebbighausen (Opladen: Westdeutscher Verlag, 1973), pp. 132–171.

29. H. Pierre Secher, "Controlling the New German Military Elite: The Political Role of the Parliamentary Defense Commissioner in the Federal Republic," *Proceedings of the American Philosophical Society* 109, no. 2 (April 1965): 63.

30. Kurt Sontheimer, *The West German Political System* (New York: Praeger, 1973), p. 172. Public opinion surveys generally find that the military is considered a rather unimportant institution when compared to the parliament, the chancellor, the courts, and even the federal bank. See Elisabeth Noelle-Neumann, ed., *The Germans: Public Opinion Polls, 1967–1980.* (Westport, CT: Greenwood Press, 1981), p. 188.

31. The German figure, however, is actually higher than that found in some other European countries such as Italy (28 percent) and Belgium (25 percent). Survey data drawn from the International Values Study cited in Elisabeth Noelle-Neumann and Renate Köcher, *Die verletzte Nation,* Stuttgart: Deutsche Verlags-Anstalt, 1987, p. 61. A 1985 study also found a low (33 percent) willingness to fight among Germans. *Euro-barometre,* no. 24, December, 1985, p. 26.

32. When Globke came under heavy criticism for his activity during the Third Reich (he wrote the legal commentaries to the infamous Nuremberg laws that legalized persecution of Jews), Adenauer refused to dismiss his most important aide.

33. Sontheimer, *The West German Political System,* p. 131.

34. Karl-Dietrich Bracher, *The German Dictatorship* (New York: Praeger, 1973), pp. 499–500.

35. In 1987, twenty years after his death and twenty-four years after his retirement, about 60 percent of West Germans in a national survey ranked Adenauer as the most successful of the five Chancellors who have preceded the current incumbent, Helmut Kohl. Helmut Schmidt with 19 percent was ranked second. EMNID survey cited in *Der Spiegel,* 41, no. 18 (April 27, 1987): 59.

36. Klaus Bölling, *Republic in Suspense* (New York: Praeger, 1965), p. 74.

37. "Die Kunst, bis an die Grenze zu gehen," *Der Spiegel,* 15 November, 1976): pp 30–34. See also Kurt Becker, "Wieviel Macht soll der Bundespräsident haben? *Die Zeit,* 19 November 1976, p. 3.

38. For key excerpts from the von Weizsäcker speech see *The New York Times,* 9 May 1985, p. A20.

39. Cited in Gerard Braunthal, "The Policy Function of the German Social Democratic Party," *Comparative Politics* 9, no. 2 (January 1977): 143.

40. Ibid.

41. Braunthal, *West German Legislative Process,* p. 231.

Policymaking Institutions II: Administration, Semipublic Institutions, and Courts

The policy process neither begins nor ends with the formal decisionmaking of government and parliament that we examined in the preceding chapter. The implementation and adjudication of policy decisions are also an integral part of government. In modern, developed political systems these functions are largely the responsibility of the state's administration, courts, and semipublic institutions. Our concern in this chapter is with these institutions and their role in the policy process.

Although Germany did not invent bureaucracy or courts, it certainly contributed heavily to their refinement and development. The Prussian civil service of the Hohenzollern emperors became a model of efficiency, dedication, and incorruptibility adopted not only throughout the Reich but in other countries as well. The German judiciary and the massive codification of civil and criminal law, completed at the turn of the century, influenced legal developments in such diverse settings as Greece and Japan.

During the past century, specific governments and regimes have come and gone, but the civil service and judiciary have remained essentially unchanged in structure and procedures. Little wonder that Germans at both elite and mass levels have had more confidence in dealing with their bureaucracy and courts than with other branches of government.[1] The legalistic-bureaucratic mentality attributed to the political culture is in part a result of the far greater stability of these institutions and hence the more extensive experience Germans have had with them.

The Federal Republic also has an extensive network of semipublic agencies that are either independent of both national and state governments or have their own separate administrative structures. These institutions—most notably the Federal Bank, the social security and health systems, and the Federal Labor Institute—play key roles in economic, social, and welfare policymaking and implementation. Our concern in this chapter is with these institutions—the state bureaucracy, semipublic institutions, and courts—and their role in the policy process.

THE DEVELOPMENT OF THE WEST GERMAN ADMINISTRATIVE AND JUDICIAL SYSTEM

The performance of the courts and state bureaucracy, defined in a narrow technical sense of getting the job done, has been good. The commitment of the bureaucracy and the judiciary to the values and processes of liberal democracy, however, has been less satisfactory. During the Weimar Republic, both institutions were at best ambivalent toward and at worst hostile to the new regime. Given their monarchical origins and the nationalist, upper-class character of their personnel, together with the association of the Weimar Republic with military defeat and foreign humiliation, these orientations should not be surprising. During the Third Reich, whatever independence and sense of integrity the judiciary and bureaucracy had were soon lost as both became tools of the dictatorship. As Arnold Brecht, himself a former high-ranking civil servant in Prussia until driven out by the Nazis, observed:

> By the end of the Hitler era the German civil service had become a worldwide epithet for irresponsible servility, for turncoat opportunism, for bureaucratic self-preservation and for an utterly undemocratic type of authoritarianism. Its renowned incorruptibility had been shown to have an unexpected limit. While its members would not be bribed individually, as a group they had surrendered to the corruption of their work by the governing party. Gone with the storm was the admiration of the world.[2]

After 1945 the Western Allies intended to purge both institutions of Nazi party members and sympathizers and reorganize them to facilitate their democratization. Yet the occupation authorities soon found that the dismissal of all party members from the bureaucracy and judiciary would bring administration to a standstill.

Thus, in the case of the civil service, although Nazis were removed from top-level leadership positions and replaced by known antifascist or "clean" civil servants, the middle and lower levels remained essentially intact and were transferred to the various local and state governments that were being formed by the military occupation. In all, about 53,000 civil servants were dismissed for party membership in the immediate postwar period, but only about 1,000 were permanently excluded from any future employment.[3] In 1951, after the restoration of partial sovereignty to the Federal Republic, a Reinstatement Act gave even most of the dismissed party members full-pension credits for service during the Third Reich and reemployment in civil service. The result was that by the early 1950s from 40 to 80 percent of officials in many departments were former party members.[4]

A similar development took place in the judiciary. Initially all courts were closed, and all Nazi party courts and special tribunals were abolished. Only those courts then devoid of Nazi influence and personnel and sanctioned by occupation authorities were reopened. At first, justice practically came to a standstill. By 1946, however, the regular system was functioning much as it had before the Nazi seizure of power.[5]

The elimination of Nazi party members from the judiciary was never accomplished. The problem was that the occupation authorities soon found that the great majority of all judicial officials, judges, and prosecutors had been in the party. Each case was decided on an individual basis, and distinctions were made between fellow travelers of varying degrees and committed Nazis. The occupation authorities, as Loewenstein reports, also discovered many non-Nazi judges seeking to protect colleagues who had been only nominal party members.[6] In spite of party membership, "if a man was a good judge, his redemption and readmission to the depleted ranks were made easy. The judicial caste had not failed its members."[7] At most, about 2,000 judicial officials lost their jobs, and only a few fanatics were permanently disqualified.

The abandonment for all practical purposes of the denazification and democratization of the civil service and judiciary was due to the Allies' desire to return to stability and normalcy as soon as possible. Countering the perceived Soviet threat to Western Europe, which heightened after the fall of Czechoslovakia and the Berlin Blockade in 1948, became more important than major internal reform in the Western zones.

Besides the absence of major personnel changes at the grassroots level, the traditional legal and administrative structure of the German state was for the most part maintained. Apart from the changing of state boundaries and the creation of several new states, city, county, and village boundaries were retained or restored to their pre-1933 form.

Denazification could also be abandoned with little short-run risk because the vast majority of former party members were more than willing to accept the rule of their new masters. Very few had actually been committed party members, and many of these had learned their lesson and were hardly inclined to subvert the new state. But neither could this generation of civil servants and judges be expected to show a genuine commitment to the ideals of liberty, equality, and the democratic process. The reform of the state administration was thus postponed and indeed, as we shall discuss, it is a task that the Republic—over forty years later—is still confronting.

STATE ADMINISTRATION

Structure

The German civil servant may work at one of several governmental levels: national, state, regional, district, county, or local. In spite of this decentralized structure of the state, civil servants generally share a common background and training, and work within a similarly structured bureaucratic framework. The occasional coordination and integration between these multiple governmental layers is in part the result of this common training and administrative framework.

German administrative units are very hierarchical but not centralized. The bureaucratic pyramid is very steep, but there is little actual direct control at the top of the activities in the middle and at the base.

At the national level there are seventeen federal ministries ranging in size from the Ministry of Finance with about 1,800 employees to the Ministry of Inner-German Relations (Bonn's relations with East Germany) with 300 employees. All ministries have a common structure, and any doubt as to what is meant by the term "hierarchical structure" should be dispelled by Table 7.1, which shows one fairly typical ministry, Economics.

Ministries are divided into four levels: executive (the minister and his state secretaries), departments, subdepartments, and sections (bureaus). The ministry's personnel are classified into five groups: (1) political officials, (2) higher service, (3) elevated upper-middle service, (4) intermediate service, and (5) simple, or lower-level, service. Also within groups 2 to 5, but usually in the lower three levels, a public employee can be classified as a *Beamter* (official) with lifetime tenure, a white-collar employee, or a manual worker. Almost all civil servants at the top two levels are officials, whereas most of those in the intermediate and lower-level service are either white-collar employees or manual workers. The elevated service, group 3, is about equally divided between Beamten and white-collar workers.

Within each organizational level, however, different types of personnel with varying ranks, job titles, and responsibilities can be found. Beginning at the top of Table 7.1, we see that the minister's two state secretaries and the eight department heads are all "political" civil servants. Thus, although they are the highest-ranking civil servants in the ministry, they can be removed, transferred, or if possible, pensioned by the minister. In spite of their formal political status, most state secretaries and ministerial directors (the rank of most department heads) are long-time tenured civil servants. If they are not retained by the minister, they must by law be transferred to another job suitable to their status. If Germany had an administrative class or *grands corps* of civil servants, as in Britain and France, they would be at this level. But there are no graduates of elite schools whose members are distributed throughout the various ministries.

The subdepartment heads (rank: *Ministerial Dirigent,* or councillor) and the section or bureau chiefs, although at two different organizational levels, are both

TABLE 7.1. HIERARCHICAL STRUCTURE OF THE MINISTRY OF ECONOMICS

Organizational Position	Employees	Service Group	Title
State secretaries	2	Political official	State secretary
Department heads	8	Political official	Ministerial director
Subdepartment heads	22	Higher service	Ministerial councillor
Section heads	131	Higher service	Varies from senior governmental councillor to ministerial councillor
Section assistants	356	Higher service	Varies from governmental councillor to governmental director
Officials	(282)		
White-collar workers	(74)		
Caseworkers	408	Elevated service	Varies from governmental inspector to senior official councillor
Officials	(268)		
White-collar workers	(140)		
Clerical and secretarial staff	611	Intermediate service	Varies from governmental assistant to official inspector
Officials	(45)		
White-collar workers	(566)		
Custodians, messengers, chauffeurs, copy machine operators	221	Simple, or low-level, service	Varies from office assistant to senior office master
Officials	(54)		
White-collar workers	(63)		
Manual workers	(104)		

	Number	Percentage
Total	1,759	
Officials	804	46
White-collar workers	851	48
Manual workers	104	6
		100

part of the higher service. They all have academic training and decision-making responsibilities within their bureau or subdepartment and are personally and legally responsible for decisions that bear their signatures. The section assistants constitute the lowest group in the higher level service. These are comparable to junior executive positions. Their titles vary depending on the length of their service and the size of their section.

The elevated service is composed largely of caseworkers, or *Sachbearbeiter*. Because the higher service (section assistants to state secretaries) requires a completed academic training, few case workers will ever enter it, even though their experience and job knowledge may make them more qualified than some of their superiors.

The intermediate-level service is made up of clerical and secretarial staff and comprises about 35 percent of most ministries' total personnel. At the bottom of the organizational ladder are those in the simple service (messengers, copy machine operators, drivers, custodians). Thus about 30 percent of a typical ministry's staff have executive or junior executive positions; another 25 percent are caseworkers; and the remaining 45 percent have clerical, secretarial, or custodial functions.

The key unit is the section, or bureau, and the key personnel are the section heads (*Referenten*). Each section is assigned responsibility for a particular policy area. The development, initiation, and supervision of ministerial policy is centered in these sections. They are the real powerhouses of West German administration, and as one frustrated reformer has put it, the section heads are the "princes" of the policymaking process within the ministries.[8]

The average section is very small, with only about three to seven members: a section head, one or two assistants, caseworkers, and clerical personnel. Overall there are about 1,700 such sections at the national level. To a large extent, national policy, as formulated in the ministries, is the sum of what these 1,700 parts produce.

Critics of Bonn's administration have focused on this hierarchic yet decentralized structure. It is, they contend, highly fragmented and discourages comprehensive policy planning or major reform initiatives that require extensive interdepartment, interministerial, or federal-state cooperation: Small sections tend to work best with small problems.[9] Since the top political officials in each ministry have so little staff, they cannot in practice exercise the control they have in theory. Expertise is at the bottom, in the sections.

The small size of each section and the practice of making the section head personally and legally responsible for the section's decisions make success or failure highly visible. Promotion is related to success. Hence sections tend to concentrate on limited, short-run projects that will in effect yield only minor modifications in an already existing policy but that will be judged as successful by superiors who approve of the existing policy. "Risky" projects will be avoided in part because they exceed a section's limited capacity but also because their failure can be easily attributed to specific individuals.

At the ministerial stage of policy development, a complex process of bargaining and negotiation takes place between the experts at the base, the section head, the department and subdepartment chiefs, and the executive (minister and state secretary). The influence of outside forces, such as interest groups, parties, and consultants, is most directly felt at the executive and department levels. The sections are relatively insulated and secure in the knowledge that they have as much, if not more, expertise than anyone else in the "house," even with the outside specialists whom the executive may call in. Shoring up the top to contend with the princes in the sections is, according to many students of the system, its most pressing need.[10] Political leadership is to initiate, oversee, coordinate, and integrate policy programs, but it does not have the necessary resources. The ministry's political leadership committed, especially in recent times, to major policy innovation is thus somewhat frustrated. The problem is not an unwillingness of the middle and lower levels to respond but an inability of political leadership to formulate and operationalize policy goals because of a lack of staff and planning capability. The problems of fragmentation and hierarchy at the national level are compounded by similar structural frameworks at the state and local levels.

Personnel

When the Federal Republic was established in 1949, many of its first civil servants came directly from either the unified (American, British, and French zones) Economics Administration in Frankfurt or the Länder bureaucracies. Early coordination between the central government and the states was thus facilitated by the common background and training of civil servants at both levels. From the beginning, the Bonn Republic had a well-trained, relatively intact bureaucracy in its service.

By the 1980s one out of almost every eight Germans was employed by the state. But only about 45 percent of this group have tenured civil servant status, and about 10 percent work at the national level. As Table 7.2 shows, Bonn employs an 11 percent of all Beamten, as compared to 78 percent for the Länder and 11 percent for local government. Moreover, most of the national-level civil servants are not employed in the federal ministries but in various offices (tax administration, weather service, air traffic control, economic agencies). Only about 20,000 civil servants are directly employed in the federal ministries. And as we have seen, most of these are not in policymaking positions. Considering the 1,600 sections chiefs and their assistants as policymakers, and adding subdepartment and department heads, the total number of civil servants with policymaking initiatives is about 3,000. All others are administrators in the strict sense of the term: They carry out the decisions of others.

German public officials at all levels are by law and custom a special group with unique privileges and obligations. The civil servant is expected to be loyal and obedient to the state and his superiors and willing to adjust his private life to the demands of the service. In exchange for this commitment to the state, the official receives lifetime tenure and a salary and benefits that enable him and his family to securely maintain a lifestyle commensurate with his rank. In short, for loyal and correct service, the Beamte receives a guarantee of lifetime security and middle-class status. Other occupational groups must take their chances in the free market economy, but the civil servant is risk-free. The postwar restoration of this privileged status, which has its origins in the age of monarchy, was opposed by American occupation authorities and the Social Democrats. Nonetheless, civil servants, through energetic and effective lobbying, were able to secure the restoration of the service to its traditional position.[11]

The conception of the civil servant as an official with a special and privileged relationship to the private citizen has certainly changed since 1949. The modern executive, unlike those during previous regimes, is now more dependent on social and political forces, specifically political parties, than on a politically independent "supreme" authority. Yet the fact that Germans have traditionally viewed the state as an institution above and superior to society still persists to some degree and gives a powerful support to the acts of the German bureaucrat.

Recruitment. Recruitment to the service is closely tied to the educational system, with each level having specific educational requirements. The higher level, still the monopoly of the university-educated, was once even more restricted in that a legal education was required. Even today, lawyers still dominate the upper ranks, and surveys have shown that they remain the most privileged of the privileged.[12] Entrance into the service, especially at higher and elevated levels, is normally limited to young candidates who are expected to make a long-term if not lifetime commitment. Most candidates must pass entrance examinations that, like those in most other European countries, test not for ability in specific positions but for general career aptitude. After admittance to the service, there is a probationary period, usually lasting from two to three

TABLE 7.2. DISTRIBUTION OF PUBLIC EMPLOYEES BY GOVERNMENTAL LEVEL AND RANK (in percentages)

Level		Rank		
	Officials	White-Collar Employees	Manual Workers	Total[a]
National	11	12	20	11
State	78	43	29	55
Local	11	45	51	34

[a] Total number of public employees including post office, railways, and other public enterprises: 3.6 million.
SOURCE: *Statistisches Jahrbuch für die Bundesrepublik Deutschland (1987)*, p. 449.

years, in which systematic in-service training is given before a final examination and eligibility for the coveted status of *Beamter auf Lebenszeit* (public official for life).

These procedures apply to all public positions that have civil service status. Little wonder that sharp distinctions are made between those in public employment with Beamte status and those without (manual workers and white-collar employees), as well as between the career civil servant and the outsider. If we add these features of the recruitment process to the hierarchic structure described earlier, we have a further explanation for the absence of major programs of innovation emanating from the established bureaucracy.

The still-dominating influence of lawyers in the higher service and the pervasive influence of legal norms and practices do, however, aid in the integration of local, state, and federal bureaucracies. Practices and procedures within the bureaucracy are explicitly prescribed both in law and in the *Common Code of Administrative Procedure,* which is only a slightly revised version of a 1926 code. This document—part office manual, part code of etiquette—is still used in some form in most German governmental offices.

Attitudes and Values. Given their background, recruitment, and structural environment, one should not be surprised that recent studies have found civil servants to be a very status-conscious, cautious group of people with, however, a firm commitment to the Republic and a growing understanding of the values and processes of liberal democracy. One survey of students' career plans found that those planning to enter the state bureaucracy deviated from average student attitudes in their emphasis on "the occupational values of job security, old age security, clearly structured tasks, and well-circumscribed demands on one's abilities and time."[13] The more independent, ambitious, achievement-oriented students were less interested in a civil service career. Not unexpectedly, bureaucrats are also very promotion-oriented, and most feel that special efforts are necessary to merit promotion.[14]

The civil servant's perception of the *political* character of his job, however, is growing. In a comparative study of top administrators (department heads), German respondents were found to be as conscious of the ways democratic politics affect their work and, conversely, of the ways their work affects the stability and effectiveness of the Bonn democracy as civil servants in Britain and even more politically aware than Italian bureaucrats.[15] A study of assistant section heads (the lowest or beginning level of the higher service) in the Economics Ministry found that most recognized and accepted the political character of their job; 67 percent perceived that they were involved "in politics" and were not just administering the laws as "neutral" agents of a state above society, parties, and parliament.[16]

This commitment to democratic principles is especially strong among younger civil servants, and there is somewhat of a generation gap in the area of political values. Younger civil servants were usually more likely to see their activity within a political context, to be less authoritarian and more personally committed to democratic party politics, and to support greater parliamentary control over the bureaucracy. Even among older age groups, however, there is little doubt that the civil service of the Bonn Republic, in contrast to that of the Weimar Republic, is committed to the political system it serves.

The civil service has also adapted to a variety of political masters since 1949 and has provided a strong element of continuity. Contrary to expectations, after twenty years of Christian Democratic rule, the civil service did not attempt any sabotage of Socialist-Liberal reforms after 1969. That many of the SPD's domestic reform programs between 1969 and 1982 did not become reality is usually attributed to factors over which the bureaucracy has little or no control: disagreements within and between the parties in the governing coalition, lack of adequate financial resources, and inadequate political leadership.

Pressures for Reform

Nonetheless, in recent years the state bureaucracy and its role in the policymaking process have come under increasing criticism. Much of this criticism focuses on its inability to adapt to new policy demands and developments especially where major innovations are needed: education, health care, transportation, land use, and regional development. Although it has served the Republic well in the reconstruction phase of the postwar period, it has not been able, the critics charge, given its present structure and mode of operation, to respond to the new, more complicated policy needs of the 1980s and beyond.[17] Specific recommendations for change or reform have centered on (1) the size of the administration, in terms of both the number of public employees and the number of administrative units; (2) the outmoded hierarchy and reward system; and (3) the absence of a system of comprehensive policy planning.

The Size of the Administration and the Number of Units. Within a physical space about the size of Oregon, there is a national government, 11 states (including West Berlin), 28 governmental districts, 327 counties, 92 cities (independent from county government), and 8,700 local communities (down from 30,000 in the 1960s). The division of labor between these units, the coordination of administrative activity, and the relationship between their size and responsibilities are insufficiently defined. Given this number of administrative units, it is not surprising that, although the number of Germans gainfully employed in the private sector has remained relatively constant since 1960, the number of public employees rose by 58 percent between 1971 and 1985.

Hierarchy and Reward System. The strict distinctions between higher, elevated, intermediate, and low or simple service levels and the privileges of lifetime tenure, free pensions, as well as the aversion to outside experts, are both expensive and outmoded and have increasingly little relationship to the actual work of administration. One study found that at least a third of the work done by academically trained higher-level civil servants could be done just as well by the caseworker at a lower level.[18] In some states, pension costs now equal the salary costs of in-service personnel. Some of the poorer states, such as the Saar, spend almost all their revenue for personnel and are dependent on federal grants for capital investment.

Inadequate Planning Capacity. The system cannot tackle big problems or foresee upcoming problems because its planning capability is inadequate. Reacting to problems is no longer sufficient, as seen in the political system's response to crises in education, the environment, health care, and urban development.

SEMIPUBLIC INSTITUTIONS

Among the semipublic institutions, the German social security and health systems, like the bureaucracy and courts, have also survived the frequent and sudden regime changes of the past century. Both were established in the 1880s by the Conservative Chancellor Otto von Bismarck, who sought to ensure that the growing German working class would support the existing monarchical regime and not the Socialists. Through these social welfare programs, Bismarck in effect tried to buy the workers' political support. The Federal Labor Institute (*Bundesanstalt für Arbeit*), located in Nuremberg, administers a nationwide network of employment offices that was established during the Weimar Republic and reemerged relatively intact after 1949. The powerful Bundesbank in Frankfurt, which is primarily responsible for monetary policy, is a postwar creation although it can trace its origins to the *Reichsbank* of the Hohenzollern Empire. These institutions assume functions performed by national governments in centralized systems such as Britain and France. In Germany they lessen the total political load carried by the national government, but they also reduce its strength. Their distance from the national and state governments has also generally shielded them from the conflicts of partisan politics.[19]

The Social Security and Health Systems

The West German welfare state is one of the most generous and comprehensive in the world. The expenditures of the health, pension, industrial accident, child support, public housing, and veterans' programs account for about a third of the national government's budget and provide Germans with over a fourth of their disposable income. The pension and health care programs are financed largely through equal employer and employee contributions. The costs of other programs, such as child support, housing and rent subsidies, and welfare, are taken from general tax revenue. German employers must pay the costs of the accident insurance program. Yet the administration of these huge programs is not carried out by either the national or state governments but by more than 1,500 social security and health funds located throughout the country. The health, or "sickness," funds cover about 90 percent of the population. They are organized by economic sector (business, agriculture, professions), occupational group, and geographic area. The social security (pension and accident) programs insure about 30 million adult Germans.

Although dating from the late nineteenth century, the programs have undergone extensive changes since the founding of the Federal Republic. The governing boards of all the funds are now based on the principle of parity representation for the various business, professional, and labor interests most concerned with the programs. After 1949 the left, or labor, wing of the ruling Christian Democratic Union, working with the trade unions and the opposition Social Democrats and enjoying the support of Chancellor Adenauer, was able to convince business interests that the confrontational class politics of the Weimar Republic should be replaced with a new emphasis on "social partnership." This required concessions from both business and labor. The trade unions gave up their majority control of the health funds, and employers did the same for the pension and accident insurance programs. Although the officials of the funds are nominally elected by their millions of members, the turnout at these *Sozialwahlen* (social welfare program elections) is very low and the slates of candidates presented by the labor unions and business and professional associations are rarely contested.

The administrative independence of the funds is limited by federal law. The size of pension payments and the taxes to pay for them, for example, are determined by the parliament. The funds do, however, have considerable discretion in setting the fee structure for physicians, the construction and management of hospitals, and the investment of pension fund capital. The concept of social partnership thus extends to the state as well. The funds, according to one authority, are "political shock absorbers," connecting "state with society because they leave it to the major economic interest groups to mediate the state's administration of major social welfare programs."[20]

The postwar emphasis on consensus and social partnership is seen most clearly in the 1957 reform of the pension system. Previous pension legislation based the size of payments largely on the individual's contributions. The 1957 law, although retaining some elements of individual insurance, linked increases in pension payments, with some time lag, to increases in the overall national wage level. This dynamic feature enabled all pensioners, regardless of their individual contribution, to share directly in the expanding national economy. The 1957 law was a political compromise. Conservative business interests and the Christian Democrats accepted its dynamic provisions (i.e., indexing pensions to the national economy), and the labor unions and the Social Democrats abandoned their preference for a more uniform, egalitarian pension scheme. The system now combines elements of individual insurance with collective welfare. In recent years, however, this postwar consensus on the pension and health systems has been strained by budgetary cutbacks, rising unemployment, and slower economic growth (see Chapter 9).

The Federal Labor Institute

The Federal Labor Institute is another semipublic institution that is assigned primary responsibility for organizing the labor market (i.e., bringing jobs and job-seekers together) and for administering the system of unemployment insurance. The institute also administers programs financed from unemployment insurance revenues that retrain workers and supplements the income of those put on short time. In its programs the institute must given special attention to the elderly, women, the handicapped, the long-term unemployed, and other special groups such as seasonal workers. The Institute, which was established in 1952, is located in Nuremberg and is under the supervision but not the direct control of the Labor Ministry in Bonn. It is governed by a president, an executive committee, and a supervisory board that has representatives from the trade unions, employers, and federal and state officials. The major guidelines determining labor policy are developed in Nuremberg and administered by 538 branch, 146 local, and 9 regional offices. Most of the unemployment compensation programs are financed by equal employer and employee contributions, which amount to about 3 percent of a worker's gross income. If the unemployment level is high, however, the federal government must subsidize the institute. Thus in certain circumstances it can be financially dependent on the federal government.

As in the case of the pension and health systems, business and labor representatives are closely involved in the work of the institute's employment offices through their membership on the institute's local, regional, and national administrative committees. The members of these committees are proposed by the trade unions, business associations, the federal government, and local government authorities.

The independence of the institute was also enhanced during the twenty-year tenure of its former president, Josef Stingl. Although a member of the conservative Christian Social Union, the Bavarian affiliate of the Christian Democrats, Stingl enjoyed the support of the trade unions and remained in office during the Social-Liberal era in Bonn. Through skillful use of the media, he established himself in the view of many West Germans as the preeminent authority on the unemployment problem and was relatively immune from criticism from Bonn. His monthly reports from Nuremberg became media events as Stingl, armed with graphs and charts, would lecture the nation, including his superiors in Bonn, on the severity of the unemployment problem.

The Bundesbank

The Bundesbank is the German national bank roughly equivalent to the American Federal Reserve or the Bank of England. It is the institution chiefly responsible for monetary policy and hence price stability. Indeed, some observers consider its chief mission to be the "guarding of West Germany's Holy Grail, a low inflation rate."[21] It is legally independent of the federal government, the states, and private interest groups. Its autonomy is greater than that of its counterparts in Britain, France, Japan, Sweden, and even the United States. Since 1982 the bank has also been directly involved in reducing the national government's deficits by transferring a portion of its profits from foreign exchange transactions to Bonn. These transfers, which since 1982 have amounted to over $25 billion, have enabled the Kohl government to reduce borrowing and cut taxes.

The power and independence of the bank reflect the strong concern about inflation held by all Germans. Twice in this century, following each World War, Germany experienced disastrous inflations that wiped out the savings of millions of citizens. Determined to keep monetary policy out of the reach of politicians, West Germany's founding fathers did not make the bank subject to any national government ministry or to the general supervision of the chancellor under his guideline power (see Chapter 6). It is also not accountable to the parliament. According to its constitution, the bank is obligated to support the government's overall economic policy, but this applies only as long as government policy, in the judgment of the bank's leadership, does not conflict with the bank's prime mission: the safeguarding of the currency. If a bank decision is opposed by the federal government, the government can delay implementation of the decision for only two weeks.

The bank is governed by two executive bodies: a directorate and a central bank council. Members of the directorate are appointed to eight-year terms by the federal president on the recommendation of the federal government. The central council mainly represents the interests of the regional branches of the bank. It is largely controlled by the regional bank presidents who are appointed by the Bundesrat on the recommendation of the respective state governments. Thus the directorate has a more national perspective, whereas the bank council tends to reflect state or regional interests.

The bank has not become a partisan political institution. Although the CDU has been in power in Bonn since 1982, there was not a single CDU supporter among the directorate's six members in 1988. The current chief executive officer is a member of the SPD. In recommending appointments to the directorate, the government has usually selected individuals who are acceptable to the banking community and generally in agreement with the main economic policy objectives of the government. Once appointed for eight-year terms, however, the directors have tended to be independent. After a careful analysis of central bank policy in West Germany, France, and Italy from 1973 to 1985, John Goodman found no evidence that the Bundesbank, in contrast to its counterparts in France and Italy, had manipulated German monetary policy for electoral purposes before the national elections of 1976, 1980, and 1983. He adds, however, that this

> finding does not reflect the absence of government interest in the setting of monetary policy. Indeed, the Chancellor and his ministers were quite conscious of the effects of monetary policy both on the economy and on their prospects for reelection. But their influence over the course of monetary policy was limited by the independent status of the German central bank.[22]

Major disagreements between the bank and the government have been rare but by no means unknown. In the late 1970s the bank initially opposed Chancellor Schmidt's plan to create a European Monetary System (EMS), which linked the deutsch mark to the currencies of several other European Community nations. The bank feared for the stability of the mark in a system where it was tied to the weaker currencies of countries with high inflation, such as France and Italy. Chancellor Schmidt was able, however, finally to convince the bank that the advantages of the EMS, such as decoupling European currencies from the unstable dollar, outweighed the possible disadvantages of rising inflation. In practice, the EMS did not restrict German monetary policy or the bank's independence.[23] On the contrary, in the view of many of Germany's European neighbors, the EMS imposed German antiinflationary discipline on its participants and promoted German trade.

In 1987 the bank became a major actor in the conflict between the United States and West Germany over international economic policy. The Reagan administration urged the Germans, as one of the world's leading trading nations, to speed up their economy in order to increase the demand for American goods and reduce the huge U.S. trade deficit. Given the Federal Republic's high unemployment, low inflation, and meager growth rate, Washington argued, there was ample room for Bonn to expand its economy through lower interest rates, tax cuts, and increased government spending. Although the Kohl government could and did cut taxes and increase spending, it had little control over interest rates, which fell largely within the domain of the Bundesbank. The bank downplayed Germany's economic influence and pointed instead to the U.S. budget deficit as the primary cause of the American trade imbalance and falling dollar.[24]

This German-American impasse became a major factor in the international financial crisis that began with the plunge of the New York stock market in October 1987. In the week preceding the October crash, the Bundesbank actually increased one of its key interest rates, and U.S. Treasury Secretary James Baker warned the West Germans that unless they stopped raising rates and restraining their economy, the United States would take no steps to prevent a drastic decline in the value of the dollar.

Responding to pressure from the Kohl government, the international financial community, and major German business interests, the bank finally lowered rates on four types of loans within six weeks after the New York stock market crisis. Until the stock market drop, however, the bank's central council was divided over the question of whether to give first priority to keeping inflation low or stimulating the economy. The council's faction for low inflation, composed largely of regional bankers less concerned about international factors and more about the effects of inflation on their institutions, held the upper hand. The sharp drop in the dollar and stock prices, however, increased the influence of the bank's growth faction, which was led by the president of the bank, Otto Pöhl.[25] This incident clearly shows the limitations placed on the national government by the power of the semipublic institutions.

THE JUDICIARY AND THE COURT SYSTEM

Contributing to the complexity and highly organized character of German social, economic, and political life are the courts and the judiciary, which play a major role in adjudicating the entire process. As Donald P. Kommers has pointed out, "There is hardly an area of human relations in Germany untouched by some rule, order or regulation."[26] For example, the opening and closing hours of shops and stores and the nighttime working hours of bakers are fixed by law. Kommers has even found a Bavarian ordinance that *requires* parents to keep their children quiet each afternoon between 1:00 and 3:00.[27] Whether Germans are simply more inclined to settle their disputes by legal means rather than through informal negotiations and bargaining or whether it is because of the relatively extensive court system available to them, they are a very law- and court-minded people.

The Character of German Law

Like that of most of its Western European neighbors, German law was fundamentally influenced by the Roman legal codes introduced by Italian jurists during the Middle Ages and by the Napoleonic Code enforced in the Rhineland during the French occupation in the nineteenth century. After the founding of the empire in 1871, the civil and criminal codes were reorganized and in some cases rewritten by teams of legal scholars. This massive work was completed by the turn of the century. Although relatively few changes have been made in the civil code since then, the criminal code since the early 1950s has been in a process of major revision.

These codes form the basis of Germany's unified legal system. Although political institutions are decentralized and fragmented, German law is the same in all states of the federation. Thus, unlike the situation under American federalism, laws regarding such matters as bankruptcy, divorce, criminal offenses, and extradition do not vary from state to state.

The codified character of German law also means that, unlike countries using the Anglo-American legal system, there is *no judge-made, or common, law*. The judge in a codified system, in theory at least, is only to administer and apply the codes, fitting the particular case to the existing body of law as found in them. The German judge may not set precedents, and thus make law, but must be only a neutral administrator of the existing codes. He does not have to make law; all the law that is needed is already in the codes. This conviction that the judge is not an independent actor in the judicial process but merely an administrator lies at the base of the still dominant philosophy of legal positivism, or analytical jurisprudence. Legal positivism contends that existing general law as found in the codes sufficiently encompasses all the rights and duties of citizens. In other words, judicial input or review is not necessary. The law supposedly offers the citizen the best protection against the arbitrary exercise of power by political authorities. Politics, according to this philosophy, must be kept strictly distinct from law.

Although in theory the judge is a neutral administrator, according to the rules of procedure, he is not a disinterested referee or umpire of court proceedings but is to take an active role in fitting the law to the facts of the particular case and ensuring that all relevant facts become known. Court observers accustomed to the Anglo-American system would be surprised by the active, inquisitorial posture assumed by the German judge. At times he seems to be working with the prosecution against the defendant. But if one assumes, as the German legal system does, that it is the duty of all participants to discern the truth or facts of the case in order to ensure a just application of the law, this activist orientation of the judge is to be expected. Unlike the Anglo-American system, the process is not one of *advocacy,* with defense and prosecution each presenting their side of the case as forcefully and persuasively as possible with the judge or jury making the final decision. It is more *inquisitorial,* with all participants—defense, prosecution, and judge—expected to join together in a mutual search for the truth, the real facts of the case.

Many critics of the German legal system have focused on this legal philosophy as the root cause of the judiciary's tragic, if not scandalous, behavior during the Third Reich. By claiming to be only neutral administrators of the law, German judges disclaimed any responsibility for judging the contents of the laws they were to administer. According to legal positivism, the judge is a "cog in the wheel of judicial administration, unmoved by feeling or even conscience."[28]

This philosophy also grants no legitimacy to any other type of law, such as natural or common law, which does not emanate from the sovereign state through its official representatives. The state is thus the only source of law. In this sense, positivism is quite supportive of the statist mentality—that is, the setting of state above society—attributed by many to the German political culture.

The Judiciary

Socialization and Recruitment. In Germany, as in other continental European states, there has been traditionally a close relationship between the court system and the state bureaucracy. Nearly all German judges, with the exception of those in specialized courts and the relatively few (about 500 out of 15,000) at the federal level, are appointed by the state ministers of justice. They are thus civil servants with roughly the same salaries, rank, tenure, and promotion structures as the Beamte in the higher service. Indeed, during the empire and the Weimar Republic, judges were not distinguished at all from higher-level civil servants. In the Federal Republic, however, a separate set of regulations for judges, designed to ensure judicial independence, was introduced. Nonetheless, structurally at least, the judge remains very much a part of the bureaucratic hierarchy. Starting at the lowest level (the local courts), he will be promoted on the basis of recommendations from his superiors. Independence and individual initiative are not encouraged by this system.

A German judge, unlike many of his American counterparts, has in most cases chosen a lifetime career and will not enter private practice and rarely even goes into the prosecuting end of judicial administration. There is a strict separation between bench and bar. After about $3\frac{1}{2}$ years of legal study, all prospective lawyers and judges take a state examination. If he passes this test, the student becomes a *Referendar*, a sort of apprentice or junior jurist, and begins a $2\frac{1}{2}$-year period of training in ordinary courts, administrative courts, as an attorney, and in the office of a public prosecutor—thus gaining experience in all major areas of the profession. After this practical experience, he must take a second state examination that, if passed, qualifies him to practice law. At this point (about the age of twenty-five to twenty-eight), the individual must make a career decision: private practice, a business or corporation career, the civil service, or the judiciary. Those who enter private practice as attorneys or who work for corporations (about 50 percent of the total) can and do switch from job to job, but those who enter state service must commit themselves to the judiciary, the prosecutor's office, or the regular civil service. Those who embark on a judicial career must then go through an additional three-year probationary period before receiving lifetime tenure as a judge and beginning the ascent up the judicial ladder. Once so committed, the German judge has little contact with other lawyers not in the judicial track, with the possible exception of those in the prosecutor's office.

Judges come from predominantly middle-class or upper-middle-class backgrounds. One study found that about half of all judges come from the top 5 percent of the population in terms of socioeconomic background; only about 6 percent of the judiciary come from working-class families, although the working class constitutes about 40 percent of the population.[29]

Attitudes and Values. Taken together, the socioeconomic background, recruitment, and professional socialization of judges would seem to make for a rather conservative group oriented toward the status quo. In the sense of supporting the status quo (that is, a middle-class liberal Republic), the judges are "conservative." Opposition to the values of liberal democracy, much less hostility to the Republic à la Weimar, are hardly to be found, at least not in studies of judges' attitudes and values. In one extensive study based on a representative sample of federal and state judges, it was found that all but 5 percent supported one or more of the three democratic political parties.[30] Almost 40 percent of the judges sampled said they would personally participate in a political demonstration if they were in agreement with its goals.[31]

In more specific policy areas, judges tended to take a mildly center-right position. Over 40 percent of the sample, for example, would support an employer lockout during a labor dispute, yet only 15 percent think striking workers are justified in preventing nonstrikers from entering the factory. Although 52 percent see a danger to the Republic from the radical left, only 16 percent view extreme right-wing groups as a present danger.[32] Almost 80 percent of the judges approve of the "education of the young in such a manner that they adapt to the existing order", and a solid 60 percent also support the "classless comprehensive school."[33] Similarly, they show strong support for both "safeguarding the independent middle class" (90 percent) and the "expansion of workers participation in management" (72 percent). Their socioeconomic views can thus hardly be termed reactionary or even solidly traditional; judges could clearly adjust to either a Socialist or Christian Democratic government, and indeed they have.

As in the case of the civil servants, age differences are important in explaining responses to these questions. Among judges who were trained after 1945, the willingness to participate personally in political demonstrations, for example, was almost 60 percent; among those over 50, only about 25 percent would demonstrate.[34] Those judges born before 1911, most of whom had been educated during the turbulent 1930s and the Third Reich, were three times more likely to reject the expansion of workers' participation in industry than were jurists trained after 1945. Although almost 40 percent of this latter group disagreed with the statement "The young should be educated so that they adapt to the existing order," only 10 percent of the judges over 50 years of age disagreed with the statement.[35] The different age groups did not differ significantly, however, in their positive, supportive attitudes toward the basic institutions and processes of the Republic.

Court Structure

In addition to a unified body of law, all regular German courts follow the same rules of procedure. The structure of the courts, however, is decentralized. Unlike in the United States, there is no separate system of federal and state courts. With the exception of the seven national high courts of appeal, all regular tribunals are state courts, and although national law outlines the basic organization of the judiciary, the courts are established and administered by state statutes. The other significant characteristics of the German structure are the collegial nature of most tribunals and the extensive system of specialized courts.

Regular (civil and criminal) courts are organized on four levels: local, district, appellate, and federal. The roughly 600 local courts (*Amtsgerichte*) are usually staffed by a single judge (in criminal cases the judge will be assisted by two lay judges chosen randomly from local citizens) and are located in most small to medium-sized towns. Local courts have jurisdiction over minor civil matters and petty criminal offenses and also perform some administrative functions (bankruptcy supervision, administering estates, appointing guardians).

At the next level are ninety-three district courts. These are appellate courts for the *Amtsgerichte*, but they also have original jurisdiction over most major civil and criminal matters. All district court cases are tried by panels of three to five judges. There are several panels at this level, and each tends to specialize on different types of cases. The final court of appeal below the national level is the

Oberlandesgericht (state appellate court). These twenty courts, with the exception of cases involving treason and anticonstitutional activity, take cases only on appeal. In Germany, an appeal involves both a reexamination of the facts in a case and its procedural and legal aspects. These courts are also divided into panels of three to five judges, with each panel specializing on different types of cases. The final appellate court in the regular system is the federal appeals court at Karlsruhe (not to be confused with the federal constitutional court, discussed later, which is also located at Karlsruhe). This is a very large tribunal with over 100 judges divided into over twenty panels or senates (see Table 7.3).

The specialized court system is also decentralized. Courts dealing with administrative, social welfare, and labor matters operate at three levels—district, appellate, and national—with the national court serving as the final court of appeal. Specialized courts dealing with fiscal and tax matters operate only at the state and national levels.

In their respective areas, these courts dispense relatively speedy and inexpensive justice. If a citizen or a group feels that any state official or agency has acted illegally or arbitrarily, the case goes to an administrative court. Recently, the administrative court system has been the major recourse for opponents of nuclear power.[36] The regular court system does not allow class action (*Verbandsklage*) suits and will grant standing to an environmental group

TABLE 7.3. THE GERMAN COURT STRUCTURE AND JUDICIARY

Court	Number	Number of Judges
Regular Courts[a]	664	12,768
Local	(551)	
District	(93)	
Appellate	(20)	
Specialized Courts (state control)	197	3,747
Administrative courts	(36)	(1,680)
Social courts	(51)	(962)
Labor courts	(96)	(648)
Fiscal courts	(14)	(457)
Federal Courts		
Federal appeals court	1	114
Federal administrative court	1	52
Federal labor court	1	5
Federal social court	1	0
Federal fiscal (finance) court	1	52
Federal patent court	1	206
Federal constitutional court	1	16
Totals (national)	868(7)	17,020(505)

[a] Civil and criminal cases.

SOURCE: *Statistisches Jahrbuch für die Bundesrepublik Deutschland, 1987* (Stuttgart and Mainz:Kohlhammer Verlag, 1987), p. 336.

only when its rights and those of its members are directly affected. The numerous permits and procedures required for the construction of a nuclear plant offers these groups, however, an opportunity to challenge the government in the administrative court on a variety of technical legal grounds. In 1972 it was the federal administrative court that ruled that safety must take precedence over economic and technical questions in the construction of nuclear plants. In 1976 it was again an administrative court that blocked the building of a controversial plant in Baden-Württemberg (in the village of Wyhl).

Specific disputes involving the social security, health, or welfare system are tried in a "social" court. Similarly labor-management problems, usually involving problems arising from collective bargaining agreements, are dealt with in labor courts. In the specialized courts, professional judges sit with lay members; in the case of labor courts, for example, these lay members are selected by employers and employees.

These institutions thus adjudicate matters that would be resolved either out of court or in the nonspecialized regular courts in the United States. To an extent, the readiness of Germans to go to court is due to the fact that they have so many available. Their presence also encourages the cautious, legalistic approach to administration so characteristic of the German bureaucracy. Knowing that their mistakes may quickly find them in some court makes civil servants more concerned about the legal correctness of their actions and less concerned about the political implications of such actions.

Judicial Review and the Federal Constitutional Court

All courts and judges are engaged in politics, but a court is most political when it strikes down the acts of other governmental bodies, usually those of the executive or the legislature. In the continental legal tradition, judicial review, the authority of courts to nullify legislative or executive acts on constitutional grounds, has been an alien concept. It has been regarded as an undemocratic infringment on the right of popular sovereignty as expressed in parliamentary acts or as contradictory to the principles of legal positivism that assign only an administrative role to judges. Although the practice of constitutional review, whereby courts resolved disputes between different levels of government or determined the validity of constitutional amendments, had some historic precedent in Germany, the acceptance of the principle of judicial review is essentially a twentieth-century and specifically postwar development.[37]

The framers of the Basic Law, desiring to check and balance governmental authority as much as possible, were in general agreement on granting the courts the power of judicial review and on establishing a specific national-level court as the final arbiter in constitutional questions. American occupation authorities, with the U.S. supreme court in mind, also supported such an institution.

The result was Articles 93 and 94 of the Basic Law, which established the constitutional court, assigned its competency and jurisdiction, and defined its composition. The court was a new addition to the postwar legal system and has become the most political of all German courts. It is assigned the functions of judicial review, the adjudication of disputes between state and federal political institutions, the protection of individual civil rights as guaranteed in the constitution, and the responsibility for protecting the constitutional and democratic order against groups and individuals seeking to overthrow it. In this latter area, the constitutional court has the right to ban such groups and their activities. These powers make the court unique in German judicial history.

The constitutional court is also distinct from other courts in organization and composition. Unlike state and national courts, which are administratively dependent on their respective justice ministers, the constitutional court is administratively independent. It hires, fires, and supervises all its employees, and justices are exempt from the administrative rules and regulations applicable to their colleagues on state and federal courts. Indeed, not even the parliament can impeach a constitutional court justice; only the federal president, upon a motion from the court itself, can remove a justice.[38] The court is financially autonomous. Like the two houses of parliament, it draws up its own budget, negotiating directly with the finance ministry and the parliament's judiciary committees.[39]

The unique position of the constitutional court and its explicitly political character is most apparent in the selection of its members. Half of the sixteen judges are selected by the Bundesrat (the upper house), and half by the Bundestag (the lower house); in each case a candidate must have at least a two-thirds majority. These selection provisions ensure that both state and party/political factors will play an important role and that they further enhance the unique character of the court. The Bundestag's candidates are chosen by a special judicial selection committee, an elite group composed of leading members of all parties in proportion to their strength in the chamber. The Bundestag parties attempt to influence the appointment of judges by presenting lists of candidates to the committee, although legally they cannot instruct their members on the committee how to vote.[40] The Bundesrat's eight appointees are elected in a bloc vote from nominees proposed by its judiciary committee. Since the two houses cannot nominate the same judges, there is an ad hoc conference committee that coordinates the process. In the Bundesrat, as discussed in Chapter 6, each state's delegation votes en bloc on instructions from its government. This ensures that state governments will have a direct influence on the selection process, and interstate bargaining on nominees is quite common especially on appointees to the court's second chamber, which will handle most states' rights cases.

It is not difficult for knowledgeable students of the constitutional court to determine how each appointee got his job. Although there is a lot of open political horse trading and occasionally bitter conflicts in the selection process, the quality of appointees has been high.[41] The Bundesrat has usually preferred high-level civil servants with excellent records in state administration. The lower house tends to nominate active politicians and judges from other federal courts. Both houses have recently drawn more candidates from their own ranks, that is, state justice ministers and leading members of the judicial selection committee. Membership on the court is regarded as a very prestigious appointment, and the quality of candidates is indicative of the status this new institution now has in the political system. Its strong penetration by state governments and parties also sets it apart from the traditional judiciary and makes it clearly a child of the Republic.

The constitutional court's sixteen members (reduced from the original twenty-five) are divided into two senates, or chambers. Election is to a specific chamber and members may not transfer. Each senate is administratively separate from the other and has its own areas of specialization. The first senate's jurisdiction includes all cases dealing with basic liberties covered by Articles 1 to 20 of the Basic Law and constitutional complaints involving these articles. The second senate is responsible for constitutional conflicts between different levels of government (federal-state, state-state) as well as a variety of specific political matters (political parties, election disputes, anticonstitutional activity, international law disputes, political parties, election issues).

Decisions. In its forty-year history, the constitutional court has made its mark as an independent guardian of the democratic constitution, a protector of human rights, and an adjudicator of German federalism. By the mid-1980s, it had interpreted about half of the constitution's 151 articles, and in about 340 cases involving the constitutionality of legislation had invalidated 54 federal and 35 state laws.[42] In its early decisions such as the *Southwest* case (1951), a dispute over state boundaries comparable to the landmark American cases of *Marbury* v. *Madison* and *McCulloch* v. *Maryland,* the constitutional court established its authority as the supreme source of constitutional interpretation, clearly departed from legal positivism in granting legitimacy to certain "higher" or natural-law principles, and set forth fundamental principles, such as federalism, democracy, and the rule of law, that are superior to all other constitutional or legislative provisions.

More than any other postwar institution, the constitutional court enunciated the view that the Federal Republic is a militant democracy whose democratic political parties are the chief instrument for the translation of public opinion into public policy. The concept of the party state, discussed in Chapter 4, owes much to the opinions of the constitutional court. The controversial banning of the Communist and neo-Nazi *Sozialistische Reichspartei* in the 1950s was also an expression of this concept of militant democracy.

The court has also not shirked from conflict with the government and top executive leadership. When Adenauer attempted to form a second television network that would have been under national control, the constitutional court, responding to state claims that such a network violated the reserved rights of the Länder to govern their own cultural affairs, struck down the legislation. The cries of protest from the chancellor's office left little doubt that the court was doing its job.

In other significant political decisions, the court has upheld the constitutionality of the 1970 treaties with the Soviet Union and Poland, struck down the abortion law passed by the Socialist-Liberal government in 1974, essentially upheld the hard-line position on radicals in public employment taken by the chancellor and minister presidents in 1972, ruled that the 1976 codetermination law was constitutional, and in 1983 ordered major changes in the census law. In the case of the abortion decision, it was the reformist, center-left position that was rejected.

Like those of its American counterpart, the constitutional court's decisions have sometimes been controversial, and charges have been made that the court has failed to exercise judicial restraint and attempted to usurp legislative functions. To students of judicial review, especially as practiced by the American supreme court, these charges are very familiar. Although disputes about court decisions are usually couched in legal terms, both supporters and critics of the court's decisions have ample political reasons for their positions. In other words, it all depends on whose ox is gored. Public support for the constitutional court is strong. A 1979 survey found that 83 percent of the adult population had "trust" in the institution, a higher level than that found for the parliament (67 percent), the churches (65 percent), or the universities (59 percent).[43] There is no doubt that the court has become a legitimate component of the political system, and its decisions have been accepted and complied with by both winners and losers.[44]

Reform of the Legal System and Judiciary

Perhaps with the examples of the constitutional court in mind, a growing number of judges and legal scholars have advocated a thorough reform of the judiciary and the legal codes. The issue is not, as during the immediate postwar years, the commitment of judges to the principles of the Republic but the rigidity and conservatism of the court structure (and some judges) as well as the outmoded irrelevant character of many provisions of the nineteenth-century civil and criminal codes.

Numerous proposals for the reform of the legal profession and especially the judiciary have been made. Most critics have focused on changes in legal education and the replacement of the still dominant philosophy of positivism with one that stresses judicial independence and makes the judge consciously "internalize those democratic values which, according to the constitution, are to determine social, economic and political life."[45] The judge is to be aware of the political character of his activity and to recognize his individual responsibility, not to the bureaucratic hierarchy but to the constitution. This concept of the political judge is still controversial in the Federal Republic, and the changes in judicial values that it assumes will take far longer than the revision of the codes.

The revision and modernization of the criminal code have been underway since the 1950s.[46] A government-sponsored commission on criminal code reform began work in 1954, and in 1962 draft legislation was presented to the Bundestag. Independent of the government's commission, fourteen professors of criminal law presented numerous alternative bills, generally more progressive, to the parliament's special committee on criminal law reform. In 1965 a "small" reform of the code, incorporating some of the proposals of both groups, was passed that expanded the rights of the defendant and his counsel and limited the imposition of "investigatory arrest," or imprisonment, before a formal filing of charges. In May 1969 a "large" reform bill was passed that (1) eliminated the *Zuchthaus* (the maximum security penitentiary with no rehabilitation or psychological counseling programs); all sentences are now served in *Gefängnissen*, prisons that are, in theory at least, oriented toward rehabilitation; (2) restricted and in many cases eliminated the imposition of short (under six months) prison terms, replacing them with monetary fines; and (3) no longer treats homosexual relations between consenting adults, blasphemy, or adultery as criminal offenses. A second major reform bill introduced in 1969 was passed in 1981. It introduced major changes in court procedures and the establishment of extensive psychotherapeutic institutions for habitual criminals. A third bill, approved in 1970, expands the citizen's right to demonstrate against constitutional institutions. Finally, a reform of the code's provisions dealing with pornography and abortion was passed in 1974. The abortion provisions, however, as discussed in Chapter 3, were invalidated by the constitutional court a year later. In 1976 the Bundestag passed yet another abortion law that met the court's objections. Most other reform bills dealing with sexual crimes, marriage, and the family, as well as the relationship between the judicial bureaucracy and the rest of the legal profession, were passed by the early 1980s. Although reforms in divorce and abortion law have provoked controversy, this enormously difficult and complex task of code reform has, for the most part, had general support.

SUMMARY AND CONCLUSION

The administrative and judicial institutions of the Federal Republic have provided an important element of continuity between the postwar democracy and earlier political systems. As in the past, they have adapted to new political events and situations with few difficulties. Moreover, the process of generational change seems to be producing younger civil servants and lawyers who do not pay simply lip service to the Republic but are genuinely committed to its principles and ideals.

During the reconstruction phase of the postwar period, from 1945 to about 1965, these institutions, faced with straightforward, relatively routine policy tasks, performed well. Their ability to adapt to the new quantitative and qualitative demands of modern policymaking, however, has been seriously questioned in recent years. It is the fragmented, decentralized, ad hoc character of policymaking and administration that concerns many students of German governmental institutions.

On the other hand, when one considers the circumstances of the Republic's founding, the pressures of Allied military occupiers, and the experiences with the centralized, "efficient" Third Reich, the present structure does not seem inefficient or irrational, at least to many foreign observers. Where some see fragmentation, others see pluralism, and there is little doubt that postwar decentralization has provided many opportunities for practicing the art of compromise and bargaining so essential to conflict management in a modern democracy. Also, some planners and reformers want a stronger, centralized political system that would be far more committed to basic social and economic change (others would say revolution) than most Germans seem to prefer. The construction, then, of a synthesis between the legitimate demands of reformist and traditionalist administrative and judicial interests has now become a major task for the political system.

NOTES

1. Gabriel A. Almond and Sidney Verba, *The Civic Culture* (Princeton: Princeton University Press, 1963), pp. 189 ff.
2. Arnold Brecht, "Personnel Management," in *Governing Postwar Germany*, ed. Edward H. Litchfield (Ithaca: Cornell University Press, 1953), p. 264.
3. Ibid., p. 267.
4. Ibid.
5. Karl Loewenstein, "Justice," in *Governing Postwar Germany*, pp. 236–262.
6. Ibid. p. 248.
7. Ibid.
8. Reimut Jochimsen, "Integriertes System," *Bulletin: Presse- und Informationsamt der Bundesregierung*, no. 97 (16 July 1970), p. 953.
9. Renate Mayntz and Fritz W. Scharpf, *Policy-Making in the German Federal Bureaucracy* (New York, Amsterdam: Elsevier, 1975), pp. 69–76.
10. Ibid., pp. 77 ff.
11. Werner Thieme, "Das Stiefkind des Staates," *Die Zeit*, (18 September 1970), p. 60.
12. Gerhard Brinkmann, "Die Diskriminierung der Nicht-Juristen im allgemeinen höheren Verwaltungsdienst der Bundesrepublik Deutschland," *Zeitschrift für die gesamte Staatswissenschaft* 129 (1973): 150–167; and Bärbel Steinkemper, *Klassische und politische Bürokraten in der Ministerialverwaltung der Bundesrepublik Deutschland* (Cologne: Carl Heymans Verlag, 1974), p. 20.
13. Mayntz and Scharpf, *Policy-Making*, pp. 53 ff.
14. Niklas Luhmann and Renate Mayntz, *Personal im öffentlichen Dienst* (Baden-Baden: Nomos Verlagsgesellschaft, 1973), pp. 56 ff.
15. Robert D. Putnam, "The Political Attitudes of Senior Civil Servants in Western Europe: A Preliminary Report," *British Journal of Political Science* 3 (1973): 257–290.
16. Eberhard Moths and Monika Wulf-Mathies, *Des Bürgers teuere Diener* (Karlsruhe: Verlag C. F. Mueller, 1973), p. 59.
17. Volkward Wrage, "Entwicklungstendenzen und aktuelle Probleme der Deutschen Öffentlichen Verwaltung," *Politische Vierteljahresschrift* 12, no. 2 (July 1971): 264–282.

18. Moths and Wulf-Mathies, *Des Bürgers teuere Diener*, p. 58.
19. Peter J. Katzenstein, *Policy and Politics in West Germany. The Growth of a Semi-Sovereign State* (Philadelphia: Temple University Press, 1987), Chapter 1.
20. Katzenstein, p. 58.
21. Katzenstein, p. 60.
22. John B. Goodman, "Monetary Politics in France, Italy and Germany: 1973–1985". Unpublished paper, Graduate School of Business Administration, Harvard University, September 27, 1987, p. 23.
23. Ibid, p. 12.
24. *New York Times*, November 19, 1987, p. D8; December 3, 1987, p. D2.
25. *New York Times*, October 30, 1987, p. D7; November 5, 1987, p. D1.
26. Donald P. Kommers, *Judicial Politics in West Germany* (Beverly Hills, CA and London: Sage Publications, 1976), p. 50.
27. Ibid.
28. Kommers, *Judicial Politics*, p. 44.
29. Theo Rasehorn, "Die dritte Gewalt in der zweiten Republik," *Aus Politik und Zeitgeschichte*, no. 39 (27 September 1975), p. 5.
30. Manfred Riegel, "Political Attitudes and Perceptions of the Political System by Judges in West Germany," (Paper, IX World Congress of the International Political Science Association, Montreal, 1973), p. 2a.
31. Ibid., p. 9.
32. Ibid., p. 8.
33. Ibid., p. 7a.
34. Ibid., p. 11.
35. Ibid.
36. Dorothy Nelkin and Michael Pollak, "French and German Courts on Nuclear Power," *Bulletin of the Atomic Scientists*, May 1980, p. 37. It has also been suggested that administrative court judges are more likely to be concerned with the citizens' rights against the state, rather than the general interest, than their counterparts in the regular court system. Some of the younger administrative court judges were also part of the student protest movement of the 1960s. According to a leading environmental lawyer: "Judges with a left ideology will usually try to find a job in the administrative rather than the civil courts." Cited in Nelkin and Pollak, p. 41.
37. Kommers, *Judicial Politics*, p. 29. During the Weimar Republic the *Reichsgericht* (the highest general court in the Weimar system), capitalizing on the ambiguity of the constitution in this area, did in fact strike down legislation on constitutional grounds, especially between 1921 and 1929. Most state courts at this time also accepted judicial review in theory, although they rarely used it to nullify legislative acts. Thus there was some tradition, albeit fragmentary, for this principle.
38. Ibid., p. 85.
39. Ibid., pp. 91–97.
40. Ibid., p. 114.
41. Ibid., pp. 120–144.
42. Ibid., pp. 207, 215.
43. January 1979 EMNID survey cited in Winfried Ockenfels and Baldur Wagner, *Signale in die achtziger Jahre* (Munich and Vienna: Günter Olzog Verlag, 1980), p. 28.
44. The success of the constitutional court is related to the performance of the overall system of which it is a part. Because the judges are selected by legislative institutions,

political and ideological considerations have played a role. However, the dominant political parties have shared a general consensus on the basic values, norms, and institutions of the Republic, including the types of people who are to serve on the court. A breakdown in this consensus would also over time undermine the court's representativeness and legitimacy. See Nevil Johnson, "The Interdependence of Law and Politics: Judges and the Constitution in West Germany," *West European Politics* 5, no. 3 (July 1982): 249, for a discussion of this point.

45. Rudolf Wassermann, "Zur politischen Funktion der Rechtssprechung," *Aus Politik und Zeitgeschichte,* no. 47 (23 November 1974), p. 3.

46. Albin Eser, "The Politics of Criminal Law Reform: Germany," *American Journal of Comparative Law* 21, no. 2 (Spring 1973): 245–262.

CHAPTER 8

Subnational Units: Federalism and Local Government

The federal structure of the Republic, which corresponds to German political tradition as well as to the wishes of postwar Allied military occupiers, ensures that the formulation and implementation of policy, together with the recruitment of political leaders, are not concentrated at the national level. More than any other major West European state, the Federal Republic has decentralized and fragmented political power. Indeed, as discussed in the preceding chapter, a growing number of experts contend that power and authority are too decentralized and compartmentalized.[1] Thus, unlike in Britain, France, Italy, and other states, the *devolution* of power is really not an issue in West Germany; more important is its *consolidation*. At no time in modern German history has any central authority been powerful enough to structure the constituent parts—that is, the subnational units into which Europe's German-speaking people have been grouped—in the *best intersets* of the whole. Thus the search for an equilibrium between national and subnational interests continues.

THE DEVELOPMENT OF GERMAN FEDERALISM

The German Reich founded in 1871 was composed of twenty-five historic German states that voluntarily entered into a federation. These entities, however, were grossly unequal in size and population. Seventeen of them combined made up less than 1 percent of the total area of the Reich and less than 10 percent of the total population. Prussia was by far the largest unit in the federation, with two-thirds of its area and population.

The unity of this newly formed Reich was tenuous. Some of the member states had in fact been forced into the federation by a combination of military

200

defeat at the hands of Prussia and the power politics practiced with consummate skill by Bismarck.[2] The remarkable industrial and economic growth that followed unification temporarily stilled opposition to Prussian dominance and reduced particularistic sentiment. Germany's defeat in World War I and the political, social, and economic unrest that plagued the postwar Weimar Republic brought forth a variety of individuals and groups in areas such as Bavaria and the Rhineland who demanded the end of the centralized Reich and the restoration of full sovereignty to the constituent states. In some cases, foreign governments (especially France) aided the forces of particularism. The Nazis, who ironically in their early years found common ground with the separatists in their opposition to the Republic, abolished state government and imposed a centralized administration on the Third Reich.

The destruction of the Nazi system and postwar military occupation returned the forces of decentralization to a dominant position. All Germany's conquerors wanted a decentralized postwar Germany in some form: The French would have preferred a completely dismantled Reich composed of several independent states, none of which would be powerful enough ever to threaten France again. American occupiers, having considerable experience with federal structures, urged an American-type system. And the British, although more centralist-oriented than the Americans or French, also envisioned a decentralized postwar Germany. Among the Germans, opposition to a strong federal system was mostly limited to the SPD and to those Christian Democrats in the Soviet zone, which incorporated most of prewar Prussia.

With the emerging cold war and East-West division of Germany, the influence of centrist elements waned, and by 1949 there was little significant West German opposition to plans for a decentralized state. Indeed, Western occupiers could count on German support for federalism in their occupation zones because the zones included the historically most particularistic and anti-Prussian segments of the former Reich: Bavaria, the Rhineland, the province of Hanover, and the Hanseatic cities of Hamburg and Bremen. The framers of the Basic Law were also largely state-level politicians or former Weimar politicos, who since 1946 had to renew their political careers at the state level. Thus the delegates to the parliamentary council were a very states'-rights-oriented group.

The Basic Law ensures major state influence in three ways: (1) through powers reserved to them (education, police and internal security, administration of justice, supervision of the mass communications media); (2) through their responsibility to administer federal law including the collection of most taxes; and (3) through their direct representation in the parliament (the Bundesrat). Since 1969 the states are also equal participants with the federal government in certain joint tasks enumerated by Article 91a of the Basic Law: higher education, regional economic development, and agricultural reform. Thus, in addition to their own reserved powers, the states have either direct or indirect influence on all national legislation. In only a few policy areas, such as defense and foreign affairs, does the national government not have to consider the views of the states in either the making or implementation of policy.

STATE-LEVEL POLITICS

Unity and Diversity among German States

The ten states (eleven with West Berlin) differ in tradition, size, population, and socioeconomic resources. Only three of the states—Bavaria and the two city-states of Hamburg and Bremen—existed as separate political entities before 1945. The remaining Länder were created by Allied occupiers, in many cases to the consternation of tradition-conscious Germans. In the American zone two new states, Hesse and Baden-Württemberg, were formed.[3] In the French zone, on the left bank of the Rhine, another new state, the Rhineland-Palatinate, was created from territories that had earlier been provinces of Prussia, Bavaria, and Hesse. Other former Prussian territories in the west were used by the British occupation to form North Rhine–Westphalia. In the north, some previously independent areas and still more Prussian provinces were rearranged by the British to make the two new states of Schleswig-Holstein and Lower Saxony. In 1957 the Saar region, which had been under French control since 1945, returned to Germany after a plebiscite and became the tenth Land. Finally, West Berlin, which may or may not be a state depending on one's interpretation of wartime and postwar statements and agreements of the occupation powers, as well as East and West German counterclaims, has existed de facto since 1949.

The most populous of the states is by far North Rhine–Westphalia. Incorporating the Rhine-Ruhr region, this Land, with about 28 percent of the country's total population, is one of the most prosperous in the Republic. Politics in this state have been competitive since 1946 with relatively close elections and alternations of government and opposition parties. From 1966 to 1980 a Socialist-Liberal coalition governed in Düsseldorf with, however, a strong CDU in opposition. In the 1980 and 1985 state elections the SPD received an absolute majority of seats in the state parliament and now governs alone.

The largest state in area and second largest in population is Bavaria. Left intact after the war, Bavaria is without question the most particularistic of the states. If there are any American-style states' rights advocates left in the Federal Republic, they are in this heavily Catholic, tradition-conscious region that has been marching to a slightly different beat from the rest of Germany even long before the Federal Republic. Bavaria entered the Bismarckian Reich in 1871 only after receiving special concessions (its own beer tax among them), and it was a hotbed of separatist and extremist sentiment during the Weimar Republic.

In spite of their separatist traditions and strong support of federalism, the Bavarians, and especially the ideologically committed among them in the Christian Social Union, in many ways consider themselves the guardians of *das Deutschtum* ("Germanness") in an increasingly cosmopolitan and integrated Western Europe. It was Bavarian television that, alone among German networks, refused to televise "Sesame Street" because even its German version was too "American" and presented models and behavior patterns foreign to Bavarian children and not particularly desirable at that. Bavaria also unsuccessfully contested the constitutionality of the Basic Treaty before the federal constitutional court in 1974, arguing that the pact with East Germany violated the preamble to the Basic Law, which commits the Republic to the reunification in peace and freedom of all Germans. Bavaria is a strong one-party-dominant state. The Christian Social Union (CSU) has been the strongest single party in all but one of ten postwar state elections and has governed either alone or in coalition for all but four years since 1946.

The third largest Land in population, with 9.3 million inhabitants, is the southwest state of Baden-Württemberg. More religiously balanced than Bavaria, its politics have usually been controlled by center-right parties, most often the CDU in coalition with the Free Democrats. Grand Coalitions between the CDU and SPD, however, have also governed at various times, and since 1969 the CDU has had sufficient strength to govern alone. Overall, then, it has been a somewhat more competitive state than Bavaria.

Lower Saxony is the fourth most populous state and the third largest in area. A heavily Protestant (80 percent) Land with a high concentration of refugees and a strong rural component to its economy, Lower Saxony has had generally competitive party politics in the postwar period. The Christian Democrats have governed since 1976.

The remaining six states, Hesse, the Rhineland-Palatinate, the Saar, Schleswig-Holstein, Hamburg, and Bremen, all have fewer than 6 million inhabitants. Both Schleswig-Holstein and the Rhineland have significant rural, small-town populations and are two of the poorest states from the standpoint of per capita income. The CDU has frequently dominated state politics in both, however, in coalition with the Free Democrats. Hesse is a heavily industrialized Protestant Land with some Catholic enclaves. It has until recently been an SPD stronghold. The cities of Hamburg and Bremen, both largely Protestant, are two of the most prosperous states in the system. The SPD has been the strongest party in both cities but has governed frequently in coalition with the Free Democrats. The Saar is primarily an industrial area with, however, a large Catholic population, and its politics have been dominated by the CDU in occasional coalitions with the FDP. In the 1985 state election, however, the Social Democrats, for the first time in the postwar history of the Saar, won an absolute majority of seats in the state's parliament.

Thus, as Table 8.1 shows, the ten states range in population from Bremen with less than a million inhabitants to North Rhine–Westphalia with a population of almost 17 million. Their area varies from Bavaria's 70,500 square kilometers to Hamburg's and Bremen's combined 110 square kilometers. Per capita GNP ranges from about $13,000 in Schleswig-Holstein to almost $29,000 in Hamburg. Politically the Social Democrats have been the strongest party in Hesse, Hamburg, Bremen, and Berlin; the CDU/CSU has dominated politics in Bavaria, the Rhineland-Palatinate, Schleswig-Holstein, Baden-Württemberg, and the Saar. Competitive party politics have been most prevalent in North Rhine–Westphalia and Lower Saxony.

TABLE 8.1. THE LÄNDER OF THE FEDERAL REPUBLIC

Land	1984 Population (millions)	Area (thousands of sq. km.)	Population (per sq. km.)	Gross National Product Total ($ billion)[b]	Gross National Product Pro-portion of Total	Gross National Product Per Capital ($ thousand)	% Foreign Residents	% of Work Force in Agri-culture (1986)	% Roman Catholic	1988 Governing Party or Coalition	Capital
North Rhine-Westphalia	16.7	34.1	490	262.5	27	15.4	8	3	52	SPD	Düsseldorf
Bavaria	11.0	70.5	155	165.2	17	15.7	6	8	70	CSU	Munich
Baden-Württemberg	9.3	35.8	269	155.3	16	16.8	9	5	47	CDU	Stuttgart
Lower Saxony	7.2	47.4	152	97.2	10	13.2	4	7	20	CDU-FDP	Hanover
Hesse	5.5	21.1	265	87.5	9	17.2	9	3	33	CDU-FDP	Wiesbaden
Rhineland-Palatinate	3.6	19.8	183	48.6	5	14.2	5	6	56	CDU-FDP	Mainz
Schleswig-Holstein	2.6	15.7	167	38.9	4	12.9	3	5	6	SPD	Kiel
Hamburg	1.6	.7	2,286	48.6	5	28.8	11	—	8	SPD-FDP	Hamburg
Saar	1.1	2.6	411	19.4	2	13.9	4	2	74	SPD	Saarbrücken
Bremen	.7	.4	1,696	9.7	1	20.7	7	—	10	SPD	Bremen
West Berlin[a]	1.8	.5	3,600	38.9	4	19.6	14	—	12	CDU-FDP	—
Total	61.1	248.6	245.5	971.8	100	15.2	7	4.7	45		

[a] West Berlin is still under four-power (U.S., Soviet Union, Britain, and France) status.
[b] $1 = DM2.00.

Since the late 1970s, the southern states have experie
growth and less unemployment than the northern states.
microelectronic, robotics, and aerospace industries are in th
Bavaria and Baden Württemberg, whereas the declining st
sectors of the economy are concentrated in the north. By 198
the south averaged about 6 percent compared to over 10 p _ _ in northern
states such as North-Rhine–Westphalia and Schleswig-Holstein.

The Constitutional Structure of the States

The Basic Law requires that the "constitutional order in the Länder states . . .
conform to the principles of republican, democratic and social government based
on the rule of law" (Article 28, paragraph 1). The specific form of government,
including the questions of whether the legislature is to be bicameral or
unicameral and the executive directly or indirectly elected, is left to the
discretion of the states. With the exception of Bavaria, all states have unicameral
legislatures with an executive (Ministerpräsident and cabinet) responsible to it.
Most states have also adopted the personalized proportional electoral law
described in Chapter 5. State-level cabinets are composed of from eight to ten
ministers. In addition to the classic ministries of finance, education, health,
justice, and internal affairs, each state has several ministries whose activities
reflect its special characteristics (for example, the Rhineland-Palatinate's wine
ministry and ministries for ports and harbors in Hamburg and Bremen).

As in Bonn, coalition governments have been common in the Länder. In the
case of the larger states, the coalition alignments have usually been similar to
those at the national level to ensure the government in Bonn adequate support in
the Bundesrat for its program. This practice demonstrates the integrating effect
that political parties can have in a federal system. It began in the 1950s when
Adenauer sought to compel all CDU state parties to leave coalitions with the
Socialists and conform to the Bonn pattern of governing alone if possible or with
other middle-class parties.[4] By the end of the decade, all state governments were
controlled by either the CDU and its allies or the Social Democrats.

The waning of Adenauer's influence, CDU/CSU intraparty conflicts, and the
greater acceptability of the SPD as a partner to the Free Democrats, and in some
cases the Union itself, led to the breakdown of this pattern in the early 1960s.
After the formation of the Grand Coalition in Bonn in 1966, almost all possible
types of party alignments could be found in the states. There were Grand
Coalitions (SPD-CDU) in Baden-Württemberg and Lower Saxony; CDU/CSU-
FDP alignments in Schleswig-Holstein, the Rhineland-Palatinate, and the Saar;
SPD-FDP coalitions in North Rhine–Westphalia, Hamburg, and Bremen; as well
as single-party governments in Bavaria (CSU) and Hesse (SPD). After the
formation of the national SPD-FDP coalition in 1969, coalition governments at
the state level again became consistent with the Bonn pattern: Either the
SPD-FDP governed in coalition (Hesse, Hamburg, Bremen, Lower Saxony,
North Rhine–Westphalia), or the Christian Democrats governed alone (Bavaria,

land-Palatinate, the Saar, Baden-Wurttemberg, Schleswig-Holstein). After /6, however, a mixed pattern returned as the Christian Democrats and Free Democrats formed coalition governments in Lower Saxony and the Saar.

The return of the Christian Democrats to power in Bonn in 1982 was not followed by any major changes in the partisan composition of state governments consistent with the national CDU/FDP coalition. In states such as Lower Saxony, Bavaria, and the Rhineland-Palatinate that were governed by the CDU, the Free Democrats fell below the 5 percent mark and were not represented in the state parliament. In Baden-Württemberg, where the CDU has an absolute majority, the Free Democrats were not needed as a coalition partner.

Party Systems

The simplification of the national party system, discussed in Chapter 4, has been paralleled at the state level. During the early postwar years and into the 1950s, small regional parties played an important role in several states, principally Lower Saxony (the refugee party and the German party), Bavaria (the Bavarian party) and North Rhine–Westphalia (the *Zentrum*). Their disappearance by the early 1960s reduced the particularistic or regional component and intensified the nationalization of state politics. Nonetheless, it is still easier for potential new national parties to test the water and make a national impact by first concentrating on the state level. This was the strategy pursued by the right-wing National Democratic party during the 1960s. By gaining representation in state parliaments, the party secured a foothold and received nationwide attention far sooner than if it had concentrated on national elections. Even in this case, the substance and direction of the party's appeal were national, and the NPD's defeat in the 1969 election also ended its string of successes in state elections. In no state election after 1969 did it secure more than 5 percent of the vote. A similar strategy was followed by the Environmentalist, or Green, political party in 1980. In two Länder, Bremen and Baden-Württemberg, the Greens cleared the 5 percent hurdle and attracted nationwide attention.

State-level party systems also increase the sociological and ideological diversity of the national parties. For example, the impetus for the transformation of the SPD during the late 1950s came from those SPD state organizations that were in power. Indeed, the SPD was able to endure twenty years of national opposition without becoming a radical, extremist sect partly because it held power in several states where it had to deal with concrete policy problems. In this sense, state-level politics kept the SPD in the mainstream of national political life. In the case of the CDU/CSU, the federal system increased the national influence of the Union's right wing by providing it with a power base in Bavaria. In a unitary system, the Bavarian component of the party would have far less impact on the national organization than it now has under a federal structure.

Electoral Politics in the States

Since the early 1960s, state elections, especially in the larger Länder, have increasingly become indicators or tests of the electorate's mood toward national parties, leaders, and issues. They can also have a direct effect on national politics by altering the party alignment in the Bundesrat.

As in congressional elections in the United States, the party or parties in power in Bonn generally lose support in these elections, usually held in off years. The results of state elections can also have an effect on the stability of the governing coalition in Bonn and its leadership. The resignation of Willy Brandt in 1974 was related to poor SPD showings in state elections after 1972. It was not until CDU defeats in state elections following the 1961 national vote that the Union finally urged Adenauer's retirement. Likewise, the defeat of the CDU in the election in North Rhine–Westphalia was instrumental in the fall of the Erhard government in 1966. The governmental crisis in April-May 1972, which produced the first vote of no confidence in the Republic's history, was also precipitated by the results of a state election in Baden-Württemberg. It was the collapse of an SPD-FDP government in Hanover (Lower Saxony) in January 1976 that gave the Christian Democrats renewed hope at the national level and solidified the position of the moderate Helmut Kohl as the party's 1976 chancellor candidate.

These consequences of state elections are largely the result of campaign strategies adopted by the parties, which have increasingly used state polls as tests of current support for national policies. The state elections of 1971 and 1972 were widely treated as referenda on the government's Ostpolitik. When the Free Democrats lost representation in two state parliaments in June 1970, thus weakening its already precarious position in Bonn, the SPD used the Hesse and Bavarian state elections in November of that year to bolster its junior partner by discreetly encouraging its supporters in these states not to let the FDP go under the 5 percent mark. The Free Democrats did indeed get enough "votes on loan" from the SPD actually to increase its proportion of the vote in both states. The 1986 state election in Lower Saxony was widely considered a test election for the 1987 national vote. When the SPD failed to win in this state, its standings in the national polls dropped. Losses in two other elections in 1986 forced the Social Democrats to change their entire 1987 campaign strategy.

The infusion of national personalities and issues into state campaigns may also explain the relatively high turnout in these elections, which has averaged about 70 percent since the early 1950s. In some cases, a party may not want to "nationalize" a state election because of unfavorable national conditions. Chancellor Schmidt, for example, expecting the SPD to lose votes because of the Brandt crisis, tried to stay out of state campaigns after his accession to the chancellorship. Because of Chancellor Kohl's declining popularity, the Christian Democrats in 1986 sought to reduce his role in state campaigns. Nonetheless, the opposition may well compel national leaders to come out and fight the electoral battle in the provinces. Thus, in spite of the occasional presence of genuine state factors in elections, they have increasingly become part of the national political struggle.[5]

Leaders and Policies

The style of state *Ministerpräsidenten* (minister-presidents, or chief executives) has ranged from the strong father figure to a low-key bureaucratic approach. The postwar Ministerpräsidenten of Hesse (Georg-August Zinn), Hamburg (Max Brauer), and Bremen (Wilhelm Kaisen), and the former chief executive of Bavaria (Alfons Goppel) are representative of the father-figure type. Most Ministerpräsidenten, however, have been relatively colorless administrators with extensive careers in local and state party organizations as their most common background characteristic.

Three of the Republic's six chancellors (Kiesinger, Brandt, and Kohl) were state chief executives before assuming the top spot in Bonn. The current chancellor, Helmut Kohl, was minister-president of the Rhineland-Palatinate. Another prominent figure in the Kohl government, Finance Minister Gerhard Stoltenberg, was chief executive of Schleswig-Holstein from 1971 to 1982. The current state leaders in North Rhine–Westphalia (SPD), the Saar (SPD), and Baden-Württemberg (CDU) are also considered future chancellor material. Leadership experience at the state level, as opposed to parliamentary experience in Bonn, may become more common for future chancellor candidates.

The major issues of state politics tend to focus on those areas where the states have primary responsibility: education, police and law enforcement, environmental questions, the supervision of radio and television, and the organization and regulation of the bureaucracy. The remainder of state activity tends to be the rather routine administration of policies formulated at the national level, albeit with state input.

The states have varied considerably in their treatment of educational matters. During the 1950s and 1960s, the issue of separate schools for Protestant and Catholic children, discussed in Chapter 4, was a major problem in those states with large Catholic populations. The reform of secondary and university-level education has also varied, with CDU/CSU states such as Bavaria and the Rhineland-Palatinate being decidedly less enthusiastic about the comprehensive school and democratized universities than SPD states like Hesse and North Rhine–Westphalia. Also, as discussed in Chapter 3, the treatment of radicals in public employment varies considerably beween conservative CDU states and liberal SPD states.

A clearer picture of state policy activities and the federal-state division of labor is provided by Table 8.2, which shows the expenditures of state and national governments by policy areas. Although the national government has almost sole responsibility for defense, internal security (police) is primarily a state

TABLE 8.2. EXPENDITURES OF STATE AND NATIONAL GOVERNMENTS BY POLICY AREA (in percentages)

Policy Area	Level	
	National	State
Social security, health, and welfare	32	8
Defense	20	—
Education	5	31
Police and administration of justice	1	10
General administration	4	6
Grants and other transfer payments	10	17
Transportation and communication	7	5
Housing	1	5
Energy and water resources	3	3
Economic enterprises	4	3
Agriculture	1	2
Debt service	12	10
	100	100

SOURCE: Statistisches Jahrbuch, 1987, p. 431.

function. In the area of social welfare, Bonn spends about four times as much as the states. Education has clearly been the prerogative of the states, and it still consumes about a third of all expenditures. Nonetheless, federal efforts to gain a foothold in the education area are evident by the $13.2 billion Bonn spent in 1987. Both levels are also the dispensers of public largesse to other levels of government. In the case of the states, about one of every five marks goes to local government in the form of grants. The grants of the federal government (10 percent of expenditures) go largely to the states, but the local communities are also the recipients of some grants from Bonn.

Federal-State Integration: Revenue Sharing

The Basic Law commits the Federal Republic to the maintenance of a "unity of living standards" between the various states of the federation. This is accomplished largely through money. Financial relations between the states and the federal government are very complex. They involve the following:

1. Vertical equalization (federal payments to poorer states).
2. The sharing of common tax revenues between the states and federal government.
3. Horizontal equalization (payments to poorer states by richer ones).
4. Intergovernmental grants and subsidies for various special and joint projects, as well as federal payments to the states to defray the costs of administering federal law.

German revenue sharing, especially on Bonn's part, has been designed to consolidate the structure and process of policymaking.[6] Although Bonn receives about 55 percent of all tax revenues, it is responsible for only about 45 percent of all public expenditures, including national defense. The states and local communities, on the other hand, spend more than they receive in taxes, with Bonn making up most of the difference. This financial leverage has enabled Bonn to effect some coordination in areas such as education, regional economic development, and social welfare programs.

The states, however, have steadily struggled for a larger piece of the tax pie and hence greater independence from Bonn. At present, the states do receive an equal share of the biggest source of tax revenue, the individual and corporate income tax (division: 40 percent each to Bonn and the states, 20 percent to the cities). Only a third of the second-biggest money raiser, the value-added tax (a form of sales tax levied on products and services at each stage in the production and distribution process as value is added to the good or service) goes to the states (see Table 8.3). Bonn receives about 95 percent of its income from taxes, but they account for only 70 percent of state revenues; the difference of 25 percent is, in a way, the margin of state dependency on the national government. For Bonn, on the other hand, it is a means to facilitate integration and consolidation. Neither side is satisfied with the present arrangement, and the struggle over the distribution of tax revenues continues.

TABLE 8.3. SOURCES OF TAX REVENUES BY GOVERNMENTAL LEVEL
(in percentages)

	Level		
Source	National	State	Local
Individual and corporate income taxes	36	58	40
Value-added tax	29	26	—
Gewerbesteuer[a]	—	—	42
Oil and gasoline tax	15	—	—
Tobacco	9	—	—
Automobile tax	—	8	—
Capital and inheritance tax	—	5	—
Custom duties	3	—	—
Liquor and beer tax	4	2	—
"Bagatelle" taxes (coffee, sugar, dogs, amusement)	1	—	1
Payroll tax	—	—	7
Property tax	—	—	9
Other	3	1	1
	100	100	100
	($124 billion)	($ 117 billion)	($77 billion)

[a] See p. 214.

SOURCE: *Statistisches Jahrbuch, 1987, pp. 430, 434, 438–439.*

THE FUTURE OF FEDERALISM

Some students of the German policy process consider the federal structure of the Republic as an impediment to efficient government and social and economic progress. Federalism is viewed as old-fashioned, something out of the nineteenth century that now frustrates future-oriented reforms and innovations. Opinion polls have also shown some support for more coordination and a stronger central government.

The states have generally opposed most efforts at planning and administrative reform (discussed in Chapter 7) fearing a loss of power and funds. In the "joint projects" program dealing with higher education, regional economic development, and health care, they opposed giving Bonn any significant coordinating authority but conceded only a framework planning function to the national government. They have also opposed increased authority for Bonn on questions of water and air pollution. Thus, for example, Bonn is being held responsible by neighboring countries such as Switzerland and the Netherlands for the pollution of the Rhine, but because of federalism, its power to make and enforce stricter pollution control laws is very limited.[7]

The weakness of the federal system was also noticeable in the inability of the police to apprehend many terrorists responsible for the robberies, kidnappings, and murders that plagued the Federal Republic in the 1970s. The structure of German law enforcement—largely as a consequence of experiences with the centralized Nazi police state—is very decentralized. Police powers are largely reserved to the states, which have been reluctant to concede any major responsibility to the federal government. Because terrorists do not respect state boundaries, the inadequate coordination and communication among the states and between them and the federal government was a major factor in the poor record of law enforcement agencies in dealing with small but well-organized terrorist groups. It was only after national law enforcement agencies, such as the Federal Criminal Office and the Office for the Protection of the Constitution, were strengthened that significant progress in the apprehension of terrorists was made.

One solution to these problems is the consolidation of the federal system through a reduction in the number of states from the present ten to five or six units of roughly similar size, population, and economic resources. Such a federal structure would greatly reduce, if not eliminate, the poor state–rich state problem and hence the need for Bonn and the richer states to pay subsidies or equalization money to the poorer states. Realignment and consolidation would also end the veto power now enjoyed by even the smallest state in many joint federal-state undertakings. Fewer but stronger states, however, would probably increase the assertiveness of the Bundesrat. The adoption of any realignment would require a constitutional amendment and a majority of two-thirds in both houses of parliament; hence, without bipartisan support, realignment is impossible.

LOCAL GOVERNMENT

Germany has a long tradition of local self-government. Many cities proudly trace their independence to the Middle Ages, before the establishment of the nation-state. Although the consolidation of monarchical rule, especially in Prussia, later reduced the autonomy of cities, the reforms of Freiherr vom Stein, which followed Napoleon's defeat of Prussia, revived local independence. The Weimar Constitution also gave all communities the right of self-government. During the Weimar Republic three types of local self-government were common: (1) a single council system fusing both legislative and executive functions (most prevalent in southern Germany); (2) a strong mayor form in which an elected council appointed a mayor with long tenure to perform executive functions—for example, Konrad Adenauer, mayor of Cologne from 1917 to 1933; (3) a bicameral municipal council according to which the lower house, directly elected, invested executive power in a board of magistrates, which served as the upper chamber.[8]

Local elections and self-government were abolished by the Nazis in the Municipal Government Act of 1935, and all local officials were appointed by higher-level Nazi party or governmental agencies. Committed to a grass-roots approach to postwar democratization, Allied occupation powers restored and actually strengthened local self-government after 1945. The Basic Law (Article 28) guarantees local communities "the right to regulate, under their own responsibility and within the limits of the laws, all the affairs of the local community."

Structures and Functions

There are about 8,500 local communities (*Gemeinden*) in the Federal Republic, ranging in size from towns and villages of less than 10,000 inhabitants to large cities (*Grosstädte*) of 1 million or more. Until the 1960s, the number of local communities approached 30,000, but local government reform in many states has consolidated most units with fewer than 8,000 inhabitants. Generally there are four types of local government, but all have an elected council (*Stadtrat* or *Gemeinderat*) in common.[9] Within each state, local government structures are uniform: In Lower Saxony, Hesse, and North Rhine–Westphalia, this council delegates executive and administrative authority to an appointed city manager (*Stadtdirektor*). In Schleswig-Holstein this executive is collegial. The Rhineland-Palatinate has a dominant mayor system with the mayor responsible to the council. In Bavaria and Baden-Württemberg, the council has both executive and legislative functions but shares executive responsibility with a directly elected mayor. The city-states of Hamburg and Bremen have a governing senate, which selects the mayor. Elections to these councils, which range in size from about 6 to as many as 75 members, usually take place every four years.

The primary organs of county (*Kreis*) governments are an elected council (*Kreistag*) and an executive official, the *Landrat,* chosen by the council, except in

Bavaria, where he is directly elected. Only 87 cities are *kreisfrei* (that is, not within the jurisdiction of a county). The *Landrat* is a type of county manager supervising local administration, especially those local activities performed on behalf of the state government. If a local community within a county disagrees with county policies, it can challenge them in the administrative or constitutional court. The character of local-state relations is determined by each state's local government constitution (*Gemeindeverfassung*).

Generally, local politics tend to be more personalistic than those at the state or national level. People know more about local problems, feel they have some influence, and are more likely to vote in local elections because of the candidate's personality rather than his party label. About 80 percent of voters in local elections, for example, report that they personally know the candidate they supported.

The belief that local government is largely a matter of nonpolitical administration and hence not appropriate for party politics is widespread. As a concession to this attitude, political parties frequently nominate well-known local figures who are not party members. Most candidates try to deemphasize their party affiliation and stress their concern for the particular community. The small size of most communities also enables personal relationships to remain determinants of political relationships. In local elections, the national parties must sometimes compete with two types of local voter groups: relatively stable local *Rathaus* (city hall) parties with a formal program and organization; and more loosely structured voter groups that are formed for specific elections and then disband. In some states these local "antiparties" ("Citizen Unions," "Free Voters Associations") have secured as much as 25 percent of the vote.

In spite of the partisan structure of local elections, especially in large cities, there is little empirical evidence to suggest that major policy differences in German cities are the result of party/political factors. Rhetorically the parties do differ in their approach to local government. The SPD supports a so-called municipal socialism with publicly owned utilities, hospitals, and cultural centers favored over private control of such institutions. The SPD has also advocated municipal control of land and large housing projects whereas, in theory at least, the Christian Democrats support individual property and home ownership. A recent empirical study, however, relating policy outputs in fields such as housing and education to local party control, found few differences that could be explained by party/political factors.[10] Indeed, it was found that in the twelve CDU cities, there was more public housing than in the SPD strongholds.[11] However, some moderate relationships between SPD or CDU party control and city spending policies were found at the local level. The SPD cities are slightly more activist, expansionist, and collectivist than CDU city governments.

There are two types of local government functions: the so-called compulsory responsibilities (for example, schools, fire protection, streets, and sanitation) and transferred responsibilities, activities carried out for the Länder or national government (for example, tax collection, health care, and housing). In spite of recent administrative reforms that reduced the number of communities, many are still too small to carry out these responsibilties independently. County government and regional local associations with pooled resources assume many of these functions. Regional associations of local communities are a relatively recent innovation and have been assigned an important role in plans for regional economic development.

Although local self-government is constitutionally guaranteed, this independence is considerably limited by local dependence on federal and, especially, state grants as well as tax revenues from industrial enterprises. Only about a third of local government revenues comes from taxes, mainly from (since 1969) its share of the income tax (20 percent) and the *Gewerbesteuer*, a tax on the production and capital investment of commercial and industrial firms. Property taxes, the major source of local government revenue in the United States, account for only about 9 percent of tax revenue for German communities. The low return on property levies is primarily a result of assessment rates that are kept artificially low by federal law for reasons of social policy. Also, large proportions of land located in the communities, such as public housing projects, defense installations, and other government-owned property, are tax-exempt.

Besides taxes and grants, the fees charged by the cities for their services (water, electricity, public transportation, gas, refuse collection) constitute another major source of local government revenue. Generally, German cities offer a broader range of services than their American counterparts: publicly owned utilities, public transportation, city-run banks, markets, breweries, and an extensive range of cultural activities (operas, repertory theater, orchestras, festivals, adult education). These latter services are heavily subsidized by local, state, and federal governments. Admission prices to the opera, for example, cover only about 30 percent of costs.[12]

THE URBAN CRISIS, WEST GERMAN STYLE

Like local communities in other advanced industrial societies, German local government in the 1980s is heavily indebted, is facing rising demands for goods and services, and in many areas, is structurally outmoded.

Mounting Financial Deficits

Although the 1971 finance reform gave the cities a larger share of tax revenues, thus saving many of them from bankruptcy, rising personnel and construction costs brought several dozen urban areas to the brink of financial collapse a few years later. Between 1961 and 1974 the new debts of local government increased by 400 percent, as compared to about 150 percent for state and national governments.[13] Two-thirds of all local government investment is done with borrowed money, and about a third of its tax revenues is consumed by debt service.[14]

The increased demand for more and better public services and their increased cost, coupled with an inadequate tax distribution system, are largely responsible for this financial dilemma. Yet poor planning and accounting procedures on the part of local government are also involved. Cost overruns on major urban projects are common. Munich, for example, spent $100 million more than planned for a new cultural center. Cologne built a stretch of subway line, which was later found to be ill-suited for transportation and is now used for growing mushrooms.[15]

Social Democratic domination of many large cities and the right of city employees to hold legislative positions have produced a political style in these areas not unlike the party machine politics once characteristic of most large American cities. In Berlin, for example, the SPD party organization and the SPD-controlled city administration became so interlocked that it was difficult to separate the two. Two-thirds of the SPD's delegation in the West Berlin parliament were employees of the city, and 87 percent of the parliament's internal affairs committee, which plays a key role in salary and wage determination, were themselves city employees. This *Verfilzung* (literally "entanglement") of governmental bureaucracy and party is one reason why local governments have been the least likely to hold the line against the wage demands of public officials.

Urban Transport

European cities were never built for automobiles, nor did the planners of cities rebuilt after the war plan for the mass motorized society that was to emerge in the 1960s. After attempting to construct streets and freeways to accommodate cars, most urban planners now believe it is financially and ecologically impossible for the German city and the private automobile to coexist. The historical core of many German cities is already badly damaged, and streets still remain jammed and parking facilities woefully inadequate. These conditions leave mass public transport as the only alternative. To make this appealing to the car-loving Germans, however, will also require new capital that the cities simply do not have.

Housing and Land Use

Existing zoning regulations and the postwar commitment to a free-market economy encouraged widespread urban land speculation, and a booming economy meant that highly profitable projects such as office buildings and apartment houses received priority over parks, playgrounds, and low-cost public housing. City governments, greatly dependent on the Gewerbesteuer for revenue, were forced into competition for new industry. By catering to industry, cities also neglected public services such as schools, hospitals, homes for the elderly, and the environment. In Hanover, for example, to secure a large IBM assembly plant the city developed at public expense large tracts of prime park and recreational land, which was then offered to IBM as a plant site. When the firm later pulled out of the deal, the pitfalls of such catering to private interests became painfully apparent to the community. With continued economic prosperity, prices for urban land skyrocketed and speculators made huge, windfall profits. In some cities, radical students and Young Socialists, to dramatize the situation, seized unoccupied private apartment buildings and turned them over to homeless, disadvantaged families.

By the late 1970s in many large German cities, the shortage of low- or moderate-cost housing became acute. The high price of land and soaring interest rates sharply reduced new construction. Access to government-subsidized public housing favored older families who already had been in public housing or on waiting lists. Young people moving into the cities had to face the high rents in private housing. In some cities, however, groups of homeless students and other young people simply occupied vacant houses and apartment buildings. By early 1981 these urban squatters had taken over more than 500 buildings in 50 urban areas. The squatters' movement has also been accompanied by frequent demonstrations and in some cases clashes with police and mass arrests. In Nuremberg, a youth center suspected by police of being an organizational center of the movement was raided and 141 young people arrested. The immediate cause for the raid was a street demonstration emanating from the youth center that resulted in only minor damage. This type of mass arrest conjured up for some memories of another era, and the Nuremberg action was condemned by many judges, prosecutors, and the media throughout the Republic as a violation of individual rights. Although most of the demonstrators were soon released, the incident reflects the hard-line approach to protest movements taken by some authorities who have attempted to link the urban squatters to the terrorist scene.[16]

These problems are to a great extent the result of inadequate urban and regional planning in the postwar period. German urban policymakers understandably wanted to rebuild as quickly as possible; comprehensive long-range planning was not a priority. The emergence of urban citizen initiative groups, discussed in Chapter 3, illustrates the extent to which established local political institutions have been unable to meet the more sophisticated demands for change they now face.

SUMMARY AND CONCLUSION

West German federalism and local self-government are largely the expression of a historically rooted particularism and the disastrous experiences with the centralized Third Reich. Like the Basic Law, of which they are a part, these structures are primarily oriented to the past and the avoidance of the errors of former regimes. Their future utility is now a topic of serious political debate. At issue is not the abolition of the federal system or local self-government but their modernization. This involves at a minimum the consolidation and realignment of state and local units, their support for more cooperative policy programs with the national government, and their acceptance of a greater federal role in areas traditionally reserved to them: education, economic development, the police, the administration of justice, and the protection of the environment.

In many areas federalism has been a positive force in the Republic's postwar development. It has enhanced the internal diversity of the political parties, has provided at times an opportunity for policy innovation, and has enabled Bonn to avoid the disadvantages of a large centralized bureaucracy.[17] But West Germany today is a far more integrated society than any of its predecessors, and it now confronts policy problems that are more complex and national in scope. The popular support that the Republic now enjoys is in large part the result of its performance. The question is whether this performance level can be maintained in the future with the structures and processes of the past.

NOTES

1. Fritz W. Scharpf, "Politische Durchsetzbarkeit Innerer Reformen Im Pluralistisch-Demokratischen Gemeinwesen der Bundesrepublik" (Berlin: International Institute for Management, 1973), pp. 33 ff.
2. Rudolf Hrbek, "Das Problem der Neugliederung des Bundesgebiets," *Aus Politik und Zeitgeschichte,* no. 46 (13 November 1971).
3. Between 1946 and 1951 Baden-Württemberg was divided into three separate units that were merged after a plebiscite.
4. Arnold J. Heidenheimer, "Federalism and the Party System: The Case of West Germany," *American Political Science Review* 52 (1958): 808–828.
5. Geoffrey Pridham, "A Nationalization Process? Federal Politics and State Elections in West Germany," *Government and Opposition* 8, no. 4 (Fall 1973): 455–472.
6. Robert L. Rothweiler, "Revenue Sharing in the Federal Republic of Germany," *Publius* 2, no. 1 (Spring 1972): 4–25.
7. It must be noted, however, that other countries also bear considerable responsibility for the condition of the river. The Swiss city of Basel, for example, still does not have a sewage treatment plant. The sodium mines in Alsace (France) are another source of pollution.
8. Linda L. Dolive, "Electoral Politics at the Local Level in the German Federal Republic" (Ph.D. dissertation, University of Florida, 1972), p. 29.
9. A rarely cited provision of the constitution (Article 28) does permit local communities to be governed by citizen assemblies (town meetings) instead of by elected, representative bodies. Few if any communities, however, have made use of this form of direct democracy at the local level. Referendums are also possible in seven of the eleven states. They are not allowed in Schleswig-Holstein, Lower Saxony, Hamburg, and West Berlin.
10. Robert C. Fried, "Party and Policy in West German Cities," *American Political Science Review,* 70, no. 9 (March 1976): 17–24.
11. Ibid.
12. Sanford Rakoff and Gunther Schaefer, "Local Government Expenditures in the Federal Republic of Germany and the United States" (Paper presented at the annual meeting of the American Political Science Association, Chicago, 1974).
13. Wolfgang Hoffmann, "Stadtväter in Not," *Die Zeit,* 18 October 1974, p. 39.
14. Horst Bieber, "Die fünf Plagen der Städte," *Die Zeit,* 4 May 1973, p. 32.

15. Hoffmann, "Stadtväter."*Die Zeit,* 4 April 1985, p. 19.
16. *Die Zeit,* 27 March 1981, pp. 3–4.
17. In their study of nuclear energy policy in France and Germany, Nelkin and Pollak found that Germany's decentralized political/administrative structure, in contrast to French centralization, was a major factor in the relatively greater success of the German antinuclear movement. In Germany "intra-governmental conflicts are inevitable—between, for example, regional and national governments, or between environmental agencies and the ministry of economics. The anti-nuclear movement increased its own influence by exacerbating such intra-administrative conflicts." Dorothy Nelkin and Michael Pollak, *The Atom Besieged* (Cambridge, MA: MIT Press, 1981), p. 182.

CHAPTER 9

Conclusion: The German Polity Faces the Future

The Federal Republic has now existed twice as long as the Weimar Republic (1919–1933) and Hitler's Thousand-Year Reich (1933–1945). Never before in German history has a liberal republic functioned as successfully or endured as long as the "provisional" Bonn system we have examined in the preceding chapters. Within a constitutional framework rather hastily constructed in 1948 and 1949, West Germany has become a legitimate and increasingly dynamic democracy. This is an impressive accomplishment, and as Richard Löwenthal has observed, it is a "German political miracle" at least as significant as, if not more than, the famous postwar "economic miracle."[1]

Although a complex variety of attitudinal changes, discussed in Chapter 3, have been taking place since the immediate postwar years (changes largely in the direction of learning and internalizing the values and procedures of liberal democracy), major institutional and policy shifts have been much slower in coming. Most German political leaders have been reluctant to embark on significant policy innovations before a solid consensus on the Republic itself is established. As a result, by the 1980s, the political agenda of West Germany contained an abundance of unfinished business. In this chapter we examine several policy areas where major changes have recently taken place or are currently being debated.

CHANGE IN FOREIGN POLICY

In spite of its many successes, the Federal Republic has not achieved what in 1949 was ostensibly its foremost policy goal: the reunification of Germany in "peace and freedom." Since the late 1960s, this goal and its realization have been redefined in the light of events and the realities of postwar European and world politics.

As discussed in Chapter 1, the creation of the Federal Republic from the three Western occupation zones took place in response to the perceived Soviet threat to Western European security. The Republic's origins then were inextricably connected with the cold war and the resultant ideology of anticommunism and containment. More than any other Western European state, the Federal Republic under Adenauer supported the American hard-line policy of strength against the Soviet Union. This was thought by many West Germans, and especially Adenauer, to be the price necessary for the Republic's integration and acceptance into the Western alliance. Adenauer, the chief if not sole architect of postwar foreign policy, sought this integration into the West before any serious consideration of reunification with the Soviet occupied zone.[2] The official position was indeed that unification could take place only through a policy of strength and confrontation with the Soviet Union—that is, through full support of postwar American foreign policy.

Many Germans recognized that a close alliance with the United States was indispensable to the *security* of the Federal Republic, but the relationship between the American alliance and *reunification* was less clear. From the outset, significant groups within the SPD, the Free Democrats, and even the CDU saw Adenauer's policy as one that would seal the division of Germany. They pointed out that the reunification issue was in fact a special problem the Germans had with the Russians. All claims to the contrary, a reunified Germany was not in the interests of any other country, East or West, except Germany. In short, if reunification was the foremost goal of the Republic's foreign policy, it should not have counted on much assistance from the Western Allies.

The spectacular electoral triumphs of Adenauer and the CDU in 1953 and 1957, however, clearly indicated that West German voters, although still paying lip service to reunification, as did Adenauer, nonetheless preferred economic prosperity and constitutional government within their territory to the hope of reunification with the Soviet zone of occupation. In short, the electorate supported Adenauer's foreign policy of Western integration and were willing to accept his assurances that somehow, at some future point, it would bring about reunification. In the meantime, they were saying, "No experiments."

A reevaluation of this foreign policy did not begin until the early 1960s when some party leaders, most notably from the SPD and FDP, began to advocate new departures in foreign policy. The impetus for this reassessment came above all from the construction of the Berlin Wall in August 1961 and its resultant American acceptance as a fait accompli. This American reaction was interpreted by many Germans as proof that the cold war policies of strength and rollback were by 1961 empty rhetoric. After thirteen years of Adenauer's leadership and his rigid anticommunism, Germany was no closer to reunification than in 1949 and was still isolated from Eastern Europe and the Soviet Union. The policies of Adenauer had not led to a lessening of the totalitarian character of the East German regime. Bonn's claim to be the sole legitimate representative of the German people and the adamant refusal to recognize the GDR did nothing to improve the day-to-day lives of the 17 million Germans in East Germany for whom Bonn claimed to speak. Finally, Berlin in 1961 remained just as isolated and vulnerable to Soviet pressures as at the time of the blockade.

The beginnings of the new foreign policy were modest. Following Adenauer's departure in 1963, West German trade missions were opened in Romania, Bulgaria, and Hungary. At the behest of the FDP, Chancellor Erhard's government initiated programs of technical and cultural exchange between the two German states. In 1966, Social Democratic leaders proposed a series of discussions with East German party leaders that were rejected only at the last moment by East Berlin.

It was not, however, until the formation of the Grand Coalition in December 1966 that Ostpolitik acquired momentum. The establishment of full diplomatic relations with Romania in 1967 meant the de facto end of the policy of refusing to maintain diplomatic relations with any state that recognized East Germany (the Hallstein doctrine), because Romania recognized East Germany. Foreign Minister Willy Brandt and the other SPD ministers in the Kiesinger cabinet then advocated recognition of and full diplomatic relations with Yugoslavia, a step that was opposed by the CDU/CSU members of the government, including Chancellor Kiesinger. A 1967 East German proposal for inner-German discussions at the chancellor level was rejected by the cabinet only after a threatened revolt by the right wing of the Christian Democrats. In addition, at its 1967 convention the small opposition party, the Free Democrats, essentially supported the policies of Brandt and even went further by proposing the outright recognition of East Germany. During its period in opposition, the foreign policy of the FDP had been converging with that of the Social Democrats, a development of fundamental importance after the election of 1969.

At the SPD's party conference in 1968, a resolution was passed that called for the recognition of East Germany but stopped short of acknowledging the GDR as a "foreign state." As the 1969 election approached, the coalition partners in the government (SPD and CDU/CSU) became increasingly polarized over any new foreign policy initiatives.

After the 1969 election, the Social Democrats and their new partner, the Free Democrats, were in basic agreement on the necessity for new departures in foreign policy, and work was begun immediately following the formation of a new government led by Willy Brandt. Within a year after the election, the treaty normalizing relations with the Soviet Union was signed, albeit with a provision that the treaty would not be submitted for parliamentary ratification until a satisfactory agreement was reached by the four powers (the United States, Great Britain, France, and the Soviet Union) over the status of Berlin. In December 1970 a treaty with Poland that essentially recognized the Oder-Neisse line as Poland's western border was also completed. Then in September 1972 a Basic Treaty with East Germany normalizing relations between the two German states and calling for the exchange of representatives, but wihholding full diplomatic recognition, was concluded. Finally, Bonn's relations with Czechoslovakia were also normalized in a treay signed in December 1973 and ratified by the parliament in June 1974.

The ratification of the Russian and Polish treaties did not take place until after the unsuccessful opposition attempt to topple the Brandt government in April 1972. The federal election in November 1972 left little doubt that a solid majority of West Germans approved of the new foreign policy.

As Figure 9.1 shows, a gradual yet decisive change had been taking place since the 1950s in West German public opinion toward the Republic's eastern borders. Between 1951 and 1972 the proportion of West Germans supporting the recognition of the Oder-Neisse line, and hence the acceptance of Germany's postwar border, increased from only 8 percent in 1951 to 61 percent by 1972. And although 80 percent of the adult population in 1951 opposed any acceptance of the postwar status quo, by 1972 this had dropped to only 18 percent. The largest increases in support for acceptance took place between 1965 and 1967 (27 percent to 46 percent) and 1969 and 1970 (42 percent to 58 percent). It appears that in the first case the public was responding to the foreign policy innovations of the Grand Coalition, and in 1970 it was reacting positively to the treaties with the Soviet Union and Poland. The difficult question of whether German policymakers were leading or following public opinion cannot be resolved with these data, but they do show that West German leaders in the late

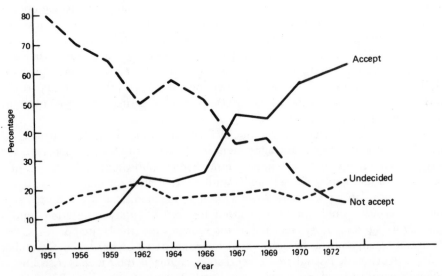

Figure 9.1. Change in popular attitudes toward acceptance of the German-Polish border (Oder-Neisse line). *(From Jahrbuch 5:525).*

1960s were making policy within a context of public opinion that was far more favorable to innovation than it had been a decade earlier.

Opposition to Ostpolitik was centered in the CDU/CSU and especially its Bavarian wing (CSU). It was Bavaria that petitioned the federal constitutional court for a judgment on the constitutionality of the treaties. The court rejected the petition on the grounds that the treaties were a political matter between the government and opposition in parliament and did not involve the Basic Law as such. Generally the critics of Ostpolitik argued that the government had given away too much to the communist bloc states and had been overanxious to secure agreement. Although few, even in the CSU, believed that Germany could ever regain the territories east of the Oder-Neisse line (Pomerania, East Prussia, Silesia), it was suggested that the formal concession of these areas should have been matched by a corresponding communist concession at some future peace conference. Also, in negotiations over a Basic Treaty with East Germany, critics asked why the government did not make the elimination of the Wall, the rescinding of the shoot-to-kill order to GDR border guards, the release of political prisoners, and the liberalization of domestic conditions within the GDR conditions for the agreement. Above all, critics charged that the government's conceptions of communism and the international movement were naive and shortsighted. The critics rejected the government's assertion that the Soviet Union had mellowed and was genuinely interested in détente.

The government responded to CDU/CSU criticism by emphasizing that it had conceded nothing to the Soviet Union, Poland, East Germany, or Czechoslovakia that had not been already lost by Germany's defeat in World War II. The loss of territories and the expropriation and forced expulsion of Germans living in Poland and Czechoslovakia that had taken place after 1945 could not conceivably be redressed without an aggressive war, which West Germany could not and would not engage in. Also, in the government's view, no Western European ally, much less the United States, would support such a hard-line, revanchist policy.

The government essentially argued that its policies had relieved Germans of false hopes, finally creating a framework for normal relations with Eastern Europe and had thus put West Germany at the forefront of the worldwide trend toward détente, quite consistent with the policies of the United States, the Republic's most important ally, and Germany's other partners in the European community, all of whom supported Ostpolitik. Furthermore, West Germany had now clearly made less tenable the communist claims of German militarism and revanchism and put the East Germans especially on the defensive. Access to Berlin was also now guaranteed. West Germans and West Berliners could travel in the GDR; friends and families could once again come together.

These developments illustrate the extensive process of coalition building and negotiation that precedes formal policymaking and implementation in the Federal Republic. In the case of Ostpolitik, neither public opinion (including the refugees) nor a majority among the parliamentary parties was prepared to support the new approach until almost twenty years after the Republic's founding. Yet there were significant domestic pressures for change. Specifically, business and industrial groups, largely represented in the FDP, were interested in the Eastern European and Russian markets where Germany historically had played a major role. Although the SPD and especially Willy Brandt saw Ostpolitik largely in ideological/humanitarian terms, the Free Democrats, even during the 1950s, had urged an open mind on the question, largely because of their export-oriented business clientele. Another important factor was the state of East-West Relations. American interest in détente, foreshadowed by de Gaulle's contacts with Eastern Europe and the Soviet Union in the early 1960s and the British interest in a relaxation of international tension, coincided with Ostpolitik and lessened the intensity of internal and external opposition to this innovation. Some West Germans regarded this policy of reconciliation and acceptance of postwar boundaries as a betrayal of national interests and of the Basic Law itself, but to the majority of them it was the only realistic policy consistent with the maintenance of world peace, which has always taken precedence over reunification.

CHANGE IN INTER-GERMAN RELATIONS

Ostpolitik achieved its final legitimation when the Christian Democrats returned to power in 1982. Contrary to their rhetoric while in opposition, the CDU/CSU in government has both accepted and continued the policies toward Eastern Europe and the Soviet Union associated with the Socialist-Liberal regimes of Willy Brandt and Helmut Schmidt. This was dramatically shown in the summer of 1983 when the Kohl government, shortly before the chancellor's trip to Moscow for talks with Soviet leader Andropov, agreed to guarantee a $400 million credit line to East Germany. The loan guarantee became a political sensation when it was revealed that the Bavarian CSU leader, Franz-Josef Strauss, had helped to initiate the entire project. Strauss, Germany's foremost cold warrior during the 1950s and staunch opponent of Ostpolitik, had in the past consistently accused the Socialists of selling out Germany's interests to the Soviet bloc through such deals. Following the loan guarantee, Strauss also went to East Germany and met with Communist party leaders. For some of his followers this change was too difficult to accept and they left the CSU, but there now could be no doubt that Ostpolitik had become a part of the West German political consensus.

Relations between the two German states reached a new level in 1987 when Erich Honecker became the first leader of East Germany to step onto West German soil. His five-day visit, which was twice postponed through the intervention of the Soviet Union, represented a culmination of fifteen years of steadily improving relations. This period was characterized by increased economic activity financed in part through multibillion dollar credits from West Germany, extensive scientific and technological cooperation, and a sharply increased flow of visitors from East Germany to the West. In 1987 a million East Germans under the pension age were allowed to visit the Federal Republic, up from only 50,000 in 1985. The total number of East Germans who traveled to the West in 1987 rose to over 2.6 million, or about 15 percent of East Germany's total population.

For Honecker, the visit meant that the Federal Republic after forty years had finally recognized East Germany, which Bonn once derisively called the "Zone," as a sovereign and legitimate state. For Chancellor Kohl, it was an opportunity to demonstrate to West Germans that his government remained committed to bringing the divided nation together and to press the East Germans for further improvements in human rights, including rescinding the shoot-to-kill order at the West German border.

This German mini-détente has taken place in spite of the ups and downs in Bonn's relations with the Soviet Union. During the 1981–1983 controversy over the deployment of new medium range missiles in West Germany, Moscow attempted to intimidate the Federal Republic with dire threats about a "pallisade" of nuclear missiles between the two German states and a renewal of Cold War tensions. The 1987 Soviet-American treaty eliminating these weapons brought a marked improvement in German-Soviet relations, however. The Kohl government's decision to dismantle the seventy-two German-owned missiles, which the Soviets requested as part of the treaty, also improved the climate between Bonn and Moscow.

The consensus on Ostpolitik reflects the West German belief that any eventual reunification of the country depends on the Soviet Union. Both official and public opinion has welcomed the new thinking and reform policies instituted by Soviet leader, Mikhail Gorbachev, since 1985. Even Franz-Josef Strauss, following a 1988 visit to Moscow, praised the Soviet leader's policies while criticizing President Reagan as unpredictable. Public opinion studies in the late 1980s also showed the Soviet leader to be more popular in West Germany than President Reagan. The proportion of West Germans who want the Federal Republic to give equal weight in its foreign policy to both the United States and the Soviet Union, rather than to depend entirely on Washington, has increased from 41 percent in 1983 to 68 percent in 1987.[3] Clearly, the Federal Republic is now pursuing a more independent foreign policy consistent with its political maturity and its economic and strategic importance.

CONSTITUTIONAL CHANGE

The Basic Law (constitution) of the Federal Republic is essentially a backward-looking document conditioned primarily by the determination to avoid the errors of the Weimar Republic's constitution which, it is widely believed, aided the Nazi seizure of power. In this sense, it is also a negative document.

In addition, few of its framers expected the constitution or the Republic to last very long. The unanticipated longevity of the system coupled with the provisional character of its constitution has necessitated relatively frequent amendments. The Basic Law can be amended by a two-thirds vote of both the Bundestag and Bundesrat. Between 1949 and 1985, thirty-one amendments were approved, as compared to only twenty-six amendments to the American Constitution beween 1776 and 1989. Most of these amendments dealt with intergovernmental (federal, state, local) relations, especially the distribution of tax revenues and the administration of justice. Other amendments involved national defense, the statute of limitations for war crimes, the adjustment of financial burdens associated with war losses, state boundaries, and procedures in the event of national emergencies. Many of these became necessary as the provisional character of the Republic became less and less apparent. When in 1955, for example, Germany joined the North Atlantic Treaty Organization (NATO), a constitutional amendment was needed because the original document, for obvious reasons, made no mention at all of military forces. The controversial "emergency laws" detailing the procedures to be followed in the event of a national emergency also required amendments.

The Basic Law in Article 79, as interpreted by the federal constitutional court, set limits on the amendment process. The court has ruled that any amendments directly affecting the federal structure of the state (that is, the division of the federation into Länder), the rights of the states to participate in the national legislative process, or the civil rights contained in Articles 1 and 20 are not permitted.

Since the late 1960s, a growing number of constitutional scholars and political leaders have been considering the possibility of a new constitution.[4] Such a document would presumably require the direct popular election of a constituent assembly, which would draft a document that would then have to be ratified by the electorate.

One problem a new constitution must address is the legal status of the Republic. Through the Ostpolitik treaties with the Soviet Union, Poland, East Germany, and Czechoslovakia and its approval of the European Security Agreement at Helsinki in 1975, the Federal Republic has legally accepted the permanence of its borders with Eastern Europe, including East Germany. Should those constitutional provisions committing the Republic to reunification be removed? Should its claim to be the sole legitimate successor to the German Reich be abandoned? By the 1980s, the government's official position was one of accepting the reality of two German states existing within one nation; and it still seeks, officially at least, the peaceful reunification of this "one nation" at some point in the future.

The European Community

West Germany was a charter member and enthusiastic supporter of the postwar European movement. Whether it was the Common Market, the Defense Community, or any other European organization, German participation could always be counted on. All democratic parties supported "Europe" and expressed the hope for an eventual political unification of the continent. Europe was, and to a large extent still is, an "OK" concept. Strong support for Europe was one way of forgetting about being German after 1945 and of reestablishing relations with Germany's neighbors. It was also highly advantageous to the German economy.

Progress toward European unification has been most apparent in the economic field. Germany had little difficulty with either the European customs union or the common external tariff policy of the Common Market. The efforts of French President de Gaulle during the 1960s to make the internal structure of the Community and its foreign policy conform to his views did, however, put the Republic between Washington and Paris and complicated West Germany's foreign policy. The Gaullist vision of Europe also prompted a miniconflict between the Atlanticist (pro-American) and Gaullist wings of the then-ruling Christian Democratic Union.

European issues have had little partisan political impact. Relations with Brussels (the administrative center of the European Community) were mainly the responsibility of one department in the economics ministry and in general were treated as a largely technical issue. The establishment of a common agricultural price support and marketing structure in 1967 did, however, provoke political controversy, as farmers concerned about competition from France and other more efficient agricultural producers protested. Yet all parties made great efforts to support the farmers, so this problem did not become a partisan policy issue.

The lions share of agricultural policymaking now takes place in Brussels. In some fields, the economics and finance ministries must work within the context of European policy. In addition, the Bundestag now examines proposed European Community regulations in its committees. Major interest groups, especially in agriculture and business, also have contacts in Brussels, and several Länder even have representatives in Europe's "capital."

In recent years, the European Community has also attempted to develop common trade policies for its members. This has led to numerous European-American disputes over steel, high technology, and agriculture. As a key member of the Community, West Germany plays a major role in the formulation of these policies. Yet, as Gebhard Schweigler has noted, "Bonn is able to escape direct blame for controversial trade policies by pursuing them together with its European partners, and, if need be, by hiding, as it were, behind the decision-making process in Brussels."[5] The Community also provides Bonn with a means to reduce the suspicion that a powerful West Germany still evokes among some of its neighbors.

Nonetheless, national autonomy is still very much preserved in the councils of the European movement. Various German governments have been critical of the costs of the Brussels bureaucracy and are wary about any agreements that would commit the Federal Republic to extensive financial support for the poorer members. Yet the Republic remains committed to the eventual political unification of Europe, which in any form would require major constitutional changes.

POLICY ISSUES AND PROCESSES

As the preceding chapters have shown, the Federal Republic is a complex political system characterized by the presence of several power centers. The national executive with its control over the civil service initiates the broad outlines of policy, but it cannot secure the approval of its policy proposals or their implementation without at least the tacit prior approval of other actors in the political system: the major interest groups, the extraparliamentary organizations of the governing parties, the back benchers in the legislature, the states, the semipublic institutions such as the Bundesbank, and even the opposition party when it has a majority of the delegates in the Bundesrat. Strong opposition by any of these actors will greatly hinder the efforts of the government and chancellor to determine the main guidelines of policy.

Successful policymaking must be accomplished within the framework of the politicoeconomic consensus that has emerged during the past forty years. This means that the system resists any efforts at introducing major innovations within a relatively short time. Change tends to be gradual and incremental, and rarely will it have a redistributive effect. The issue of codetermination, for example, has been a policy problem throughout most of the Republic's history. Codetermination—the right of workers and other employees to share in a firm's decisionmaking process through equal representation on its supervisory board—was a key element in the SPD program in 1969 when it became the major partner in a coalition with the FDP and again in 1972 when this coalition secured a comfortable parliamentary majority. In spite of these favorable political conditions, the new codetermination law that finally went into effect in 1976 did not give a firm's workers parity with capital and management. Attempts to change the tax system in the direction of more progressive rates have also been stymied, partly by the opposition of the small coalition partner but also through the efforts of well-organized interest groups that have extensive contacts with governmental ministries.

The postwar German economic record—low inflation and unemployment, steady economic growth—is one result of a consensus-oriented political leadership and policy process. In a recent seven-nation study, Germany ranked third in expenditures but also third highest in taxes.[6] At the same time, the social welfare system (pensions, health insurance) has helped to maintain a high level of demand. Germany also ranked high in capital investment, which provided for an adequte number of new jobs.

In comparison with six other advanced industrial societies:

> Germany attained the best trade-off (the lowest inflation and jobless rates) because labor unions sought moderate wage increases, concentrated industries accepted the need for import-export competition, and the government enacted monetary and fiscal policies that stimulated moderately high aggregate demand—neither high enough to cause rapid price rises nor sufficiently low to produce high joblessness.[7]

The disastrous experience with inflation in the 1920s and the real economic gains in the postwar period have made all parties sensitive and responsive to inflationary problems.

The extensive welfare state has also been part of this consensus. The Basic Law states that the Federal Republic is a *sozialer* state, or state obligated to establish and maintain basic social welfare rights. Thus governmental policies designed to provide full employment, education, housing, child support payments, social security, and health care have not been for the most part matters of partisan conflict over the issue of whether the government should be involved in these areas but, rather, the *extent* of governmental activity. Partisan debates about these issues have tended to revolve around problems of detail and administration.

In recent years, however, both the Socialist governments of Helmut Schmidt and the Christian Democratic coalition of Helmut Kohl, responding to the sluggish economy and reduced state revenues, have made significant cuts in West Germany's extensive social welfare system. Since 1979 the dynamic pension system, first introduced in 1957, which linked pension increases to wage and salary raises, has been trimmed. Pension increases are now only indirectly connected to net wage and salary gains. Moreover, since 1984 retirees must pay a portion of the costs for their health insurance. The national health insurance program, once one of the most generous in Western Europe, has also encountered fiscal problems. Since 1983, hospital patients must pay part of the costs of their stay. Prescription drugs under the system are also no longer free; the patient must pay about $1 toward the cost of each prescription. Workers' compensation payments have also been reduced. Many student aid programs have been converted from stipends to loans. Child allowances (*Kindergeld*), tax-free payments by the state to parents, were cut back, especially for higher-income groups.

These reductions in the welfare state have been accompanied by strong protests from labor unions, student organizations, and other affected groups. Thus far, however, the cutbacks have been only marginal. Critics of Bonn's social programs argue that the entire structure of the welfare state must be fundamentally reformed if the spiraling costs are to be controlled.[8] Even with the recent reductions, these social programs still consume a third of the gross national product. Since 1960, expenditures for the welfare state have grown at a far greater rate than the economy that must finance it. Economic conservatives in the Federal Republic contend that spending for social programs is consuming capital that is badly needed to modernize the economy and prepare Germany for the high-tech future. Supporters of the welfare state respond by citing the large inequities in capital resources, the defense budget, and the numerous tax advantages and subsidies given to upper-income groups. To try to dismantle the welfare state, they warn, would endanger "social peace" and induce a "class struggle" mentality reminiscent of past periods in German history.[9]

Since the early 1980s, the combination of slow economic growth, high unemployment, and cuts in social welfare programs has produced a growing poverty problem. The "new poverty," as Germans term it, refers especially to the condition of the long-term unemployed, divorced women with children, low-income pensioners, and refugees seeking asylum. The proportion of unemployed who have been jobless for more than one year has risen from 16 percent in 1981 to 36 percent in 1985. The longer a worker is unemployed, the lower his or her level of support. After one year (24 months for older workers), unemployment compensation, which is based on employer-employee contributions and amounts to about two-thirds of the worker's prior wages, ceases and is replaced by unemployment aid. These payments are about 15 to 17 percent less than unemployment compensation and require an examination of the applicant's personal finances.

Once a worker's eligibility for this support is exhausted, the only alternative is the general welfare system. These payments, however, are lower still (by about 7 percent) than the unemployment aid and require a needs or means test. Between 1981 and 1986, the proportion of unemployed workers in the top tier (wage-based unemployment compensation) has dropped from 57 percent to 38 percent, whereas the unemployed workers dependent on either unemployment aid or welfare has grown from 43 percent to 52 percent.[10] It is now estimated that about 5 percent of the population, or about 3 million people, live below the poverty line.[11]

Socioeconomic Redistribution

Policies of redistribution, which in essence involve taking goods and benefits from one group or individual and giving them to others, are among the most controversial in any political system. Traditionally in European politics, redistribution has been associated with images of class struggle and even revolution. Thus far in the Federal Republic there have been few redistributive policies actually put into practice. The extensive social welfare system, the dynamic pension system, and the health care program are largely financed by employer and employee contributions and not from general government tax revenue. Bonn does not for the most part take from the rich and give to the poor. Business or employer contributions to health and pension systems are viewed as business expenses and passed on to consumers via higher prices. When a proposed policy such as codetermination or a more equitable distribution of capital resources (*Vermögensbildung*) or the reform of vocational education begins to assume a redistributive character, it encounters difficulty in the policymaking process.

The aversion of even Social Democratic leaders to redistributive policies thus far is in part the result of the continued expansion of the economy. As long as the pie continues to get larger, they have seen little reason to engage in the type of conflict necessary to pass redistributive legislation. There is also some evidence that most German voters would not support such measures.

One important means of redistribution is through the tax system. While in power (1969–1982), the SPD often discussed the institution of a more progressive tax system (that is, taxing higher incomes at a still higher rate than lower incomes) although its proposals were always modified or softened either through the opposition of its coalition partners, the middle-class Free Democrats, or the Christian Democrats through their position in the Bundesrat. It is thus not surprising that studies of the distribution of national wealth during the last thirty years found little real redistribution.[12]

Since the early 1970s, most of the nations of Western Europe have experienced a slowdown or a halt in their economic growth; the pie is not getting as big as fast anymore. West Germany has not escaped the higher inflation, increased unemployment, and decline in economic growth of its neighbors. Higher energy costs are responsible for much of this development, but the rising costs of the welfare state are also involved. Under conditions of increasing scarcity, which will also characterize the Federal Republic, the frequency and intensity of demand for more redistributive policies will increase.

Increased Popular Participation in the Policymaking Process

West Germans are among the best politically informed citizens in any modern democracy. Their levels of voting participation are also extremely high. Although they have never completely fulfilled the claims of their proponents in the United States, devices such as the referendum, recall, and the direct primary are now being considered as means to expand the plebiscitary dimension of the constitutional framework. The success of local citizen initiative groups, discussed in Chapter 3, also suggests to some observers that the formal participatory opportunities for West German citizens should be expanded.

The established policymaking institutions and political leaders in the parties, parliament, and bureaucracy have, however, thus far been ill-prepared for the style and policy demands of the citizen groups. When in 1977 a national coalition of citizen action groups secured a court order halting the construction of a large nuclear power plant, the first major success of citizen groups at a national level, party and government leaders reacted with shock and dire warnings about this new "extraparliamentary" force. Even former Chancellor Willy Brandt, who in his 1969 governmental program told Germans they should "risk more democracy," has expressed his dismay at the nontraditional tactics of the citizen organizations. Brandt, like other party leaders, would prefer that the citizen groups work through the existing party and state channels.

The ranks of the citizen initiative groups have continued to grow. By 1983 their total membership exceeded that of the major political parties. In addition to the Greens, the antinuclear, environmental message is now also heard at the leadership levels of the established parties. Most SPD state organizations now oppose any expansion of nuclear power plant construction, and antinuclear factions have been identified in the parliamentary delegations of the FDP and even the CDU/CSU. The success of the Greens in 1983 ensures that environmental issues and the related problems of citizen participation will continue to be prominent in German politics.

By the mid-1980s public concern about environmental problems, as measured in public opinion polls, approached that shown for major economic issues such as unemployment.[13] From modest beginnings in the early 1970s, sparked largely by the issue of nuclear power, the environmental movement has now secured a firm position in the Federal Republic's political structure. The success of the movement in attracting public attention and support is due above all to the inability of the traditional political forces to deal with a growing number of severe problems: acid rain, fuel emissions, hazardous waste disposal, ground and surface water pollution. In the mid-1980s the neglect of these problems led to a development that shocked the great majority of Germans: The country's fabled forests were dying. Water and air pollution, acid rain, and exhaust emissions had, according to government estimates, damaged almost half of all trees. *Waldsterben* (the death of the forest) became a major national issue whose political impact was greater than the nuclear power controversy of the 1970s. The center-right government of Chancellor Kohl, which only a few years earlier had dismissed the environmental movement as a noisy, left-wing sect, moved quickly to develop programs to deal with the forest issue. In 1984 a long-time demand of environmentalists—the introduction of lead-free gasoline—was enacted into law.

A variety of proposals have been made to increase citizen influence in the political process, many of them familiar to American students: the direct primary as a means of democratizing the political parties; the introduction of referenda so that issues of great concern, such as nuclear power, could receive direct popular input; more responsibility given to local governments, especially in the education and urban planning fields; and the extension of citizens' rights to petition and recall public officials. For some critics of the present "limited middle-class" democracy, however, the question of citizenship participation in policymaking can be resolved only if the *economy* and *society* are first *democratized*. Codetermination in industry is viewed by some as the beginning of such an economic democratization. The worker, according to this argument, cannot be expected to become an involved, active citizen if taught through job and school experiences to be a subject, follow orders, and let the interests of those above in the economic hierarchy determine when and how to perform the job. Real political democracy is thus seen as dependent on economic and social democracy.

Thus far there are few indications that the existing codetermination legislation has produced this type of new citizen. Nonetheless, the issue of participation and the related area of socioeconomic democratization will remain important. The SPD left and many of the Greens are committed to overcoming what they see as the contradiction between the ideal of equality and the reality of stratification and inequality in the Federal Republic.

Conceptions of Democracy

One of the classic questions of democratic political theory is whether democracy is largely a set of political and governmental *procedures* and *arrangements*—such as "one-man, one-vote" and civil rights and liberties, with the emphasis on limited governmental interference in socioeconomic affairs—or a way of life with clear prescriptions for *social and economic justice and equality* as well as political equality. This question has been debated intensively in recent years in West Germany, particularly as it relates to the present constitution. Generally, the Christian Democrats have viewed democracy largely in political or procedural terms. They contend that the Basic Law established and supports only this limited version of democracy. They view the democratic state founded in the Basic Law as realized and argue that the foremost goal of any government now must be to maintain it against "radicals," especially those who desire a socialist or communist society with a planned economy and the abolition of private property. Some Christian Democrats have indeed suggested that the Basic Law condones only a capitalist market economy and that to oppose the Republic's present economic system, based on free enterprise and private property, is to oppose the Republic itself. The Social Democrats and the Greens argue that because of the crass inequalities in wealth, status, and power in the Republic, the Basic Law is far from realized. They suggest that the best means of both maintaining the democratic political system and fully realizing its potential is through social and economic reforms, largely in the direction of more social equality and economic security, which will in turn give more genuine freedom to more citizens. They reject the position that the constitution ordains any particular economic system but instead say it requires policies aiming at social and economic reform.

This is, of course, not a uniquely German debate. In some form it is being conducted in every modern democracy.[14] It is becoming a more prominent feature of the political and electoral struggle in Germany, however.

The German Experience and Political Development

The West German polity in the 1980s is also grappling with other policy problems common to advanced industrial societies: the energy crisis; the maintenance of civil liberties against an increasingly inquisitive state bureaucracy; and the classic economic tasks of full employment, moderate economic growth, and stable prices. Like her Western European neighbors, Germany also has an articulate group of scholars and political activists who seriously question whether the liberal democratic political systems of late capitalist societies can resolve these and other problems without eventually turning to a system of state or collective ownership of the means of production. West Germany may also have to confront several external problems that could threaten political stability, such as Soviet pressure in Central Europe or a major economic crisis in the European Community.

Without denying the importance of these present and possible future problems, the Federal Republic, unlike the Weimar Republic, has established a record of performance and a reserve of cultural support that should enable it to resolve these questions at least as effectively as other Western societies. Bonn is no longer a fair-weather or provisional democracy.

The postwar German experience illustrates that a nation can overcome or change its political culture within a relatively short time. Democratic political stability does not necessarily require the centuries-long evolution characteristic of the classical democracies of Great Britain and the United States. Postwar Germany should also alert students of development to the importance of system performance or effectiveness, especially in the early years of a country's development. National ideologies, symbols, power, and prestige are not substitutes for meeting concrete popular demands for social change and economic stability. Finally, the German political experience, which once brought Germans the scorn and contempt of civilized mankind, can also give us reason for optimism and faith in the ability of people to use democratic politics to better their lives and those of their neighbors.

NOTES

1. Richard Löwenthal, "Prolog: Dauer und Verwandlung," in *Die zweite Republik,* ed. Richard Löwenthal and Hans-Peter Schwarz (Stuttgart: Seewald Verlag, 1974), p. 9.
2. Richard Löwenthal, "Vom kalten Krieg zur Ostpolitik," in *Die zweite Republik,* pp. 604–699.
3. Institut für angewandte Sozialforschung, *Politogramm, Bundestagswahl 1987,* Bad Godesberg, 1987, p. 103. The proportion of voters who opted for the "rely only on the United States" approach dropped from 47 percent in 1983 to 27 percent in 1987.
4. Rudolf Schuster, "Ein neues Grundgesetz? Überlegungen zur geforderten Verfassungsreform," in *Demokratisches System und politische Praxis der Bundesrepublik,* ed. Gerhard Lehmbruch et al. (München: Piper Verlag, 1971). pp. 127–142. See also Hans Peter Ipsen, "Über das Grundgesetz nach 25 Jahren," *Die öffentliche Verwaltung* 27, no. 9 (May 1974): 289–293.
5. Gebhard Schweigler, *West German Foreign Policy: The Domestic Setting* (New York: Praeger, 1984), p. 21.
6. Charles F. Andrain, *Politics and Economic Policy in Western Democracies* (North Scituate, MA: Duxbury Press, 1980), pp. 212–228.
7. Ibid., p. 167.
8. Michael Jungblut, "Der Sozialstaat wird zum Moloch," *Die Zeit,* 7 December 1984, p. 1.
9. There is little public support for cutting back on the general pattern of welfare services. When asked in 1987 whether the social welfare program should be expanded, maintained at its present level, or cut back, only 8 percent of a national sample of voters supported a reduction in the welfare system. The argument is frequently heard among some CDU and FDP supporters that social programs restrict individual intiative and achievement. This argument was supported by only 12 percent of CDU voters and 4 percent of FDP supporters. Infas, *Politogramm, Bundestagswahl 1987,* p. 91.
10. *Die Zeit,* vol. 41, no. 26 (1986), p. 44.
11. Erika Martens, "Klassengesellschaft neuer Art," *Die Zeit,* vol. 40, no. 22 (1985), p. 9.
12. *Der Spiegel,* 2 June 1980, p. 84 ff.
13. Emnid surveys cited in *Der Spiegel,* 29 October 1984, pp. 40 ff.
14. See Robert D. Putnam, *The Beliefs of Politicians* (New Haven: Yale University Press, 1973) for an illuminating discussion of this problem within the British and Italian political systems.

Select Bibliography

The following listing is selected from the English language literature on postwar German politics. Those students with a command of the German language are directed to the various footnotes in this book. The major German language surveys of West German politics, Thomas Ellwein's *Das Regierungssystem der Bundesrepublik Deutschland*, 6th ed. (Cologne and Opladen: Westdeutscher Verlag, 1983), and Eckhard Jesse's *Die Demokratie der Bundesrepublik Deutschland*, 7th ed. (Berlin: Colloquium Verlag, 1986) are important sources. For current developments, the weekly newspaper, *Die Zeit*, is recommended. Parliamentary proceedings are well covered in another weekly, *Das Parlament*.

CHAPTER 1: THE HISTORICAL SETTING

Barraclough, Geoffrey, *The Origins of Modern Germany*. New York: Capricorn Books, 1963, reprint.

Botting, Douglas. *From the Ruins of the Reich, Germany 1945–1949*. New York: Crown Publishers, 1985.

Bracher, Karl Dietrich. *The German Dictatorship*. New York: Praeger, 1970.

Broszat, Martin. *The Hitler State*. London and White Plains, NY: Longman, 1981.

Calleo, David. *The German Problem Reconsidered*. Cambridge and New York: Cambridge University Press, 1978.

Childers, Thomas. *The Nazi Voter*. Chapel Hill and London: University of North Carolina Press, 1983.

Craig, Gordon A. *The Germans*. New York: Putnam, 1982.

———. *Germany, 1866–1945*. New York: Oxford University Press, 1978.

Detweiler, Donald S. *Germany: A Short History*. Carbondale: Southern Illinois University Press, 1976.

Epstein, Klaus. *The Genesis of German Conservatism.* Princeton: Princeton University Press, 1966.

———. "The German Problem, 1945–50." *World Politics* 20, no. 2 (January 1968): 279–300.

Fest, Joachim. *Hitler.* New York: Random House, 1975.

Friedrich, Carl J. "The Legacies of the Occupation of Germany." In *Public Policy,* edited by John D. Montgomery and Albert O. Hirschman. Cambridge, MA: Harvard University Press, 1968, p. 1–26.

Gillis, John R. "Germany." In *Crisis of Political Development in Europe and the United States,* edited by Raymond Grew. Princeton: Princeton University Press, 1978, pp. 313–345.

Grosser, Alfred. *Germany in Our Time.* New York: Praeger, 1973.

Hamilton, Richard F. *Who Voted for Hitler?* Princeton: Princeton University Press, 1982.

Holborn, Hajo. *A History of Modern Germany, 1840–1945.* New York: Knopf, 1970.

Krieger, Leonard. "The Inter-Regnum in Germany: March–August 1945." *Political Science Quarterly* 64, no. 4 (December 1949): 507–532.

———. "The Potential for Democratization in Occupied Germany: A Problem in Historical Projection." In *Public Policy,* edited by John D. Montgomery and Albert O. Hirschman. Cambridge, MA: Harvard University Press, 1968, pp. 27–58.

Laqueur, Walter, *Weimar, A Cultural History.* New York: Putnam, 1974.

Lepsius, M. Rainer. "From Fragmented Party Democracy to Government by Emergency Decree and National Socialist Takeover: Germany" In *The Breakdown of Democratic Regimes: Europe,* edited by Juan J. Linz and Alfred Stephan. Baltimore and London: Johns Hopkins University Press, 1978, pp. 34–79.

Litchfield, Edward, ed. *Governing Postwar Germany.* Ithaca: Cornell University Press, 1953.

Merkl, Peter H. *The Origins of the West German Republic.* New York: Oxford University Press, 1965.

Peterson, Edward N. *The American Occupation of Germany: Retreat to Victory.* Detroit: Wayne State University Press, 1977.

Rittberger, Volker. "Revolution and Pseudo-Democratization: The Formation of the Weimar Republic." In *Crisis, Choice and Change,* edited by Gabriel A. Almond et al. Boston: Little, Brown, 1973, pp. 285–396.

Sanford, Gregory W. *From Hitler to Ulbricht: The Communist Reconstruction of East Germany 1945–46.* Princeton: Princeton University Press, 1983.

Speer, Albert. *Inside the Third Reich.* New York: Macmillan, 1968.

Tent, James F. *Mission on the Rhine: Reeducation and Denazification in American-Occupied Germany.* Princeton: Princeton University Press, 1983.

Turner, Henry Ashby, Jr. *The Two Germanies Since 1945.* New Haven: Yale University Press, 1987.

CHAPTER 2: THE SOCIAL AND ECONOMIC SETTING

Ardagh, John. *Germany and the Germans.* New York: Harper & Row, 1987.

Bessel, Richard. "Eastern Germany as a Structural Problem in the Weimar Republic." *Social History* 3 (1978): 199–218.

Dickinson, Robert E. *Germany: A General and Regional Geography.* 2d ed. London: Methuen, 1964.

Dyson, Kenneth H. F. "The Politics of Economic Management in West Germany." *West European Politics* 4, no. 2 (May 1981): 35–55.

————. "The Politics of Corporate Crises in West Germany." *West European Politics* 7, no. 1 (January 1984): 24–46.

Frye, Charles E., "The Third Reich and the Second Republic: National Socialism's Impact upon German Democracy." *Western Political Quarterly* 21, no. 4 (December 1968): 668–681.

Heidenheimer, Arnold J. "The Politics of Educational Reform." *Comparative Education Review* 18, no. 3 (October 1974): 388–410.

Kloten, Norbert, Ketterer, Karl-Heinz, and Vollmer, Rainer. "West Germany's Stabilization Performance." in *The Politics of Inflation and Economic Stagnation,* edited by Leon N. Lindberg and Charles S. Maier. Washington, DC: The Brookings Institution, 1985, pp. 353–402.

Knott, Jack H. *Managing the German Economy: Budgetary Politics in a Federal State.* Lexington, MA: Lexington Books, 1981.

Laqueur, Walter. *Germany Today.* Boston: Little, Brown, 1985.

Medley, Richard. "Inflation Policy in Germany: The Institutional and Political Determinants." In *The Politics of Inflation: A Comparative Analysis,* edited by Richard Medley. New York and Oxford: Pergamon Press, 1982, pp. 127–153.

Roskamp, Karl W. *Capital Formation in West Germany.* Detroit: Wayne State University Press, 1965.

Schelsky, Helmut. "The Family in Germany." *Marriage and Family Living* 16, no. 4 (November 1954): 330–342.

Schnitzer, Martin. *East and West Germany: A Comparative Economic Analysis.* New York: Praeger, 1972.

Schoenbaum, David. *Hitler's Social Revolution.* New York: Doubleday, 1966.

Stokes, William S., Jr. "Emancipation: The Politics of West German Education." *The Review of Politics* 42 (1980): 191–215.

Webber, Douglas. "Combatting and Acquiescing in Unemployment? Crisis Management in Sweden and West Germany." *West European Politics* 6, no. 1 (January 1983): 23–43.

Weiler, Hans N. "West Germany: Educational Policy as Compensatory Legitimation." In *Politics and Education,* edited by R. Murray Thomas. New York and Oxford: Pergamon Press, 1983, pp. 33–54.

Williams, Arthur. "Pluralism in the West German Media: The Press Broadcasting and Cable." *West European Politics* 8, no. 2 (April 1985): 84–103.

CHAPTER 3: POLITICAL CULTURE, PARTICIPATION, AND CIVIL LIBERTIES

Baker, Kendall L., Dalton, Russell, and Hildebrandt, Kai. *Germany Transformed.* Cambridge: Harvard University Press, 1981.

Becker, Jillian. *Hitler's Children: The Story of the Baader-Meinhof Terrorist Gang.* Philadelphia and New York: Lippincott, 1977.

Bunn, Ronald F. *German Politics and the Spiegel Affair.* Baton Rouge: Louisiana State University Press, 1968.

Conradt, David P. "West Germany: A Remade Political Culture?" *Comparative Political Studies* 7, no. 2 (July 1974): 222–238.

———. "Changing German Political Culture." In *The Civil Culture Revisited,* edited by Gabriel A. Almond and Sidney Verba. Boston: Little, Brown, 1980, pp. 212–272.

———. "Political Culture: Legitimacy and Participation." *West European Politics* 4, no. 2 (May 1981): 18–34.

Dahrendorf, Ralf. *Society and Democracy in Germany.* New York: Doubleday, 1969.

Dyson, Kenneth H. F. "Anti-Communism in the Federal Republic of Germany: The Case of the 'Berufsverbot.'" *Parliamentary Affairs* 27, no. 2 (January 1975): 51–67.

Franz, Gerhard. "Economic Aspirations, Well-Being and Political Support in Recession and Boom Periods: The Case of West Germany." *European Journal of Political Research,* 14, nos. 1 and 2 (1986): 97–112.

Hartmann, Heinz. *Authority and Organization in German Management.* Princeton: Princeton University Press, 1959.

Haug, Frigga. "The Women's Movement in West Germany." *The New Left Review,* no. 195 (January/February 1986): pp. 59ff.

Herf, Jeffrey. "War, Peace and Intellectuals. The West German Peace Movement." *International Security* 10, no. 4 (Spring 1986): 172–200.

Helm, Jutta A. "Citizen Lobbies in West Germany." In *Western European Party Systems,* edited by Peter H. Merkl. New York: Free Press, 1980, pp. 576–596.

Hoskin, Marilyn. "Public Opinion and the Foreign Worker. Traditional and Nontraditional Bases in West Germany." *Comparative Politics* 17, no. 2 (January 1985): 193–210.

———. "Integration or Nonintegration of Foreign Workers: Four Theories." *Political Psychology* 5, no. 4 (December 1985): 661–685.

Jennings, M. Kent. "The Variable Nature of Generational Conflict: Some Examples from West Germany." *Comparative Political Studies* 9, no. 2 (July 1976): 171–188.

Krieger, Leonard. *The German Idea of Freedom.* Chicago: University of Chicago Press, 1957.

Langguth, Gerd. "Origins and Aims of Terrorism in Europe." *Aussenpolitik* 37, no. 2 (1986): 163–175.

Lepsius, M. Rainer. "The Nation and the Nationalism in Germany." *Social Research* 52, no. 1 (Spring 1985): 43–64.

Lederer, Gerda. "Trends in Authoritarianism: A Study of Adolescents in West Germany and the United States Since 1945." *Journal of Cross-Cultural Psychology* 13, no. 3 (September 1982): 299–314.

Merritt, Richard L. "The Student Protest Movement in West Berlin." *Comparative Politics* 1, no. 4 (July 1969): 516–533.

Meulemann, Heiner. "Value Change in West Germany, 1950–1980: Integrating the Empirical Evidence." *Social Science Information* 22, nos. 4 and 5 (1983): 777–800.

Mushaben, Joyce Marie. "Anti-Politics and Successor Generations: The Role of Youth in the West and East German Peace Movements." *Journal of Political and Military Sociology* 12, no. 1 (Spring 1984): 171–190.

———. "The Forum: New Dimensions of Youth Protest in Western Europe." *Journal of Political and Military Sociology* 11, no. 1 (Spring 1983): 123–144.

Nelkin, Dorothy, and Pollak, Michael. *The Atom Besieged: Extraparliamentary Dissent in France and Germany.* Cambridge, MA: MIT Press, 1981.

Noelle-Neumann, Elisabeth. *The Germans: Public Opinion Polls, 1967–1980.* Westport, CT., and London: Greenwood Press, 1981.

Noelle-Neumann, Erich Peter and Elisabeth. *The Germans, 1947–1966.* Allensbach am Bodensee: Verlag für Demoskopie, 1967.

Oppenheim, A. N. *Civic Education and Participation in Democracy.* Beverly Hills and London: Sage Publications, 1977.

Pines, Maya. "Unlearning Blind Obedience in German Schools." *Psychology Today* 15, no. 5 (May 1981): pp. 59 ff.

Rabinbach, Anson, and Zipes, Jack. (eds.). *Germans and Jews Since the Holocaust.* New York: Holmes and Meier, 1986.

Rist, Ray C. *Guestworkers in Germany: The Prospects for Pluralism.* New York: Praeger, 1978.

Schoonmaker, Donald. "Novelist and Social Scientist: Contrasting Views of Today's West German Political System." *Polity* 14, no. 3 (Spring 1982): 414–470.

Schram, Glenn. "Ideology and Politics: The *Rechtsstaat* Idea in West Germany." *Journal of Politics* 33 (February 1971): 133–157.

Schweigler, Gebhard. *National Consciousness in Divided Germany.* Beverly Hills and London: Sage Publications, 1975.

———. "Anti-Americanism in Germany." *Washington Quarterly* 9, no. 1 (Winter 1986): 67–84.

Shell, Kurt L. "Extraparliamentay Opposition in Postwar Germany." *Comparative Politics* 2, no. 4 (July 1970): 653–680.

Stern, Fritz. *The Failure of Illiberalism: Essays on the Political Culture of Modern Germany.* Chicago: University of Chicago Press, 1975.

Szabo, Stephen F. *The Successor Generation: International Perspectives of Postwar Europeans.* London: Butterworths, 1983.

Verba, Sidney. "Germany: The Remaking of Political Culture." In *Political Culture and Political Development,* edited by Sidney Verba and Lucien Pye. Princeton: Princeton University Press, 1965, pp. 130–170.

Weil, Frederick D. "Tolerance of Free Speech in the United States and West Germany, 1970–79: An Analysis of Public Opinion Survey Data." *Social Forces* 60, no. 4 (June 1982); 973–992.

CHAPTER 4: THE PARTY SYSTEM AND THE REPRESENTATION OF INTERESTS

Alexis, Marion. "Neo-Corporatism and Industrial Relations: The Case of the German Trade Unions." *West European Politics* 6, no. 1 (January 1983): 75–92.

Andrlik, Erich. "The Farmers and the State: Agricultural Interests in West German Politics." *West European Politics* 4, no. 1 (January 1981): 104–119.

Brandt, Willy. *In Exile.* London: Oswald Wolff, 1971.

Braunthal, Gerard. *The Federation of Germany Industry in Politics.* Ithaca: Cornell University Press, 1965.

———. "The West German Social Democrats: Factionalism at the Local Level." *West European Politics* 7, no. 1 (January 1984): 47–64.

————. *The West German Social Democrats, 1969–1982: Profile of a Party in Power.* Boulder, Colorado: Westview Press, 1983.

————. "Social Democratic–Green Coalitions in West Germany: Prospects for a New Alliance." *German Studies Review* 9, no. 3 (October 1986): 569–597.

Broughton, David, and Emil Kirchner. "Germany: The FDP in Transition—Again." *Parliamentary Affairs,* 37, no. 2 (Spring 1984): 183–98.

Buerklin, Wilhelm P. "The German Greens. The Post-Industrial, Non-Established and the Party System." *International Political Science Review* 6, no. 4 (October 1985): 463–481.

————. "The Split Between the Established and the Non-Established Left in Germany." *European Journal of Political Research* 13 (1985); 283–293.

————. "Governing Left Parties Frustrating the Radical Non-Established Left: The Rise and Inevitable Decline of the Greens." *European Sociological Review* 3, no. 2 (September 1987): 109–26.

Capra, Fritjof, and Spretnak, Charlene. *Green Politics: The Global Promise.* New York: Dutton, 1984.

Chalmers, Douglas A. *The Social Democratic Party of Germany.* New Haven: Yale University Press, 1964.

Chandler, William M., and Alan Siaroff, "Postindustrial Politics in Germany and the Origins of the Greens." *Comparative Politics* 18, no. 3 (April 1986): 303–325.

Conradt, David P. *The West German Party System.* Beverly Hills and London: Sage Publications, 1972.

————. "The End of an Era in West Germany." *Current History* 81 (1982): 405–408, 438.

Diamant, Alfred, "Democratizing the Workplace: The Myth and Reality of *Mitbestimmung* in the Federal Republic of Germany." In *Worker Self-Management in Industry. The West European Experience,* edited by G. David Garson. New York and London: Praeger, 1977, pp. 25–48.

Doering, Herbert, and Smith, Gordon, eds. *Party Government and Political Culture in Western Germany.* New York: St. Martin's, 1982.

Edinger, Lewis J. *Kurt Schumacher: A Study in Personality and Political Behavior.* Stanford: Stanford University Press, 1965.

Esser, Josef. "State, Business and Trade Unions in West Germany after the 'Political Wende'." *West European Politics* 9, no. 2 (April 1986): 198–214.

Feist, Ursula, and Liepelt Klaus. "New Elites in Old Parties: Observations on a Side Effect of German Educational Reform." *International Political Science Review* 4, no. 1 (1983): 71–83.

Gourevitch, Peter *et al. Unions and Economic Crisis: Britain, West Germany and Sweden.* London: Allen and Unwin, 1984.

Heidenheimer, Arnold J. *Adenauer and the CDU.* The Hague: Martinus Nijhoff, 1960.

Kaltefleiter, Werner. "Legitimacy Crisis of the German Party System?" In *Western European Party Systems,* edited by Peter H. Merkl. New York: Free Press, 1980, pp. 597–608.

Kirchheimer, Otto. "Germany: The Vanishing Opposition." In *Political Opposition in Western Democracies,* edited by Robert A. Dahl. New Haven: Yale University Press, 1966, pp. 237–259.

Koeble, Thomas A. "Trade Unionists, Party Activists, and Politicians: The Struggle for Power over Party Rules in the British Labour Party and the West Social Democratic Party." *Comparative Politics* 19, no. 3 (April 1987): 253–266.

Linz, Juan. "Cleavage and Consensus in West German Politics: The Early Fifties." In *Party*

Systems and Voter Alignments: Cross-National Perspectives, edited by S. M. Lipset and S. Rokkan. New York: Free Press, 1966, pp. 283–316.

Markham, James M. "Germany's Volatile Greens." *New York Times Magazine,* 13 February 1983, pp. 37 ff.

Markovits, Andrei S., and Allen, Christopher S. "Power and Dissent: The Trade Unions in the Federal Republic of Germany Re-Examined." *West European Politics* 3 (1980): 68–86.

Markovits, Andrei S. *The Politics of West German Trade Unions: Activist Challenges and Accommodationist Responses.* Cambridge: Cambridge Unviersity Press, 1986.

Müller-Rommel, Ferdinand. "Social Movements and the Greens: New Internal Politics in Germany." *European Journal of Political Research* 13, no. 1 (March 1985): 53–67.

Pridham, Geoffrey. *Christian Democracy in Western Germany.* New York and London: St. Martin's, 1977.

Pulzer, Peter G. J. "The German Party System in the Sixties." *Political Studies* 19 (1971): 1–17.

———. "Responsible Party Government and Stable Coalition: The Case of the German Federal Republic." *Political Studies* 26 (1978): 181–208.

Silvia, Stephen J. "The West German Labor Law Controversy: A Struggle for the Factory of the Future." *Comparative Politics* 20, no. 2 (January 1988): 155–173.

Smith, Gordon. "West Germany and the Politics of Centrality." *Government and Opposition* 11, no. 4 (Autumn 1976): 387–407.

Spotts, Frederic. *The Churches and Politics in Germany.* Middletown: Wesleyan University Press, 1973.

Stone, Deborah A. *The Limits of Professional Power: National Health Care in the Federal Republic of Germany.* Chicago: University of Chicago Press, 1981.

Webber, Douglas. "A Relationship of 'Critical Partnership'? Capital and the Social-Liberal Coalition in West Germany." *West European Politics* 6, no. 2 (April 1983): 61–86.

Willey, Richard J. "Trade Unions and Political Parties in the Federal Republic of Germany." *Industrial and Labor Relations Review* 28 (October 1974): 38–59.

Woodall, Jean. "The Dilemma of Youth Unemployment: Trade Union Responses in the Federal Republic of Germany, the U.K. and France." *West European Politics* 9, no. 3 (July 1986): 429–447.

Yost, David, and Glad, Thomas. "West German Party Politics and Theater Nuclear Modernization since 1977." *Armed Forces and Society* (1982): 525–560.

CHAPTER 5: ELECTIONS AND VOTING BEHAVIOR

Barnes, S. H., et al. "The German Party System and the 1961 Federal Election." *American Political Science Review* 56 (1962): 899–914.

Cerny, Karl, ed. *West Germany at the Polls.* Washington, DC: American Enterprise Institute, 1978.

———. *West Germany at the Polls: The 1980 and 1983 Federal Elections.* Durham: Duke University Press, forthcoming 1989.

Conradt, David P., and Lambert, Dwight. "Party System, Social Structure and Competitive Politics in West Germany." *Comparative Politics* 7, no. 1 (October 1974): 61–86.

Conradt, David P., and Dalton, Russell J. "The West German Electorate and the Party

System: Continuity and Change in the 1980s." *Review of Politics* 50, no. 1 (January 1988): 3–29.

Edinger, Lewis J. "Political Change in Germany: The Federal Republic after the 1969 Election." *Comparative Politics* 2, no. 4 (July 1970): 549–578.

Edinger, Lewis, J., and Luebke, Paul, Jr. "Grass-Roots Electoral Politics in the German Federal Republic." *Comparative Politics* 3, no. 4 (July 1971): 463–498.

Farrell, D. M., and Wortmann, M. "Party Strategies in the Electoral Market: Political Marketing in West Germany, Britain and Ireland." *European Journal of Political Research* 15, no. 3 (1987): 297–318.

Irving, R. E. M., and Paterson, W. E. "The West German Parliamentary Election of November, 1972" *Parliamentary Affairs* 26, no. 2 (1973), pp. 218–239.

––––––. "The *Machtwechsel* of 1982–83: A Significant Landmark in the Political and Constitutional History of West Germany." *Parliamentary Affairs* 36, no. 4 (Autumn 1983): 417–435.

Klingemann, Hans-Dieter. "Germany". In *Electoral Change in Western Democracies,* edited by Ivor Crewe and David Denver. New York: St. Martin's Press, 1985, pp. 230–263.

Klingemann, Hans-Dieter, and Pappi, Franz-Urban. "The 1969 Bundestag Election in the Federal Republic of Germany: An Analysis of Voting Behavior." *Comparative Politics* 2, no. 4 (July 1970): 523–548.

Kuechler, Manfred. "Maximizing Utility at the Polls?" *European Journal of Political Research* 14, nos. 1 and 2 (1986): 81–95.

Lewis-Beck, Michael. "Comparative Economic Voting: Britain, France, Germany, Italy." *American Journal of Political Science* 30, no. 2 (May 1986): 315–346.

Markovits, Andrei S. "West Germany's Political Future: The 1983 Bundestag Election." *Socialist Review* 13, no. 4 (July-August 1983): 67–98.

Norpoth, Helmut. "Choosing a Coalition Partner. Mass Preference and Elite Decisions in West Germany." *Comparative Political Studies* 12 (1980): 424–440.

––––––. "The Making of a More Partisan Electorate in West Germany." *British Journal of Political Science* 14, no. 1 (January 1984); 52–71.

Urwin, Derek W. "Germany: Continuity and Change in Electoral Politics." In *Electoral Behavior: A Comparative Handbook,* edited by Richard Rose. New York: Free Press, pp. 109–170.

CHAPTER 6: POLICYMAKING INSTITUTIONS I: PARLIAMENT AND EXECUTIVE

Braunthal, Gerard. "The Policy Function of the German Social Democratic Party." *Comparative Politics* 9 no. 2 (January 1977): 127–146.

––––––. *The West German Legislative Process.* Ithaca and London: Cornell University Press, 1972.

Burkett, Tony, and Schuettemeyer, S. *The West German Parliament.* London: Butterworths, 1982.

Conradt, David P. "Chancellor Kohl's Center Coalition." *Current History* 85, no. 514 (November 1986): 357–360, 389–391.

Dyson, Kenneth H. F. *Party, State and Bureaucracy in Western Germany.* Beverly Hills and London: Sage, 1978.

Grande, Edger. "Neoconservatism and Conservative-Liberal Economic Policy in West Germany." *European Journal of Political Research* 15, (1987): 281–296.

Johnson, Nevil. *Government in the Federal Republic of Germany: The Executive at Work.* London: Pergamon, 1973.

Loewenberg, Gerhard, ed. *Modern Parliaments, Change or Decline?* Chicago and New York: Aldine-Atherton, 1971.

———. *Parliament in the German Political System.* Ithaca and London: Cornell University Press, 1966.

Mayntz, Renate. "Executive Leadership in Germany: Dispersion of Power or 'Kanzler Demokratie'?" In *Presidents and Prime Ministers,* edited by Richard Rose and Ezra N. Suleiman. Washington, DC: American Enterprise Institute, 1980, pp. 139–170.

Merkl, Peter H. "Executive-Legislative Federalism in West Germany." *American Political Science Review* 53, no. 3 (September 1959): 732–741.

Paterson, William. "The Chancellor and His Party: Political Leadership in the Federal Republic." *West European Politics* 4, no. 2 (May 1981): 3–17.

———. "The SPD After Brandt's Fall—Change or Continuity?" *Government and Opposition* 10, no. 2 (Spring 1975): 167–188.

Pinney, Edward L. *Federalism, Bureaucracy, and Party Politics in Western Germany: The Role of the Bundesrat.* Chapel Hill: University of North Carolina Press, 1963.

Prittie, Terence. *Adenauer.* London: Stacey, 1971.

Safran, William. *Veto-Group Politics: The Case of Health Insurance Reform in West Germany.* San Francisco: Chandler, 1967.

Schmidt, Helmut. *Perspectives on Politics.* Boulder, CO: Westview Press, 1982.

Schmidt, Manfred G. "The Politics of Domestic Reform in the Federal Republic of Germany." *Politics and Society* 8 (1979): 165–200.

CHAPTER 7: POLICYMAKING INSTITUTIONS II: ADMINISTRATION, SEMIPUBLIC INSTITUTIONS, AND COURTS

Aberbach, Joel et al. *Bureaucrats and Politicians in Western Democracies.* Cambridge, MA: Harvard University Press, 1981.

Alber, Jens. "Germany." In *Growth to Limits,* edited by Peter Flora. Berlin: Walter de Gruyter and Co., 1988 (Vol. 2), pp. 1–154.

Blair, J. M. *Federalism and Judicial Review in West Germany.* London and New York: Oxford University Press, 1981.

Dyson, Kenneth H. F. "Planning and the Federal Chancellor's Office in the West German Federal Government." *Political Studies* 21, no. 3 (1973): 348–362.

———. "Improving Policy-Making in Bonn: Why the Central Planners Failed." *Journal of Management Studies* 12, no. 2 (May 1975): 157–174.

Eser, Albin, "The Politics of Criminal Law Reform: Germany." *American Journal of Comparative Law* 21, no. 2 (Spring 1973): 245–262.

Hanf, Kenneth. "Administrative Developments in East and West Germany: Stirrings of Reform." *Political Studies* 21, no. 1 (1973): 35–44.

Heidenheimer, Arnold J. "The Politics of Educational Reform: Explaining Different Outcomes of School Comprehensivization Attempts in Sweden and West Germany." *Comparative Education Review* 13, no. 3 (October 1974): 388–410.

Herz, John H. "Political Views of the West German Civil Service." In *West German Leadership and Foreign Policy,* edited by Hans Speier and W. Phillips Davison. Evanston, IL: Row, Peterson, 1957, pp. 96–135.

Jacob, Herbert. *German Administration Since Bismarck: Central Authority Versus Local Autonomy.* New Haven: Yale University Press, 1963.

Johnson, Nevil. "The Interdependence of Law and Politics: Judges and the Constitution in West Germany." *West European Politics* 5, no. 3 (July 1982): 236–252.

Kommers, Donald P. *Judicial Politics in West Germany: A Study of the Federal Constitutional Court.* Beverly Hills and London: Sage, 1976.

Landfried, Christine. "The Impact of the German Federal Constitutional Court on Politics and Policy Output." *Government and Opposition* 20, no. 4 (Autumn 1985): 522–541.

Lee, Orlan, and Robertson, T. A. *"Moral Order" and the Criminal Law, Reform Efforts in the United States and West Germany.* The Hague: Martinus Nijhoff, 1973.

Mayntz, Renate. "German Federal Bureaucrats: A Functional Elite Between Politics and Administration." In *Higher Civil Servants in the Policymaking Process: A Comparative Exploration,* edited by Ezra Suleiman. New York: Holmes and Meier, 1983, pp. 145–174.

Mayntz, Renate, and Scharpf, Fritz W. *Policymaking in the German Federal Bureaucracy.* New York: Elsevier, 1975.

———. "The Higher Civil Service of the Federal Republic of Germany." In *The Higher*

Putnam, Robert D. "The Political Attitudes of Senior Civil Servants in Western Europe: A Preliminary Report." *British Journal of Political Science* 3, no. 2 (July 1973): 257–290.

Rueschemeyer, Dietrich. *Lawyers and Their Society.* Cambridge, MA: Harvard University Press, 1973.

Schram, Glenn, N. "The Recruitment of Judges for the West German Federal Courts." *American Journal of Comparative Law* 21, no. 4 (Fall 1973): 691–711.

CHAPTER 8: SUBNATIONAL UNITS: FEDERALISM AND LOCAL GOVERNMENT

Billerbeck, Rudolf. "Socialists in Urban Politics: The German Case." *Social Research* 47 (1980): 114–140.

Cole, R. Taylor. "Federalism and Universities in West Germany: Recent Trends." *American Journal of Comparative Law* 21, no. 1 (Winter 1973): 45–68.

Fried, Robert C. "Politics, Economics, and Federalism: Aspects of Urban Government in Austria, Germany and Switzerland." In *Comparative Community Politics,* edited by Terry Clark. Beverly Hills and London: Sage Publications, 1974, pp. 313–350.

Fried, Robert C. "Party and Policy in West German Cities." *American Political Science Review* 70, no. 4 (March 1976): 11–24.

Gunlicks, Arthur B. "Administrative Centralization and Decentralization in the Making and Remaking of Modern Germany." *The Review of Politics* 46, no. 3 (July 1984): 323–345.

———. *Local Government in the German Federal System.* Durham, NC: Duke University Press, 1986.

Heidenheimer, Arnold J. "Federalism and the Party System: The Case of West Germany." *American Political Science Review* 52 (1958): 808–828.

Lehmbruch, Gerhard. "Party and Federation in Germany: A Developmental Dilemma." *Government and Opposition* 13 (1978): 151–177.

Pridham, Geoffrey. "A Nationalization Process? Federal Politics and State Elections in West Germany." *Government and Opposition* 8, no. 4 (Fall 1973): 455–472.

Rose, Richard, ed. *The Management of Urban Change in Britain and Germany.* Beverly Hills and London: Sage Publications, 1974.

Rothweiler, Robert L. "Revenue Sharing in the Federal Republic of Germany." *Publius* 2, no. 1 (Spring 1972): 4–25.

von Beyme, Klaus. "West Germany: Federalism." *International Political Science Review* 5, no. 4 (1984): 381–396.

Weiler, Conrad J., Jr. "Metropolitan Reorganization in West Germany." *Publius* 2, no. 1 (Spring 1972): 26–68.

Wilensky, Harold L. *The Welfare State and Equality.* Berkeley: University of California Press, 1975.

CHAPTER 9; CONCLUSION: THE GERMAN POLITY FACES THE FUTURE

Asmus, Ronald D. "Is There a Peace Movement in the GDR?" *Orbis* 27, no. 2 (Summer 1983): 301–342.

Barnet, Richard J. *The Alliance: America-Europe-Japan. Makers of the Postwar World.* New York: Simon & Schuster, 1983.

Bell, Daniel. *The Coming of Post-Industrial Society.* New York: Basic Books, 1973.

Bulmer, Simon, and Paterson, William. *The Federal Republic of Germany and the European Community.* London: Allen and Unwin, 1987.

Crozier, Michel et al. *The Crisis of Democracy.* New York: New York University Press, 1975.

Dean, Jonathan. "Directions in Inner-German Relations." *Orbis* 29, no. 3 (Fall 1985): 609–632.

Feld, Werner. *The European Community in World Affairs.* Port Washington, NY: Alfred Co., 1976.

Garthoff, Raymond L. "The NATO Decision on Theater Nuclear Forces." *Political Science Quarterly* 98, no. 2 (Summer 1983): 197–214.

Gatzke, Hans W. *Germany and the United States.* Cambridge, MA: Harvard University Press, 1980.

Griffith, William E. "Bonn and Washington: From Deterioration to Crisis." *Orbis* 26, no. 1 (Spring 1982): 117–133.

Hanrieder, Wolfram F. *The Stable Crisis.* New York: Harper & Row, 1970.

Hardach, Karl. *The Political Economy of Germany in the Twentieth Century.* Berkeley: University of California Press, 1980.

Helm, Jutta. "Co-Determination in West Germany: What Difference Does It Make?" *West European Politics* 9, no. 1 (January, 1986): 32–53.

Joffe, Josef. "The Foreign Policy of the German Federal Republic." In *Foreign Policy in World Politics,* edited by Roy C. Macridis. Englewood Cliffs, NJ: Prentice-Hall, 1976, pp. 117–151.

Katzenstein, Peter J. *Policy and Politics in West Germany. The Growth of a Semi-Sovereign State.* Philadelphia: Temple University Press, 1987.

Kelleher, Catherine McArdle. "The Defense Policy of the Federal Republic of Germany." In *The Defense Policies of Nations,* edited by Douglas J. Murray and Paul R. Viotti. Baltimore and London: Johns Hopkins University Press, 1982, pp. 268–296.

Lindberg, Leon. *Politics and the Future of Industrial Society.* New York: David McKay, 1976.

McAdams, A. James. "Surviving the Missiles: The GDR and the Future of Inter-German Relations." *Orbis* 27, no. 2 (Summer 1983): 343–370.

———. "Inter-German Detente: A New Balance." *Foreign Affairs* 65, no. 1 (Fall 1986): 136–153.

Mellenthin, F. W., Stolfi, R. H. S. et al. *NATO under Attack.* Durham, NC: Duke University Press, 1984.

Morgan, Roger. "Dimensions of West German Foreign Policy." *West European Politics* 4, no. 2 (May 1981): 87–111.

———. *West Germany's Foreign Policy Agenda.* Beverly Hills and London: Sage Publications, 1978.

Rattinger, Hans. "The Federal Republic of Germany: Much Ado about (Almost) Nothing." In *The Public and Atlantic Defense,* edited by Gregory Flynn and Hans Rattinger. Totowa, NJ: Rowman and Allanheld, 1985, pp. 101–174.

Riemer, Jeremiah M. "West German Crisis Management: Stability and Change in the Post Keynesian Age." In *Political Economy in Advanced Industrial Societies,* edited by Norman J. Vig and Stephen E. Schier. New York and London: Holmes and Meier, 1985, pp. 229–254.

Schweigler, Gebhard. *West German Foreign Policy: The Domestic Setting.* New York: Praeger, 1984.

Tilford, Roger. *The Ostpolitik and Political Change in Germany.* Lexington, MA: Heath, 1975.

Whetten, Lawrence L. *Germany's Ostpolitik.* New York: Oxford University Press, 1971.

Appendix
The Basic Law of the Federal Republic

This is an abridged version of the Basic Law as amended, containing only the most important provisions and including sections mentioned in the book.*

I. BASIC RIGHTS

Article 1 (Protection of human dignity)

(1) The dignity of man shall be inviolable. To respect and protect it shall be the duty of all state authority.

(2) The German people therefore acknowledge inviolable and inalienable human rights as the basis of every community, of peace, and of justice in the world.

(3) The following basic rights shall bind the legislature, the executive, and the judiciary as directly enforceable law.

Article 2 (Rights of liberty)

(1) Everyone shall have the right to the free development of his personality insofar as he does not violate the rights of others or offend against the constitutional order or the moral code.

(2) Everyone shall have the right to life and to inviolability of his person. The liberty of the individual shall be inviolable. These rights may only be encroached upon pursuant to a law.

---

* Based on an English translation provided by the Press and Information Office of the federal government of West Germany.

Article 3 (Equality before the law)

(1) All persons shall be equal before the law.

(2) Men and women shall have equal rights.

(3) No one may be prejudiced or favored because of his sex, his parentage, his race, his language, his homeland and origin, his faith, or his religious or political opinions.

Article 4 (Freedom of faith and creed)

(1) Freedom of faith, of conscience, and freedom of creed, religious or ideological (weltanschaulich), shall be inviolable.

(2) The undisturbed practice of religion is guaranteed.

(3) No one may be compelled against his conscience to render war service involving the use of arms. Details shall be regulated by a federal law.

Article 5 (Freedom of expression)

(1) Everyone shall have the right freely to express and diseeminate his opinion by speech, writing, and pictures and freely to inform himself from generally accessible sources. Freedom of the press and freedom of reporting by means of broadcasts and films are guaranteed. There shall be no censorship.

(2) These rights are limited by the provisions of the general laws, the provisions of law for the protection of youth, and by the right to inviolability of personal honor.

(3) Art and science, research and teaching, shall be free. Freedom of teaching shall not absolve from loyalty to the constitution.

Article 8 (Freedom of assembly)

(1) All Germans shall have the right to assemble peaceably and unarmed without prior notification or permission.

(2) With regard to open-air meetings this right may be restricted by or pursuant to a law.

Article 9 (Freedom of association)

(1) All Germans shall have the right to form associations and societies.

(2) Associations, the purposes or activities of which conflict with criminal laws or which are directed against the constitutional order or the concept of international understanding, are prohibited.

(3) The right to form associations to safeguard and improve working and economic conditions is guaranteed to everyone and to all trades, occupations, and professions.

Agreements which restrict or seek to impair this right shall be null and void; measures directed to this end shall be illegal.

Article 11 (Freedom of movement)

(1) All Germans shall enjoy freedom of movement throughout the federal territory.

(2) This right may be restricted only by or pursuant to a law and one in cases in which an adequate basis of existence is lacking and special burdens would arise to the community as a result thereof, or in which such restriction is necessary to avert an imminent danger to the existence of the free democratic basic order of the Federation or a Land, to combat the danger of epidemics, to deal with natural disasters or particularly grave accidents, to protect young people from neglect, or to prevent crime.

Article 12 (Right to choose trade, occupation or profession)

(1) All Germans shall have the right freely to choose their trade, occupation, or profession, their place of work, and their place of training. The practice of trades, occupations, and professions may be regulated by or pursuant to a law.

(2) No specific occupation may be imposed on any person except within the framework of a traditional compulsory public service that applies generally and equally to all.

(3) Forced labor may be imposed only on persons deprived of their liberty by court sentence.

Article 12a (Liability to military and other service)

(1) Men who have attained the age of eighteen years may be required to serve in the Armed Forces, in the Federal Border Guard, or in a Civil Defense organization.

(2) A person who refuses, on grounds of conscience, to render war service involving the use of arms may be required to render a substitute service. The duration of such substitute service shall not exceed the duration of military service. Details shall be regulated by a law which shall not interfere with the freedom of conscience and must also provide for the possibility of a substitute service not connected with units of the Armed Forces or of the Federal Border Guard.

Article 13 (Inviolability of the home)

(1) The home shall be inviolable.

(2) Searches may be ordered only by a judge or, in the event of danger in delay,

by other organs as provided by law and may be carried out only in the form prescribed by law.

(3) In all other respects, this inviolability may not be encroached upon or restricted except to avert a common danger or a mortal danger to individuals, or, pursuant to a law, to prevent imminent danger to public safety and order, especially to alleviate the housing shortage, to combat the danger of epidemics, or to protect endangered juveniles.

Article 14 (Property, Right of inheritance, Expropriation)

(1) Property and the right of inheritance are guaranteed. Their content and limits shall be determined by the laws.

(2) Property imposes duties. Its use should also serve the public weal.

(3) Expropriation shall be permitted only in the public weal. It may be effected only by or pursuant to a law which shall provide for the nature and extent of the compensation. Such compensation shall be determined by establishing an equitable balance between the public interest and the interests of those affected. In case of dispute regarding the amount of compensation, recourse may be had to the ordinary courts.

Article 15 (Socialization)

Land, natural resources, and means of production may for the purpose of socialization be transferred to public ownership or other forms of publicly controlled economy by a law which shall provide for the nature and extent of compensation. In respect of such compensation the third and fourth sentences of paragraph (3) of Article 14 shall apply mutatis mutandis.

Article 16 (Deprivation of citizenship, Extradition, Right of asylum)

(1) No one may be deprived of his German citizenship. Loss of citizenship may arise only pursuant to a law, and against the will of the person affected only if such person does not thereby become stateless.

(2) No German may be extradited to a foreign country. Persons persecuted on political grounds shall enjoy the right to asylum.

Article 17 (Right of petition)

Everyone shall have the right individually or jointly with others to address written requests or complaints to the appropriate agencies and to parliamentary bodies.

Article 19 (Restriction of basic rights)

(1) In so far as a basic right may, under this Basic Law, be restricted by or pursuant to a law, such law must apply generally and not solely to an individual case. Furthermore, such law must name the basic right, indicating the Article concerned.

(2) In no case may the essential content of a basic right be encroached upon.

II. THE FEDERATION AND THE CONSTITUENT STATES (LÄNDER)

Article 20 (Basic principles of the Constitution—Right to resist)

(1) The Federal Republic of Germany is a democratic and social federal state.

(2) All state authority emanates from the people. It shall be exercised by the people by means of elections and voting and by specific legislative, executive, and judicial organs.

(3) Legislation shall be subject to the constitutional order; the executive and the judiciary shall be bound by law and justice.

(4) All Germans shall have the right to resist any person or persons seeking to abolish that constitutional order, should no other remedy be possible.

Article 21 (Political parties)

(1) The political parties shall take part in forming the political will of the people. They may be freely established. Their internal organization must conform to democratic principles. They must publicly account for the sources of their funds.

(2) Parties which, by reason of their aims or the behavior of their adherents, seek to impair or abolish the free democratic basic order or to endanger the existence of the Federal Republic of Germany, shall be unconstitutional. The Federal Constitutional Court shall decide on the question of unconstitutionality.

(3) Details shall be regulated by federal laws.

Article 28 (Federal guarantee of Länder constitutions)

(1) The constitutional order in the Länder must conform to the principles of republican, democratic, and social government based on the rule of law, within the meaning of this Basic Law. In each of the Länder, counties (Kreise), and communes (Gemeinden), the people must be represented by a body chosen in general, direct, free, equal, and secret elections. In the communes the assembly of the commune may take the place of an elected body.

(2) The communes must be guaranteed the right to regulate under their own responsibility all the affairs of the local community within the limits set by law. The associations of communes (Gemeindeverbände) shall also have the right of self-government in accordance with the law and within the limits of the functions assigned to them by law.

(3) The Federation shall ensure that the constitutional order of the Länder conforms to the basic rights and to the provisions of paragraphs (1) and (2) of this Article.

Article 30 (Functions of the Länder)

The exercise of governmental powers and the discharge of governmental functions shall be incumbent on the Länder in so far as this Basic Law does not otherwise prescribe or permit.

Article 31 (Priority of federal law)

Federal law shall override Land law.

Article 32 (Foreign relations)

(1) Relations with foreign states shall be conducted by the Federation.

(2) Before the conclusion of a treaty affecting the special circumstances of a Land, that Land must be consulted in sufficient time.

(3) In so far as the Länder have power to legislate, they may, with the consent of the Federal Government, conclude treaties with foreign states.

Article 35 (Legal, administrative, and police assistance)

(1) All federal and land authorities shall render each other legal and administrative assistance.

(2) In order to maintain or to restore public security or order, a Land may, in cases of particular importance, call upon forces and facilities of the Federal Border Guard to assist its police if, without this assistance, the police could not, or only with considerable difficulty, fulfill a task. In order to deal with a natural disaster or an especially grave accident, a Land may request the assistance of the police forces of other Länder or of forces and facilities of other administrative authorities or of the Federal Border Guard or the Armed Forces.

(3) If the natural disaster or the accident endangers a region larger than a Land, the Federal Government may, in so far as this is necessary effectively to deal with such danger, instruct the Land governments to place their police forces at the disposal of other Länder, and may commit units of the Federal Border Guard or the Armed Forces to support the police forces. Measures taken by the Federal

Government pursuant to the first sentence of this paragraph must be revoked at any time upon the request of the Bundesrat, and in any case without delay upon removal of the danger.

III. THE FEDERAL PARLIAMENT (BUNDESTAG)

Article 38 (Elections)

(1) The deputies to the German Bundestag shall be elected in general, direct, free, equal, and secret elections. They shall be representatives of the whole people, not bound by orders and instructions, and shall be subject only to their conscience.

(2) Anyone who has attained the age of eighteen years shall be entitled to vote; anyone who has attained full legal age shall be eligible for election.

(3) Details shall be regulated by a federal law.

Article 39 (Assembly and legislative term)

(1) The Bundestag shall be elected for a four-year term. Its legislative term shall end with the assembly of a new Bundestag. The new election shall be held at the earliest forty-five, at the latest forty-seven, months after the beginning of the legislative term. If the Bundestag is dissolved the new election shall be held within sixty days.

(2) The Bundestag shall assemble at the latest on the thirtieth day after the election.

(3) The Bundestag shall determine the termination and resumption of its meetings. The President of the Bundestag may convene it at an earlier date. He must do so if one third of its members or the Federal President or the Federal Chancellor so demand.

Article 43 (Presence of the Federal Government)

(1) The Bundestag and its committees may demand the presence of any member of the Federal Government.

(2) The members of the Bundesrat or of the Federal Government as well as persons commissioned by them shall have access to all meetings of the Bundestag and its committees. They must be heard at any time.

Article 44 (Committees of investigation)

(1) The Bundestag shall have the right, and upon the motion of one fourth of its members the duty, to set up a committee of investigation which shall take the requisite evidence at public hearings. The public may be excluded.

(2) The rules of criminal procedure shall apply mutatis mutandis to the taking of evidence. The privacy of posts and telecommunications shall remain unaffected.

(3) Courts and administrative authorities shall be bound to render legal and administrative assistance.

(4) The decisions of committees of investigation shall not be subject to judicial consideration. The courts shall be free to evaluate and judge the facts on which the investigation is based.

Article 47 (Right of deputies to refuse to give evidence)

Deputies may refuse to give evidence concerning persons who have confided facts to them in their capacity as deputies, or to whom they have confided facts in such capacity, as well as concerning these facts themselves. To the extent that this right to refuse to give evidence exists, no seizure of documents shall be permissible.

IV. THE COUNCIL OF CONSTITUENT STATES (BUNDESRAT)

Article 50 (Function)

The Länder shall participate through the Bundesrat in the legislation and administration of the Federation.

Article 51 (Composition)

(1) The Bundesrat shall consist of members of the Land governments which appoint and recall them. Other members of such governments may act as substitutes.

(2) Each Land shall have at least three votes; Länder with more than two million inhabitants shall have four, Länder with more than six million inhabitants five votes.

(3) Each Land may delegate as many members as it has votes. The votes of each Land may be cast only as a block vote and only by members present or their substitutes.

Article 53 (Participation of the Federal Government)

The members of the Federal Government shall have the right, and on demand the duty, to attend the meetings of the Bundesrat and of its committees. They must be heard at any time. The Bundesrat must be currently kept informed by the Federal Government of the conduct of affairs.

Article 53a

(1) Two-thirds of the members of the Joint Committee shall be deputies of the Bundestag and one-third shall be members of the Bundesrat. The Bundestag shall delegate its deputies in proportion to the sizes of its parliamentary groups; such deputies must not be members of the Federal Government. Each Land shall be represented by a Bundesrat member of its choice; these members shall not be bound by instructions. The establishment of the Joint Committee and its procedures shall be regulated by rules of procedure to be adopted by the Bundestag and requiring the consent of the Bundesrat.

(2) The Federal Government must inform the Joint Committee about its plans in respect of a state of defense. The rights of the Bundestag and its committees under paragraph (1) of Article 43 shall not be affected by the provision of this paragraph.

V. THE FEDERAL PRESIDENT

Article 54 (Election by the Federal Convention)

(1) The Federal President shall be elected, without debate, by the Federal Convention (Bundesversammlung). Every German shall be eligible who is entitled to vote for Bundestag candidates and has attained the age of forty years.

(2) The term of office of the Federal President shall be five years. Reelection for a consecutive term shall be permitted only once.

(3) The Federal Convention shall consist of the members of the Bundestag and an equal number of members elected by the diets of the Länder according to the principles of proportional representation.

(4) The Federal Convention shall meet not later than thirty days before the expiration of the term of office of the Federal President or, in the case of premature termination, not later than thirty days after that date. It shall be convened by the President of the Bundestag.

(5) After the expiration of a legislative term, the period specified in the first sentence of paragraph (4) of this Article shall begin with the first meeting of the Bundestag.

(6) The person receiving the votes of the majority of the members of the Federal Convention shall be elected. If such majority is not obtained by any candidate in two ballots, the candidate who receives the largest number of votes in the next ballot shall be elected.

VI. THE FEDERAL GOVERNMENT

Article 62 (Composition)

The Federal Government shall consist of the Federal Chancellor and the Federal Ministers.

Article 63 (Election of the Federal Chancellor— Dissolution of the Bundestag)

(1) The Federal Chancellor shall be elected, without debate, by the Bundestag upon the proposal of the Federal President.

(2) The person obtaining the votes of the majority of the members of the Bundestag shall be elected. The person elected must be appointed by the Federal President.

(3) If the person proposed is not elected, the Bundestag may elect within fourteen days of the ballot a Federal Chancellor by more than one-half of its members.

(4) If no candidate has been elected within this period, a new ballot shall take place without delay, in which the person obtaining the largest number of votes shall be elected. If the person elected has obtained the votes of the majority of the members of the Bundestag, the Federal President must appoint him within seven days of the election. If the person elected did not obtain such a majority, the Federal President must within seven days either appoint him or dissolve the Bundestag.

Article 64 (Appointment of Federal Ministers)

(1) The Federal Ministers shall be appointed and dismissed by the Federal President upon the proposal of the Federal Chancellor.

Article 65 (Distribution of responsibility)

The Federal Chancellor shall determine, and be responsible for, the general policy guidelines. Within the limits set by these guidelines, each Federal Minister shall conduct the affairs of his department autonomously and on his own responsibility. The Federal Government shall decide on differences of opinion between Federal Ministers. The Federal Chancellor shall conduct the affairs of the Federal Government in accordance with rules of procedure adopted by it and approved by the Federal President.

Article 65a (Power of command over Armed Forces)

Power of command in respect of the Armed Forces shall be vested in the Federal Minister of Defense. . . .

Article 67 (Vote of no confidence)

(1) The Bundestag can express its lack of confidence in the Federal Chancellor only by electing a successor with the majority of its members and by requesting the Federal President to dismiss the Federal Chancellor. The Federal President must comply with the request and appoint the person elected.

(2) Forty-eight hours must elapse between the motion and the election.

Article 68 (Vote of confidence—Dissolution of the Bundestag)

(1) If a motion of the Federal Chancellor for a vote of confidence is not assented to by the majority of the members of the Bundestag, the Federal president may, upon the proposal of the Federal Chancellor, dissolve the Bundestag within twenty-one days. The right to dissolve shall lapse as soon as the Bundestag with the majority of its members elects another Federal Chancellor.

(2) Forty-eight hours must elapse between the motion and the vote thereon.

Article 70 (Legislation of the Federation and the Länder)

(1) The Länder shall have the right to legislate insofar as this Basic Law does not confer legislative power on the Federation.

(2) The division of competence between the Federation and the Länder shall be determined by the provisions of this Basic Law concerning exclusive and concurrent powers.

Article 71 (Exclusive legislation of the Federation, definition)

In matters within the exclusive legislative power of the Federation, the Länder shall have power to legislate only if, and to the extent that, a federal law explicitly so authorizes them.

Article 72 (Concurrent legislation of the Federation, definition)

(1) In matters within concurrent legislative powers, the Länder shall have power to legislate as long as, and to the extent that, the Federation does not exercise its right to legislate.

(2) The Federation shall have the right to legislate in these matters to the extent that a need for regulation by federal legislation exists because:

    1. a matter cannot be effectively regulated by the legislation of individual Länder, or

2. the regulation of a matter by a Land law might prejudice the interests of other Länder or of the people as a whole, or
3. the maintenance of legal or economic unity, especially the maintenance of uniformity of living conditions beyond the territory of any one land, necessitates such regulation.

Article 76 (Bills)

(1) Bills shall be introduced in the Bundestag by the Federal Government or by members of the Bundestag or by the Bundesrat.

(2) Bills of the Federal Government shall be submitted first to the Bundesrat. The Bundesrat shall be entitled to state its position on such bills within six weeks. A bill exceptionally submitted to the Bundesrat as being particularly urgent by the Federal Government may be submitted by the latter to the Bundestag three weeks later, even though the Federal Government may not yet have received the statement of the Bundesrat's position; such statement shall be transmitted to the Bundestag by the Federal Government without delay upon its receipt.

(3) Bills of the Bundesrat shall be submitted to the Bundestag by the Federal Government within three months. In doing so, the Federal Government must state its own view.

Article 77 (Procedure concerning adopted bills—Objection of the Bundesrat)

(1) Bills intended to become federal laws shall require adoption by the Bundestag. Upon their adoption they shall, without delay, be transmitted to the Bundesrat by the President of the Bundestag.

(2) The Bundesrat may, within three weeks of the receipt of the adopted bill, demand that a committee for joint consideration of bills, composed of members of the Bundestag and members of the Bundesrat, be convened. The composition and the procedure of this committee shall be regulated by rules of procedure to be adopted by the Bundestag and requiring the consent of the Bundesrat. The members of the Bundesrat on this committee shall not be bound by instructions. If the consent of the Bundesrat is required for a bill to become a law, the convening of this committee may also be demanded by the Bundestag or the Federal Government. Should the committee propose any amendment to the adopted bill, the Bundestag must again vote on the bill.

(3) In so far as the consent of the Bundesrat is not required for a bill to become a law, the Bundesrat may, when the proceedings under paragraph (2) of this Article are completed, enter an objection within two weeks against a bill adopted by the Bundestag. This period shall begin, in the case of the last sentence of paragraph (2) of this Article, on the receipt of the bill as readopted by the Bundestag, and in all other cases on the receipt of a communication from the chairman of the committee provided for in paragraph (2) of this Article, to the effect that the committee's proceedings have been concluded.

(4) If the objection was adopted with the majority of the votes of the Bundesrat, it can be rejected by a decision of the majority of the members of the Bundestag. If the Bundesrat adopted the objection with a majority of at least two-thirds of its votes, its rejection by the Bundestag shall require a majority of two-thirds, including at least the majority of the members of the Bundestag.

Article 78 (Conditions for passing of federal laws)

A bill adopted by the Bundestag shall become a law if the Bundesrat consents to it, or fails to make a demand pursuant to paragraph (2) of Article 77, or fails to enter an objection within the period stipulated in paragraph (3) of Article 77, or withdraws such objection, or if the objection is overridden by the Bundestag.

Article 79 (Amendment of the Basic Law)

(1) This Basic Law can be amended only by laws which expressly amend or supplement the text thereof. In respect of international treaties the subject of which is a peace settlement, the preparation of a peace settlement, or the abolition of an occupation regime, or which are designed to serve the defense of the Federal Republic, it shall be sufficient, for the purpose of clarifying that the provisions of this Basic Law do not preclude the conclusion and entry into force of such treaties, to effect a supplementation of the text of this Basic Law confined to such clarification.

(2) Any such law shall require the affirmative vote of two-thirds of the members of the Bundestag and two-thirds of the votes of the Bundesrat.

(3) Amendments of this Basic Law affecting the division of the Federation into Länder, the participation on principle of the Länder in legislation, or the basic principles laid down in Articles 1 and 20, shall be inadmissible.

Article 80 (Issue of ordinances having force of law)

(1) The Federal Government, a Federal Minister, or the Land governments may be authorized by a law to issue ordinances having the force of law (Rechtsverordnungen). The content, purpose, and scope of the authorization so conferred must be set forth in such law. This legal basis must be stated in the ordinance. If a law provides that such authorization may be delegated, such delegation shall require another ordinance having the force of law.

(2) The consent of the Bundesrat shall be required, unless otherwise provided by federal legislation, for ordinances having the force of law issued by the Federal Government or a Federal Minister concerning basic rules for the use of facilities of the federal railroads and of postal and telecommunication services, or charges therefor, or concerning the construction and operation of railroads, as well as for

ordinances having the force of law issued pursuant to federal laws that require the consent of the Bundesrat or that are executed by the Länder as agents of the Federation or as matters of their own concern.

Article 80a (State of tension)

(1) Where this Basic Law or a federal law on defense, including the protection of the civilian population, stipulates that legal provisions may only be applied in accordance with this Article, their application shall, except when a state of defense exists, be admissible only after the Bundestag has determined that a state of tension (Spannungsfall) exists or if it has specifically approved such application. In respect of the cases mentioned in the first sentence of paragraph (5) and the second sentence of paragraph (6) of Article 12a, such determination of a state of tension and such specific approval shall require a two-thirds majority of the votes cast.

(2) Any measures taken by virtue of legal provisions enacted under paragraph (1) of this Article shall be revoked whenever the Bundestag so requests.

(3) In derogation of paragraph (1) of this Article, the application of such legal provisions shall also be admissible by virtue of, and in accordance with, a decision taken with the consent of the Federal Government by an international organ within the framework of a treaty of alliance. Any measures taken pursuant to this paragraph shall be revoked whenever the Bundestag so requests with the majority of its members.

Article 81 (State of legislative emergency)

(1) Should, in the circumstances of Article 68, the Bundestag not be dissolved, the Federal President may, at the request of the Federal Government and with the consent of the Bundesrat, declare a state of legislative emergency with respect to a bill, if the Bundestag rejects the bill although the Federal Government has declared it to be urgent. The same shall apply if a bill has been rejected although the Federal Chancellor had combined with it the motion under Article 68.

(2) If, after a state of legislative emergency has been declared, the Bundestag again rejects the bill or adopts it in a version stated to be unacceptable to the Federal Government, the bill shall be deemed to have become a law to the extent that the Bundesrat consents to it. The same shall apply if the bill is not passed by the Bundestag within four weeks of its reintroduction.

(3) During the term of office of a Federal Chancellor, any other bill rejected by the Bundestag may become a law in accordance with paragraphs (1) and (2) of this Article within a period of six months after the first declaration of a state of legislative emergency. After the expiration of this period, a further declaration of a state of legislative emergency shall be inadmissible during the term of office of the same Federal Chancellor.

(4) This Basic Law may not be amended or repealed or suspended in whole or in part by a law enacted pursuant to paragraph (2) of this Article.

VIII. THE EXECUTION OF FEDERAL LAWS AND THE FEDERAL ADMINISTRATION

Article 83 (Execution of federal laws by the Länder)

The Länder shall execute federal laws as matters of their own concern in so far as this Basic Law does not otherwise provide or permit.

Article 84 (Land administration and Federal Government supervision)

(1) Where the Länder execute federal laws as matters of their own concern, they shall provide for the establishment of the requisite authorities and the regulation of administrative procedures in so far as federal laws consented to by the Bundesrat do not otherwise provide.

(2) The Federal Government may, with the consent of the Bundesrat, issue pertinent general administrative rules.

(3) The Federal Government shall exercise supervision to ensure that the Länder execute the federal laws in accordance with applicable law. For this purpose the Federal Government may send commissioners to the highest Land authorities and with their consent, or if such consent is refused, with the consent of the Bundesrat, also to subordinate authorities.

(4) Should any shortcomings which the Federal Government has found to exist in the execution of federal laws in the Länder not be corrected, the Bundesrat shall decide, on the application of the Federal Government or the Land concerned, whether such land has violated applicable law. The decision of the Bundesrat may be challenged in the Federal Constitutional Court.

(5) With a view to the execution of federal laws, the Federal Government may be authorized by a federal law requiring the consent of the Bundesrat to issue individual instructions for particular cases. They shall be addressed to the highest Land authorities unless the Federal Government considers the matters urgent.

Article 85 (Execution by Länder as agents of the Federation)

(1) Where the Länder execute federal laws as agents of the Federation, the establishment of the requisite authorities shall remain the concern of the Länder except insofar as federal laws consented to by the Bundesrat otherwise provide.

(2) The Federal Government may, with the consent of the Bundesrat, issue pertinent general administrative rules. It may regulate the uniform training of civil servants (Beamte) and other salaried public employees (Angestellte). The

heads of authorities at the intermediate level shall be appointed with its agreement.

(3) The land authorities shall be subject to the instructions of the appropriate highest federal authorities. Such instructions shall be addressed to the highest Land authorities unless the Federal Government considers the matter urgent. Execution of the instructions shall be ensured by the highest Land authorities.

(4) Federal supervision shall extend to conformity with law and appropriateness of execution. The Federal Government may, for this purpose, require the submission of reports and documents and send commissioners to all authorities.

Article 86 (Direct federal administration)

(1) Where the Federation executes laws by means of direct federal administration or by federal corporate bodies or institutions under public law, the Federal Government shall, insofar as the law concerned contains no special provision, issue pertinent general administrative rules. The Federal Government shall provide for the establishment of the requisite authorities insofar as the law concerned does not otherwise provide.

Federal frontier protection authorities, central offices for police information and communications, for the criminal police, and for the compilation of data for the purposes of protection of the constitution and protection against efforts in the Federal territory which, by the use of force or actions in preparation for the use of force, endanger the foreign interests of the Federal Republic of Germany may be established by federal legislation.

(2) Social insurance institutions whose sphere of competence extends beyond the territory of one Land shall be administered as federal corporate bodies under public law.

(3) In addition, autonomous federal higher authorities as well as federal corporate bodies and institutions under public law may be established by federal legislation for matters in which the Federation has the power to legislate. If new functions arise for the Federation in matters in which it has the power to legislate, federal authorities at the intermediate and lower levels may be established, in case of urgent need, with the consent of the Bundesrat and of the majority of the members of the Bundestag.

Article 87a (Build-up, strength, use, and functions of the Armed Forces)

(1) The Federation shall build up Armed Forces for defense purposes. Their numerical strength and general organizational structure shall be shown in the budget.

(2) Apart from defense, the Armed Forces may only be used to the extent explicitly permitted by this Basic Law.

(3) While the state of defense or a state of tension exits, the Armed Forces shall have the power to protect civilian property and discharge functions of traffic control insofar as this is necessary for the performance of their defense mission. Moreover, the Armed Forces may, when a state of defense or a state of tension exists, be entrusted with the protection of civilian property in support of police measures; in this event the Armed Forces shall cooperate with the competent authorities.

(4) In order to avert any imminent danger to the existence or to the free democratic basic order of the Federation or a Land, the Federal Government may, should conditions as envisaged in paragraph (2) of Article 91 obtain and the police forces and the Federal Border Guard be inadequate, use the Armed Forces to support the police and the Federal Border Guard in the protection of civilian property and in combating organized and militarily armed insurgents. Any such use of Armed Forces must be discontinued whenever the Bundestag or the Bundesrat so requests.

VIIa. JOINT TASKS

Article 91a (Definition of joint tasks)

(1) The Federation shall participate in the discharge of the following responsibilities of the Länder, provided that such responsibilities are important to society as a whole and that federal participation is necessary for the improvement of living conditions (joint tasks):

1. expansion and construction of institutions of higher education including university clinics;
2. improvement of regional economic structures;
3. improvement of the agrarian structure and of coast preservation.

(2) Joint tasks shall be defined in detail by federal legislation requiring the consent of the Bundesrat. Such legislation should include general principles governing the discharge of joint tasks.

(3) Such legislation shall provide for the procedure and the institutions required for joint overall planning. The inclusion of a project in the overall planning shall require the consent of the Land in which it is to be carried out.

(4) In cases to which items 1 and 2 of paragraph (1) of this Article apply, the Federation shall meet one-half of the expenditure in each Land. In cases to which item 3 of paragraph (1) of this Article applies, the Federation shall meet at least one-half of the expenditure, and such proportion shall be the same for all the Länder. Details shall be regulated by legislation. Provision of funds shall be subject to appropriation in the budgets of the Federation and the Länder.

(5) The Federal Government and the Bundesrat shall be informed about the execution of joint tasks, should they so demand.

Article 91b (Cooperation of Federation and Länder in educational planning and in research)

The Federation and the Länder may pursuant to agreements cooperate in educational planning and in the promotion of institutions and projects of scientific research of supraregional importance. The apportionment of costs shall be regulated in the pertinent agreements.

IX. THE ADMINISTRATION OF JUSTICE

Article 92 (Court organization)

Judicial power shall be vested in the judges; it shall be exercised by the Federal Constitutional Court, by the federal courts provided for in this Basic Law, and by the courts of the Länder.

Article 93 (Federal Constitutional Court, competency)

(1) The Federal Constitutional Court shall decide:
1. on the interpretation of the Basic Law in the event of disputes concerning the extent of the rights and duties of a highest federal organ or of other parties concerned who have been vested with rights of their own by this Basic Law or by rules of procedure of a highest federal organ;
2. in case of differences of opinion or doubts on the formal and material compatibility of federal law or Land law with this Basic Law, or on the compatibility of Land law with other federal law, at the request of the Federal Government, of a Land government, or of one-third of the Bundestag members;
3. in case of differences of opinion on the rights and duties of the Federation and the Länder, particularly in the execution of federal law by the Länder and in the exercise of federal supervision;
4. on other disputes involving public law, between the Federation and the Länder, between different Länder or within a Land, unless recourse to another court exists;
4a. on complaints of unconstitutionality, which may be entered by any person who claims that one of his basic rights or one of his rights under paragraph (4) of Article 20, under Article 33, 38, 101, 103, or 104 has been violated by public authority.
4b. on complaints of unconstitutionality, entered by communes or associations of communes on the ground that their right to self-government

under Article 28 has been violated by a law other than a Land law open to complaint to the respective Land constitutional court;

5. in other cases provided for in this Basic Law.

(2) The Federal Constitutional Court shall also act in such other cases as are assigned to it by federal legislation.

Article 94 (Federal Constitutional Court, composition)

(1) The Federal Constitutional Court shall consist of federal judges and other members. Half of the members of the Federal Constitutional Court shall be elected by the Bundestag and half by the Bundesrat. They may not be members of the Bundestag, the Bundesrat, the Federal Government, nor of any of the corresponding organs of a Land.

(2) The constitution and procedure of the Federal Constitutional Court shall be regulated by a federal law which shall specify in what cases its decisions shall have the force of law. Such law may require that all other legal remedies must have been exhausted before any such complaint of unconstitutionality can be entered, and may make provision for a special procedure as to admissibility.

Article 97 (Independence of the judges)

(1) The judges shall be independent and subject only to the law.

(2) Judges appointed permanently on a full-time basis in established positions cannot against their will be dismissed or permanently or temporarily suspended from office or given a different function or retired before the expiration of their term of office except by virtue of a judicial decision and only on the grounds and in the form provided for by law. Legislation may set age limits for the retirement of judges appointed for life. In the event of changes in the structure of courts or in districts of jurisdiction, judges may be transferred to another court or removed from office, provided they retain their full salary.

Article 102 (Abolition of capital punishment)

Capital punishment shall be abolished.

Article 103 (Basic rights in the courts)

(1) In the courts everyone shall be entitled to a hearing in accordance with the law.

(2) An act can be punished only if it was an offense against the law before the act was committed.

(3) No one may be punished for the same act more than once under general penal legislation.

Article 104 (Legal guarantees in the event of deprivation of liberty)

(1) The liberty of the individual may be restricted only by virtue of a formal law and only with due regard to the forms prescribed therein. Detained persons may not be subjected to mental nor to physical ill-treatment.

(2) Only judges may decide on the admissibility or continuation of any deprivation of liberty. Where such deprivation is not based on the order of a judge, a judicial decision must be obtained without delay. The police may hold no one on their own authority in their own custody longer than the end of the day after the day of apprehension. Details shall be regulated by legislation.

(3) Any person provisionally detained on suspicion of having committed an offense must be brought before a judge not later than the day following the day of apprehension; the judge shall inform him of the reasons for the detention, examine him, and give him an opportunity to raise objections. The judge must, without delay, either issue a warrant of arrest setting forth the reasons therefor or order his release from detention.

(4) A relative or a person enjoying the confidence of the person detained must be notified without delay of any judicial decision ordering or continuing his deprivation of liberty.

Article 107 (Financial equalization)

(2) Federal legislation shall ensure a reasonable equalization between financially strong and financially weak Länder, due account being taken of the financial capacity and financial requirements of communes and associations of communes. Such legislation shall specify the conditions governing equalization claims of Länder entitled to equalization payments and equalization liabilities of Länder owing equalization payments as well as the criteria for determining the amounts of equalization payments. Such legislation may also provide for grants to be made by the Federation from federal funds to financially weak Länder in order to complement the coverage of their general financial requirements (complemental grants).

Index

Abortion, 71, 111, 168, 195–196. *See also* Women

Adenauer, Konrad
  chancellor democracy and, 151–153, 156–157, 168
  Christian Democratic Union and, 86–87
  Federal Constitutional Court and, 194–195
  foreign policy and, 220–221
  foundation of, 84
  influence on state politics, 205
  as mayor of Cologne, 212
  relations with Bundestag, 138, 145

Administration. *See* Civil service

Administrative Courts, 191–192
  nuclear power and, 198n.36

Age, 31–33, 129–130. *See also* Generational differences

Agriculture, 20–21, 108–109. *See also* Interest groups; Common Agricultural Policy
  reforms in, 201

Antisystem parties, 119. *See also* Radicals
  banning of, 83–84

Authoritarianism in family, 33–35

Baader-Meinhof band, 75. *See also* Terrorism

Baden-Württemberg, 203

Bad Godesberg program, 91–92. *See also* Social Democratic party

Baker, James, 186

Basic Law (constitution)
  amendments to, 225–226
  attitudes toward, 16
  biconfessional schools and, 110
  Bundesrat (Federal Council) and, 148–150
  Bundestag (Federal Diet) and, 140–141
  civil liberties in, 59–60
  constitutional position of states (Länder) in, 148–150, 201
  economic system and, 233
  Federal Constitutional Court and, 193
  function of federal chancellor in, 151–153
  function of federal president in, 164–165
  local government and, 212
  origins of, 16–17

Basic Law (*continued*)
  positive vote of no-confidence in,
    152–153
  suffrage and, 116
  text of, 247–266
Basic Treaty, 203, 221–222. *See also*
    Ostpolitik
Bavaria, 203
Berlin
  relationship to *Ostpolitik,* 221
  status of, 202, 221–222, 223
  Verfilzung (entanglement) in, 215
  Bismarck, Otto von, 3–5, 148, 201
Bitburg affair, 48–49
  Chancellor Kohl and, 163–164
Brandt, Willy, 90–94. *See also Ostpolitik*
  as chancellor, 159–161, 168, 207,
    222
  citizen initiative groups and, 231
Brauer, Max, 208
Brecht, Arnold, 173
Bremen, 203–204
Bundesbank (Federal Bank) 173,
    184–186, 228
  New York Stock Market and, 186
Bundesrat (Federal Council), 4
  divided parliamentary control of,
    150–151
  expansion of veto power, 149–150
  legislation and, 167–169
  structure, membership, organization
    of, 148–149
Bundestag (Federal Diet)
  legislation and, 167–169
  post-Adenauer era and, 145–147
  public attitudes toward, 147
  structure, membership, functions of,
    139–145
Bureaucracy. *See* Civil Service

Cabinet ministers, federal, 142, 144,
    151–155. *See also* Federal Cabinet
Cable television, 40
Campaign finance, 113n.8, 123–124

Candidate selection, 119–122. *See also*
    Bundestag
Capital resources, distribution of, 26,
    27–29
Carstens, Karl, 166
Catholic church and Christian
    Democratic Union, 111. *See also*
    Churches
Census, and civil liberties, 63–64
Centralization, administrative need for,
    201, 211
Chancellor. *See* Federal chancellor
Chancellor, role of in Second Reich,
    3–4
Chernobyl accident
  and the Greens, 100–101
  and 1987 election, 135
Christian Democratic Union (CDU). *See
    also* Elections, federal; Kohl,
    Helmut
  formation of, 85–89
  membership of, 86
  as opposition party, 87–89
  Ostpolitik and, 224–225
  policies of, 85–86
  return to power of, 89, 224
Christian Social Union (CSU), 85. *See
    also* Bavaria; Strauss, Franz Josef
  Ostpolitik and, 224–225
  relationship to CDU, 88
Churches, 29–30
  attendance at, 29
  political influence of, 109–110
  political programs of, 109–112
Cities
  financial deficits of, 214–215
  housing shortage (squatters) in,
    215–216
  party politics in, 213–214
  public services of, 214
  transportation in, 215
  zoning and land use regulations in,
    215–216
Citizen initiative groups, 57–59,

231–232. *See also* Green political party; Political participation
for voters, 122–123
Civil liberties
awareness of, 59–60
census and, 63–64
Federal Constitutional Court and, 194–195
Civil servants. *See also* Radicals
Bundesrat and, 149
Bundestag committees and, 170n.3
as Bundestag deputies, 142
judiciary and, 188–189
political attitudes of, 180–181
Civil service
planning capacity of, 182
recruitment for, 179–180
reform of, 181–182;
stability of, 172–173
structure of, 175–178, 181
Class structure
economic inequality in, 22–23, 26–27
educational system and, 35–37
Coalition governments, 97, 125–126.
See also Grand Coalition
in the states, 205–206
Co-determination law, 105–106, 160.
See also Trade unions
policy process and, 228
socioeconomic redistribution and, 230
Common Agricultural Policy (CAP), 109, 227
Communist party, 76–77. *See also* Radical left
at national elections, 76, 125
during Weimar Republic, 6, 7
Communities (*Gemeinden*). *See also* Local government
organization of, 212.
Comprehensive school, 37. *See also* Educational system
Concerted Action, 103
Conference committee, 169
Conflict, attitudes toward, 53–54

Constitution. *See* Basic Law
Constitutional Court. *See* Federal Constitutional Court
Corporate guilds, 101–102. *See also* Interest groups
Corporatism, 103
County (*Kreis*) government, 212–213
Courts. *See* Judiciary

Dahrendorf, Ralf, 53
Decentralization, historical pattern, 2–3
Defense council, 156
DeGaulle, Charles, 227
Democratic values, attitudes toward, 53–55. *See also* Political culture
Democracy, conceptions of, 232–233
Denazification, 14
civil service and, 173–174
Diffuse support, 53, 55
Direct democracy. *See also* Green political party; Political participation
citizen initiative groups and, 58–59
Basic Law and, 231–232.
Ditfurth, Jutta, 69, 122
Divorce laws, 110–111

East Germany. *See* German Democratic Republic
Ebert, Friedrich (foundation), 84
Economics ministry, 154
structure of, 176
Economy, performance of, 24–26
Educational system
basic structure of, 35–37
confessional schools and, 110
proposals for reform of, 36–37
role of states in, 37
Elections
federal
of 1949, 86, 90, 124, 125
of 1953, 87, 90, 124, 125
of 1957, 87, 90, 124, 125
of 1961, 87, 91, 124

Elections (*continued*)
  of 1965, 87, 91, 124
  of 1969, 87, 93, 124, 221
  of 1972, 87, 93, 105, 118, 119,
    124, 222
  of 1976, 88, 93, 124, 126
  of 1980, 88, 93–94, 98, 111, 124,
    126
  of 1983, 89, 94–95, 99, 100, 124,
    127
  of 1987, 89–90, 95–96, 99, 101,
    117, 118, 124, 134–135
  turnout, 56, 124
  local, 213
  state, 207–208
Electoral law, 117–119, 205
Electoral politics, in states, 207–208
Emergency laws, 58, 79n.30
Emergency powers
  Federal president and, 164
  role of parliament and, 145
  in Second Reich, 4
  in Weimar Republic, 7
Erhard, Ludwig, 86–87, 157–158, 207.
    See also Federal chancellor
European Community, 226–227. *See also*
    Common Agricultural Policy
European Economic Community
    (Common Market), 227
European monetary system (EMS), 186
Evangelical Church in Germany (EKD),
    111–112. *See also* Churches
Exports, importance of, 19–20

Family structure, 34–36. *See also* Voting
    behavior
  party preference and, 32–33
Federal Assembly, 164
Federal Cabinet, 138, 141, 144,
    153–155, 167–168
Federal Chancellor, 138–139, 144–145,
    151–153. *See also* Positive vote of
    no-confidence
  chancellor democracy and, 153–164

legislation and, 167–168
  military and, 155–156
Federal Chancellor's Office, 153
Federal Constitutional Court. *See also*
    Basic Law
  civil liberties and, 63–64, 192
  decisions of, 194–195, 223, 226
  independence of, 193
  policy making and, 194–195
Federal Council. *See* Bundesrat
Federal Diet. *See* Bundestag
Federal Labor Institute, 173, 184
Federal President, 164–166
Federal Republic of Germany
  attitudes toward, 50–53
  formation of, 14–17
  legal status of, 225–226
  legitimacy of, 50–53
  provisional character of, 46–47, 146
Federal structure, reform of, 211
Federation of German Employer
    Associations (BDA), 104. *See also*
    Interest groups
Flick affair, 39, 124, 136–137n.5. *See
    also* Lambsdorff, Otto von
Foreign policy. *See also* Ostpolitik
  European unification and, 47–48,
    226–227
  public opinion and, 222–223
  relationship to United States and,
    47–48
Foreign workers, 65–67
  German citizenship and, 80n.47
Fraktionen (caucuses), 141. *See also*
    Bundestag
Free Democratic party (FDP). *See also*
    Elections, federal
  in Brandt government, 160–161, 168
  in coalitions with Christian
    Democratic Union, 97–99
  electoral law and, 96
  finances of, 113n.8
  internal divisions of, 97
  in party system, 97–98

Generational differences in political
    attitudes, 32–33, 71–72. *See also*
    Family structure
Genscher, Hans-Dietrich, 98–99. *See
    also* Free Democratic party
German Democratic Republic (GDR).
    See also Basic Treaty
    formation of, 15–16
    recognition of, 221–222
    relations with, 224–225
German Federation of Labor (DGB). *See*
    Trade unions
German Industrial and Trade
    Conference (DIHT), 104. *See also*
    Interest groups
Globke, Hans, 156, 171n.32
Glotz, Peter, 94
Goodman, John, 185
Gorbachev, Mikhail, 225
Goppel, Alfons, 208
Grand Coalition (1966–1969), 92–93
    Bundestag and, 145–146
    Ostpolitik, 221
    states and, 205
Grass, Günter, 57, 123
Green Front, 108–109. *See also* Interest
    groups
Green political party, 99–101,
    126–127. *See also* Peace
    movement; Civil liberties
    census and, 63–64
    electoral system and, 119
    finances of, 123
    state elections and, 206
    women and, 68–69
    youth and, 32, 129–130

Habermas, Jurgen, 49
Hallstein doctrine, 221
Hamburg, 203–204, 205
Health care system, 182–184
    costs of, 229
Hearings of Bundestag committees,
    145–146. *See also* Bundestag

Heinemann, Gustav, 165
Hennis, Wilhelm, 84
Hesse, 203–204
Heuss, Theodor, 165
Hindenburg, Paul von, 7–8. *See also*
    Weimar Republic
Historikerstreit (Historians Dispute),
    48–49
Hitler, Adolf, 6–7. *See also* National
    Socialism
    attitudes toward, 9–12, 51–61
Honecker, Erich, 224–225

Ideology of electorate, 127–128
Income
    sex differentials in, 69
    structure of, 26
Independent deputies, 141. *See also*
    Bundestag
Industrial interests and political parties,
    103–104. *See also* Flick affair
Inflation, 24–26, 228–229
Interest groups
    agriculture, 20–21, 108–109
    Bundestag and, 142–143
    business, 20, 103–105; 106–107
    candidate recruitment and, 120–121
    churches, 29–30, 109–112
    governmental bureaucracy and,
        101–103
    labor, 105–108
Interest in politics, general pattern,
    56–57

Jewish congregations, 109
Judicial review, 192–192. *See also*
    Federal Constitutional Court
    Judiciary
    attitudes and values, 189–190
    court structure and, 190–192
    reform of, 195–196
    socialization and recruitment of,
        188–189
    Third Reich and, 174, 188

Kaisen, Wilhelm, 208
Kapp Putsch, 6
Kiesinger, Kurt-Georg, 158–159. *See also* Grand Coalition
Kohl, Helmut. *See also* Christian Democratic Union
   Bitburg affair and, 48
   Christian Democratic Union and, 87–90
   as federal chancellor, 163–164
   as minister president, 208
   population and, 41n.1
   private television and, 40
   trade unions and, 108
   US-Soviet relations and, 164
   youth and, 72
Kommers, Donald P., 187
Krieger, Leonard, 59

Labor unions. *See* Trade unions
Labor management relations, 107–108, 114n.17
LaFontaine, Oscar, 95
Lambsdorff, Otto Count von, 85, 124
Land use, zoning regulations and, 215–216
Late capitalist societies, 233
Legal codes, 187. *See also* Judiciary
Legal process, role of social class in, 59–60
Legislation
   Bundesrat and, 148–149, 168–169
   Bundestag and, 144–145, 168–169
   initiation process of, 167–168
   role of executive in, 147, 168–169
Legitimacy of Federal Republic. *See* Federal Republic of Germany
Liberalism, 2–5. *See also* Free Democratic party
Local government, 212–214
Loewenberg, Gerhard, 143
Loewenstein, Karl, 174
Lower Saxony, 203–204
Ludendorff, Erich, 5, 9
Lübke, Heinrich, 165

Marcuse, Herbert, 79
Military, attitudes toward, 155–156
Ministerpräsident, 205, 208. *See also* States
Monarchy, attitudes toward, 50

Nagle, John D., 142
National Democratic party (NPD), 73–74, 206. *See also* Radicals
National identity, sense of, 45–50
National politics and state elections, 207–208
National pride, sense of, 49–50
National socialism. *See also Historikerstreit*
   attitudes of Germans toward, 11–12, 48–49
   capitalism and, 8–9, 28–29
   family and, 33–34
   origins of, 8–10
NATO missile decision
   Green political party and, 72, 79n.32 100, 127, 134–135
   Helmut Kohl and, 163–164
   Helmut Schmidt and, 162
   military and, 156
   national identity and, 47–48
   peace movement and, 58
   Social Democratic party and, 134
Naumann, Friedrich (foundation), 84
Neue Heimat scandal, 39, 107
New poverty, 229–230
North Rhine Westphalia, 39, 202
Nuremberg, mass arrest in, 216. *See also* Cities

Occupation government, 12–16, 173–174. *See also* Basic Law
Oder-Neisse line, 13, 222–223. *See also* Basic Law
Office for the Protection of the Constitution, 63, 73, 211
Opposition party, attitudes toward, 53–55, 133
Ostpolitik (Eastern policy). *See also*

Brandt, Willy; Social Democratic party
beginnings of, 92, 221–225
Christian Democratic Union and, 224–225
constitutionality of, 195
detente and, 224
Free Democratic party and, 221, 224
national identity and, 47
and 1969 election, 92
opposition to, 223
support from business and, 224–225
treaties with Eastern Europe and, 160, 221–222

Parliament: attitudes toward, 54–55, 147
in Frankfurt, 3
in Second Reich, 4. See also Bundesrat; Bundestag; Legislation; Reichstag
Parliamentary Council (1948), 16, 201
Parliamentary investigations, 144–145
Particularism, 22, 201. See also States
Parties, political. See also Christian Democratic Union; Free Democratic party; Green political party; Social Democratic party
attitudes toward, 84–85
in Basic Law, 83–84, 251
influence on media of, 39–40
origins of, 82–83.
Party discipline in parliament, 141–142
Party identification of voters, 33
Party membership, 57
Party preference, 128–129
Party state, 82–85
Party systems in states, 206–207
Peace movement, 58
Green political party and, 99–101
Helmut Schmidt and, 94–95, 162
military and, 156
Social Democratic party and, 94–95
Pöhl, Otto, 186
Police, 201, 211

Political culture
Americanization of, 46, 48
antisystem sentiment and, 50–51
changes in 52–55, 234
conflict and, 53–54
definition of, 44
democratic values and, 53–55
elites and, 55
European Community and, 47, 49–50
founding of Federal Republic and, 16–17, 45–46
leadership and, 46, 51
national division and, 47
national identity and, 45–50
national pride and, 49–50
occupation and, 44
party competition and, 53–54
performance of system and, 51, 53
political education and, 51
privatization and, 15–16, 32–33
representation and parliament and, 54–55
reunification and, 47
Weimar Republic and, 44
Political development, 233–234
past political systems and, 50–51
Political participation. See also Citizen initiative groups; Interest in politics; Political culture; Voting behavior
new forms of, 57–59, 231–232
voter involvement in campaigns, 122–123.
Population of Federal Republic, 18–19, 204
Pornography laws, 110–111, 196
Positive vote of no confidence, 151–152. See also Bundestag; Federal Chancellor
President. See Federal President Press, 38–39. See also Television and radio
Proportional electoral system, 117–119. See also Electoral law; Free Democratic party

Prussia, rise of, 2–4. *See also* Bismarck, Otto von

Question hour in Bundestag, 144

Radical left, 40, 73, 74–77. *See also* Grand Coalition; Political culture; Terrorism; Young Socialists
extra-parliamentary opposition and, 75
parliamentary system and, 74
Radical right, 73–74. *See also* National Democratic party (NPD); Political culture
Radicals. *See also* Civil service
civil liberties and, 61–63, 75
in civil service, 62–63, 195, 208
Rau, Johannes, 95
Reagan, Ronald, 48, 163, 225
Rechtsstaat, 59. *See also* Civil liberties; Political culture
Redistribution, socioeconomic, 230–231
Refugees, 72–73. *See also* Population of Federal Republic
Regional economic development, 201, 205
Reichstag, 82. *See also* Bundestag; Parliament
during Second Reich, 139
Religion. *See also* Churches
beliefs in, 29–30
party preference and, 129–130, 132
Reunification of East and West Germany. *See also* Foreign policy; *Ostpolitik*
attitudes toward, 47
Basic Law and, 226, 227
Western Allies and, 223
Revenue sharing, 209–210
Revolutionary Cells, 76. *See also* Terrorism
Rhineland Palatinate, 62, 203–204

Saar, 63, 203–204
Scheel, Walter, 98, 160, 165–166. *See also* Free Democratic party; *Ostpolitik*
Schiller, Karl, 90, 92
Schleswig-Holstein, 203–204
Schmidt, Helmut
as federal chancellor, 161–162
Free Democratic party and, 99
NATO missiles and, 94–95, 161–162
in Social Democratic party, 93–94
Schools. *See* Educational system
Schumacher, Kurt, 90. *See also* Social Democratic party
Schweigler, Gebhard, 227
Seidel, Hans (foundation), 84
Semipublic institutions, 182–186
Small parties, 125. *See also* Electoral law
Social class, 22–23
capital resources and, 27–29
education and, 35–37
income structure and, 26
voting behavior and, 129–132
Social Democratic party (SPD). *See also* Elections, federal
missiles and, 94–95
New Left and, 93–94
private television and, 40
program of, 90–92, 133–134
public image of, 90–91
state organization of, 207–208
Socialism, decline of in postwar period, 105–106
Social security system: 182–184
reductions in, 229
Sociodemographic structure and voting, 129–130. *See also* Voting behavior
Sontheimer, Kurt, 82
Spartakus League, 5–6
Specialized court system, 191–192
Spiegel affair, 60–61. *See also Neue Heimat* scandal; Flick affair
Springer, Axel, 38, 40
States (Länder). *See also* Bundesrat; Educational system; Police

constitutional structure of, 205–207
economic equalization between,
    21–22, 209–210
education and, 37, 201
influence of, 201
leaders of, 208–209
origins of, 208–209
religious schools and, 110–111
Statism, 8, 83
attitudes toward, 133
Stingl, Josef, 184. *See also* Federal Labor
    Institute
Strikes, 107–108, 114n.17
Stoltenberg, Gerhard, 154, 208
Strauss, Franz-Josef, 61, 88–90, 126,
    134, 224. *See also* Christian
    Democratic Union; Christian
    Social Union; *Spiegel* affair

Tax collection, 201, 209–210, 214. *See
    also* Revenue sharing; States
Television and radio, 39–40,
    122–123, 194–195
Terrorism, 50, 75–76, 216. *See also*
    Police; Radicals
Ticket splitting, 118–119. *See also*
    Voting behavior
Trade unions, 105–108. *See also* Interest
    groups
Kohl government and, 108
Social Democratic party and, 106,
    113n.14

Unemployment, 24–26, 228–230
1983 election and, 25
voting behavior and, 134–135
Unification of Germany, 1–4
Universities, 36–37. *See also* Educational
    system
Urbanization, 19, 214–216. *See also*
    Cities

Value added tax, 210
Vogel, Jochen, 94. *See also* Social
    Democratic party

Vote of no confidence, 144–145, 152,
    170–171n.25. *See also* Bundestag;
    Positive vote of no confidence
Voting behavior. *See also* Elections,
    federal; Elections, state
candidates, 119–122
issues, 134–135
party policies and, 133–134
registration rules, 116
social change and, 130–132.

Waldsterben (death of forest), 232
Wehner, Herbert, 90, 92. *See also* Social
    Democratic party
Weimar Republic (1919–1933). *See also*
    National Socialism; Political
    culture
constitution of, 6, 139–140
failure of, 7–9
leadership of, 8
political culture of, 44
political parties of, 7
Weizsäcker, Richard von, 166. *See also*
    Federal President
West Germany. *See* Federal Republic of
    Germany
Women. *See also* Abortion; Population of
    Federal Republic
discrimination against, 69–70
party preference of, 68, 130
in public office, 68–69
social and legal status of, 19, 69, 71

Young Socialists, 93. *See also* Social
    Democratic party
Youth
attitudes toward, 71–72
in political organizations, 72
unemployment and, 72

Zinn, Georg-August, 208